"This book is an invitation to another book: Holy Scripture. In *Biblical Reasoning*, Jamieson and Wittman make what might be called an exegetical confession: Scripture is God's word that reveals and redeems to the end that readers are brought into relationship. God speaks so God's creatures finally see God. Trinitarian and christological doctrine, in this economy, is not a movement away from the biblical texts but rather the theological grammar that flows from and returns the reader to the canonical voice of God, the Father who sends the Son and the Spirit. *Tolle lege, tolle lege*: take up and read this book, for the sake of taking up and reading the other one."

—**Jonathan A. Linebaugh**, University of Cambridge; fellow, Jesus College

"Theology needs to be exegetical and contemplative, though a whole host of pressures draw attention elsewhere. *Biblical Reasoning* helps alert us to where we should focus and equips us to do so with competence and care. I hope it's read widely by students and those who long to go back to school with the Scriptures."

—**Michael Allen**, Reformed Theological Seminary

"Does biblical exegesis, when done with modern tools, collapse the classical dogmatic consensus on the Trinity and Christ? Jamieson and Wittman show us why the answer is no through a careful introduction to what Scripture is, what hearing Scripture's truth involves, and why the realities of the Trinity and the incarnation are biblical. This book requires the attention of all catholic (and Catholic) Christians. The movement founded by the great John Webster rises to new heights with this book!"

—**Matthew Levering**, Mundelein Seminary

"God's self-presentation to us in Scripture is the path to God's self-presentation to us in the beatific vision. For this reason, biblical interpretation is never merely a matter of attending to the various historical, literary, and theological features of the text. If biblical interpretation is to fulfill its divinely appointed end, we must learn to recognize the face of God in Holy Scripture (Ps. 27:8). In this profoundly learned, instructive, and helpful work, Bobby Jamieson and Tyler Wittman outline and exemplify a number of well-tried exegetical principles and tools for discerning in Scripture the glory of God in the face of Jesus Christ. This is a book of generational significance that deserves to be read by all teachers and serious students of the Bible."

—**Scott R. Swain**, Reformed Theological Seminary

# BIBLICAL REASONING

## CHRISTOLOGICAL AND TRINITARIAN
## RULES FOR EXEGESIS

# R. B. JAMIESON
## AND TYLER R. WITTMAN

**Baker Academic**

*a division of Baker Publishing Group*
Grand Rapids, Michigan

© 2022 by Robert Bruce Jamieson III and Tyler R. Wittman

Published by Baker Academic
a division of Baker Publishing Group
PO Box 6287, Grand Rapids, MI 49516-6287
www.bakeracademic.com

Printed in the United States of America

Library of Congress Cataloging-in-Publication Data
Names: Jamieson, R. B., 1986– author. | Wittman, Tyler, author.
Title: Biblical reasoning : christological and trinitarian rules for exegesis / R. B. Jamieson and
    Tyler R. Wittman.
Description: Grand Rapids, Michigan : Baker Academic, a division of Baker Publishing Group,
    [2022] | Includes bibliographical references and index.
Identifiers: LCCN 2021057337 | ISBN 9781540964670 (paperback) | ISBN 9781540965608
    (casebound) | ISBN 9781493436651 (pdf ) | ISBN 9781493436644 (ebook)
Subjects: LCSH: Bible—Criticism, interpretation, etc. | Bible—Theology. | Jesus Christ—Person
    and offices. | Trinity.
Classification: LCC BS511.3 .J36 2022 | DDC 220.6—dc23/eng/20220120
LC record available at https://lccn.loc.gov/2021057337

Baker Publishing Group publications use paper produced from sustainable forestry practices and post-consumer waste whenever possible.

22   23   24   25   26   27   28        7   6   5   4   3   2   1

All the knowledge imparted by faith revolves around these two points, the divinity of the Trinity and the humanity of Christ.

—Thomas Aquinas,
*Compendium of Theology*

You have to learn to speak sky with an earth tongue.

—Ursula K. Le Guin,
*Always Coming Home*

# Contents

# Acknowledgments

The writing of this book began in the relative calm of 2019 and was frustrated by the many upheavals of the years since. Despite the challenges of writing during a complex global crisis, we have been reminded that contemplating the mystery of the Trinity sustains us in ways that more "practical" concerns do not.

Thanks are due, first, to the whole team at Baker Academic. We are grateful for their embrace of and enthusiasm for this work and for their skillful assistance throughout. We especially want to thank our editors, Dave Nelson and Tim West, and the other members of Baker's editorial team for improving the book in many ways and granting us generous leeway in its form and scope. We are indebted to Michael Allen, Scott Swain, and Fred Sanders for advocating for and encouraging this project, and are doubly indebted to Fred for incisive comments on, and fortifying encouragement of, chapter 9.

We also thank those who read and commented on portions of the manuscript: Alex Arrell, Rodney Evans, Caleb Greggson, Ryan Hurd, Jonathan Keisling, Vincent Kajuma, David Larson, Tim Stanton, and Ben Robin. Special thanks go to Nick Gardner for astute comments on the whole manuscript and to David Moser for insightful, generative reflections on chapters 7 and 8.

We are heartily grateful to Richard McBee for allowing his striking, evocative work *Jacob's Dream* to illumine the book's cover.

Finally, we would like to thank our Lord Jesus Christ and the teachers he has graciously provided to the church who shaped this book's ideas. He has answered our prayers that this book would see the light of day; now we wait confidently, praying that it will bear some good fruit.

Bobby Jamieson would like to thank Eric Beach for reading and discussing several primary sources that proved seminal, and the students in my June 2021 class on biblical reasoning at Bethlehem Seminary for their enriching engagement with an early draft of the book. I am especially grateful to Capitol Hill Baptist Church for generous sabbaticals in the summers of 2019 and 2021, in which I was able to draft and revise most of my half of the book. I'm deeply grateful to my friend and coauthor Tyler for a fruitful decade of theological sharpening that joyfully intensified in these past three years. I also thank Mark Dever for his generous support of my writing, and, last because opposite of least, my wife, Kristin, and our four delightful children for making writing a joyful family project. Χάρις τῷ θεῷ.

Tyler Wittman would like to thank the students and colleagues who generously encouraged this book. Thanks are especially due to the many friends old and new who saw us through some very trying months and transitions amid the pandemic, which delayed and even imperiled the book. I'm particularly thankful for Jamie Dew, whose belief in and encouragement of my academic pursuits has been a lifeline. Thanks also to my friend Bobby, whose good humor and intelligence made this book better than it would've been otherwise. Where would I be without my wife, Jessie? Her resolute support, patient listening as ideas took shape, and feedback left me acutely aware of my own poverty, but also my wealth. The cheerful optimism of our four children is a constant source of inspiration. Life is much more than writing books, and for this I'm deeply grateful.

# Abbreviations

Clines. 9 vols. Sheffield: Sheffield Phoenix, 1993–2016.

Denzinger   Denzinger, Heinrich. *Compendium of Creeds, Definitions, and Declarations on Matters of Faith and Morals.* Edited by Peter Hünermann, Robert Fastiggi, and Anne Englund Nash. 43rd ed. San Francisco: Ignatius, 2012.

esp.   especially

FC   Fathers of the Church

FTECS   Foundations of Theological Exegesis and Christian Spirituality

GNO   *Gregorii Nysseni Opera.* Edited by Werner Jaeger et al. Leiden: Brill, 1921–.

HTR   *Harvard Theological Review*

ICC   International Critical Commentary

IJST   *International Journal of Systematic Theology*

ITC   International Theological Commentary

JBL   *Journal of Biblical Literature*

JECS   *Journal of Early Christian Studies*

JETS   *Journal of the Evangelical Theological Society*

JRT   *Journal of Reformed Theology*

JSem   *Journal for Semitics*

JSNT   *Journal for the Study of the New Testament*

JSNTSup   Journal for the Study of the New Testament Supplement Series

JSOTSup   Journal for the Study of the Old Testament Supplement Series

JTI   *Journal of Theological Interpretation*

JTS   *Journal of Theological Studies*

KD   *Kerygma und Dogma*

KEK   Kritisch-exegetischer Kommentar über das Neue Testament

LCL   Loeb Classical Library

LHBOTS   Library of Hebrew Bible / Old Testament Studies

LNTS   Library of New Testament Studies

LXX   Septuagint

MT   Masoretic Text

NAC   New American Commentary

NETS   Pietersma, Albert, and Benjamin G. Wright, eds. *A New English Translation of the Septuagint: And the Other Greek Translations Traditionally Included under That Title.* New York: Oxford University Press, 2007.

NICNT   New International Commentary on the New Testament

NIDNTT   *New International Dictionary of New Testament Theology.* Edited by Colin Brown. 4 vols. Grand Rapids: Zondervan, 1975–78.

NIGTC   New International Greek Testament Commentary

NovTSup   Supplements to Novum Testamentum

NPNF[2]   *Nicene and Post-Nicene Fathers*, Series 2

NSD   New Studies in Dogmatics

NT   New Testament

NTS   *New Testament Studies*

OECS   Oxford Early Christian Studies

OECT   Oxford Early Christian Texts

OSAT   Oxford Studies in Analytic Theology

OSHT   Oxford Studies in Historical Theology

OT   Old Testament

OTM   Oxford Theological Monographs

par.   parallels

| | | | |
|---|---|---|---|
| PG | Patrologia Graeca [= *Patrologiae Cursus Completus. Series Graeca*]. Edited by J.-P. Migne. 162 vols. Paris, 1857–86. | | *Opera Omnia*, vols. 13–20. Translated by Laurence Shapcote. Steubenville, OH: Emmaus Academic, 2018. |
| PNTC | Pillar New Testament Commentary | StPatr | *Studia Patristica* |
| PPS | Popular Patristics Series | THKNT | Theologischer Handkommentar zum Neuen Testament |
| RB | *Revue Biblique* | TLNT | *Theological Lexicon of the New Testament*. C. Spicq. Translated and edited by J. D. Ernest. 3 vols. Peabody, MA: Hendrickson, 1994. |
| RSPT | *Revue des Sciences Philosophiques et Théologiques* | | |
| RTL | *Revue Théologique de Louvain* | | |
| SBLMS | Society of Biblical Literature Monograph Series | TynBul | *Tyndale Bulletin* |
| | | VC | *Vigiliae Christianae* |
| SBLSBS | Society of Biblical Literature Sources for Biblical Study | VCSup | Supplements to Vigiliae Christianae |
| SC | Sources Chrétiennes | WBC | Word Biblical Commentary |
| SCDS | Studies in Christian Doctrine and Scripture | WSA | The Works of Saint Augustine |
| | | WUNT | Wissenschaftliche Untersuchungen zum Neuen Testament |
| SCG | Thomas Aquinas, *Summa contra Gentiles* | ZECNT | Zondervan Exegetical Commentary on the New Testament |
| SHT | Studies in Historical Theology | | |
| SJT | *Scottish Journal of Theology* | | |
| SNTSMS | Society for New Testament Studies Monograph Series | ZNW | *Zeitschrift für die neutestamentliche Wissenschaft* |
| SPhiloA | *Studia Philonica Annual* | | |
| STh | Thomas Aquinas, *Summa Theologiae*. In *Latin-English* | | |

# Note on Sources

Citations from the biblical commentaries of Thomas Aquinas come from the Latin-English *Opera Omnia*, published by Emmaus Academic (2018–). In this book we cite these sources as *Commentary on 1 Corinthians* or *Commentary on the Gospel of St. John* and so forth, followed by the standard reference to lecture, part, and section. References to other of Aquinas's works are from the same *Opera Omnia*, unless otherwise noted. Similarly, citations from the biblical commentaries of John Calvin are all drawn from the Calvin Translation Society edition from the mid-nineteenth century. We have chosen to cite these by title and the biblical verse Calvin is commenting on (e.g., *Commentary on Jeremiah* 33:34). Though these methods may not be standard in every way, we believe they will enable readers to find the original texts easily, regardless of the versions available to them. Translations of modern sources in other languages are the authors' own.

# Introduction

## Theology for Better Exegesis

I n this entryway to the book we introduce its goal, the resources on which it draws, and the plan by which it progresses. We conclude by commenting briefly on the book's audiences and authors.

## Goal

Our goal in this book is to assemble a toolkit for biblical reasoning. The toolkit's goal is to enable better exegesis. The goal of that exegesis is, ultimately, to see God.

Hence, by "better exegesis" we mean exegesis that is not only more adequate to the text itself but also, especially, more adequate to the ultimate reality to which the text bears witness and more adequate to the text's ultimate goal. That reality is the triune God and that goal is the sight of God's face that will eternally satisfy our souls.

What is "biblical reasoning"? We take the phrase and framework from a seminal essay by John Webster.[1] According to Webster, biblical reasoning is "the redeemed intellect's reflective apprehension of God's gospel address through the embassy of Scripture, enabled and corrected by God's presence, and having fellowship with him as its end."[2] Webster distinguishes within biblical reasoning two overlapping, mutually informing modes of reasoning:

1. Webster, "Biblical Reasoning."
2. Webster, "Biblical Reasoning," 128.

exegetical and dogmatic. Exegetical reasoning is the act of "following the words of the text." This act is theologically and epistemologically primary. To run in the wake of the apostles and prophets is every theologian's chief obligation and should be their chief delight.[3] Dogmatic reasoning "produces a conceptual representation of what reason has learned from its exegetical following of the scriptural text. In dogmatics, the 'matter' of prophetic and apostolic speech is set out in a different idiom, anatomized."[4] Exegetical reasoning attends to the order and flow of the text, following its twists and turns; dogmatic reasoning attends to the theological claims of the text, looking along and with the text to discern the ultimate reality to which it bears witness. Neither is complete without the other; both move from and toward one another in a continual, mutually informative exchange. Dogmatic reasoning enables readers of Scripture to locate major concerns of the text quickly and easily, to perceive Scripture "in its full scope as an unfolding of the one divine economy," to see Scripture's unity and interrelations, and to discern its proportions. With this sense of scope and proportion that dogmatic reasoning provides, exegetical reasoning is better equipped to discover the fullness present in discrete prophetic and apostolic discourses.[5] Embracing both intellectual activities in an organic process, "biblical reasoning" keeps them from neglecting each other.

On Webster's reckoning, theology is therefore not a movement *away* from Scripture toward some distant logical synthesis. Instead, theology thinks from Scripture, with Scripture, and to Scripture. Scripture is thus systematic theology's origin and goal.[6] When rightly pursued, theology comes from and returns to Scripture in order to hear and confess ever more faithfully God's gospel address, which has fellowship with God in Christ as its end. Hence, biblical reasoning maintains a continual concern for personal knowledge of, and conformity to, Scripture's ultimate subject matter. In turn, the organic processes of exegetical and dogmatic reasoning are both oriented toward, and critically normed by, the triune God. As we will argue in the first three chapters, biblical reasoning is therefore that form of attention to Holy Scripture that is taught by God, teaches about God, and leads to God.

In our adopting the mantle of "biblical reasoning," one of our key concerns is to rightly relate what should not be kept separate: exegesis and systematic theology. To introduce this central theme, we will consider a common model for relating these two and indicate respects in which we aim to improve upon

---

3. Webster, "Biblical Reasoning," 130.
4. Webster, "Biblical Reasoning," 130–31.
5. Webster, "Biblical Reasoning," 131.
6. Webster, "Principles of Systematic Theology," 148.

it.[7] Many construe the relation between exegesis and doctrine as that between raw material and its development. For instance, in an exegetical work on the Trinity, Ben Witherington and Laura Ice assert that the NT provides "raw data" that the church's theologians later synthesized into a "developed doctrine of the Trinity."[8] There is more than an element of truth in this model. Further, all analogies have limits, and we should not push this one beyond its intended scope. However, the notion of doctrine as the development of raw biblical or exegetical material has significant liabilities and is at least potentially misleading. It implies a one-way arrow from exegesis to doctrine: from raw material to finished product, from foundation to superstructure. It also implies a substantive, material difference between the respective products of each. No one would mistake a car for its unassembled constituent components. Further, it also implies that systematic theology in some sense improves upon the undeveloped deliverances of Scripture.

Hence, this model obscures two key aspects of the symbiotic relationship between exegetical and dogmatic reasoning that this work will develop and defend. First, as we will discuss further below, there is a crucial sense in which exegetical and dogmatic reasoning say the same thing in different words. To put it more formally: when rightly defined and practiced, the goals and products of exegetical and dogmatic reasoning harmonize, complement, and inform each other. Each aims at understanding and representing the apostles' and prophets' witness to the reality of God and the relation of all things to God. Second, rather than implying a one-way arrow from exegesis to dogmatics, a proper construal of their relationship recognizes two-way traffic between them. Dogmatic judgments and concepts that are properly derived from exegesis can enrich and direct exegesis. Dogmatic reasoning is every bit as much a mode of reading Scripture as exegetical reasoning. As the Heidelberg Reformer Zacharias Ursinus put it, the purpose of studying doctrine is "that we may be well prepared for the reading, understanding, and exposition of the holy Scriptures. For as the doctrine of the catechism and

---

7. Our discussion is informed by that of Swain, "The Bible and the Trinity in Recent Thought," 39–40.

8. Witherington and Ice, *The Shadow of the Almighty*, xi. Similarly, though in a more subjective, experiential idiom, see Fee, "Paul and the Trinity," 51. Cf. also Vos, "The Idea of Biblical Theology as a Science and as a Theological Discipline," 7, who describes the role of the "contents of revelation" in the discipline of systematic theology as "the material for a human work of classifying and systematizing according to logical principles." See the instructive critique of Vos's position in Webster, "Principles of Systematic Theology," 146–48. While the work of systematic theology is certainly a human work of classifying (as exegesis and biblical theology are as well), it is structured not by "logical principles" but by the triune God and the economy of his works. Systematic theology is therefore no less concerned than other disciplines with the historical sequence of God's works.

Common Places are taken out of the Scriptures, and are directed by them as their rule, so they again lead us, as it were, by the hand to the Scriptures."[9]

As much or perhaps more than they erect a superstructure upon Scripture, dogmatic judgments discern just the reverse: a substructure. Rather than climbing out of the text, dogmatic judgments, as it were, plunge beneath the surface of the text's discrete assertions. In other words, dogmatic reasoning discerns what must be the case if everything Scripture says is true.[10] Further, rather than treating dogmatics as an intellectual development that, at least implicitly, improves upon the raw material of Scripture, we will treat theology as the grammar of Scripture.[11] As Scott Swain observes, "What we have in the Bible is well-formed Trinitarian discourse: primary, normative, fluent."[12] Dogmatic reasoning attends to this primary discourse in order to discern its conceptual order and inner connections and comment reflectively on it. By way of analogy, consider the kindergarten-level sentence "She hit the ball to him." There is a sense in which the grammatical terms "subject," "verb," "object," and "indirect object" add nothing to the text. They simply describe the words of the sentence in their ordered syntactical relations. Yet the grammatical analysis operates at a higher level of abstraction than the sentence itself. The words are all longer and take more work to understand and relate. However, this abstraction and conceptualization serves understanding. The grammatical terms grant purchase on the text so that one can understand not only what it says but also why it is ordered and formed as it is. Similarly, when understood as grammar, dogmatic concepts and judgments cannot improve upon the text but only enable us to understand why it is ordered and formed as it is.

Toward this end, throughout the book we will assemble a biblical reasoning toolkit—or, more precisely, a biblical reasoning "rule-kit." The body of the book articulates a set of theological principles and their corresponding exegetical rules.[13] Each principle is a doctrinal commitment, a constituent element of the catholic Christian faith. Each rule turns an aspect of that principle into an exegetical guideline and guardrail, "operationalizing" a theological principle for exegetical purposes. If the principles articulate the grammar of Scripture, then the rules merely show us how to read Scripture with the grain of its own grammar. Our articulation and development of these principles

---

9. Ursinus, *Commentary on the Heidelberg Catechism*, 10.
10. Similarly, S. R. Holmes, "Scripture in Liturgy and Theology," 117.
11. For theology as "grammar" in this sense, see, e.g., Young and Ford, *Meaning and Truth in 2 Corinthians*, 256; Bayer, *Theology the Lutheran Way*, 81, 94–96, 125–26, 170.
12. Swain, "The Bible and the Trinity in Recent Thought," 40.
13. For a full table of the rules and principles, see the appendix.

is deliberately spare. We aim to offer not exhaustive doctrinal discussion of these core Christian teachings but only their exegetical on-ramps.

Speaking of exegesis, ours will receive much help from learned, contemporary, historically minded biblical scholarship. At the same time, we will frequently dissent from common presuppositions of, and conclusions widely held by, modern biblical scholars. Further, while we cannot justify every exegetical decision to the extent that we would if this were a biblical studies monograph, we aim to make exegetical arguments that professional biblical scholars will take seriously.

Our principles and rules cluster primarily around two mutually illuminating foci: the Trinity and the person of Christ. Why this dual focus? The first reason is material. The identity of the God who speaks in his Word and saves us by sending his Son and Spirit is at the heart of God's gospel address. To penetrate more deeply into the gospel is to penetrate more deeply into the mysteries of the Trinity and the Son's incarnation, and vice versa. Another reason for our focus on Christ and the Trinity is that this is where the divorce between biblical studies and theology has been felt most painfully. Creedal Christian teaching about the person of Christ and the Trinity enjoys broad ecumenical consensus. These central doctrines define and distinguish the Christian faith. Yet these are among the doctrines treated with most skepticism by the contemporary biblical studies guild. The breach between theology and exegesis that we aim to help repair is widest here.

Talk of theological "rules" for exegesis may cause some biblical scholars to balk. Shouldn't exegesis be protected from prior dogmatic commitments? Hasn't historical criticism freed Scripture from the shackles of creedal constraint?[14] To offer an initial response to this concern, we would distinguish between two kinds of rules, which we might call extrinsic and intrinsic. An extrinsic rule is imposed from without. A nearby street has a speed limit of twenty-five miles per hour. That limit could easily be revised up or down by the relevant authority. By contrast, consider the link between life and breath in human beings. It is a rule that a living human being breathes. Where you see someone breathing, there you see someone living. No dead person breathes. No breath, no life; no life, no breath. This rule enables rapid, reliable judgments about what a situation calls for. If someone is suddenly unable to breathe, that must be remedied, or grave consequences will quickly follow. The rule "breath = life" is not extrinsic but intrinsic. It derives from the material

---

14. Moberly, *The Bible, Theology, and Faith*, 5: "It is common knowledge that modern biblical criticism only became a recognizable discipline through the process of explicit severing of the Bible from classic theological formulations." Watson, "Trinity and Community," 169, offers grounds for skepticism of this scholarly anti-trinitarianism.

constitution of a human being. One of the primary arguments of this book is that the exegetical rules we will promulgate are not extrinsic but intrinsic. They derive from, and therefore rightly regulate our dealings with, the material content of Scripture.

Hence, we aim to show that these doctrines are more biblical than many think and that a right reading of Scripture requires more theology than many are willing to grant. Because they are distilled from a right reading of Scripture, classical doctrines about Christ and the Trinity constitute a well-stocked keychain that can open exegetical doors that would otherwise remain shut in the face of modern exegetical conventions.

## Resources

In laying out a series of theologically molded rules for exegesis, we are self-consciously following in the footsteps of Augustine, especially his work *The Trinity*. Further, by deriving exegetical rules from theological principles, we are recovering and redeploying an approach that flourished in ancient Christian hermeneutical handbooks such as Tyconius's *Liber regularum*.[15] More broadly, this work is an act of critically retrieving the kind of theological culture that shaped biblical interpretation in the fourth century.[16] Specifically, we aim to retrieve key elements of the theological anthropology and exegetical practices that proved integral to the formation of fourth-century trinitarian theology and many of the christological decisions in the following centuries.

Two caveats are important here. First, "retrieval" is not naïve nostalgia for a golden era that never existed. Instead, it is a matter of standing within a stream of thought as an active and critical, not passive and partisan, participant. We aim to retrieve some of the exegetical practices from the fourth and fifth centuries that have had enduring appeal, but not uncritically.[17] At

15. See Toom, "Early Christian Handbooks on Interpretation." We are critically appropriating the distinction between "principles" and "rules" from Froehlich, *Sensing the Scriptures*, 17–20. As we employ this distinction, principles are the grammar and source of the ways various parts of Scripture speak as they do about God and Christ. The rules are guidelines that correspond to these principles and are therefore intrinsic to Scripture itself.

16. For an account of pro-Nicene theological culture, see Ayres, *Nicaea and Its Legacy*, esp. 414–25.

17. Why critically retrieve fourth- and fifth-century exegetical practices? As Sanders, *The Triune God*, 177, puts it, "It is senseless to try to retain the result of the early church's holistic interpretation of Scripture—the perception of the biblical doctrine of the Trinity—without cultivating, in a way appropriate for our own time, the interpretative practice that produced that result." Too often, theologians attempt to repeat the findings of the early centuries without inhabiting the exegesis and culture that shaped those findings, or by maintaining too combative a stance toward the real gains made in modern biblical interpretation.

several points we attempt to provide these practices with a more solid footing in Scripture, and in this we are undoubtedly and gratefully shaped by modern biblical interpretation.[18] Second, we aim to retrieve the spiritually formative and moral dimensions of exegesis. God's gospel address in Scripture generates the kind of theological culture in which the reader is not a neutral subject dissecting the text as an inert object. If God speaks in Scripture, then reading Scripture is a matter of listening to God. The reader is therefore a proper object of theological reflection. Theological exegesis is, minimally, textual interpretation that reflects on the nature and ends of the reader in light of the God who addresses us in Scripture.[19]

In terms of modern thinkers, in addition to John Webster we owe a special debt to David Yeago and Kavin Rowe. In a widely influential essay, Yeago has argued that biblical exegesis stands to benefit from distinguishing between concepts and judgments.[20] In the simplest terms, a judgment is what a biblical text or theologian is saying about God, and a concept is the way the text or theologian is saying it. Yeago's point is that one can render essentially the same judgment using a variety of concepts.[21] While not identical in every respect, there is a crucial sense in which Nicaea's *homoousios* and Paul's "form of God" (Phil. 2:6) say the same thing about Jesus.

In a series of insightful essays, Kavin Rowe has developed a closely complementary framework of "biblical pressure."[22] As we will discuss more fully in chapters to follow, in Rowe's account, "the biblical text is not inert but instead exerts a pressure ('coercion') upon its interpreters and asserts itself within theological reflection and discourse such that there is (or can be) a profound continuity, grounded in the subject matter itself, between the biblical text and traditional Christian exegesis and theological formulation."[23] The pressure of Scripture not only enables but requires us to confess that the one God of Israel is the triune God who reveals himself in Jesus. Hence, "The ontological judgments of the early ecumenical Creeds were the only satisfying and

---

18. See here Sanders, *The Triune God*, 155–89. Sanders rightly eschews a simplistic turning back of the clock and embraces the contributions of modern biblical scholarship, especially its "enhanced literary sensibility and alertness to narrative reasoning." However, we must use these contributions "better, more fully, and more strategically" (179).

19. See here esp. Webster, "Hermeneutics in Modern Theology"; also Sarisky, *Reading the Bible Theologically*, 198–238.

20. Yeago, "The New Testament and the Nicene Dogma."

21. A qualifier such as "essentially" is crucial; see Yeago's subsequent clarifications in "The Bible," 64–65.

22. Rowe, "Biblical Pressure and Trinitarian Hermeneutics"; Rowe, "Luke and the Trinity"; Rowe, "For Future Generations"; Rowe, "The Trinity in the Letters of St Paul and Hebrews."

23. Rowe, "Biblical Pressure and Trinitarian Hermeneutics," 308.

indeed logical outcome of the claims of the New Testament read together with the Old."[24]

The metaphor of pressure implies agent, object, means, and purpose. God is the agent. His redeemed people are the object. Scripture wielded by the enlivening Spirit and reflected on by regenerated reason is the means. Finally, the purpose is transformative knowledge and covenantal fellowship with the triune God, with the beatific vision as the ultimate fruition of this purpose. As we deploy and develop Rowe's metaphor throughout the book, we will offer close readings of how Scripture characterizes each of these elements in God's economy of divine teaching.

Some readers may wonder whether the book they are holding is a work of "Theological Interpretation of Scripture" (TIS). Certainly we have learned much from, and appreciate many elements of, work that has been done under that heading. If someone were to apply that label to our work, we would offer little objection, though we would also see little gain. We find the phrase to be overly broad, with little descriptive value.[25] Further, we are far more interested in doing theological interpretation than in theorizing it.[26] Theological interpretation is justified by its exegetical children; by the fruits of our readings you may know us.

## Plan

The first three chapters locate biblical reasoning within the economy of divine teaching, in which the nature and ends of Scripture and its readers come to light. These chapters form something of a methodological preamble to the book, with principles and rules that warrant the procedure that the rest of the book undertakes. Chapters 4–9 will then generally follow a four-part structure: biblical pressure, theological grammar, the rule or rules, and exegetical application of the rule(s). Chapter 10 recapitulates and seals the argument of the entire book, applying the full "rule-kit" to the exegesis of a single passage, John 5:17–30.

After theologically describing the teleology of Scripture's readers and the shape of God's teaching activity in the first two chapters, in chapter 3 we

24. Rowe, "Biblical Pressure and Trinitarian Hermeneutics," 308. We will discuss all these matters in far more detail in chap. 3.

25. In appreciating the fruits of TIS while being skeptical of its utility as a rallying cry, our perspective resonates with that of M. Allen, "Systematic Theology and Biblical Theology—Part Two," 349–51, who sympathetically evaluates TIS as a "crisis measure."

26. While we crafted our agenda independently of it and only read the article late in this book's writing, there is a sense in which our entire work answers Wesley Hill's recent call for not just theological interpretation but specifically doctrinal exegesis. See Hill, "In Defense of 'Doctrinal Exegesis.'"

consider the ontology and function of Scripture within that activity. There we will explain in more detail what biblical reasoning looks like in practice. In chapter 4 we articulate a principle and a rule that mark God's qualitative difference from all things as their creator and that remind us to read Scripture's depictions of God in a manner befitting the canon's witness to his holy, infinite, transcendent existence. After thus considering God with regard to his singular essence, our remaining principles and rules consider God with regard to the distinction of persons in the Trinity. In this respect, our order of expounding these rules follows the order of the two Testaments. Chapters 5 and 6 will develop trinitarian rules for exegesis, chapters 7 and 8 christological ones, and then chapter 9 considers the Son and the Spirit from the standpoint of their relations to the other divine persons. The first three rules form the indispensable foundation for and background of the last seven, and the last seven enable us to articulate the identity of the Father, Son, and Spirit in ways that fit with the first three.

## Audiences and Authors

The intended audience of this book includes both biblical scholars and theologians. For most of the church's history, those were two names for one thing. But over the past four centuries, tall, durable walls have been erected between what are now considered two disciplines.[27] We hope to engage practitioners of both. We aim to convince biblical scholars that exegesis requires more theology than they commonly admit, and we aim to convince theologians that theology requires more exegesis than they typically do.[28] While the disciplinary division between biblical studies and theology has some heuristic and practical value, we believe that, all told, it does more harm than good.[29] Hence, following Webster, we instead distinguish between exegetical and dogmatic reasoning as two primary elements in the larger task of "biblical reasoning."

Depending on which side of the disciplinary divide a reader's training and interests fall, parts of the book may call for patience. Biblical scholars who have little concern for theological place-setting may want to skim or skip the first three chapters and begin in earnest either with the latter half of chapter 3

---

27. For an important slice of the relevant history, see Legaspi, *The Death of Scripture and the Rise of Biblical Studies*.

28. For the latter point, see esp. Watson, "The Scope of Hermeneutics," 74. Watson's broader comments on the consequences of the policed boundary between biblical studies and theology are penetrating (72–74).

29. On the deleterious consequences of the divisions between biblical studies and theology and between Old and New Testament scholarship, see Watson, *Text and Truth*, 6.

or with chapter 4. Then again, perhaps such readers stand to profit the most from the theological provocations of the first three chapters. The argument is cumulative and builds on itself; the whole can persuade far better than any of the parts taken alone. Those who skip the first part yet go on to find the exegesis and theological reasoning of later chapters worth consideration may wish to double back for the larger context. Conversely, those who skim for doctrinal portions while skipping the exegesis will miss the argument entirely.

This book not only has two audiences; it also has two authors. The "we" throughout this book will be not conventional, much less royal, but real. This book synthesizes the sensitivities and skills of one author trained in systematic theology and one in biblical studies. Tyler Wittman drafted chapters 1–6 and the conclusion; R. B. Jamieson drafted chapters 7–10 and this introduction. While we have thoroughly revised each other's chapters, we have not imposed a strict uniformity of style. Given our differing primary vocations, one might notice more Latin scholasticisms in the earlier chapters and more sermonic illustrations in the later chapters. Nevertheless, we both fully endorse the full product.

# PART ONE

---

# BIBLICAL
# REASONING

# 1

# Seek His Face Always

## The End of Biblical Reasoning

**Principle 1:** Holy Scripture presupposes and fosters readers whose end is the vision of Christ's glory, and therein eternal life. Biblical reasoning must be ordered to this same end.

In this initial chapter we consider one of the primary goals of Scripture and the exegetical means of attaining this goal. Destinations, after all, determine pilgrimages. Likewise, construction materials cohere because of what they build, and an education is more than busy work only in light of a curriculum with particular goals. All of these examples point out the fact that to steer things appropriately we must first know the end (*telos*) at which we aim. Hence, we must first consider the end of biblical reasoning so that we may aim at it.

This distinction between an end and our aiming points to how "ends" are distinct from "purposes" in at least one crucial respect. The end of something is grounded in its nature, whereas any given purpose is grounded in a will. Ends are objective and purposes more subjective. Sometimes purposes align with ends, but not always. For instance, a toddler may purpose that a toilet serve as a bathtub for his father's Bible. Yet that toilet remains fit for some things and unfit for others; the end of the toilet—not to mention the Bible—clashes with these toddlerian purposes. Other examples are ready to hand: no one brushes their teeth with motor oil; people do not go to the airport to purchase groceries; penguins are useless when you need a doctor (and vice versa). Why? Given what these things are, they flourish in the pursuit of certain ends and flounder in other pursuits. Given the ends of these things, some purposes are fitting and others are not. So too with the reading of Scripture. But we can grasp how ends bear upon our reading of Scripture only if we have some idea of our own ends as readers and of Scripture's ends in light of what God is doing in and through it for his people. Crucially, these ends must be discerned not from general psychological, anthropological, or sociological analysis but from the overall shape of the Christian faith.

Our purpose in this chapter will therefore be to begin laying the foundation for the project of "biblical reasoning" that this book proposes. Starting with "ends," we are concerned here with justifying and elucidating our first principle: *Holy Scripture presupposes and fosters readers whose end is the vision of Christ's glory, and therein eternal life. Biblical reasoning must be ordered to this same end.* The following chapters will build on this end, looking backward and forward to it as the destination of our exegetical and theological activity.

We start by looking at Christ and what certain key moments of his teaching suggest about the chief end of his disciples, which is summarized in the concept of the beatific vision, or the sight of God that renders us blessed. Then we will explore how this same end requires that we undergo the purification of our vision through faith that works by love. Finally, we will consider how faith and sight are distinguished and yet related, especially in the notion of contemplation, which is both shaped by exegesis and shapes exegesis.

## Beholding Christ's Glory

We often hear a great deal about approaching the Bible with a hermeneutic centered on some fundamental theme like the gospel, salvation history, or even Christ. But in such discussions far less tends to be said about the truths on which even these themes are centered. If our reading of Scripture is going to center on something, it should be on what is central, and nothing is more central in Scripture than the triune God. It is not going too far to say that ignorance of the Trinity is ignorance of the gospel.[1] Thomas Aquinas voices a common opinion when he says, "All the knowledge imparted by faith revolves

---

1. Johann Gerhard: "If we are ignorant of or deny the mystery of the Trinity, we are ignorant of or deny the entire economy [οἰκονομία, i.e., administration] of salvation" (*Theological Commonplaces* III.1.7).

around these two points, the divinity of the Trinity and the humanity of Christ."[2] Understanding the significance of Christ's humanity requires a full view of his mission, which encompasses his life, death, resurrection, ascension, and continuing reign from heaven. Further, to know Christ is to know him as both man and God and so to perceive that he is one with the Father and the Holy Spirit. Hence, a deep understanding of Christ leads us to knowledge of the triune God. Conversely, knowledge of the Trinity is impossible apart from faith in Christ. In order to know one, we must know the other, such that Scripture tends to be theocentric and Christocentric in one breath.

Scripture displays this theocentric and Christocentric focus explicitly. After all, Aquinas's comment is a gloss on Jesus's prayer, "This is eternal life, that they know you, the only true God, and Jesus Christ whom you have sent" (John 17:3). Eternal life consists in knowledge of God, not just any knowledge but specifically that which is found in and through Jesus Christ. These words come toward the end of Jesus's high priestly prayer, building up to the climactic moments of his betrayal and crucifixion in the Gospel of John. Where the other Gospels narrate the Lord's Supper before Christ's passion, John instead gives us a lengthy discourse soaked through with important teaching on the centrality of Christ, the workings of the Trinity, and how these truths bear upon our discipleship (John 13:31–17:26). Occupying such a prominent place, knowledge of the triune God in Christ must be crucial and therefore worth pursuing. This is reinforced by the progression of Jesus's concluding prayer, which consists of six requests that culminate with a petition that his disciples would see his eternal, divine glory: "Father, I desire that they also, whom you have given me, may be with me where I am, to see my glory that you have given me because you loved me before the foundation of the world" (John 17:24; cf. 17:5).[3] This statement provides a window into the hope of John's Gospel and arguably all of Scripture: that its readers will come to see the glory of Christ.[4] The biblical metaphor of vision, about which we will say more below, here functions to tie together how the only true God will

---

2. Aquinas, *Compendium of Theology* 1.2. For similar statements, see Augustine, *The Trinity* 1.5; Turretin, *Institutes of Elenctic Theology* 13.6.1.

3. This final request stands apart, since "I desire" (θέλω; John 17:24) lays greater stress on the petition than the previous "I ask" (ἐρωτῶ; 17:9, 15, 20); cf. Bengel, *Gnomon of the New Testament*, 2:467. Our presentation of glory and the vision of God in John's Gospel is indebted to Filtvedt, "The Transcendence and Visibility of the Father in the Gospel of John"; Chibici-Revneanu, *Die Herrlichkeit des Verherrlichten*, 512–631; Nielsen, "The Narrative Structures of Glory and Glorification in the Fourth Gospel."

4. Hence, Jörg Frey concludes, "The goal of the Fourth Gospel's distinctive presentation of Christ is that believers of later times see Jesus' δόξα (17.24)" (*The Glory of the Crucified One*, 258).

be known as his glory is seen in the Christ he has sent. Stepping back for a moment to canvass what Scripture says about seeing God and how this is concentrated in Christ's glory will begin to orient this book's approach to its subject matter.

Jesus's prayer prompts two questions that are relevant to our inquiry. First, why does Jesus relate knowledge of himself and God the Father to vision, and why is this so important to John's Gospel and the story of Israel? Second, what does all this suggest about how we should pursue this knowledge through Scripture? Answering each of these questions will serve to paint in broad strokes the orientation of the following chapters. As we shall see, our overall goal for exegetically investigating the doctrines of the Trinity and Christology is to pursue, prayerfully, a vision of the risen Christ's glory through faith.

### The Beatific Vision

The answer to the first question depends on the kind of knowledge under discussion. The goodness of the gospel's news is not only that we sinners are reconciled to God through Jesus Christ but also that we are promised future glory in the resurrection (Rom. 8:30; Phil. 3:21; 1 Cor. 15). Intrinsic to this glory is a full knowledge and enjoyment of God, which Scripture often portrays through metaphors of sight and vision. Paul, for instance, parallels sight with knowledge when speaking of this future glory: "For now we see only a reflection as in a mirror, but then face to face. Now I know in part, but then I will know fully, as I am fully known" (1 Cor. 13:12 CSB; cf. Num. 12:8; 1 John 3:6). For this reason Christians speak of the "beatific vision," the eschatological vision of God that beatifies or renders us blessed. Theologians have long debated what blessedness is, but at its core blessedness is our highest hope, and it consists in an intimate communion with God that quiets our hearts' deepest longings and fills us with everlasting joy.[5] Scripture expresses this hope through a variety of metaphors pertaining to light and glory, riches and treasures, Sabbath rest, and even the absence of sin and evil, as well as hunger and thirst.[6] But through all of these, vision is central. Intrinsic to blessedness is this mysterious vision of God.[7]

The hope of beholding God is expressed throughout the OT:

---

5. Griffiths, *Decreation*, 217, provides a spare definition: "Beatitude . . . is an umbrella-word for whatever it is that constitutes the final and unsurpassable good for human creatures." The vision of God is intrinsic to blessedness since vision begets conformity to God, sufficiency in God, and full knowledge of God (Polanus, *Syntagma theologiae christianae* 1.9).

6. See the catena of imagery and themes in Turretin, *Institutes of Elenctic Theology* 20.8.18–21.

7. See *Synopsis purioris theologiae* 39.33; 40.17.

- "As for me, I shall behold your face in righteousness; when I awake, I shall be satisfied with your likeness" (Ps. 17:15).
- "The LORD is righteous; he loves righteous deeds; the upright shall behold his face" (Ps. 11:7).
- "Your eyes will behold the king in his beauty" (Isa. 33:17).
- "In my flesh I shall see God, whom I shall see for myself, and my eyes shall behold, and not another" (Job 19:26–27).[8]

And often this longing is juxtaposed with notions of presence and joy: "In your presence there is fullness of joy; at your right hand are pleasures forevermore" (Ps. 16:11); "One thing have I asked of the LORD, that will I seek after: that I may dwell in the house of the LORD all the days of my life, to gaze upon the beauty of the LORD and to inquire in his temple" (Ps. 27:4). From these witnesses alone, we conclude that the vision of God is something uniquely to be hoped for ("one thing") and even something that may only happen fully in the flesh ("when I awake"; "in my flesh").[9]

However, the hope of seeing God seems paradoxical. How may one see God if he is invisible? God is the one "who dwells in unapproachable light, whom no one has ever seen or can see" (1 Tim. 6:16; 1:17; 1 John 4:12).[10] The closer we get to the heart of biblical eschatology, the more this knot loosens. Throughout Scripture, God is clearly free to make himself visible in some manner when he pleases. Scripture does not shy away from the apparent oddity of this fact, expressing the tension explicitly when Moses is described as "seeing him who is invisible" (Heb. 11:27). In the aftermath of the exodus, Moses initially beholds God with the seventy elders of Israel on the mountain, before going further up the mountain on his own to enter the cloud of glory and speak with God (Exod. 24:9–18). Later, Moses speaks with God "face to face" in the tent of meeting on Israel's behalf (Exod. 33:11; Deut. 34:10). These moments peak dramatically with Moses's request to see God's glory, at which point God warns him, "You cannot see my face, for man shall not see me and live" (Exod. 33:18–20). While Moses has spoken to God face-to-face, this somehow has not involved seeing God's face. God nevertheless makes a concession of sorts and renders himself visible to Moses *indirectly*: "You shall see my back, but my face shall not be seen" (Exod. 33:23). What this

---

8. On the bodily language of God's face and appearance, see Miller, *The Lord of the Psalms*, 32–38.

9. On theophanic psalms, see Kraus, *Theology of the Psalms*, 38–39.

10. Among contemporary theologians, Katherine Sonderegger gives forceful expression to God's invisibility in *Systematic Theology*, vol. 1, *The Doctrine of God*. See also Bavinck, *Reformed Dogmatics*, 2:29–52.

half-refusal suggests is that even though Moses has beheld God and spoken to God face-to-face, he has nevertheless not yet seen God's face directly.[11] Moses reinforces some such distinction when recounting Israel's experience at Sinai: "You heard the sound of words, but saw no form; there was only a voice" (Deut. 4:12).[12] Furthermore, no other prophet arose in Israel like Moses, "whom the LORD knew face to face" (Deut. 34:10). If no one saw God as intensely as Moses and yet even Moses only had an indirect vision, then why do we hope to see God "face to face" (1 Cor. 13:12)?

### The Invisible God's Visibility

There are hints in these episodes that, like a good teacher, God leads Moses step-by-step into a deeper friendship that ultimately points beyond Moses to something more to come. Retrospectively, we know that this "something more" is the new covenant whose mediator is Jesus Christ and whose promise is God's outpoured Spirit. The one mediator of the new covenant is like Moses, but better. Moses asked to see God's glory, but Jesus is this glory (Exod. 33:18; John 1:14; Heb. 1:3). Moses encountered God's glory in the tabernacle, but Jesus is the Word who "became flesh and tabernacled among us" (John 1:14; Exod. 33:7).[13] Moses could only see God's glory indirectly, from behind, as God tells him, "There is a place by me where you shall stand on the rock, and while my glory passes by I will put you in a cleft of the rock, and I will cover you with my hand until I have passed by" (Exod. 33:21–22). Whether the rock is the teaching of Christ one finds in the church or Christ himself, God's glory now encounters us in the man Jesus Christ.[14] Specifically, we now behold the glory of God "passing by" in Christ's person, both in his

11. Gregory of Nyssa and Augustine both observe from this fact that Moses was unable to see God "according to God's true being" (ὡς ἐκεῖνός ἐστι) or "as He is," meaning God's incomprehensible essence; Moses nevertheless genuinely knew God. See Gregory of Nyssa, *The Life of Moses* 2.230 (Malherbe and Ferguson, 114; GNO 7/1:114); Augustine, *Letter* 147.20 (WSA II/2:329); cf. also Gregory of Nazianzus, *Oration* 28.3 (PPS 23:39).

12. In this respect, DeLapp, *Theophanic "Type-Scenes" in the Pentateuch*, 139, is correct to observe that Deuteronomy "provides a commentary for reading the narrative" at Sinai, which includes a "warning not to remember the scene as one including YHWH's form *in se*." Something similar would apply to Jacob's report of seeing God at the Jabbok, because what he saw was "a man" (Gen. 32:24; Hosea 12:4).

13. By "tabernacled" (ἐσκήνωσεν; cf. σκηνή in Exod. 25:9; 33:7 LXX), John hints at the incarnation as the fulfillment of the temple, and so records Jesus's explicit identification of himself with the temple in the following chapter (John 2:18–22).

14. For Augustine, the "rock" is Peter, the place is the church, and the glory that passes by is the humanity of Christ (*The Trinity* 2.30 [WSA I/5:122–23]). Gregory of Nazianzus construes the rock as "God the Word incarnate for us" (*Oration* 28.3 [PPS 23:39]; cf. Gregory of Nyssa, *Life of Moses* 2.244).

earthly ministry and in his cross and resurrection (John 12:28).[15] Consideration of each point will serve to demonstrate how it is that the invisible God stoops down for us to behold him.

First, God's glory becomes visible as it "passes by" in Christ's ministry. Consider Mark's portrait, in which, long before the disciples can "see" Jesus as the revelation of God, Jesus first sees them. As the disciples crossed the sea, Jesus "saw" the trouble of their passage through the winds, even amidst the darkness of the night. In view of their trouble, Jesus walks out to them intending "to pass by them" (Mark 6:48). As on the mountain, so also on the sea God passes by and reveals his glory (cf. 1 Kings 19:11).[16] Christ can reveal God's glory in this way because he has seen God uniquely: "No one has ever seen God; the only begotten God, who is in the bosom of the Father, he has made him known" (John 1:18 AT); no one "has seen the Father except he who is from God; he has seen the Father" (John 6:46). More than this, God's glory is now visible in the face of Christ, "the image of the invisible God," such that those who see him see the Father (Col. 1:15; cf. John 14:9).

Second, God's glory also "passes by" us in Christ's cross, resurrection, and ascension. In this respect especially, the *visio Dei* that we are given overturns any expectations we might naturally have. Isaiah speaks of the Servant's suffering as "without glory" (ἀδοξήσει [*adoxēsei*]; Isa. 52:14 LXX), but Jesus identifies himself as this Servant and makes his crucifixion the decisive revelation of God's glory (δόξα, *doxa*). Speaking of his glorification by the Father in being lifted up on the cross, Jesus says that "whoever sees me sees him who sent me" (John 12:45).[17] When we understand these words in their larger context, Jesus is saying that God's glory will especially be seen in his inglorious crucifixion: "When you have lifted up the Son of Man, then you will know that I am [ἐγώ εἰμι, *egō eimi*]" (John 8:28).[18] But however central the cross is,

15. On this unity of the cross and resurrection in John's Gospel, see Schnelle, "Cross and Resurrection in the Gospel of John"; Moloney, *Love in the Gospel of John*, 92–98.

16. Marcus, *Mark 1–8*, 426, notes that "pass by" (παρελθεῖν) functions "almost" as a technical term for divine revelations in the LXX, being supplied in some instances where the corresponding verb was lacking in the MT (e.g., Gen. 32:31–32; Dan. 12:1). Further OT context reinforces this: only God "trampled the waves of the sea" and elusively "passes by me," says Job (Job 9:8, 11). Hence, it comes as no surprise that in this episode on the sea Jesus alludes to the burning bush: "Take heart, I am [ἐγώ εἰμι]. Do not be afraid" (Mark 6:50 AT; cf. Exod. 3:14).

17. See Filtvedt, "The Transcendence and Visibility of the Father in the Gospel of John," 111–16.

18. As John shows in his use of Isaiah, Christ's being "lifted up" (ὑψώσητε) reveals God's glory (John 12:27–43). Of the four times that being "lifted up" and "exalted" are used together in Isaiah, three describe YHWH (Isa. 6:1; 33:10; 57:15), suggesting that these terms in conjunction are unique to God, who gives his glory to no other (Isa. 42:8; 48:11). The other instance describes the suffering Servant: "Behold, my servant shall act wisely; he shall be high and

there are other elements of the Son's glorification, since his resurrection and ascension return him to the glory he enjoyed with the Father before the world began (John 17:5). Even in Mark's story, Jesus comes to the disciples around "the fourth watch of the night" (Mark 6:48), or dawn, which Mark elsewhere uses as a poetic allusion to the resurrection: the darkness of Jesus's crucifixion is rolled back only with the rising of the sun on the third day (Mark 15:33; 16:2).[19] We truly "see" God's glory in Christ's cross when we understand his death and resurrection as an act of love, the Son laying down and taking up his own life for his sheep (John 10:18; cf. 2:19). God's visibility is found in Jesus Christ crucified and risen or it is not found at all. We may see the Father in Christ, so we may not see him elsewhere or by other means. In Christ's resurrection and ascension, then, God's glory passes before us from Christ's grave to the Father's right hand. Just so, God confirms that he is "merciful and gracious, slow to anger, and abounding in steadfast love and faithfulness, keeping steadfast love for thousands, forgiving iniquity and transgression and sin, but who will by no means clear the guilty" (Exod. 34:6–7).

The importance of Christ's Spirit further emphasizes this concentration of God's visibility in the crucified and risen Jesus. There are hints in Moses's ministry pointing us in this direction, as when he finds himself inadequate to mediate between God and Israel, and so wishes that all God's people were anointed with God's Spirit (Num. 11:29). God then apportions some of Moses's anointing to seventy elders who help to share his burden (Num. 11:16–30). This anticipates the new covenant promise, fulfilled at Pentecost, of the Holy Spirit being poured out on all God's people (Joel 2:28–29). Paul points to the Spirit's significance when discussing how seeing God's glory in Christ outweighs the glory of the old covenant. Moses's ministry was written on mere tablets of stone and, because he spoke to God face-to-face, was still glorious enough that the Israelites could not gaze upon him without a veil (2 Cor. 3:7–13; Exod. 34:25–29). But the new covenant is better because the Spirit writes on "tablets of human hearts" (2 Cor. 3:3; cf. Jer. 31:31–33; Ezek. 11:19–20; 36:26–27). For God's people, then, the indwelling Spirit removes the "veil" so that we may see God's glory in the mirror of Christ's flesh: "We

---

lifted up, and shall be exalted" (Isa. 52:13). John incorporates these associations in depicting the "glory" revealed on Christ's cross, which Isaiah "saw" (John 12:41), which reinforces that the Servant belongs to the identity of YHWH. See, further, Brendsel, *"Isaiah Saw His Glory,"* 123–34; also C. H. Williams, "Johannine Christology and Prophetic Traditions."

19. The detail about the women arriving at the tomb "when the sun had risen" (Mark 16:2) has clear symbolic significance against the background of the OT. For example, in David's last words about "the son of Jesse . . . the man who was raised [ἀνέστησεν] on high, the anointed [χριστὸν] of the God of Jacob," he says God "dawns on them [Israel] like the morning light" (2 Sam. 23:1–4 LXX). For this and other examples, see Marcus, *Mark 8–16,* 1083–84.

all, with unveiled face, beholding as in a mirror the glory of the Lord, are being transformed into the same image from glory to glory, just as by the Spirit of the Lord" (2 Cor. 3:18 NKJV). The Holy Spirit has "shone in our hearts to give the light of the knowledge of the glory of God in the face of Jesus Christ" (2 Cor. 4:6).

God's Spirit enables us to behold God's glory in Christ crucified. This eschatological work has a transformative effect on our lives now but will be complete only in the resurrection. Jesus's desire for his disciples to see him, while primarily referring to a future vision, is nevertheless something held out to them now because they are already in one sense with him where he is by virtue of the Spirit's presence.[20] What we grasp by faith in this life, we will behold by sight in the next: the man Jesus, the Lamb of God, the King in his beauty (cf. John 1:29; 3:14–15; 19:5). This sight of God will be no terror because we will be friends with God, holy as God is holy. The canon's conclusion seals this hope's importance when, at God's renewal of all things, his servants "will see his face, and his name will be on their foreheads" (Rev. 22:4). To behold God is the startling possibility opened by the actuality of God's self-diffusing light. The Son, who is Light from Light and is light itself (αὐτοφώς, *autophōs*), shines in the darkness of our hearts by his Spirit so that we may see him together with the Father and the Spirit as the God who dwells in unapproachable light. Christ is the pure radiance of God himself making us pure, so that in God's light we may see light (Ps. 36:9).

Much more could be said about the beatific vision, but this much suffices for our current purposes. Knowing God in Christ has a transforming effect because this knowledge is connected to the vision of Christ's glory, which will be consummated at the end of all things. Beholding God in the face of Christ in the new creation, we will enjoy life eternal, perpetual peace, joy, and rest. This is our telos. God created us for his own glory, certainly, but God's glory elicits our glorification. Irenaeus expresses the unity of these truths eloquently: "For the glory of God is the living human, but the life of the human is the vision of God. Indeed, if the manifestation of God through creation gives life to all things living on earth, much more does the revelation of the Father by the Word give life to those who see God."[21]

We exist so that we might see God, intimately commune with him, and become decorated in his light. Before discussing how this telos bears on exegetical reason, we must first grasp something of how it bears on our lives. The vision of God is eschatological, after all. So how does it concern us now?

---

20. Chibici-Revneanu, *Die Herrlichkeit des Verherrlichten*, 304.
21. Irenaeus, *Against Heresies* 4.20.7 (SC 100.648 [AT]).

## Ascesis and Vision-Shaped Attention

What the vision of God as our telos helps us to see is that we are attention-shaped creatures. Where our attention goes, our affections and actions follow. Various forms of this insight fuel portraits of the Christian life that emphasize an attentiveness to "heavenly" things with a corresponding, though qualified, detachment from this world. Qualified, because the detachment in question is a fruit of evangelical freedom from the tyranny of mundane goods, their empty promises and narrow possibilities. As C. S. Lewis observes, "If you read history you will find that the Christians who did most for the present world were just those who thought most of the next."[22] A great "cloud of witnesses" would agree (Heb. 11:2–12:2). Since the Christian's hope is to see Christ's glory, then this heavenly frame focuses our attentions upward and reorders our loves and priorities. It structures our relationship with God and others and shapes how we suffer, lament, pray, pursue and receive temporal goods, and more.[23]

Such reorientation involves elements of ascesis, the denial and disciplining of those impulses that would draw our attention away from Christ's glory. In one of the concluding moments to a central section of the Sermon on the Mount, Jesus warns his listeners against treasuring things of this earth, for "where your treasure is, there your heart will be also" (Matt. 6:21).[24] He extends this exhortation into the metaphor of vision: "The eye is the lamp of the body. So if your eye is healthy [or "simple," ἁπλοῦς, *haplous*], your whole body will be full of light, but if your eye is bad [or "wicked"], your whole body will be full of darkness. If then the light in you is darkness, how great is the darkness!" (Matt. 6:22–23; cf. Luke 11:34–36). The point is that our hearts' attentions are morally determined, since whether we are full of light or darkness depends on where our treasure is and how that affects our lives.[25] To be "simple" we must become wholehearted in our attentiveness and devotion to God. To do this we must take not only every thought but also every desire captive to Christ. Wholeheartedness, or simplicity of heart, focuses our attention and love on God and leads to acts of generosity (part of the meaning of ἁπλότης [*haplotēs*], "simplicity"), whereas a wicked attention is torn from

22. C. S. Lewis, *Mere Christianity*, 134.
23. See esp. M. Allen, *Grounded in Heaven*, 89–132. It is also true that actions sharpen our attentions and desires, leading us to discover new things about our attentions, the things they focus on, and why. Nevertheless, it remains true that our hearts' attentions hold a certain pride of place in shaping who we are and what we do.
24. Pennington, *The Sermon on the Mount and Human Flourishing*, 237–44.
25. Allison, "The Eye Is the Lamp of the Body (Matthew 6.22–23=Luke 11.34–36)," esp. 76–78.

God by love of self, and thus is "double-minded" (James 1:8).[26] Hence, our attentions may be products of either sin's darkness or the light of grace, which comes from God: "For it is you who light my lamp; the LORD my God lightens my darkness" (Ps. 18:28). The exegetical relevance of these observations goes beyond the fact that our attention needs to be focused on the right object. In addition, the reader must become a particular kind of person to have this rightly ordered attention. In order to read with the kind of attention that corresponds to our telos, we need eyes that are simple, pure, and full of light.

Indeed, no small part of our discipleship consists in cultivating a vision-shaped attention through pursuit of the moral conditions suggested by Jesus's words about our eyes:

- "Blessed are the pure in heart, for they shall see God" (Matt. 5:8).
- Without holiness "no one will see the Lord" (Heb. 12:14).
- "Everyone who thus hopes in him purifies himself as he is pure" (1 John 3:3).
- "With the purified you showed yourself pure" (Ps. 18:26; cf. 2 Sam. 22:27; Dan. 12:10).[27]

However, these are not symbols for mere moral and intellectual virtues. Something far more radical is in view. Purity and holiness are important especially as they concern the knowledge of God in Christ because, under the sway of sin, our attentions are constantly dragged down toward created things. Therefore, so are our thoughts about God. Given these circumstances, Augustine cautions us that idolatry inevitably results if we seek God with our own resources and desires, even if they rise to the highest cultural standards of intellectual and moral excellence.[28] The problem is that we are sinners whose loves stretch out to the wrong things, or the right things in the wrong ways, and whose pride looks for ways to think and speak (or not) about God apart from the embarrassment of Christ's cross. Our souls are sick, and so we need a remedy that reaches as deep as the problem; we need to have our "sickly gaze" purified and our loves reordered.[29] Hence, "Our minds must be purified so that they

---

26. On the moral significance of simplicity in Scripture, see Spicq, "La vertu du simplicité dans l'ancien et le nouveau testament."

27. For an informed overview of historical approaches to the beatific vision, centered on interpretations of Matt. 5:8, see Allison, "Seeing God (Matt. 5:8)," in *Studies in Matthew*, 43–63.

28. Augustine, *The Trinity* 1.1; *On Christian Teaching* 1.9.

29. Augustine, *The Trinity* 1.2 (WSA I/5:66); *Tractates on the Gospel of John* 1.19. This is a common emphasis in the fathers: "For one who is not pure to lay hold of pure things is dangerous, just as it is for weak eyes to look at the sun's brightness" (Gregory of Nazianzus, *Oration* 27.3 [PPS 23:27]; on this theme, see Beeley, *Gregory of Nazianzus on the Trinity and*

are able to perceive that light and then hold fast to it."[30] For these reasons, he notes, "What calls for all our efforts in this life is the healing of the eyes of our hearts, with which God is to be seen."[31]

Augustine recognizes, however, that our purification is not something we can muster up with our own strenuous effort. In order for us to perceive God's glory in the crucified and risen Christ, God himself must purify our hearts' vision: "The only thing to cleanse the wicked and the proud is the blood of the just man and the humility of God; to contemplate God, which by nature we are not, we would have to be cleansed by him who became what by nature we are and what by sin we are not."[32] In sin we "fall short of the glory of God" and therefore cannot perceive God's glory in the person of Christ (Rom. 3:23).[33] Hence, to perceive Christ's glory, we need Christ: "Christ loved the church and gave himself up for her, that he might sanctify her, having cleansed her by the washing of water with the word, so that he might present the church to himself in splendor, without spot or wrinkle or any such thing, that she might be holy and without blemish" (Eph. 5:25–27); he "gave himself for us to redeem us from all lawlessness and to purify for himself a people for his own possession who are zealous for good works" (Titus 2:14). His self-giving, from the cross to his entrance into God's presence in heaven, is therefore an act of "making purification for sins" (Heb. 1:3; 1 John 1:7). All the regulations for purity in the old covenant pointed to Christ because of their merely provisional nature, but by his blood and the washing of regeneration, those who belong to Christ and are united to him may "draw near with a true heart in full assurance of faith, with our hearts sprinkled clean from an evil conscience and our bodies washed with pure water" (Heb. 10:22; cf. Titus 3:5; 1 Pet. 3:21).

Though in sin we fall short of God's glory, by faith in Christ "we rejoice in hope of the glory of God" (Rom. 5:2). We are therefore purified "by faith" (Acts 15:9) and the righteousness that comes through it (Rom. 4:13). As unbelief and impurity are treated synonymously (Titus 1:15), so too are faith and

---

the *Knowledge of God*, 65–90). Cyril of Alexandria likewise comments: "Those who have a pure heart would surely be none other than those who, by union with God through the Son in the Spirit, have abandoned all love of the flesh and have driven worldly pleasure as far away as possible, who have denied their own lives, as it were, and have offered themselves only to the will of the Spirit, living a pure life completely devoted to Christ" (*Commentary on John* 11.12, on John 17:24 [Maxwell, 2:308]).

30. Augustine, *On Christian Teaching* 1.10 (Green, 12).
31. Augustine, *Sermon* 88.5 (WSA III/3:422).
32. Augustine, *The Trinity* 4.4 (WSA I/5:155).
33. On the extent of our defilement and God's provision for purification, which is one part of our sanctification, see Owen, *Pneumatologia*, 4.4–5 (*Works* 3:422–67).

purity, from which acts of love follow: "Having purified your souls by your obedience to the truth for a sincere brotherly love, love one another earnestly from a pure heart" (1 Pet. 1:22). The obedience in question is the "obedience of faith" (Rom. 1:5; 10:16; 16:26), often tested and confirmed in its purity by trials and suffering (1 Pet. 1:6–7). Faith is in this sense the instrumental cause of our purification, not on account of faith as such, but on account of its object: faith receives the purifying work of Christ and his Spirit. Peter says of the gentiles: "God . . . by giving them the Holy Spirit . . . cleansed their hearts by faith" (Acts 15:8–9). It is the person and work of Christ, and the gift of the Holy Spirit this work secures, that are the center of gravity—not the act of faith as such. Faith, as it were, opens the heart's mouth and draws in the Spirit (πνεῦμα [*pneuma*], "breath").[34] And the Spirit in turn draws us into the life of God as adopted children and away from the life of the flesh. Because faith entails repentance, reconciliation, and humility, it trains our attention on what is above and away from what is below, including what is earthly in us.[35] Faith thus lifts our attention to Christ and his kingdom: "Seek the things that are above, where Christ is, seated at the right hand of God. Set your minds on the things that are above, not on the things that are on earth" (Col. 3:1–2).[36] These imperatives imply knowledge that begets desire. The more we see Christ's beauty, the more beautiful we will find him, and we become like what we love and worship.[37]

The connection with love is important, because love is the flowering of an active faith. Where faith introduces knowledge of something, love propels us toward an even greater intimacy with it. Love, after all, is a unitive force that assimilates the lover to the beloved. Faith in Christ therefore redirects our love toward him and conforms us to his image, reorienting our attention to the "things that are above." If faith did not work by love in this way, it would not be saving faith but mere "knowledge about" God, which leaves us defenseless against the many things that can cloud our vision. But since it is more than mere cognition, faith involves the will's assent and trust, and on this account moves us to hope and love. Hence, when the eschatological vision of God shapes our attention by faith, it is imperative to "put to death

---

34. Cf. Gregory of Nazianzus, *Oration* 6.1 (FC 107:3).
35. Calvin, *Institutes of the Christian Religion* 3.7.1.
36. The same thought is expressed elsewhere: "We look not to the things that are seen but to the things that are unseen. For the things that are seen are transient, but the things that are unseen are eternal" (2 Cor. 4:18); "For those who live according to the flesh set their minds on the things of the flesh, but those who live according to the Spirit set their minds on the things of the Spirit" (Rom. 8:5; cf. Phil. 2:5).
37. Beale, *We Become What We Worship*; Lints, *Identity and Idolatry*.

. . . what is earthly" and "put on" the virtues of the kingdom (Col. 3:5–17; cf. Phil. 3:8–16).

God begins our purification through faith and will consummate it at Christ's return. Your life is "hidden with Christ in God," Paul says, and when "Christ who is your life appears, then you also will appear with him in glory" (Col. 3:3–4). In this framework, what propels our pursuit of holiness is eschatological hope rather than some nostalgia for innocence.[38] All of this is possible because the saints have a foretaste of this hope now: "Like the Israelites, they have some clusters of Canaan's grapes, some of the fruits of the good land by the way, as a specimen and pledge of what they shall enjoy when they come into that better country."[39] Among such "fruits" are those of the Spirit, who is the guarantee of our inheritance and therefore the one who enables us to behold Christ by faith in this life (Gal. 5:22–24; Eph. 1:13–14). By holding on to Christ, faith follows God's glory as it passes by, from the face of Moses, to the shores of Galilee, through the hall of Pontius Pilate, into the darkness of Golgotha and Joseph of Arimathea's tomb, spanning the depths of the dead and the heights of the Father's right hand.

Disciples of Christ are called to behold his glory as the crucified and risen emissary of the Father. Far from being a merely intellectual pursuit, this calling claims our whole lives. To become those whose attentions are fixed on Christ and his kingdom, the "things that are above," we must undergo the ascetical obedience of faith. We must embrace the good news about Christ and the bad news about ourselves that this entails. We must cast ourselves at his feet, hunger and thirst for righteousness, and so work out our salvation with fear and trembling. God's grace thus prepares us for glory: "Music hath no pleasure in it unto them that cannot hear; nor the most beautiful colours unto them that cannot see. . . . Heaven itself would not be more advantageous unto persons not renewed by the Spirit of grace in this life."[40] This much is required of disciples. What does this require of our exegesis?

## Faith, Contemplation, and Exegesis

So far we have canvassed the telos of Christ's disciples and the way that leads there, through Christ and the Spirit, whom we receive by the gift of faith. In Jesus's high-priestly prayer, he desires that we "see" his glory (John 17:24; 19:35). This is only possible for those whose wayward attentions have been

---

38. M. Allen, *Grounded in Heaven*, 145–46.
39. Gill, *A Complete Body of Doctrinal and Practical Divinity* 7.11.
40. Owen, *Meditations and Discourses on the Glory of Christ* I (*Works* 1:291).

purified by Christ and the Spirit through faith. Christ must "sprinkle the doorposts of our mind, contemplation and action, with the great and saving token, with the blood of the new covenant."[41] In this final section, we need to expound a bit further the distinction between faith and sight as well as their connection, so that we may understand how faith cultivates its vision of Christ through exegetical reasoning.

### Faith and Sight

Though faith and sight are distinct, they are also both described with visual metaphors and are therefore linked together. Their distinction is clear: "We know that while we are at home in the body we are away from the Lord, for we walk by faith, not by sight" (2 Cor. 5:6-7); "Blessed are those who have not seen and yet have believed" (John 20:29). In Scripture, hope also is distinguished from sight, and linked to faith: "Hope that is seen is not hope. For who hopes for what he sees? But if we hope for what we do not see, we wait for it with patience" (Rom. 8:24–25); "Faith is the assurance of things hoped for, the conviction of things not seen" (Heb. 11:1).

The connection between faith and sight needs to be spelled out since faith is also an act of seeing or beholding: "For now we see in a mirror dimly, but then face to face" (1 Cor. 13:12); "beholding as in a mirror the glory of the Lord . . . [we all] are being transformed" (2 Cor. 3:18 NKJV). In light of what has already been said about faith and the beatific vision, we can see that faith and sight are connected in at least two ways.[42] First, as we have established, faith and sight have the same object, which is the crucified and risen Christ's glory. The difference lies in this: whereas faith beholds Christ's glory enigmatically in the gospel, the blessed vision of God beholds Christ's glory clearly and in its full splendor. In this life there are times when it is difficult to perceive Christ's glory (Job 23:8–9), when God's absence is felt more than his presence.[43] The beatific vision leaves no room for such interruptions and withdrawals. Then, "we will always be with the Lord" (1 Thess. 4:17).

Second, and beyond this, faith is connected to vision because faith leads to and is consummated in it. Especially Paul's contrasts between "partial" and "perfect" and "child" and "man" suggest that the relation between faith and sight is one of part to whole, lesser to greater (1 Cor. 13:8–12). Blessedness comes with vision, but faith already renders us blessed in the sense that it

---

41. Gregory of Nazianzus, *Oration* 16.11 (*NPNF²* 7:251).
42. Much more needs to be said to flesh out the relationship between faith and sight. See, further, Owen, *Meditations and Discourses on the Glory of Christ* XII–XIV (*Works* 1:374–415).
43. See Owen, *Meditations and Discourses on the Glory of Christ* XIII (*Works* 1:389–408).

tethers us to what is not yet: eschatological glory at the vision of God (Luke 1:45; 11:28). Faith thus relates to vision as grace does to glory, or sanctification to glorification. "Grace is nothing else than glory begun, as glory is grace consummated."[44] In its opening toward realities beyond our reach, faith latches onto an object that will one day no longer be hoped for but fully present. Glorification and blessedness are the perfection of what is only inchoate in faith; here we are transformed and renewed "day by day" (2 Cor. 4:16), and "what we will be has not yet appeared," but there our transformation will be complete and "we shall be like him" (1 John 3:2; cf. Rom. 8:29–30).

Yet the link between faith and sight is important for our happiness now. Even if full joy, peace, and rest will only be ours at the resurrection and glorification of the body, faith still offers a foretaste of these realities now: "Though you have not seen him, you love him. Though you do not now see him, you believe in him and rejoice with joy that is inexpressible and filled with glory, obtaining the outcome of your faith, the salvation of your souls" (1 Pet. 1:8–9).

## Contemplation

When attempting to explain the relation between faith and vision, many theologians have appealed to some account of "contemplation" (θεωρία, theōria) to wed the movements of reason in this life to its rest in the next. The difficulty with the concept of contemplation is just how varied, and sometimes elusive, treatments of it are.[45] That said, within most treatments one may find a common conviction that whatever else it entails and consists in, contemplation of divine realities is a spiritual vision of spiritual truth (cf. 1 Cor. 2:13). Generally, contemplation is a form of "spiritual perception," and we can understand it better by unpacking that phrase.

First, contemplation is a *spiritual* vision (θεωρία πνευματική, theōria pneumatikē) because it is a gift of the Holy Spirit, a divine sense for divine

44. Turretin, *Institutes of Elenctic Theology* 20.8.2 (Giger, 3:608). Polanus states that faith is therefore the instrumental cause of beatitude (*Syntagma theologiae christianae* 1.6 [9i]). Cyril of Alexandria illustrates the relationship between faith and sight: "When the night is dark, the bright beauty of the stars can be seen as each one sends out its light, but when the sun rises with its radiance, the partial light now disappears and the brilliance of the stars grows weak and ineffective" (*Commentary on John* 11.2, on John 16:25 [Maxwell, 2:264]). See also, e.g., Augustine, *Enchiridion* 1.5; Aquinas, *Compendium of Theology* 2.1.

45. In many authors, the "vision" (θεωρία) implied in contemplation pertains to a special perception of Scripture's deeper meaning, along with the various connections and implications of those truths (so Gregory of Nyssa) and especially the ways the mystery of Christ is disclosed therein (so Cyril of Alexandria). In general, it designates a focused form of "theological reflection" on Scripture (A. N. Williams, *Divine Sense*, 140).

truth. Something very much like this is suggested by Paul after he discusses the glory of the new covenant in contrast to the old. When he situates his own ministry within this glorious new covenant, he acknowledges that the gospel is more than veiled to some: "In their case the god of this world has blinded the minds of the unbelievers, to keep them from seeing the light of the gospel of the glory of Christ, who is the image of God" (2 Cor. 4:4). The vision in question is to a significant extent intellectual, for it is the unbelievers' *minds* that have been blinded to the light by Satan and who therefore have no sight of the truth.

Contemplation's character as a gift has at least two corollaries worth mentioning. On the one hand, it is not reserved for a religious elite or only those with certain intellectual abilities. Contemplation involves the intellect in accordance with an individual's capacities rather than bypassing them for a mystical escape from self-consciousness.[46] On the other hand, contemplation in the minimal sense defined above is not reserved for those whose ascetical heroism especially ennobles them to the light. Beholding Christ's glory in faith is a possibility freely given to us on account of Christ's objective work and our union with him by the Spirit. United thus to Christ, "we have boldness and access with confidence through our faith in him" (Eph. 3:12). Contemplation should center our attention on the drama and power of God's objective work in Christ rather than on the subjective dramas, or putative powers, of the human soul. But such concentration on *this* objective reality is possible only for saving faith, which works by love.

Second, contemplation is a spiritual perception in the sense of sight, not with the physical eyes but with the mind's eye. When theologians describe contemplation as an "intuitive knowledge," they mean something like an apprehension of the truth rather than the acts of reasoning that lead us there. This is why contemplation is also like a "gaze": we do not have to reason about the colors we perceive in a painting because they are present to us in the mere act of gazing.[47] When Jesus expresses his desire for his disciples to see him, he promises a future vision of his glory of which we have a foretaste in faith. However, the perception of contemplation is a form of spiritual insight into Christ's person that joins knowledge and affection together through faith. In this sense, "everyone who looks [θεωρῶν, *theōrōn*] on the Son and believes in him" will have "eternal life" (John 6:40). And Stephen is able to suffer like Jesus because he "gazed into heaven and saw the glory of God" (Acts 7:55).

---

46. Since the intellect's role is proportionate to an individual's cognitive capacities, contemplation is held out to all believers regardless of cognitive ability.

47. See, e.g., Augustine, *The Trinity* 15.45; Aquinas, *STh* II-II.180; Polanus, *Syntagma theologiae christianae* 1.8 (11g).

Third, contemplation is determined by our telos and therefore focuses on God's truth in and through Christ, in whom "all things hold together" and "in whom are hidden all the treasures of wisdom and knowledge" (Col. 1:17; 2:3). Christ is the Truth. Therefore truth's unity may be perceived in his light: "Everything which faith ought to contemplate is exhibited to us in Christ."[48] The telos of contemplation is the apprehension of truth, and Truth himself reigns as the Alpha and Omega. Therefore, contemplation beholds the Truth as an end in itself, needing no further justification, such as "practical" bene-fits (though there are such benefits). God uses contemplation to purge us of idolatry. This idolatry includes an idolatrous utilitarian rationality, according to which anything, even God, is interesting to us only insofar as we can "get" something more important out of it. In this respect, beholding Christ's glory in faith is supremely "useless." But uselessness is not the same as worthless-ness, because God is the fountain of all goodness, truth, and beauty. Behold-ing God is infinitely worthwhile because he is infinitely delightful. There is nothing more true, more interesting, or more worthy of our attention than God. Contemplation seeks to know and enjoy God in Christ for his own sake, because it begins in astonishment and is restless until it finds its rest in him.[49]

## Exegesis

Contemplation bears upon the task of exegesis to the extent that we seek God's face in the "face of God for now"—that is, Scripture.[50] Exegesis shapes contemplation, and contemplation shapes exegesis. We will close this chapter by teasing out both of these truths.

Exegesis shapes contemplation in the sense that, this side of the coming resurrection, we behold Christ through the testimony of his prophets and apostles as the Spirit opens our minds and hearts to give us understanding. The distinctions between faith and sight apply here. Exegetical reasoning is a discursive process that takes time and admits of fits and starts. None of this is true of the sight to which faith will one day give way. However, just as faith leads to sight, so too the discursive activity of exegesis is meant to lead to the spiritual perception of Christ's glory. What we are after in con-templation is a form of reasoning with the grain of Scripture that is open to truths transcending our natural senses, truths that require a "divine sense" to perceive. As it relates to exegesis, then, we may define contemplation as

48. Calvin, *Commentary on Ephesians* 3:12.
49. Cf. Augustine, *On Christian Teaching* 1.3–5; *Confessions* 1.1. For a brief, practical over-view of contemplation, see Brakel, *The Christian's Reasonable Service*, 1:652–58.
50. Augustine, *Sermon* 22.7 (WSA III/2:46).

follows: *Contemplation is a spiritual perception of Scripture's deepest truths relating to Christ's glory, in a manner that stirs up delight and conforms us to Christ.* Christ's "glory" here includes not only the divinity he possesses with the Father and Holy Spirit but also the whole mystery of his incarnation, passion, resurrection, and return by which that glory is made known to us.[51] Moreover, contemplation stirs up delight and effects conformity to Christ because it cultivates a knowledge characterized by friendship rather than mere acquaintance (John 15:15). Contemplation therefore engages both the intellect and the affections in response to a sight that astonishes them. Contemplation is no mere intellectual pursuit, because knowledge that leaves the affections behind carries no conviction and ends up in atheism, just as affection that leaves behind knowledge runs into superstition and sentimentalism.[52] Understanding the doctrinal content of the Christian faith is one thing; knowing and delighting in God is another. Knowledge as such is not always friendship.

In turn, contemplation shapes exegesis by intensifying its focus and broadening its reach, within the bounds of Scripture. In reading Scripture we are not called to mere observation of the text and its truths, but rather to "penetratingly reflect upon the matters themselves."[53] That is, a properly theological exegesis is one in which the reader's attention is oriented by the beatific vision and which therefore has Christ's glory as its object rather than the text or its natural properties in isolation.[54] Such exegesis is still a reasoning process, as we will see in chapter 3. It involves gathering together what the various parts of Scripture say about the glory of Christ by way of anticipation and retrospection and comparing these truths together. But it proceeds to a further step of prayerfully meditating on these truths until they form a comprehensive impression on our minds that prompts praise. Faith contemplates the deepest significance it may of such matters as Christ's divinity, his relation to the Father and the Spirit, his humanity and the mission for which he became incarnate, and more. Therefore, to behold Christ's glory we will have to see how this glory is displayed across the whole canon and how it reaches singular heights in his cross and resurrection. This contemplative exegesis will lead us to think long and hard about apparently recondite matters. Yet such matters are intrinsic to faith's object. Biblical reasoning will prove contemplative, in

---

51. Cf. Alexander of Hales, *Summa theologica* intro., q. 1, c. 3.

52. Owen, *Meditations and Discourses on the Glory of Christ* XIII (*Works* 1:401).

53. Brakel, *The Christian's Reasonable Service*, 1:653.

54. The text's natural properties—its historical and material circumstances, authorship, destination, and so forth—are part of what the text *is*, and so they *are* matters of importance for theological exegesis.

part, by how extensively and intensively it attends to this object, the crucified and risen Christ.

Contemplation by faith anticipates vision and tastes some crumbs from its banquet table. There is a promise here for exegesis: when it pursues the knowledge and enjoyment of God in Christ, it becomes a means of cultivating faith's foretaste of vision and therefore becomes a work of God's grace in our own sanctification. What else could this be but a work of grace, since orienting our attentions to confessing the truth requires a renovation of our intellect and will that only God can effect? Being renewed by God's grace, our redirected attentions become further vehicles of that grace, as they enable us to be conformed to the image of God's Son. As we focus on the crucified and risen Christ's glory, we come to a greater understanding of the only true God and Jesus Christ whom he has sent (John 17:3). This is to a large degree the purpose of John's Gospel and, implicitly, all of Scripture. The evangelist hopes that his readers would become like the "beloved disciple" and thus blessed as those who believe without having seen: "These are written so that you may believe that Jesus is the Christ, the Son of God, and that by believing you may have life in his name" (John 20:29–31).[55] After all, the beloved disciple is the one who "believed" upon seeing, not the risen Jesus, but the empty tomb (John 20:8–9). The fact that John's testimony is "written" means that it is now in textual form. It therefore demands acts of reading, hearing, and proclamation. The question posed to us as readers is whether we will be "those who have not seen and yet have believed" (John 20:29). Will our acts of reading be those of beloved disciples?

The dominant intellectual cultures of modern biblical scholarship often, though not always, resist applying the yoke of discipleship to the reading of Holy Scripture. However, understanding Scripture requires that we sit at the feet of Jesus and follow him if we are to see him (Luke 10:41–42; 24:13–35). What does this mean, and what further insight might it have for cultivating expectant exegesis? Exploring this theme is the burden of the next chapter.

---

55. See Moloney, *Love in the Gospel of John*, 170–76. John's perfect passive "are written" (γέγραπται) is intriguing for at least two reasons. First, it "objectifies the transition from orality to writing; it signals that it's indeed a work written in the past, but whose reading remains offered to every potential reader" (Zumstein, *L'Évangile selon Saint Jean*, 2:296). The book is addressed to *us*. Second, this is a verb John reserves up to this point in his Gospel for Scripture (e.g., 2:17; 6:31; 8:17), providing subtle insight into John's understanding of his own book (Keener, *The Gospel of John*, 2:1215).

# 2

# The School of Christ

## The Pedagogical Context of Biblical Reasoning

**Principle 2:** Everything Scripture says about God is part of God's meticulous and wise pedagogy, by which God adapts the form of his wisdom to educate finite and fallen creatures so that we might see his glory. Biblical reasoning fits within this larger context of divine teaching.

To seek God's face always, we must become disciples of Christ and sit at his feet so that we may learn from him about the glory he has with the Father and the Holy Spirit. As we saw in the previous chapter, Christ's disciples do this in the present through a vision-shaped attention to Holy Scripture. In this chapter, we need to explore further the overarching context for this attention, specifically how Scripture characterizes the interaction between God and its readers as a form of teaching and learning.

Indeed, according to John Calvin, Scripture is "the very school of God's children."[1] This reflects a conviction widely shared throughout the Christian church that behind every faithful human teacher stands God as the great heavenly teacher of all the saints, and Scripture as the chief means of God's instruction. Since Scripture is the curriculum and God is the teacher, disciples are students.

1. Calvin, *Institutes of the Christian Religion* 1.6.4.

But how does God teach? What are we here to learn? And how do we learn well? We will find answers to these questions if we attend more carefully to God's teaching activity, how it characterizes his covenant dealings with his people, and how that bears on our reading of Scripture. God's teaching activity with his covenant people is the wider setting within which our pursuit of Christ's glory through Scripture makes sense. This wider setting is the divine "economy," God's orderly administration of history and the cosmos, in which God stoops down to teach us, adapting his methods to our various needs to render us wise unto salvation (2 Tim. 3:15). By locating ourselves within this economy, we will understand ourselves as students of the divine pedagogy, and our approach to Scripture as an openness to divine teaching. As we will argue, our approach to Scripture is shaped by its function in the school of Christ and by his pedagogical and instructional purposes as he leads us to an ever-deeper contemplation of the eternal glory that he possesses with the Father and the Holy Spirit.

The present chapter lays the groundwork for this argument by describing the divine economy of teaching, with a focus on God's teaching activity and how it reaches its audience. The next chapter will explore Scripture as the "curriculum" of this teaching. Our present goal is to unpack the second principle of biblical reasoning: *Everything Scripture says about God is part of God's meticulous and wise pedagogy, by which God adapts the form of his wisdom to educate finite and fallen creatures so that we might see his glory. Biblical reasoning fits within this larger context of divine teaching.* We proceed in two large steps. First, we frame our understanding of God's pedagogical economy by looking at its principal agent: God the teacher. This role as teacher and pedagogue distinguishes God from his people as well as from false gods, since it displays his uniqueness and underived wisdom. Further, God's pedagogy has three general characteristics to which we must give our attention: it is adaptable, gradual, and formative. Second, because God determines to teach obstinate, rebellious students who prefer their own counsel over God's, we must look at the content and possibility of divine teaching. These two aspects go together, because the form in which God teaches us his wisdom provides the stunning solution to his recalcitrant audience: God's adaptation to his audience's needs ends up "adapting" the audience itself.

## God's Pedagogical Economy

First, we need to grasp what it means to say that our reasoning with Scripture, our learning at Christ's feet, occurs within the broader context of God's pedagogical economy. What does this mean, and what does it look like? We can begin by looking briefly at the opening chapter of 1 Timothy. Paul says Timothy should "command" others to align their teaching with the teaching of the apostles (1 Tim. 1:3). The apostolic teaching, including this command, has a particular goal: "love that issues from a pure heart and a good conscience and a sincere faith" (1:5; cf. 1:3). Paul entrusts this command to Timothy in the presence of Jesus Christ (1:18; 6:13). As Timothy fulfills this charge, he will train his congregation in godliness so that they may set their hope on its proper object, God, rather than the enticements of this world (4:10–11; 5:5–7; 6:17). If they fix their attentions firmly on God, they will avoid silly myths and speculations that detract from what Paul calls "the economy [οἰκονομία, *oikonomia*] of God that is in faith" (1:4 AT).

This perplexing phrase simultaneously embraces two ideas that we will explore here in greater depth. Specifically, "economy" may be understood both as "God's plan" (cf. Eph. 1:10) and as the "stewardship" (cf. Titus 1:7) of the gospel carried out by the ministers who teach and preach it.[2] In the sense that God's economy is his orderly plan for and administration of all things, and particularly the household that is his church (1 Tim. 3:15), God's economy is the location in which the "deposit" of heavenly teaching is handed down through the ministry of the gospel (1 Tim. 6:20).[3] Christians partake in this economy "in faith," which is to say, "through sanctification by the Spirit and belief in the truth" (2 Thess. 2:13). The human authors of Scripture, the prophets and apostles, therefore understand themselves as "stewards [οἰκονόμους, *oikonomous*] of the mysteries of God" (1 Cor. 4:1). Implicit in Paul's comments are his identity as a steward (or "economist") of teaching that he has received from God and his place within the broader economy of divine teaching.[4] To grasp Paul's description of his apostolic teaching activity as an "economist," we must understand the divine Teacher who presides over this economy and the economy itself.

---

2. See esp. Richter, *Oikonomia*, 33–92.

3. What this deposit contains is the antithesis of "pointless, empty chatter" and "what is falsely called knowledge" (1 Tim. 6:20 AT). Elsewhere such "empty chatter" is opposed to the "word of truth" (2 Tim. 2:15–16). Guarding the deposit is parallel with holding fast to "the standard [ὑποτύπωσις] of sound words" (2 Tim. 1:13 NASB) or the "pattern [τύπον] of teaching" (Rom. 6:17) that churches received from Paul and other apostles. The deposit is the apostolic teaching at the foundation of the church, and it is found in the form of a structure and pattern of teaching connecting truth with life. See Spicq, "παραγγελία, παραγγέλλω," in *TLNT* 3:9–11.

4. The metaphor of οἰκονόμοι is chiefly pedagogical, so it should not surprise that in context it also bears apocalyptic overtones. See Gladd, *Revealing the Mysterion*, 183–90; D. L. White, *Teacher of the Nations*, 73–79.

## God the Teacher and Pedagogue

The way Scripture portrays God as both teacher and pedagogue, or trainer, is a window into the broader context of God's pedagogical economy. It is by understanding the former (God as teacher) that we will understand the latter (God's economy of teaching). It should not surprise us that teaching and pedagogy characterize Christ's ministry. For instance, the Gospels extensively emphasize Jesus's role as teacher (διδάσκαλος, *didaskalos*).[5] Jesus's opponents recognize him as a teacher, but only his disciples recognize him also as Lord (Matt. 9:11; 17:24). If disciples are to be like their teacher, they will take up their cross, receive Jesus as the Father's emissary, and receive Jesus's yoke (Matt. 10:25, 38, 40; 11:29). Because the Scriptures witness to Christ, then whether we are reading the Law or the Prophets, we should "listen to him" because he is our teacher (Matt. 17:5; cf. John 5:37–47; 6:68–69).[6] Jesus's teaching activity is particularly accented in the attention Mark gives to his interpretation of Scripture and his preaching ministry (e.g., Mark 1:21–27).[7] Jesus heals the blind and deaf so that they may "see" and "hear" (Mark 7:6, 31–37; 8:22–26; cf. Isa. 29:9, 13, 18; 35:5). Also, he leads the disciples on "the way" because he fulfills Isaiah's promise about the divine teacher: "Your Teacher will not hide himself anymore, but your eyes shall see your Teacher. And your ears shall hear a word behind you, saying, 'This is the way, walk in it,' when you turn to the right or when you turn to the left" (Isa. 30:20–21; cf. Mark 1:2; Isa. 35:8–10).

Jesus's teaching activity picks up on broader themes across Scripture that identify God as the unique teacher and source of all understanding: "In your light do we see light" (Ps. 36:9). God's role as teacher highlights his divine aseity, for he teaches without being taught. "Who has measured the Spirit of the LORD, or what man shows him his counsel?" (Isa. 40:13; cf. Rom. 11:34–35; 1 Cor. 2:15). God's wisdom has no source, and so it is immeasurable and incomparable to all human understanding. There is no teacher like God, says Elihu, majestic and exalted in knowledge, wisdom, and power (Job 36:22; cf. Isa. 40:13). Hannah also extols God's incomparability in this regard: "For the LORD is a God of knowledge, and by him actions are weighed" (1 Sam. 2:3). Therefore, since God is the unique teacher

---

5. Witmer, *Divine Instruction in Early Christianity*, 110–11, elucidates this point from John 3:1–15.

6. Clement of Alexandria, *Christ the Educator* 1.11.97 (FC 23:86).

7. This leads John of la Rochelle to the observation that Mark highlights the *dignitas doctoris* of Christ because he omits much of what the other Gospels narrate in order to focus on Christ's interpretive power; see "Introduction to the Four Gospels," in McElrath, *Franciscan Christology*, 50–53.

of his people, the disciples have "one teacher" just as they have "one Father, who is in heaven" (Matt. 23:8–9). The idea here is that Jesus's unique role as teacher conforms to the uniqueness of God himself: *solus Christus* because *solus Deus*.

Complementing Jesus's role as teacher is his pedagogy, or formative training. Clement of Alexandria points to this element of God's instruction when he describes Jesus as our pedagogue (παιδαγωγός, *paidagōgos*), or educator, in the sense that he guides us "correctly to the contemplation of God, and a description of holy deeds that endure forever."[8] The distinction between pedagogy and teaching is subtle but important. In antiquity, pedagogues ("guides of little ones") or psychagogues ("guides of the soul") would conduct people toward virtue and truth through example and rhetorical persuasion. A good pedagogue knows what to say or do, when to say or do it, and how, based on the audience's needs and the educator's purposes.[9] And at the core of a good pedagogue is reliable, self-consistent character worth emulating.

Christ exemplifies the characteristics of a pedagogue broadly throughout his ministry. Just as the disciples have one Teacher and one Father, so too they have "one guide" (καθηγητής, *kathēgētēs*), in contrast to the "blind" guidance of the scribes and Pharisees (Matt. 23:10, 16, 24). Unlike hypocritical guides who say one thing and do another, Jesus's deeds are consistent with his words, and so his burden is light rather than heavy (Matt. 11:30; 23:3). Christ educates his followers chiefly with words, but also by example (Matt. 20:25–28), as well as by object lessons (Mark 8:22–33; John 13:1–20). As Augustine observes, "Even the deeds of the Word are a word for us."[10] And as we might expect by now, these deeds are meant to lead us to the vision of his glory. Unlike blind guides, Jesus can indeed lead us to the *visio Dei* because he has seen the Father (John 1:18; 6:46). More pointedly, to see Christ is to see the Father (John 14:9). This is part of what Jesus teaches us, but it is something we can perceive only by faith: "Believe me that I am in the Father and the Father is in me, or else believe on account of the works themselves" (John 14:11).

---

8. Clement of Alexandria, *Christ the Educator* 1.7.54 (FC 23:50). Justin Martyr likewise appeals to the Greeks to "be instructed by the divine Word," so that they might learn true wisdom and flee the passions of the soul (*Discourse to the Greeks* §5 [ANF 1:272]). The divine pedagogy is a widely held conviction, especially in the early church, with both formal and material significance.

9. Rylaarsdam, *John Chrysostom on Divine Pedagogy*, 18–22; Sturdevant, *The Adaptable Jesus of the Fourth Gospel*, 13–46.

10. Augustine, *Homilies on the Gospel of John* 24.2 (WSA III/12:424); Aquinas, *STh* III.40.1.*ad*3. On a related note, Jesus is the "one shepherd" of his people (John 10:16; cf. Ezek. 37:24).

Jesus's pedagogy, like his teaching activity, is a window into God's broader dealings throughout history. Being the most excellent guide of the soul, God employs a variety of pedagogical strategies for the education of his covenant people. According to Elihu, "God speaks in one way, and in two, though man does not perceive it" (Job 33:14). Hence, at times God allows us to experience suffering for the sake of our souls. Whether ordaining pain, weakness, loss of appetite, or fear of death, God "does all these things, twice, three times, with a man, to bring back his soul from the pit, that he may be lighted with the light of life" (Job 33:29–30).[11] When God spoke to the prophets, he "multiplied visions, and through the prophets gave parables" (Hosea 12:10). Through a variety of methods, images, and manners of speech, God instructs us "as he sees to be suitable to our capacities and weakness; for the Scriptures set before us various representations, which show to us the face of God."[12] This means that often God uses visible things, or sense impressions, to teach his people about invisible truths such as himself. The Holy Spirit used the earthly tabernacle as a sign of something "greater and more perfect" (Heb. 8:5; 9:11). In his conversation with Nicodemus, Jesus points to the wind—something sensible yet visible only in its effects—as an image of the Spirit's regenerative work (John 3:8). The point of these various examples is that God's pedagogy adapts according to the needs of the audience and circumstances. Some people and occasions require mysterious imagery and parables, while others require rebuke and harsh words, while yet others benefit most from gentle, kind words or merciful acts. In all of this, God kindles faith, hope, and love by revealing himself.

Situated within God's pedagogical economy, we learn quite early that God is our teacher and pedagogue. While it may seem too obvious to merit discussion, it is too important to assume. To apprehend God's pedagogy, we must perceive how, in whatever God says or does, he is seeking to sanctify his people, shape us in virtue, persuade us toward the truth and away from idolatry, and prepare us for the vision of his glory in Christ. Indeed, this is why we began our consideration of divine teaching by looking at God: the center of God's pedagogical economy is God himself, not the education of his pupils. God's pedagogy is not so much something distinct from his teaching as it is the way that God teaches. Since we are concerned in this book with divine teaching, then, we need to look more closely at the pedagogical characteristics or methods of divine teaching.

11. See, e.g., Croy, *Endurance in Suffering*; Davis, *The Place of Paideia in Hebrews' Moral Thought*.

12. Calvin, *Commentary on Hosea* 12:10. See also Rylaarsdam, *John Chrysostom on Divine Pedagogy*, 76, on how Chrysostom favors this text to demonstrate just this point.

## Characteristics of God's Pedagogy: Adaptable, Gradual, and Formative

God's pedagogy bears numerous qualities, but for our purposes we will highlight only three: its adaptability, gradual pace, and formative manner. One of the chief characteristics of God's pedagogy is his gracious *adaptation* (συγκατάβασις, *synkatabasis*), often described as condescension or accommodation. Adaptable teachers are ones who considerately tailor their teaching to the needs of the different audiences and circumstances in which they find themselves, all while maintaining a consistent character.[13] The idea is prevalent in the theological tradition, especially in discussions of the incarnation. Athanasius expresses the idea succinctly:

> For as a good teacher who cares for his students always condescends [συγκαταβαίνων, *synkatabainōn*] to teach by simpler means those who are not able to benefit from more advanced things, so also does the Word of God. . . . For since human beings, having rejected the contemplation of God and as though sunk in an abyss with their eyes held downwards, seeking God in creation and things perceptible, setting up for themselves mortal humans and demons as gods, for this reason the lover of human beings and the common Savior of all, takes to himself a body and dwells as human among . . . human beings, so that those who think that God is in things corporeal might, from what the Lord wrought through the actions of the body, know the truth and through him might consider the Father.[14]

God became flesh for the sake of those who are flesh and whose attentions are weighed down by sin, in order that he might set us free from sin and raise our attentions to him. The same can be said for all of God's teaching, down to his use of human words and categories: "Both on account of our weakness and on account of the sublimity of the things themselves, God borrows our words."[15] Even stewards of the divine pedagogy are adaptable, like Paul, who desires to be "all things to all people . . . for the sake of the gospel" (1 Cor. 9:22–23). First and foremost, however, adaptability characterizes the incarnate God himself. While adaptability is one of the most important characteristics of God's pedagogy, we must not reduce divine pedagogy to

---

13. The category was current in the broader cultures in which the NT arose. See Benin, *The Footprints of God*; Glad, *Paul and Philodemus*; Mitchell, "Pauline Accommodation and 'Condescension' (συγκατάβασις)"; Sturdevant, *The Adaptable Jesus of the Fourth Gospel*, 13–93; D. L. White, *Teacher of the Nations*, 121–24.

14. Athanasius, *On the Incarnation* 15 (PPS 44a:83); Augustine, *On Christian Teaching* 1.11.

15. Turretin, *Institutes of Elenctic Theology* 20.8.19 (Giger 3:614). See, inter alia, Bengel: "The whole style of Scripture is full of συγκατάβασις" (*Gnomon of the New Testament*, 2:277).

adaptability.[16] More needs to be said about the pedagogical economy even to see how adaptability functions as one piece of a larger whole.

The two other qualities of divine pedagogy may be illustrated from a paradigmatic episode of divine teaching, when God speaks to Israel from Mount Sinai and hands down the law. That this is an episode of divine teaching is clear: God first instructs Moses and Aaron in what to say and do (Exod. 4:15), and then he instructs Israel through the decalogue at Sinai (Exod. 20:1–17; Deut. 4:10–14; 5:6–21). Moses recalls all of this for the people and frames it in pedagogical terms: "Out of heaven he let you hear his voice, that he might discipline you" (לְיַסְּרֶךָ, ləyassərekā / παιδεῦσαί σε, paideusai se; Deut. 4:36). The law itself has a pedagogical purpose, which arguably extends all the way to its style: the wordiness and repetition of Deuteronomy sets the law before us clearly and abundantly, so that its demands and goals are inescapable.[17] Looking at what Scripture says about the law, we can see further how God's pedagogy is not only adaptable but gradual and formative as well.

Alongside its adaptability, God's pedagogy is *gradual* in the sense that God progressively leads his people to a greater understanding of who he is and what it means to be in covenant with him. Basil of Caesarea expresses this key idea when commenting on how God considers our weakness with his pedagogy throughout the old covenant: "He first trained us to see the shadows of bodies and to look at the sun in water, so that we not be blinded by wrecking ourselves on the vision of pure light."[18] In other words, God only gradually exposes us more as our eyes adjust to greater intensities of light. Much of this gradual element was covered in the previous chapter when we looked at the contrast between the ministries of Moses and Christ. But we may see it further in how Paul personifies the Mosaic law as itself a pedagogue or tutor whose job was to prepare us for and bring us to Christ, who is its telos (Gal. 3:24; Rom. 10:4). The law could not make us perfect, but it brought us to the One who can (Heb. 7:19). And in this respect, the law is simply part of God's gradual pedagogy of Israel. Indeed, throughout Israel's whole sojourn in the wilderness, God guided them by an angel, of whom God says, "My name is in him" (Exod. 23:21) and whom Paul later identifies as Christ (1 Cor. 10:9).[19]

---

16. For some important qualifications of "adaptability," see Rylaarsdam, *John Chrysostom on Divine Pedagogy*, 22–30; S. E. Harris, *God and the Teaching of Theology*, 3–8.

17. Thus Calvin, picking up a long tradition of interpretation: Blacketer, *The School of God*, 109–13.

18. Basil, *On the Holy Spirit* 14.33 (PPS 42:65).

19. We have left aside the issue of how to interpret OT theophanies, but we follow the logic of Augustine's views in *The Trinity* 3–4, where he argues that theophanies are not Christophanies but manifestations of the whole Trinity because Father, Son, and Spirit are inseparable

Clement comments: "Of old, the Word educated through Moses, and after that through the Prophets; even Moses was in fact a Prophet. For the Law was the education of children difficult to control."[20] Jesus fulfills the gradual pedagogy of the Law and the Prophets, so that we newly receive the law from him—mediated through his person, work, and teaching—as a rule for right living (Matt. 5:17).[21]

Finally, following from this normative function of the law, we can see how God's pedagogy is *formative*. The law functions this way both negatively and positively. On the one hand, through the law's requirements and our inability to obey them fully, God guides us to a knowledge of our sin (Rom. 3:20; 7:7–13).[22] On the other hand, God also educates us morally as the law leads us away from idolatry and casts us on God's mercy (Gal. 3:23).[23] In Christ, the law now serves as a rule for the Christian life when it is understood at its heart to be about the love of God and neighbor. Hence, it was given "to the *regenerate* person that in it he may have a most certain rule for his repentance and sanctification and be led to Christ by its pedagogical strength."[24] The formative elements come into view even more clearly when we set them against the background of the adaptive and gradual elements as they relate to Christ. Hence, on another mount, a new and better Moses interprets Torah in a new and better way through his "teaching" (Matt. 7:28; 5:2).[25] Jesus fulfills the Law and the Prophets (Matt. 5:17; 7:12), and so his teaching draws out most perfectly what they were intended to do: form people in the virtues of grace that they might "be perfect" like their heavenly Father (Matt. 5:48).[26] This reflects the essence of the covenant relation codified in the law: "You shall be holy, for I the LORD your God am holy" (Lev. 19:2); "You shall be blameless

---

and act inseparably. No person is more intrinsically "invisible" than another. Augustine's view has been defended most recently by Sanders, *The Triune God*, 224–26. Vermigli draws out Augustine's logic when he argues that divine apparitions in human form in the OT differ from Christ's incarnation because they do not have redemption through the cross and resurrection as their aim: *Loci Communes*, II.17.8c–e (291).

20. Clement of Alexandria, *Christ the Educator* 1.11.96 (FC 23:85); cf. Irenaeus, *Against Heresies* 4.14.2–3 (ANF 1:479).

21. This has often been termed the law's "didactic use" (*usus didacticus*). Turretin comments on how Christ fulfilled the law in three ways, "either as a doctrine by faithful preaching, solid confirmation and powerful vindication; or as a rule [*normam*] by a full and consistent keeping of it; or as a type by a perfect consummation, by exhibiting in himself the truth of the types and prophecies and the body of its shadows" (*Institutes of Elenctic Theology* 11.3.5 [Giger 2:20]).

22. This is the so-called pedagogical use (*usus paedagogicus*) of the law.

23. Aquinas, *STh* I-II.98.2; Turretin, *Institutes of Elenctic Theology* 11.3.8.

24. Heidegger, *The Concise Marrow of Theology*, 14.39.

25. Allison, *The New Moses.*

26. On the virtue-forming element of Jesus's pedagogy in the Sermon on the Mount, see Pennington, *The Sermon on the Mount and Human Flourishing.*

before the LORD your God" (Deut. 18:13). And all of this so that God's people might "behold the King in his beauty" (Isa. 33:17).

## The Problem with God's Students

Thus far we have examined the adaptive, gradual, and formative aspects of divine pedagogy. For the sake of transforming his people to be holy as he is holy and to behold him face-to-face, God adapts his teaching in accordance with his people's needs and the stages of redemptive history in which they live. At the center of the covenant formula we find the divine pedagogy expressed in a nutshell: Israel is God's and God is Israel's; therefore they should be holy as God is holy. These are truths expressed in the very Torah that is meant to train them.

Yet this same center also heightens the problem of Israel's radical need, which we see in how they respond to tests. Like a master teacher, God tests his people, most notably when "God tested Abraham" by telling him to offer Isaac as a burnt offering (Gen. 22:1; Heb. 11:17). Such testing is not temptation, because it is meant to confirm faith by guiding people away from idolatry and pride: "Do not fear, for God has come to test you, that the fear of him may be before you, that you may not sin" (Exod. 20:20; cf. Pss. 7:9; 11:4–5; 26:1–2; 1 Cor. 3:13). Examples of this testing include God's withholding the normal means of sustaining life so that he can provide for his people in an extraordinary manner, as when he rained down bread from heaven (Exod. 15:25; 16:4). When God's people fail his tests, the root cause is their wickedness, pride, foolishness, and general unteachableness (Ps. 10:4; Prov. 3:11–12; 4:1, 13). God's teaching is adaptable, gradual, and formative, but we might also say it is *resisted*.

With problems like these, the answer is not simply more teaching. The problem is not educational, as if mere ignorance were the cause of unrighteousness. According to Scripture, wickedness causes morally culpable ignorance: "People loved the darkness rather than the light because their works were evil" (John 3:19; Rom. 1:18). Further, this ignorance exacerbates a difficulty humans already face: it is all too easy for finite, corporeal creatures like us to allow our attention to stop at the signs God uses to teach us, thus failing to follow these vectors to their ultimate source in God. Suppressing the truth in unrighteousness means confusing the Creator with the creature and therefore exchanging truth for lies (Rom. 1:22–25). Such failure is open rebellion against God and his teaching: "They have turned to me their back and not their face. And though I have taught them persistently, they have not listened to receive instruction" (Jer. 32:33). Israel's need, and therefore our own, springs not only from our created and finite condition but also, more deeply, from our sinfulness. In Adam we all naturally resist God's teaching, preferring instead the counsel of the world (Prov. 15:14; Jer. 10:2).

What hope, then, do God's students have that we can be taught? How is divine teaching possible? To answer these questions, we need to consider finally how God's teaching, taking root in our hearts, solves these radical problems.

## The Content and Possibility of Divine Teaching

So far we have seen something of God's unique role and some of his methods within the economy of divine teaching. Yet in the conclusion to the previous section we came up against a fundamental, twin problem pertaining to our finitude and fallenness. Our fallenness exacerbates the difficulties already present in our finitude. If it is difficult for creatures to think of God, who is uncreated and infinite, then it is even more difficult when we run from God's instruction and seek instead to replace it with whatever fancies us. What hope is there, then, for finite and fallen creatures to come to know God?

The hope is what God announces for the wayward students of Israel, which extends to God's students today. God promises that in the new covenant, he will write his instruction on his people's hearts (Jer. 31:33). All God's people, even the children, will be taught by the Lord in an even greater way than before (Isa. 54:13). Calvin says that God "hyperbolically extols" this greater way by saying that his people will no longer need human teachers (Jer. 31:34).[27] And such is precisely what is fulfilled in Christ, our "one teacher" (Matt. 23:10), and in the gift of the Holy Spirit: "The anointing that you received from him abides in you, and you have no need that anyone should teach you" (1 John 2:27). This remains true despite the fact that Christ commissions others to carry his teaching forth to the nations (Matt. 28:19–20). These teachers do not replace Christ but steward his teaching activity (1 Cor. 4:1). Stewards within God's pedagogical economy can only plant or water, whereas God must give the growth (1 Cor. 3:6–7). Augustine thus distinguishes between the external teaching of stewards and the internal teaching of Christ: "He who teaches hearts has his chair in heaven. . . . He who teaches . . . is the inner teacher: Christ teaches; his inbreathing teaches."[28]

How is this so, and what does it say about the problem of our finitude and fallenness? How does God's adaptability address these challenges? To

27. Calvin, *Commentary on Jeremiah* 33:34.
28. Augustine, *Homilies on the First Epistle of John* 3.13 (WSA III/14:63).

ask these questions is to ask how divine teaching is possible, consideration of which will conclude our account of God's pedagogical economy.

Answers to these questions emerge in the opening argument of Paul's First Letter to the Corinthians, which has long been recognized by theologians, and increasingly by modern biblical scholars, as suffused with pedagogical and apocalyptic themes. Paul's concern is to encourage the Corinthian church to see themselves in view of their unity in Christ, rather than their favorite human apostle or teacher, and to live accordingly in generosity and love. He does so by pointing them to the scandal of Christ's cross and how it introduces a new way of being and a new way of knowing God that is at odds with ordinary ways of knowing and living. Throughout, Paul carefully blends ancient pedagogical themes and rhetorical strategies, demonstrating that he is aware of himself as a steward within a larger pedagogical economy. The argument has much to tell us about ourselves as learners and about God as teacher if we look briefly at the content and form of God's teaching and how this answers our finitude and fallenness.

### Content and Form

According to Paul, in the new covenant's central act of divine teaching, God has revealed his "hidden wisdom," which he "predestined before the ages for our glory" (1 Cor. 2:7 AT; Isa. 28:16). Paul first proclaimed God's wisdom to the Corinthian church in "the word of the cross," "Christ crucified," which is the "power and wisdom of God" (1 Cor. 1:18, 23–24). Now, among the mature, Paul proclaims this same wisdom in words taught by the Spirit, "interpreting spiritual truths to those who are spiritual" (1 Cor. 2:13). Here we begin to see both the content and form of divine teaching, which revolve around God's wisdom. When we recall our argument in the previous chapter, we see that God's wisdom is revealed in the same place as his glory: Christ's crucifixion, when he is lifted up (John 8:28; 12:45), which also includes a forward reference to his resurrection (cf. 1 Cor. 2:8; 15:1–8). Indeed, God's cruciform wisdom reveals to us "the Lord of glory" (1 Cor. 2:8).

The content of divine teaching is therefore God's wisdom, but it exists in two distinct forms: secret and hidden in the divine counsel, and publicly proclaimed in the word of Christ's cross, which enacts God's counsel (Eph. 3:11). This is why all the "treasures of wisdom and knowledge" are hidden in Christ, as if buried in a field (Col. 2:3; cf. Matt. 13:44). Since these treasures are found in Christ crucified and resurrected, the whole substance of the wisdom God wants to teach us is virtually contained in the

gospel.[29] Hence, Paul knows "nothing . . . except Jesus Christ and him crucified" (1 Cor. 2:2).

Paul's attention is not so much restricted as focused: it is not that there
is nothing else to know about God other than Christ's glorification on and
through the cross, but that whatever else there is to know is drawn from the
cross as from the deepest well. In his joy, Paul gives everything he has to buy
this field. What we learn about God, such as his perfections (e.g., wisdom and
power) or his providence (cf. Gen. 22:8), is learned at the foot of the cross:
"Christ hanging on the cross is like a teacher in his teaching chair."[30] And
if God teaches his wisdom from the cross, then the form of God's instruction must have deep pedagogical significance that requires our attention. In
God's kingdom the first shall be last and the last first. It pleases God to hide
his glory in what is inglorious. So too he hides his wisdom and power in the
guise of foolishness and weakness (Matt. 11:25–26; 1 Cor. 1:21–23; cf. 2 Cor.
4:7). Exploring two interwoven threads of Paul's complex argument will show
how God's pedagogy answers our finitude and fallenness in the same breath.

### Possibility

One thread in Paul's argument addresses how it is that an infinite God
communicates with finite creatures. We have already seen God's uniqueness
as teacher, which highlights God's aseity, since he teaches all but is taught by
none (Rom. 11:34). The uniqueness of God's teaching mirrors God's creative
relation to creatures: we are created, God is uncreated; we are finite, God is
infinite; we are taught, God is teacher. In this vein, Paul praises God's immense
and incomprehensible understanding in terms of "the depth of the riches and
wisdom and knowledge of God" (Rom. 11:33; cf. Isa. 40:13; 1 Cor. 2:16).[31]
Yet the incomprehensible God is comprehensible to himself, for the Spirit
"searches everything, even the depths of God. . . . No one comprehends the
thoughts of God except the Spirit of God" (1 Cor. 2:10–11; cf. Dan. 2:22).[32]
This perhaps echoes Jesus's claim to unique knowledge of the Father: "No
one knows the Son except the Father, and no one knows the Father except the
Son" (Matt. 11:27). Together, these statements suggest a basic truth: divine
teaching comes to us from the immeasurable depths of God's knowledge,

29. For further context on the history of interpretation regarding God's "wisdom" here, see
S. E. Harris, *God and the Teaching of Theology*, 87–103.

30. Aquinas, *Commentary on the Gospel of St. John* 19.4.2441; cf. Augustine, *Homilies on
the Gospel of John* 119.2; Aquinas, *STh* I.46.4.*resp.*

31. See Cranfield, *Romans 9–16*, 589; Schreiner, *Romans*, 633–34.

32. On the apocalyptic background, relevant to God's pedagogy as we have presented it, see
Wolff, *Der erste Brief des Paulus an die Korinther*, 58–59.

which belongs to the Father, Son, and Holy Spirit.[33] However, God wills to share this knowledge and to be known. While "no one" knows the Father except the Son, and "no one" comprehends God's thoughts except God's Spirit, nevertheless God is known to those "to whom the Son chooses to reveal him" (Matt. 11:27), and "we have received . . . the Spirit who is from God, that we might understand the things freely given us by God" (1 Cor. 2:12). The verbs here, "choose" and "freely give," show that God is known only by God's will and gift. Our knowledge is "from God" and dependent on his grace, and for this very reason we may know God's depths to the extent that God makes them known. That said, God remains inexhaustible such that we do not know God like God knows God (cf. John 6:45–46; 1:18). God is incomprehensible but not unknown.

When we proceed to inquire how finite creatures can understand the infinite God, we face the problem of our finitude directly. God's will is yet again our guide. As a recipient of God's wisdom and a steward of the divine teaching "by the will of God" (1 Cor. 1:1; 4:1), Paul speaks of "God's wisdom in a mystery, the hidden wisdom which God predestined before the ages to our glory" (1 Cor. 2:7 NASB). *God wills to teach* his hidden wisdom through prophets and apostles, for our glory. And if God wills nothing in vain, then God does not teach in vain; hence, *God wills to be understood*. But how can an infinite God be understood by finite creatures? To borrow one of Jesus's own images, how can a shepherd have rational dealings with sheep? The absurdity of the image hints at the wonder of divine teaching: somehow, the shepherd translates himself to the sheep. Like many before him, Calvin concludes that this happens as God adapts his infinite self-knowledge to finite categories and linguistic forms that we may understand. What is uncreated takes on created form. Therefore, the content of God's wisdom remains the same while we distinguish between its uncreated, infinite form and its created, finite extension toward us. But God's teaching activity is not complete simply because God speaks in categories accessible to our created minds, because we still need God's help to understand God. After all, not everyone receives the word of the cross as God's wisdom. God's instruction is still inaccessible to those who refuse God as their teacher.

This latter insight leads us to how God's wise adaptation answers our fallenness, where divine teaching really emerges in its world-toppling power. Even though God adapts the form of his wisdom for human understanding,

---

33. On the knowledge of God, see Aquinas, *STh* I.14; Mastricht, *Theoretical-Practical Theology* 1.2.13; Bavinck, *Reformed Dogmatics*, 2:191–210; on the qualities of divine and human wisdom in the history of interpretation, see S. E. Harris, *God and the Teaching of Theology*, 69–86.

this form is counterintuitive: wisdom in the guise of foolishness, power in weakness. The pedagogical significance of this is in how it serves God's purposes of creating an audience for himself. The word of the cross represents an unexpected reversal of ordinary modes of perception, both by relativizing individualistic and subjective mindsets and by upsetting standard dichotomies like power and weakness. The effect of God's disruptive word is to separate its possible recipients into three categories, which Paul depicts as offense and possibly unbelief (Isa. 8:14; 1 Pet. 2:8), disputing and mocking (Acts 17:32; 25:19), or astonishment and wonder (1 Cor. 1:24–25). Were it not for God's grace, all would belong to one of the first two groups.

Even though God teaches in a form adapted to creaturely understanding, our capacities and standards of perception are hostile to divine teaching. Hence, those clutching their preconceived standards are "perishing," and so the word of the cross sounds like lunacy to them (1 Cor. 1:18). It confounds Greeks looking for wisdom and Jews looking for spectacular displays of power (1 Cor. 1:22–23). It relativizes the elite teaching one might find from philosophers, scribes, and debaters, who all belong to "this age," like the rulers who put Christ to death (1 Cor. 1:20; 2:8).[34] With his teaching, God puts to shame all the expectations and perceptions belonging to "this age" (1 Cor. 1:20). Revealing himself outside the standard antitheses of wisdom and foolishness or power and weakness, God instead demonstrates his wisdom and power in the foolishness and weakness of Christ's cross.[35] Consequently, those who perceive the truth of the cross, who see God's glory in and through it, cannot boast in their status or achievements but only in the Lord (1 Cor. 1:26–31). There is nothing in the recipients of God's teaching that makes them fit for it, like learning, status, or prestige. As in creation, God needs no preexisting materials because he creates something new (1 Cor. 1:28). Those who respond to the word of the cross with astonishment and gratitude do so by God's grace.

This eschatological work of God is the answer to our fallenness. The apostolic teaching is "in a mystery," which is to say, "in words . . . taught by the Spirit," so that spiritual truths will only be "spiritually discerned" (1 Cor. 2:7, 13–14 NASB).[36] We understand divine teaching not by human ingenuity or

---

34. See D. L. White, *Teacher of the Nations*, 110–12. Consult Thiselton, *The First Epistle to the Corinthians*, 233–39, on the meaning of "rulers" (ἄρχων) in 1 Cor. 2:6, 8.

35. Note the specificity of all this: *God's* power and wisdom in *Christ's cross*. God does not simply initiate a dialectical pursuit of general realities like power and wisdom in their opposites; the reversal follows the pattern of the kingdom of God.

36. S. E. Harris, *God and the Teaching of Theology*, 38–44. Thiselton discusses the apocalyptic overtones in *The First Epistle to the Corinthians*, 242–45.

heroics but by the "God in heaven who reveals mysteries" (Dan. 2:28)—that is, "by the Spirit" (1 Cor. 2:10).[37] God's Spirit creates God's audience. By sovereign decree, God prepares his mysteries for those who in turn "love him" (1 Cor. 2:9; Isa. 52:15). This love, Paul says later, is patient, kind, humble, and "does not rejoice at wrongdoing, but rejoices with the truth. Love bears all things, believes all things, hopes all things, endures all things" (1 Cor. 13:6–7). In traditional language, from love spring forth the virtues required for being a good student, like docility, humility, simplicity, and more.[38] But love is the outworking of faith (Gal. 5:6). So what distinguishes the teachable from the unteachable is the same thing that separates the "mature" and "spiritual" (1 Cor. 2:6, 15) from the "infants" and merely "worldly" (2:14; 3:1)—namely, "faith" (1:21; 2:5).[39] And this is the gift of God (Eph. 2:8), which grants us the "mind of Christ" (1 Cor. 2:16). The "mind" in question here is a whole new way of perceiving, a new *habitus*.[40] According to Paul, divine teaching does not merely adapt to our finite ways of knowing but transforms our understanding. God's inward teaching creates a new mind for the Spirit to instruct. God's work of adaptation thereby finds its audience by creating it. God's adaptation is stranger and deeper than any other pedagogy. God adapts the form of his wisdom in light of his audience and their circumstances, it is true. But Christ's cross shows us that the primary reality God "adapts" is the audience itself. By God's work within we become capable of receiving his paradoxical wisdom.

What we see in Paul's argument throughout the first chapters of 1 Corinthians is how, from God's inexhaustible riches, he generously provides all things for us in Christ so that we may be taught by his Spirit (cf. 1 John 2:6). God teaches us his wisdom, but the form of his instruction weaves together the adaptive, gradual, and formative elements in a stunning synthesis. God teaches through folly that is wisdom and reveals himself in weakness that is power. In the fullness of time, at the end of a gradual economy of divine teaching, God reverses the expectations and standards of this age and ushers in the age to come. His adaptation to our needs runs deeper than our creatureliness, radically uprooting our sinful unteachableness and forming us into those who have been given understanding that we may keep ourselves

37. Brown, *The Cross and Human Transformation*, 31–64 (esp. 59–63), explores apocalyptic traditions on the Spirit's role in knowing.

38. The virtues related to being teachable are included in the ninth commandment: "You shall not bear false witness against your neighbor" (Deut. 5:20); cf. Ursinus, *Commentary on the Heidelberg Catechism*, 600–605. Another, broader discussion of the virtues required for biblical reasoning is in Bonaventure, *Collations on the Six Days* 1.2–9.

39. Fitzmyer, *First Corinthians*, 170.

40. Cf. Thiselton, *The First Epistle to the Corinthians*, 275–76.

from idols (1 John 5:20–21). All of this is conducive to what Christ desires, that we may see his glory (John 17:24). So it is that God's wisdom is decreed for our glory, that we might know the "Lord of glory" and his resurrection (1 Cor. 2:7–8; 15:3–8; Phil. 3:10–11, 21). On this basis alone is divine teaching not only possible but also efficacious and real.

## Conclusion

In this chapter we have seen that our attention to Holy Scripture occurs within the larger setting of the divine economy in which God teaches his people. Much of the foregoing is implicit in the word "doctrine," or teaching. If we recall that disciples must seek God's face always, then we may now say that we do so especially through the teachable stance we adopt toward Scripture. And to the extent that teachableness (*docilitas*) is an openness to teaching (*doctrina*), then teachable approaches to Holy Scripture are open to the heavenly doctrine of Christ the Teacher (*doctor*). Part of God's pedagogy is to create a teachable audience, such that the virtue of docility is a gift of God's grace. Calvin famously recalls how God "by a sudden conversion subdued and ordered my heart to docility."[41] The note of conversion reminds us that we may seek God's face always only if God first seeks us: "I have gone astray like a lost sheep; seek your servant" (Ps. 119:176).

Among the many things docility requires are our attention and our intention. Teachable readers of Scripture set their attentions on God, delight in him, and meditate on his Word day and night (Pss. 1:1–2; 119:16, 24, 35, 47, 62). Such attentiveness is fundamentally receptive rather than autonomous. Docility also engages our will, stirring up "the desire to learn."[42] God's wisdom and knowledge are hidden in Christ, and so teachable readers seek those treasures diligently (cf. Matt. 13:44). With the psalmist, we must pray, "With my whole heart I seek you. . . . I have stored up your word in my heart" (Ps. 119:10–11). Here as well, the teacher teaches us teachability by his example, for Jesus learned obedience by what he suffered (Heb. 5:8). Schooled by God's grace into docility, we "abandon mastery of the text," and rather seek to be mastered by the work of God in the words of God.[43] We must be open to doctrine in the sense the word acquires within God's pedagogical economy: God's teaching about himself, through himself, that has fellowship with him in eternal life as its goal. If our reading of Scripture somehow resists or curtails

41. Calvin, *Commentary on the Psalms* (CO 31:22 AT).
42. Calvin, *Institutes of the Christian Religion* 3.2.5; cf. Augustine, *On Christian Teaching* 2.9.
43. Webster, *Holy Scripture*, 101.

this goal, then it inhabits an alternate economy and sits under another teacher. For this reason, it has been necessary to examine the larger context within which the church learns from Scripture.

A word of caution, however: divine pedagogy is not a universal acid that burns through every text of Scripture, scouring the particular details away to isolate only that which is relevant to formal doctrinal concerns. We must do equal justice to texts' immediate concerns and to their function in God's pedagogy with us, contemporary readers. God tested Israel and judged their failures on the one hand, and these same events *also* serve a larger function in God's broader pedagogical economy: "Now these things happened to them as an example, but they were written down for our instruction, on whom the end of the ages has come" (1 Cor. 10:11).[44] God genuinely disciplined his people for their sins, just as they deserved. Yet these episodes are *also* part of our education, so they are preserved in the curriculum of Scripture. Stated differently: recognition of God's pedagogy does not license a form of exegesis analogous to a purely exemplarist Christology, as if everything Jesus says and does is merely some moralist tale.

Divine pedagogy is not reducible to one of its elements, whether this be its adaptive, gradual, and formative features or others besides. Rather, God's pedagogy reminds us that in everything God does for us and for our salvation—genuine acts of judgment and mercy, salvation and revelation—God is *also* carefully instructing us about himself and his will. Another way of stating the point is that all that God says and does is revelatory in some respect. This much we have articulated in our second principle above. Understanding the aim of God's pedagogy, we may more readily understand God's aim in any particular part of Scripture: to lead us to the vision of Christ's glory adaptively, gradually, and formatively. Exegesis is therefore inescapably doctrinal in the sense that it is instruction by God, our teacher and pedagogue.

44. Calvin: "It does not . . . follow from this, that these inflictions were not true chastisements from God, suited for their correction at that time, but as God then inflicted his judgments, so he designed that they should be kept everlastingly in remembrance for our instruction" (*Commentary on the Epistles of Paul the Apostle to the Corinthians* 1 Cor. 10:11).

# 3

# The Curriculum of Christ

## The Source and Practice of Biblical Reasoning

**Principle 3:** Scripture is the inspired, textual form of Christ's teaching in which he is present to his people across time and space, leading us toward wisdom.

**Rule 1:** To rightly respond to God's pedagogical pressures in his Word, read Scripture as a unity, interpreting its parts in light of the whole and understanding the whole as a harmonious testimony to God and his works.

**Rule 2:** To understand the theological grammar and syntax of Scripture, read Scripture in such a way that you learn how its various discourses both form and presuppose a larger theological vision.

In the previous two chapters we have considered the end of discipleship—that is, the beatific vision—and its context, the economy of divine teaching in which God leads us to this end. This chapter concludes part 1 by synthesizing these principles briefly and setting the stage for the rule chapters that follow in part 2. Our task in this chapter is to make explicit a claim that has so far been only implicit: the mutually informing and reciprocal, though asymmetrical, relation between exegesis and theology. Supporting this claim will be the goal of the rest of the book. In sum, we describe this mutually informing relation between exegesis and theology as "biblical reasoning," which John Webster defines as "the redeemed intellect's reflective apprehension of God's gospel address through the embassy of Scripture, enabled and corrected by God's presence, and having fellowship with him as its end."[1] The central role of Scripture, already hinted at in the previous two chapters, now needs to be made more explicit.

When we keep God's teaching activity before us, then our biblical reasoning is set within a broader economy ordered toward certain pedagogical aims. The chief end in view is the blessed vision of God's glory in Christ. By concentrating on God's teaching and pedagogy, we have grasped some of the ways by which God leads us to this vision. In general terms, God's pedagogy is adaptive, gradual, and formative. He not only speaks to us in words and deeds that creatures may understand; he also transforms his audience so that we may indeed be taught. Just as Christ bids us to behold his glory by faith in the "face of God for now"[2]—Holy Scripture—so too Scripture functions as the main text in the curriculum. As Calvin says, Scripture is the "special gift, where God, to instruct the church, not merely uses mute teachers but also opens his own most hallowed lips."[3] Holy Scripture is the voice of the Teacher himself, so it plays a central role in divine teaching.

Among other things, as we will see more clearly below, this means that biblical reasoning cannot be described without appeal to God's presence and activity. But more to our present purposes, God also teaches us through various actions authoritatively attested in Scripture and performed by Scripture.[4] To find ourselves in a pedagogical economy is to open ourselves to the many possibilities such actions set before us: to warn, reprimand, encourage, lead along, comfort, stir to action, arouse the affections, refine the understanding of faith (*intellectus fidei*), and more. While space prohibits us from developing a comprehensive theology of Scripture and its interpretation, we will now explore some of the ways in which a theology of Scripture, set within God's pedagogical economy, bears upon the task of exegesis. Thus we will begin to see how exegesis and theology relate.[5]

---

1. Webster, "Biblical Reasoning," 128. Kevin Vanhoozer has also argued for an account of "biblical reasoning" very companionable to this in *Remythologizing Theology*, 187–98.

2. Augustine, *Sermon* 22.7 (WSA III/2:46).

3. Calvin, *Institutes of the Christian Religion* 1.6.1.

4. God's revelation always employs a unity of word and act: Sanders, *The Triune God*, 37–68.

5. On the theology of Scripture, see in particular Bavinck, *Reformed Dogmatics*, 1:283–494; Warfield, *The Inspiration and Authority of the Bible*; Webster, *Holy Scripture*; Swain, *Trinity, Revelation, and Reading*.

In other words, this chapter explores Scripture's nature and its interpretation within the broader setting and practice of biblical reasoning. In the previous chapter we investigated God's pedagogy, and now we must reflect more directly, albeit briefly, on the central means Christ uses to teach his church: Scripture. In order to offer a brief account of the nature and interpretation of Scripture, we will examine Scripture's character in light of the ascended Christ's present ministry to the church and how exegesis is a response to his pedagogy and thus is open to divine teaching (*doctrina*). First, we will elucidate our third principle by looking at what the setting of biblical reasoning tells us about Scripture's nature and function. Equipped with an understanding of what Scripture is, we will then proceed in the final section to look at some consequences for the practice of biblical reasoning, which will lead to our first two rules concerning Scripture's interpretation.

## The Setting of Biblical Reasoning

In the last chapter we looked at the larger context within which we seek the Lord's face through Scripture, which is the economy of divine teaching. This section picks up where that discussion left off, looking more narrowly at Holy Scripture itself and its interpretation in light of the divine economy. Since we seek the Lord's face within an economy of divine teaching, and since we seek to meditate on Christ's glory by faith through reading Scripture, how does this divine economy inform biblical reasoning?

Answering this question requires us to look first at what Scripture is in the divine economy and only then at how that affects biblical reasoning, "the redeemed intellect's reflective apprehension" of Scripture. In this section, we will unpack our third principle, which concerns Scripture's nature and function in the economy: Scripture is the inspired, textual form of Christ's teaching in which he is present to his people across time and space, leading us toward wisdom.

### The Nature of Scripture

As we turn to consider the nature and function of Holy Scripture in the divine economy, we may learn a great deal from the portrait of Christ and Scripture in Revelation, the concluding book of the canon. The first thing to observe is how the nature of Holy Scripture is determined in no small part by the text's relation to its source. The opening of the Apocalypse tells us that it is "the revelation of Jesus Christ, which God gave him to show to his servants the things that must soon take place" (Rev. 1:1).[6] The source of the message is Jesus (Rev. 22:16), the one who reveals the Father (Luke 10:22) because he makes known what he has "seen" and "heard" from the Father (John 1:18; 15:15). John, on the other hand, is a "servant" and so his witness depends on and serves the "witness of Jesus Christ" (Rev. 1:2; cf. John 8:18). Both John and Jesus are witnesses, but in a certain order. In their witness, Jesus and John stand in a relationship of primary to secondary witness, source to receiver. Thus, John writes about what he has seen, what is, and what will take place, in conformity to the activity of Jesus, "who is and who was and who is to come" (Rev. 1:8, 19). In the first place, then, we see that Holy Scripture is a form of human witness that depends on divine witness. It is a human witness that derives from and is determined by the triune God.

Further, this human witness takes written form. The manner of John's witness is textual: in the Spirit, John hears a "loud voice like a trumpet" commanding him to "write" what he sees and to distribute it to the churches (Rev. 1:10–11).[7] The fact that John is "in the Spirit" signals the divine inspiration of his prophecy (cf. Rev. 4:2; 17:3; 21:10; Ezek. 3:12).[8] Like the prophets before him, he obeys amidst this inspiration and so provides us with the Apocalypse (cf. Jer. 1:7–9; Ezek. 2:8–3:4).[9] So too, under the Spirit's guidance, the apostles obey Christ's command to go forth into the nations, baptizing, discipling, and teaching (Matt. 28:19–20; Luke 1:1–4; John 20:30–31). The organic results of this obedience are the documents of the NT. The character of their inspiration creates an identity between God's speech and the human words of his commissioned prophets and apostles. What Scripture says, God says.[10] It is thus that Paul can say, in a representative statement, that his teaching is not merely a human word but "the word of God" (1 Thess. 2:13). This is strikingly apparent in the Apocalypse: each of the seven letters John writes to the churches, which epitomize the prophecy as a whole, is simultaneously something "the Spirit says to the churches" (Rev. 2:7, 11, 17, 29; 3:6, 13, 22) and something Jesus says (Rev. 2:1, 8, 12, 18; 3:1, 7, 14). In John's servant relation to the Lord we find that, to adapt a saying from Wallace Stegner, the Apocalypse is like the rest of Scripture, only more so: "Men spoke from God as they were carried

---

6. As the book makes clear in its overall shape, the genitive Ἰησοῦ Χριστοῦ ("of Jesus Christ") is subjective, meaning Jesus is the one doing the revealing. See Koester, *Revelation*, 211.

7. Every "loud voice" in Revelation is significant (Rev. 1:10; 8:13; 10:4; 11:12; 12:10). Each carries deep OT allusions (Exod. 19:16; 20:18; 2 Sam. 6:15; Ps. 47:5; Joel 2:1; Zech. 9:14; Heb. 12:18–19). See, further, Koester, *Revelation*, 244.

8. Bauckham, *The Theology of the Book of Revelation*, 115.

9. On this theme in Jeremiah, see Shead, *A Mouth Full of Fire*.

10. See, for instance, the detailed, illuminating, and still-relevant work of Warfield, "'It Says:' 'Scripture Says:' 'God Says.'"

along by the Holy Spirit" (2 Pet. 1:21). The inspired words of the prophets and apostles remain human, with all their essentially human characteristics. But they are also Jesus's words, the speech of the triune God himself. As such, Holy Scripture is divine self-testimony, and it occupies a unique, central place in the curriculum of God's pedagogical economy. As the church's teacher, then, Jesus Christ provides us with a mediated, textual form of his instruction, consenting "to be both embodied and expressed through letters, syllables, and sounds . . . according to the principle of adaptation" (συγκατάβασις).[11]

Beyond creating a written form of his witness through the prophets and apostles, Jesus also remains present to his people in and through that mediated speech.[12] As we soon discover, John is beholding the Son's ascended session at the right hand of the Father where, startlingly, the Son is moving freely across time and space. John turns to see the voice and sees instead "seven golden lampstands, and in the midst of the lampstands one like a son of man" (Rev. 1:12–13). This imagery pictures Christ's unrestricted presence to all the churches in two ways. First, the number seven conveys the idea of perfection or completeness (cf. Gen. 2:2–3). And as Jesus tells John, "the seven lampstands are the seven churches" in whose midst he walks (Rev. 1:20; cf. 1:13; 2:1).[13] By representing the "seven" churches, the lampstands represent *all* the churches—what the Apostles' Creed designates the one, holy, *catholic* church, which includes God's people across time and space. Second, though, lampstands were of special importance to the tabernacle's holy place. Aaron was instructed to set up the "lamps" to give light "in front of the lampstand," so that the light and fire, symbols of God's presence, would shine on the twelve loaves of showbread, which represented the twelve tribes of Israel (Num. 8:2; Lev. 24:4–6). This symbolized how, through the mediation of priests, God would bless his people and keep them, make his face shine upon them and be gracious to them, lift his face to them and grant them peace (Num. 6:24–26).[14] On a deeper level, then, the lampstands serve to underscore Christ's presence with the churches. Taken together, the imagery of seven lampstands portrays Christ's prophetic and apostolic disclosure: Jesus, with his church always, bestowing the blessing of God's presence through his priestly ministry on her behalf (Matt. 28:20; Heb. 7:25; 9:24).[15] Scripture is not, therefore, an

---

11. Maximus the Confessor, *Ambiguum* 33.2 (Constas, 2:64–65, modified).

12. As Webster observes, "Verbal inspiration is an extension of (not a replacement for) the theology of divine instruction" ("On the Inspiration of Holy Scripture," 246).

13. John also mentions the "seven lampstands" four times, possibly signifying the four corners of the earth (cf. Leithart, *Revelation 1–11*, 102).

14. Morales, *Who Shall Ascend the Mountain of the Lord?*, 15–17.

15. "Lamp" (λύχνος) is used three times in an important contrast: Babylon exploits the nations and so "the light of a lamp will shine in you no more" (Rev. 18:23); but the new Jerusalem

inert document Jesus leaves behind before taking a holiday. On the contrary, Scripture is a tool in his hands, and as such is "living and active" (Heb. 4:12).

The Apocalypse elaborates on Jesus's presence with the churches in how it sets before us his activity in his three roles as prophet, priest, and king. To see this, we need look no further than John's vision of the Lord's royal investiture in heaven upon his ascension.[16] Leading up to this vision, John sees heaven opened and hears Jesus's voice: "Come up here, and I will show you what must take place after this" (Rev. 4:1). Soon after, he sees in God's right hand a scroll sealed with seven seals and hears an angel asking if anyone is worthy to open it (Rev. 5:1–2). It is important to grasp just what the scroll is as well as who is worthy to open it and why. The scroll has elicited much commentary because it is described in various ways that allude to different scenes from the OT. It has words on the back and front, like the tablets of the law (Exod. 32:15) and Ezekiel's scroll that he had to eat (Ezek. 2:9–3:3; cf. Ps. 19:7–10). It is sealed, like Daniel's book that is not to be opened "until the time of the end" (Dan. 12:4), or Isaiah's vision that cannot be received until the day when "the deaf shall hear the words of a book, and out of their gloom and darkness the eyes of the blind shall see" (Isa. 29:18; cf. vv. 11–12).[17] The ambiguity should be allowed to say something before we move too quickly to associate the imagery with one particular reference. Indeed, all of these allusions are likely in play if the Law and the Prophets all point us to Christ (Matt. 17:3–5; Rom. 10:4). As the investiture scene plays out, we see Christ take the book in hand as the true Davidic King who keeps God's testimony close (Deut. 17:18–20; Josh. 1:7–9). It is a book of law, conquest, and prophecy: Jesus will open it to govern his covenant people (Exod. 24:1–8), to crush idols like Josiah did (2 Kings 22:8–23:25), and to reveal what has been hidden but is now open (Dan. 12:4).[18] As at the beginning of his ministry, Jesus is the one who is worthy to open and expound the scroll because he fulfills it as its substance (Luke 4:16–21; Heb. 1:2).

Crucially, Jesus is "worthy" because he is the Lamb whose blood ransomed God's people from our enemies, making us a kingdom of priests (Rev. 5:9–10).[19] His fulfillment of God's plan to exercise dominion over the cosmos through

---

will be filled with the luminous glory of God: "its lamp is the Lamb," and "by its light will the nations walk" (21:23–24; 22:5). Bauckham, *The Theology of the Book of Revelation*, 131–32. This contrast suggests that Jesus's threat of removing a lampstand (Rev. 2:5) is like his judgment of Babylon, which will be brought to nothing (Rev. 17–18).

16. On the scene as one of investiture, see Aune, *Revelation 1–5*, 336–38.

17. Aune, *Revelation 1–5*, 341–46, canvasses these many options.

18. Leithart, *Revelation 1–11*, 253–55. Scripture is thus an instance of "language in use" (Ward, *Words of Life*, 77).

19. Beale, *The Book of Revelation*, 351–55, 357–59, discusses the Passover and Isaianic background to the "lamb" imagery, as well as the significance of Jesus conquering through death.

his image bearers renders him uniquely suited to opening the Scriptures in their full scope (Ps. 8:3–8; Heb. 2:5–18; 1 Cor. 15:21–27).[20] His death and resurrection are, after all, "in accordance with the Scriptures" (1 Cor. 15:3–4). Jesus Christ uniquely reveals mysteries that otherwise would be hidden from our understanding (Eph. 1:9–10; 3:11). As prophet, Jesus speaks the word of God; as king, Jesus rules by the word of God; as our "merciful and faithful high priest" (Heb. 2:17), Jesus removes the "veil" that otherwise covers our hearts when we read Moses (2 Cor. 3:12–18; 4:6). Christ remains the "supreme expositor of divine Scripture."[21] In this ministry as our prophet, priest, and king, Jesus leads us with Scripture to behold the glory of God in his face. Scripture is therefore not just the written word of God but also an instrument in the Teacher's hands, inseparable from his presence and activity.

## The Economic Location of Scripture

So far the Apocalypse has given us a glimpse of Scripture's nature or ontology, especially as this is informed by its role in God's economy. By the Spirit's inspiration, and by the ascended Jesus's oversight, Holy Scripture is the Word of God that resides in the Lord's hands as he continues to guide and instruct his people so that we may worship him in spirit and in truth. In this light, John Webster argues that we must locate Scripture in time and space relative to the divine economy of teaching.[22] Unpacking each of these "locations" will introduce the consequences of Scripture's ontology and economic function relevant to biblical reasoning.

First, when we understand Scripture in relation to Christ's ascension and his ongoing ministry to and for the church, we acquire a greater sense of its location in time. Jesus's sovereign movement among the churches attests his identity as the eternal God, so he is not confined to the past or future. This means that the temporal location of Scripture is one in which Jesus remains present to us now. Historical-critical approaches to Scripture largely assume an account of time uninformed and uncorrected by the ascended, present, and ruling Lord. Consequently, the text is usually treated as an artifact of ancient religious culture accessible mainly to the historian's craft rather than to the disciple's faith.[23] On this reckoning, the text is located in the past. To

---

20. It is this fact that, theologically, requires the use of the *regula fidei*—a succinct summary of the apostolic proclamation—in interpretation. See Ferguson, *The Rule of Faith*; Swain, "Ruled Reading Reformed"; cf. Polanus, *Syntagma theologiae christianae* 1.45 (107c).

21. Polanus, *Syntagma theologiae christianae* 1.45 (112a–b).

22. For what follows, see Webster, "Resurrection and Scripture," in *The Domain of the Word*, 32–49.

23. Webster, "Resurrection and Scripture," 42.

be sure, this text originates in the past, replete with a material history of its composition that may be studied and analyzed with historical tools (cultural location, historical and social circumstances of authorship and reception, and so on). Yet the text is also more, in light of the Spirit's inspiration and Christ's presence: it inhabits a divine economy in which its temporal location is not merely the past but also the present, as the Lord continues to speak with these texts to his church now. Indeed, since both audiences are part of the same economy, the divide between "original" and "contemporary" audiences is really a distinction within the *one* audience that is the people of God (cf. Rom. 15:4; 1 Cor. 10:1–4).[24]

Second, just as Jesus moves freely across time, so too he is unconstrained by space and so not swallowed up by the church, much less by any one congregation or tradition. The *social location* of Scripture is therefore the universal church that the Father elects, that Jesus calls into being and fills with his presence, and that the Spirit sanctifies and animates (Eph. 1:23). Two consequences of this social location merit our attention. First, Scripture may not be absorbed into the church's practices or made dependent on the church to fill out some insufficiency. The Spirit, not the church, "carried along" the words of the prophets and apostles (2 Pet. 1:21). The Spirit gives textual form to the voice of Christ in inspiration, and the church is the hearing of that voice that the Spirit creates in illumination. The church is thus the creature of God's Word, not vice versa. Hence, Scripture demands ever new attention from the church because it contains the words of life with which the Spirit renews her. Second, readers must necessarily be "catholic," gratefully receptive to God's generous provision of teachers throughout the universal church's history and across denominational lines. "For all things are yours," Paul reminds us, whether this be Paul himself, Apollos, Peter, or any other faithful teacher, "and you are Christ's, and Christ is God's" (1 Cor. 3:21–23).[25] Exegesis should never be isolated from the wisdom of the saints, past and present, for they too are provisions of God's generous pedagogy. Biblical reasoning is that form of attention to Scripture consistent with the nature of Scripture in these temporal and social locations, licensed because of what the text is in God's pedagogical economy.

In this section we mined the Apocalypse for a representative portrait of what Scripture is and how it functions in the economy. Scripture is the scepter of the risen Lord Jesus Christ, the written form of his voice which the church hears and obeys. The inspired text is God's word because it extends

24. Sarisky, *Reading the Bible Theologically*, 217–32.
25. See S. E. Harris, *God and the Teaching of Theology*, 165–68.

the teaching activity of the risen Christ rather than competing with it. Christ is present to the church in and through the teaching of the prophets and apostles, who are stewards in his economy. In all of this, the church's great prophet, priest, and king addresses, redeems, and governs his people in order to present her spotless in his presence.

To seek the Lord's face is therefore to attend to Scripture as a communicative act in the present that incorporates us into the audience of the church past and present. Biblical reasoning finds its place primarily in the economy of divine teaching and secondarily in more proximate contexts, such as particular streams of tradition. None of these factors are barriers to sound exegesis. Instead, they are conditions for it: hearers of the Word are those addressed in *this* text, in *this* setting. Given this setting, what can we say about the practice of biblical reasoning?

## The Practice of Biblical Reasoning

Turning in this section to consider the practice of biblical reasoning, we are not turning belatedly from lighter to weightier matters. Any question about the practice of exegesis is predicated upon prior convictions about the nature and ends of interpreters as well as the nature of the text and the setting within which it may be received. Every stance on how to read rests on convictions about who is reading and what is being read. In theological terms, every scriptural hermeneutic implies an anthropology and bibliology. In the two previous chapters we have characterized readers of Scripture as *disciples* whose end is the vision of Christ's glory that he shares with the Father and the Spirit, and *students* who learn only by God's benevolent adaptation. And thus far in this chapter we have considered the nature of Scripture within the setting of biblical reasoning, the divine economy. John presents us with a picture of the ascended Christ traversing time and space, speaking to all the churches through his written self-testimony as their prophet, priest, and king, and calling forth rightly ordered praise and adoration. From Holy Scripture's status as the *viva vox Christi* (living voice of Christ) in the Apocalypse, we see how it is the *viva vox Dei* (living voice of God). Only now may we ask: Given who we are as readers and what the text is that we read, what does biblical reasoning look like?

On one level, no answer to this question would be complete without some basic considerations. Reading well requires competency in acts of listening and understanding, so exegesis is undertaken best when employing a full range of linguistic, grammatical, historical, and literary skills, all of which have intellectual standards of excellence. Moreover, given what we have said in the previous chapters, theological exegesis also involves faith, prayer, docility, humility, a love of truth, willingness to obey, and much more.[26] One standard way of describing these responsibilities is through the three steps of explication, meditation, and application.[27] In explication, the goal is to understand what the text says and how it does so through patient, loving attention to its form, details, and subject matter. This includes historical inquiry into the text's material settings as well as literary analysis of its distinctive features and place within the larger canon of Scripture, all in service of understanding its chief subject: God in Christ.[28] Meditation occurs as readers begin to internalize the sense of the text and think reflectively in its light, reading particular parts of Scripture in view of the whole canon and the collective substance of its teachings. Finally, in application the reader receives the book as the summons to discipleship that it is and responds to it.

Without attempting a full account of hermeneutics, however, what must we say about biblical reasoning in order to lay a foundation for the following chapters? In light of Scripture's nature and role as the curriculum of God's instruction, we focus on two consequences of divine teaching for the way biblical reasoning responds to Holy Scripture. Respectively, we begin by discussing Scripture's "exactness" and then examine how God's pedagogy employs the text's "pressures" to goad us toward understanding. Together, these two consequences of divine teaching provide us with a relatively simple methodological approach for relating theology and exegesis.

### Scripture's Exactness

Early Christian interpreters often spoke of Scripture's "exactness" (ἀκρίβεια, akribeia) to underscore divine teaching's intentionality, reliability, and attention to detail.[29] Exactness was considered a stylistic mark of perfection in the rhetoric and art of antiquity, so the characteristic stood out more readily to the eyes of early Christians than it does to moderns. However, something very much like it is an extension of what we have already seen of

---

26. For a representative list of such hermeneutical instructions, see Polanus, *Syntagma theologiae christianae* 1.45. More broadly in this connection, see East, "What Are the Standards of Excellence for Theological Interpretation of Scripture?"

27. Different but companionable recent examples include the following: Yeago, "The Bible"; Swain, *Trinity, Revelation, and Reading*, 125–36; Sarisky, *Reading the Bible Theologically*, 294–326.

28. Cf. Alexander of Hales, *Summa theologica* intro., q. 1, c. 3, vol. 1:6.

29. On this motif in the fathers, see Rylaarsdam, *John Chrysostom on Divine Pedagogy*, 114–15; Margerie, *The Greek Fathers*, 199–205; Martens, *Origen and Scripture*, 168–81; Ernest, *The Bible in Athanasius of Alexandria*, 168–69.

God's pedagogy. Since Scripture is an element of divine teaching, it shares the communicative virtues of its inspiring Author and sanctified, inspired authors. Hence, in various ways, Scripture meticulously and purposefully communicates God's holy teaching. There are hints of this in Luke, who claims that his orderly account of the gospel events is the product of carefully (ἀκριβῶς, *akribōs*) attending to them (Luke 1:3). Moreover, exactness characterizes the teaching of Apollos, who "spoke and taught accurately the things concerning Jesus," though Priscilla and Aquilla "explained to him the way of God more accurately" (Acts 18:25–26; cf. 23:15, 20; 24:22). Luke also depicts Paul's Jewish education and religious observance as exacting (Acts 22:3; 26:5). These stewards in the divine economy exhibited exactness in their teaching and lives because they were concerned to pass on what they were taught in the way they were taught it. God tells John to write "because these words are faithful and true," thus conforming the very words of the prophecy to God's own character (Rev. 21:5; 22:18–19; cf. 15:3; 19:9; 22:6). This exactness in teaching is due to God's adaptability; God knows that it is good for his people not to be taught haphazardly. Employing various human authors, God's pedagogy is characterized by a meticulous rhetoric that encompasses the agrarian and poetic as much as the emotional and rational dimensions of human existence. But just what does this exactness mean for biblical reasoning?

God's teaching is exact in at least two senses important for our study. First, God chooses his words carefully rather than leaving us to sort through mishaps and slips of the tongue. Second, what is taught carries a degree of precision that we must grasp. The first sense is a consequence of Scripture's ontology—namely, that it is an instrument of divine teaching. The principle here is that, as a good teacher, Christ does not mislead or act carelessly in word or deed—even when speaking through prophets and apostles. In Scripture, God "speaks exactly what He thinks, and thinks exactly what He speaks."[30] Thus John's Apocalypse concludes with the warning to neither take away nor add to the prophecy of his book, and by inference the same prohibition applies to the whole of Scripture (Rev. 22:18–19; cf. Deut. 4:2; Prov. 30:5–6). Because God's teaching employs exact words and phrases as much as the interrelations between different books and the two Testaments, all of it rewards exacting attention by student-disciples. The consequences for exegesis are that readers should expect nothing misleading, nothing superfluous, and nothing finally contradictory (though apparent contradictions and paradoxes

---

30. Irenaeus, *Against Heresies* 2.28.5 (*ANF* 1:400); cf. also Gregory of Nazianzus, *Oration* 2.105 (*NPNF*² 7:205).

abound).[31] Chrysostom's advice is representative: "Let us act so as to interpret everything precisely and instruct you not to pass by even a brief phrase or a single syllable contained in the Holy Scriptures. After all, they are not simply words, but words of the Holy Spirit, and hence the treasure to be found in even a single syllable is great."[32] Every word of Scripture is an implement of God's pedagogy. Readers should therefore be conscious of our limitations and yet hopeful that even those bits of Scripture that confuse us have some deeper significance.[33] Faced with something inexplicable, we cannot write it off as a mere product of the circumstances surrounding its human authorship or a remnant of crude editorial layers of tradition. Rather we must learn to see God's meticulous wisdom in preserving these difficulties, which are there "to wear Adam down and let Christ's glorious grace shine through."[34] God intends to form us in patience, sometimes even by confounding us.

The second sense is broader: what Scripture teaches possesses an extent of exactitude regarding its subject, God in Christ, that the reader must discern, approximate, and never transgress. The first consequence of this for biblical reasoning in the following chapters will be our willingness to allow *that* Scripture leads us to consider and confess matters pertaining to the vision of Christ's glory. God's instruction leads us to contemplate such realities as God's eternal life, though it does so with an exactness in Scripture that our understanding must *approximate*. As the church has listened attentively to Scripture in this regard, inevitably it has used extrabiblical language to paraphrase what it has heard. The term "Trinity" is a prime example, since it is "a word certainly unwritten as to its syllables, but most evidently written as to its meaning."[35] The exegetical use of theological and metaphysical concepts like being, nature, and relations, for example, can only be warranted if such concepts help us to approximate the precision of Scripture itself.

It is important not to overestimate or overstate what theology does at this point. In David Yeago's seminal treatment of theological exegesis, he distinguishes concepts and judgments: "The same judgement can be rendered in a variety of conceptual terms."[36] For example, despite their different historical settings, Paul's affirmation of the Son's equality with the Father, expressed

---

31. All paradoxes are apparent contradictions, but not all apparent contradictions are paradoxes (e.g., apparent discrepancies in number, order, and narration).

32. John Chrysostom, *Homilies on Genesis* 15.3 (FC 74:195).

33. Bavinck, *Reformed Dogmatics*, 1:439–48.

34. Augustine, *The Trinity* 2.1 (WSA I/5:97).

35. Mastricht, *Theoretical-Practical Theology* 1.2.24.vi. The anti-trinitarian Michael Servetus argued that the Trinity was unbiblical partly because concepts like person, essence, and trinity did not occur to Scripture's authors. Servetus, *De Trinitatis erroribus, libri septem*, 1.33, 44, 58.

36. Yeago, "The New Testament and the Nicene Dogma," 159.

with the concept of "the form of God" (Phil. 2:6), says something substantially, though not exactly, the same as Nicaea's "of the same being" (ὁμοούσιος, *homoousios*).[37] The subjects under consideration in each text are identical: Jesus of Nazareth. The intimate relation of Jesus to the Father is "logically equivalent" in each text. And both affirmations share a common overarching framework of belief and practice—namely, Jesus's divinity as the warrant for Christians' worship of him.[38] The judgments are substantially the same (Jesus is God), though the concepts are not (form of God, *homoousios*). In this light, the continuity between Scripture and later theological formulas "must be sought at the level of judgements and not at the level of concepts."[39] Yeago's is a salutary account, so long as we remember that the meaning of biblical concepts may not be reduced to the individual judgments they facilitate, and that we do not improve upon Scripture when we identify particular judgments and conceptualize them with nonbiblical idioms.[40] Thus, theological concepts are best thought of as approximations of Scripture's native precision and clarity rather than improvements on the Bible's raw materials.

The second consequence is that the extent of Scripture's exactness structures *how far* we can take our contemplation of the God who dwells in unapproachable light (1 Tim. 6:16). As theology traces the movement of divine teaching, absorbs it, and responds with confession and praise, it attempts to follow Scripture's precision. Because it adopts a "rhetoric of effacement" before Scripture, biblical reasoning may confidently attempt precision concerning the things about which Scripture speaks.[41] We adhere to Scripture's teaching as much as its silences. Calvin's admonition is sound: "Let us use great caution that neither our thoughts nor our speech go beyond the limits to which the Word of God itself extends."[42] This is not to say there is more virtue in silence than in speech or that speculative theology, rightly understood, is inherently depraved. Speculation, after all, is looking deeply into what is there to be seen. To see well, we must avoid spiritual nearsightedness as much as

---

37. Yeago, "The Bible," 64–65n22.
38. Yeago, "The New Testament and the Nicene Dogma," 160.
39. Yeago, "The New Testament and the Nicene Dogma," 159.
40. Sarisky, "Judgements in Scripture and the Creed"; cf. Webster, *Holy Scripture*, 117–20. It is worth making two further clarifications regarding "judgments" in light of the previous chapters. First, the idiom of judgment alongside concept should not mislead: biblical judgments are gifts of divine teaching rather than achievements of human spontaneity. Second, as deliverances of the divine pedagogy leading us to the vision of Christ's glory, biblical judgments have a truth value that is not merely "regulative" (cf. Kant, *Critique of Pure Reason*, A633–34/B661–62).
41. Webster, *The Culture of Theology*, 76–78.
42. Calvin, *Institutes of the Christian Religion* 1.13.21; cf. Cyril of Jerusalem, *Catechetical Lecture* 16.24 (NPNF² 7:121); Gregory of Nazianzus, *Oration* 27.3.

farsightedness. Theology may err by not going far enough as much as by going too far; students should neither lag behind nor get ahead of their Teacher.

Finding these limits is not a simple task. It is less of a science than an art acquired through consciously inhabiting the culture formed by God's pedagogy. At minimum, discerning Scripture's exactness—how far Scripture takes our contemplation of transcendent realities—is something that occurs through exegesis itself. Scripture's sufficiency extends to the standard of "precision" that theology seeks. Readers should beware of adopting a foreign criterion of precision or of parking our attention somewhere beyond or short of what God teaches. Theological exegesis does its job when it submits to the measure given by its object. In this way, theological reason follows wherever the Shepherd leads with a precision answering to his voice rather than to another.

### Scripture's Pressure

Because Scripture is the risen Christ's active instruction, biblical reasoning pays exacting attention to it as the rule that binds us to our Lord's voice. With such attentiveness, exegesis will rightly expect that, in Scripture, the Lord has spoken and continues to speak. Moreover, attentive exegesis will acknowledge there can be no mastery of divine teaching, only submission to it in all of its scriptural heights and depths. Yet how do we get from the arresting imagery of the Apocalypse, much less the earthy material of Leviticus, to the place where we suddenly feel the need for lofty doctrinal constructions about being, relations, natures, and so forth? How should we attempt, prayerfully, to correspond to the exactness of divine teaching?

For our purposes, we may restrict ourselves to a general preview of the exegetical theory and practice that will constitute the rest of the book. Biblical reasoning follows Scripture's exactness as it attends to God's pedagogy in Scripture, thereby learning its fundamental grammar. C. Kavin Rowe's treatment of Scripture's "pressure" or "coercion" is helpful in this regard. Scripture is not inert, according to Rowe, but exerts a coercion on its readers "such that there is (or can be) a profound continuity, grounded in the subject matter itself, between the biblical text and traditional Christian exegesis and theological formulation."[43] Rowe extracts the idea of pressure from the organic relation between the Testaments because both testify to the same subject matter—that is, the same God: "The two-testament canon read as one book pressures its interpreters to make ontological judgments about the trinitarian nature of the one God *ad intra* on the basis of its narration of the act and

---

43. Rowe, "Biblical Pressure and Trinitarian Hermeneutics," 308.

identity of the biblical God *ad extra*."[44] Against the backdrop of the OT's insistence on God's unity and unique glory, the NT's teaching about Christ pressures us toward trinitarian theology in ways that it would not on its own. To absorb the full force of Scripture's canonical pressures, we must reckon with the primary reality behind and above not only the text but all of history.[45] This leads us to recognize that the unity of both Testaments is rooted not simply in their primary referent but in their primary acting subject: God. Therefore, the idea of "biblical pressure" ultimately leads us to conclude that "it is the presence of God himself in his Word that wills and moves us to speak in this way about God."[46] This should not surprise us by now, especially in light of the Apocalypse's portrait of Scripture in the hands of the risen Christ. Hence, through the discourse of the two-testament canon, God pressures us in pedagogically diverse ways to acknowledge divine teaching. Every rightfully perceived "pressure" is thus the effect of God's pedagogy, goading us toward wisdom (*sapientia*).[47] We may now formulate our first rule: *To rightly respond to God's pedagogical pressures in his Word, read Scripture as a unity, interpreting its parts in light of the whole and understanding the whole as a harmonious testimony to God and his works.*[48] But what more might be said about how God pressures us toward certain interpretative decisions and theological judgments?

The category of "pressure" helps us to see how exegesis leads to theology, not only warranting but also encouraging doctrinal formulation and recognition. For Rowe, the most important exegetical question to ask at this point is "how." For instance, NT claims about the worship of Jesus (e.g., Matt. 2:2, 11) alongside the OT's insistence on worshiping God alone (Deut. 6:13–15) force us to answer questions of an ontological nature, such as "how" a Jewish man belongs to the identity of the one God of Israel. Or we may return to our text from earlier: *How is it* that the Apocalypse portrays Jesus the slain Lamb being worshiped (Rev. 5:12–13) alongside the angels' refusal to accept worship, which is due God alone (19:10; 22:8–9)? A strictly historical analysis of the text tethered to its material settings can certainly tell us *what*

---

44. Rowe, "Biblical Pressure and Trinitarian Hermeneutics," 308. Sanders, *The Triune God*, 119, offers a lapidary axiom: "Only the pan-economic is trans-economic, and vice versa."

45. Rowe, "Biblical Pressure and Trinitarian Hermeneutics," 311.

46. Rowe, "Biblical Pressure and Trinitarian Hermeneutics," 309.

47. See Aquinas, *STh* II-II.9.4.

48. Irenaeus explicates rules such as this one in response to Valentinian Gnosticism. See Margerie, *The Greek Fathers*, 55–56. See also Tertullian, *Against Praxeas* 20: "[Modalists] would have the entire revelation of both Testaments yield to . . . three passages, whereas the only proper course is to understand the few statements in light of the many" (*ANF* 3:615); Augustine, *The Trinity* 1.14; *On Christian Teaching* 2.6–7.

is being said (at least according to the author of Revelation): Jesus belongs to the identity of God, he is not an angel, and so on. But faith's movement toward understanding requires us to see more than the bare facts. We must press on to perceive their inner unity because "the kinds of questions raised by the pressure of the biblical text cannot be settled from within the noetic resources of the text's historical surroundings."[49] Scripture's pressure prods us to ask not only *what* is being said but *how* these things can be said coherently.

Hence, we must ask *how* it is theologically possible—not simply histori- cally, religiously, or culturally possible—that a crucified man can be worshiped legitimately. Do the various affirmations of the Apocalypse, not to mention the broader complex of moves made across the canon concerning God and Jesus Christ, resolve into an ultimate coherence? Perceiving and conceiving this ultimate coherence is the work of theology, understood minimally as reflection on and exposition of the implicit presuppositions of the prophetic and apostolic discourse. This coherence and these presuppositions belong to the larger theological vision of which these particular texts are a part.

In this sense, theology is the grammar of divine teaching. To ask the ques- tion "how" is to seek the grammatical structure that enables us to perceive the coherence of Scripture's various and particular ways of speaking about God in Christ. In this case, where a Jewish man is rendered worship that belongs to God alone, the doctrines of the Trinity and Christ's two natures provide the necessary grammar. Exegesis thus enjoys an epistemological primacy over theology because there can be no abstract or immediate knowledge of doctrine that is not drawn from careful attention to the texture and shape of biblical discourse.[50]

Once recognized, the grammatical structure that displays the coherence of Scripture's particular discourses helps us in turn to understand divine teach- ing more intelligibly. That is, theology helps us read Scripture. The grammar with which Scripture speaks—in our case, of its teaching about Christ and the Trinity—grants hermeneutical purchase on both individual texts and their larger canonical horizon. Doctrine functions this way because it is formulated a posteriori, on the basis of careful exegesis, rather than a priori, imposed on the text from elsewhere. Rowe concludes by reflecting on the relationship between theology and exegesis:

> To interpret the Bible in light of the doctrine of the Trinity does not, therefore, distort its basic content but penetrates to its core with respect to the reality of the divine identity, the living God outside of the text known truly and fully in

49. Rowe, "For Future Generations," 199.
50. Rowe, "For Future Generations," 200.

Jesus Christ. . . . Thus, to read the Bible in light of later trinitarian dogma is to read the Bible in light of the reality of God himself as he has pressured us through his Word, that is, his speaking, to speak about him.[51]

Exegesis leads to doctrine, and doctrine returns to exegesis after absorbing the text's pressures. Such theology-informed exegesis seeks deeper resonances that also serve as critical tests for whether the doctrinal understanding achieved is indeed the best frame of reference. On this reckoning, theology is the grammar of Scripture. Hence, we may formulate our second rule: *To understand the theological grammar and syntax of Scripture, read Scripture in such a way that you learn how its various discourses both form and presuppose a larger theological vision.*

The argument of this book is in broad agreement with Rowe's account of "pressure" as we have explained it. Exegesis attends to God's pedagogical presence in his Word. The pedagogical pressure of this Word lifts our attention to the glory of Christ and the Trinity, which is the ultimate frame of reference for understanding why the biblical texts operate the way they do with regard to any subject. Once perceived, our understanding of God helps us in turn to understand the speech of God: Holy Scripture. Theology and exegesis therefore stand in a mutually informative, albeit asymmetrical, relationship. Exegesis funds doctrinal understanding, which returns to Scripture with a greater subjective apprehension of its scope, unity, thematic coherence, and interrelations. However, doctrinal understanding does not reform Scripture, improve on it, or cast it aside to enjoy unmediated access to its subject matter (*res*). Theology instead returns to Scripture to be nourished and corrected, because faith's understanding also "lives by every word that comes from the mouth of the LORD" (Deut. 8:3). The church therefore rereads Scripture because it has no other way of being.

## Conclusion

The context of divine teaching is how the church has always understood revelation, Scripture, and the receptive interpretive culture that the Spirit's presence generates as the church listens to God's Word. Consider the concluding words of the Council of Chalcedon's *definitio* concerning the hypostatic union: "He is not split or divided into two Persons, but he is one and the same only begotten Son, God the Word, the Lord Jesus Christ, as formerly the prophets and later Jesus Christ himself have taught [ἐξεπαίδευσεν, *exepaideusen*] us

51. Rowe, "Biblical Pressure and Trinitarian Hermeneutics," 311–12.

about him and as has been handed down [παραδέδωκε, *paradedōke*] to us by the creed of the Fathers."[52] With Luther, we must say that "Christ is above all teachers and councils,"[53] while recognizing that Christ also employs other teachers in the economy of his teaching. This economy, and no other, locates our own acts of reading and response. In reading Scripture we respond not to an inert textual artifact of religious culture but to the Lord Jesus Christ in his sacred writings. Biblical reasoning is that form of attention to Holy Scripture that is taught by God, teaches about God, and leads to God. Undertaken in faith, with a sense of gratitude and awe before God's presence, our theological exegesis should gravitate toward the eschatological vision of Christ's glory that he possesses with the Father. We carry out this work by paying exacting attention to divine teaching. Biblical reasoning submits to Scripture's pressures in order to grasp the grammar of the whole canon and thereby seek the only One who can turn our faith into sight.

We may conclude by returning to where we began to look at the intended effect of reading the Apocalypse, and by extension all of Holy Scripture. Those who read and hear the Apocalypse are "blessed" (Rev. 1:3), as are those who keep it and worship God, whose robes are washed in the blood of the Lamb, and who neither take away from nor add to the prophecy; these will enter the city and partake of the tree of life (Rev. 22:6–19; cf. 7:14). None of this leaves room for disinterested readers of Scripture. Indeed, such clues from the prologue and epilogue suggest that the text has a liturgical structure, incorporating the reader(s) into the prophecy, as well as the worship given to the triune God.[54] John's opening doxology includes himself with the churches to whom the letters are sent, speaking of God who "loves us" and "has freed us," and "made us a kingdom" (Rev. 1:5–6). He also announces the churches' hope that the Lord "is coming with the clouds" (1:7). Both the doxology and expectation elicit the congregational response, "Amen" (1:6, 7). Finally, the Lord affirms all of this as one who is in their midst: "I am the Alpha and the Omega . . . who is and who was and who is to come, the Almighty" (1:8).

The Apocalypse's epilogue reiterates many of these same features: blessings and warnings to the readers, confirmations of the Lord's presence and rule, invitations to confession and adoration, and congregational response. "He who testifies to these things says, 'Surely I am coming soon.' Amen. Come, Lord Jesus!" (Rev. 22:20). The implied reader is therefore also an implied

---

52. Denzinger §302.

53. Luther, *On the Councils and the Churches* (1539), in *Luther's Works*, 41:136.

54. For what follows, see W. G. Campbell, "Apocalypse johannique et adoratuer implicite," who also makes several pertinent observations on the cultic atmosphere of Rev. 4–5 and its inclusion of the implied reader/worshiper.

worshiper, one who participates in the reconciliation that the risen and present Jesus announces in the words of his appointed witness. Upon reading and hearing the "revelation of Jesus Christ" announced with his "loud voice" through what John has written, we too are being led to the vision of God's face (22:4). We are being summoned to join the heavenly liturgy. If we are aware of what is happening, then our response should match John's: "I fell at his feet as though dead." Yet we must also remember that Jesus lays his hands on us too and says, "Fear not" (Rev. 1:17; Matt. 17:7).

# PART TWO

# CHRISTOLOGICAL and TRINITARIAN RULES for EXEGESIS

# 4

# Worthy Are You

## Understanding Scripture as Honoring God

**Principle 4:** God, who is the creator of all things *ex nihilo*, is holy, infinite, and unchangeable. Since God is qualitatively distinct from all things, he therefore differs from creatures differently than creatures differ from one another.

**Rule 3:** Biblical discourse about God should be understood in a way appropriate to its object, so read Scripture's depictions of God in a manner that fits the canonical portrait of God's holy name and his creation of all things out of nothing.

Previous chapters have explored biblical reasoning's preliminary considerations: its implied anthropology and telos, its economic setting and the nature of its textual source, as well as the kinds of rational acts it involves. We have seen that biblical reasoning's goal is to enable us to "gaze upon the beauty of the Lord" (Ps. 27:4). We are now well positioned to explore the kinds of exegesis that biblical reasoning enables and requires. The present chapter expounds our fourth principle and third rule together because they are coordinated with one another. Our principle concerns the qualitative distinction between God the creator and all else, arising from Scripture's witness to God's fullness and how this is reflected in his dignity as creator. The rule that follows from this concerns what is "fitting for God" (θεοπρέπης, *theoprepēs*) or what is "worthy of God" (*digno Dei*). With this rule the doctrine of God itself becomes an exegetical tool. In light of what Scripture says about God and creation—that God is eternal, holy, and qualitatively distinct from all things, which he created "out of nothing"—then how do we understand passages of Scripture that suggest, for instance, that God changes his mind or that God has a body? Such passages present a much more humanlike God than we might expect from what Scripture says elsewhere. So how do we reconcile these and adjudicate the apparent discrepancies between them? This rule for what is "God-befitting" guides our reading of Scripture by giving us a standard for the coherence of its varied and apparently conflicting portrayals of God.

As a guide for reading religious texts, the rule concerning what is "worthy" of God has its remote origins in the Greek philosopher Xenophanes, who criticized the licentious depiction of the gods in foundational texts for Greek culture and education, such as Homer's *Iliad*.[1] These gods are scandalously humanlike. They steal from one another, lie, fornicate, and generally behave like troublesome humans writ large. For Xenophanes, these depictions were unbecoming of true divinity and therefore unworthy of imitation. His solution was to demythologize these passages in a way "befitting" true divinity and thus serviceable to the formation of virtuous Greek citizens. Hence, his idea of God's true being became a hermeneutical tool used to interpret the problematic texts in question: in light of the true God's freedom from passions and depravity, texts suggesting otherwise had to be read in a way "befitting" God's divine nature and thus stripped of their mythological dross.

For their own, different theological and pedagogical reasons, early Christian theologians found a similar need to employ the contemplative understanding of God as a guide to the proper interpretation of Scripture. Clement of Alexandria speaks to the importance of this rule when he notes people's tendency to make God or gods in their own image, not only physically but also morally: "For instance, the barbarians make them brutal and savage, the Greeks milder, but subject to passion."[2] In the terms of Scripture, the problem is that we children of Adam project ourselves when thinking and speaking about God: we paint a picture on the stars of what we most desire or value and dub it "god."[3] As we do so, we construct a god who vouches for our own

1. See Jaeger, *The Theology of the Greek Philosophers*; Sheridan, *Language for God in Patristic Tradition*.

2. Clement of Alexandria, *Stromateis* 7.4.22, in *Miscellanies Book VII* (trans. Hort and Mayor). Clement is here drawing from Xenophanes explicitly.

3. The problem is thus associated with Ludwig Feuerbach's accusation that Christian theology is essentially anthropology in disguise, a form of "projection." For discussion, see Vanhoozer, *Remythologizing Theology*, 17–23.

perverse agendas and construals of the good life. Consequently, we end up with distorted portraits of what is worthy of God (what is "godly") and the life that reflects this (the godly life). Inevitably, how we live reflects who we believe God to be (or who we believe to be "God"), just as our vision of God affects our vision of what is the godly life. But prone as we are to projection, how do we acquire an objective understanding of God and therefore of what is worthy of God?

Objectivity is not easily won and quickly slips from our grasp. We must seek again and again to shut off our projectors so that the light of God's true revelation of himself can shine into our darkened minds and hearts. At minimum this requires looking away from ourselves and looking to Christ, the Image to which we must be conformed, our Teacher whom we must hear and obey, our Guide to godliness (cf. 2 Cor. 4:4; Col. 1:15; 2 Pet. 1:4). In his own way, this is what Clement does. Since Christ is "without sin, without blame, without passion of soul, God immaculate in form of man, accomplishing His Father's will," then we must try "to resemble Him in spirit as far as we are able."[4] Hence, through Christ "we become like God through a likeness of virtue."[5] Against the backdrop of what and who God is by nature, we may discern what is becoming of us by grace, all of which is seen in Christ, the righteous God and righteous man in one. Because God is holy and without passion, so too is Christ, and so too should we be as we imitate God in Christ.

Traditionally, appeal to the "God-fittingness" rule adjudicates scriptural language about God as metaphorical in some instances or anthropomorphic or allegorical in others, all in service of receiving Scripture's overall portrait of God's divine nature for the sake of our contemplation and imitation (2 Pet. 1:3–11; Lev. 19:2). Our imitation of God through virtue and the exemplar of this imitation, God's divine nature, illuminate one another so that godly interpretation of Scripture "honors" God and promotes Christian virtue in the same breath.[6] Godliness is therefore key to becoming a better reader of Scripture's sacred mysteries, because what befits us by grace reflects what befits God by nature, and vice versa.[7] So as we strive to imitate Christ, we will grow as readers of Scripture because we will grow in our honoring of God's divine nature, which is what our rule ultimately concerns.

4. Clement of Alexandria, *Christ the Educator* 1.2.4 (FC 23:5).
5. Clement of Alexandria, *Christ the Educator* 1.12.99 (FC 23:88).
6. Clement of Alexandria, *Stromateis* 7.1.3–4.
7. The notion of θεοπρέπεια carries the sense not only of what is God-befitting but also of *pietas* or *religio*; cf. Wollebius, *Compendium theologiae Christianae* 2.4. We return to this below when discussing the God-fittingness rule.

The biblical basis for this rule has often been implicit at best, leaving the idea of what is "worthy of God" open to the criticism that it owes more to extrabiblical philosophical concerns than to Scripture's narrative of God reconciling the world to himself in Christ. Moreover, the rule represents an intuition out of step with most biblical scholarship because of its strong claims about God's perfect life. Therefore, our first priority in this chapter will be to demonstrate this rule's consonance with Scripture. In this chapter we will articulate a version of this rule by coordinating it with Christian teaching about creation.

First, we look at how Scripture pressures us toward the theological insight of the Creator's qualitative distinction from all things, articulated especially in the foundational doctrine of creation "out of nothing" (*ex nihilo*). We will focus on this doctrine because it is itself a mirror of what Scripture says about God's majesty, freedom, and transcendence. Then we will turn to consider how this doctrine bears upon the task of exegesis. This will require a careful evaluation of biblical language that appears to clash with God's qualitative distinction from creation and his intrinsic fullness and blessedness. In a concluding case study, we will apply our rule to the OT's widespread language of God "relenting" or "regretting," looking at how biblical reasoning focuses our attention by broadening it. In the end, we will see that this rule sharpens the eyes of faith to perceive the glory of Christ.

## The Pressures of the Heavenly Liturgy: God and Creation in Revelation 4

In this section we will see how Scripture guides us to recognize God's qualitative distinction from creation, especially as this has been articulated in the doctrine of creation *ex nihilo*. Creation out of nothing arises indirectly from Scripture, specifically as it reflects what Scripture pressures us to affirm about God alongside what it has to say about creation itself. For especially illuminating teaching on God and creation we may return to the Apocalypse, a book in which creation "is not simply one motif alongside others, but an absolutely fundamental motif."[8] Specifically, the heavenly liturgy to the Creator in John's vision of the throne room (Rev. 4:1–11) pressures us to frame God's worthiness and dignity in relation to creation *ex nihilo*. From there we will develop the implicit "grammar" behind these various pressures, developing our principle.

After hearing the letters to the seven churches, John is ushered into the heavenly throne room, where he witnesses concentric circles of theophany

8. Hahn, "Die Schöpfungsthematik in der Johannesoffenbarung," 611.

and praise. Together these circles portray God's glory as the creator and his creatures' response in worship. Before we can understand what these circles represent, however, we are struck by the majesty of what John beholds. John's language echoes his own sense of awe: rather than speaking directly of who sits upon the throne, he instead speaks thirteen times simply of "the throne" (Rev. 3:21; 4:2, 4–6; 9–10). The vision's eclectic coterie of worshipers is described as either "around" or "before" or "in the midst of" the throne, but in any case they are oriented to it and so are we. "Flashes of lightning, and rumblings and peals of thunder" come "from the throne," reminiscent of the theophany at Sinai (Rev. 4:5; Exod. 19:16). The same God who showed himself to Moses without being seen is here seen by John in a similarly indirect way. John will only speak obliquely about the "one seated on the throne" (Rev. 4:2). Throughout the opening verses of Revelation 4, John uses "like" (ὅμοιος, *homoios*) to approximate what he sees with his language and visual metaphors: "He who sat there appeared like jasper and carnelian, and round the throne was a halo that looked like an emerald" (4:3 AT); the sea was "like crystal" (4:6) and the four living creatures "like" various animals (4:7). Things are like this and like that; no words are adequate for what John sees. The whole vision is apophatic, in contrast to the more ornate theophanies of his literary sources (Ezek. 1; Dan. 7; Isa. 6). This throne vision is an austere reflection "on the Eternal Light through the mirror of the worshipping host of heaven."[9] Even apart from what John sees, the *way* he sees leaves us with a sense of God's sheer transcendence and sublimity.

Just what this transcendence and sublimity mean is suggested as we discover *what* John sees. At the heart of these concentric circles is the "halo [ἶρις, *iris*] that looked like an emerald" around the One seated on the throne (Rev. 4:3 AT).[10] This glorious nimbus surrounds God's throne, rippling outward and eliciting praise from the living creatures and the twenty-four elders (4:6–11).[11] In each of their hymns we find a response to God's glory displayed in John's rich metaphors. Together these hymns frame the notion of God's worthiness around God's unique nature and his creative activity. Briefly considering three main elements of these hymns will suffice to show their pressures before considering their implicit grammar in the following section.

---

9. Caird, *The Revelation of Saint John*, 63; see, further, Bauckham, *The Theology of the Book of Revelation*, 40–47; Leithart, *Revelation 1–11*, 220–25.
10. For ἶρις as "halo" rather than "rainbow," see Swete, *The Apocalypse of St. John*, 67; Prigent, *Commentary on the Apocalypse of St. John*, 226.
11. On the identities of the "living creatures" and the "elders," see Aune, *Revelation 1–5*, 287–92, 297–301; Leithart, *Revelation 1–11*, 229–45.

## *"Holy, Holy, Holy Is the Lord God Almighty"*

The first hymn belongs to the creatures in the second circle around the luminous cloud, immediately facing the One seated on the throne. These creatures, likely the cherubim, praise God in a way that recalls Isaiah's seraphim: "Holy, holy, holy is the Lord God Almighty, who was and is and is to come!" (Rev. 4:8; Isa. 6:3). This series of three triads is an abridged theology of God's identity and being that grounds the subsequent response of the twenty-four elders. The two key elements are the threefold declaration of God's holiness and the gloss on the divine name.

First, the revelation of God's holiness entails many things, but here it characterizes God's transcendence and sublimity. However difficult it may be to define, holiness communicates at minimum the idea of God's distinctiveness, purity, and devotion to his own glory. Thus holiness grounds the self-consistency of God in all his actions, even his devotion to his covenant people. According to Johann Albrecht Bengel, holiness summarizes God's nature: "Holiness is glory concealed, glory is holiness revealed."[12] God's holiness is God himself and is therefore unlike any other (Exod. 15:11; 1 Sam. 2:2; Isa. 40:25).

The cherubim's threefold praise of God's holiness follows Isaiah and emphasizes this holiness than which none greater can be conceived. In Hebrew, the twofold repetition of a word already expresses unparalleled totality, like the "pit pits" into which some kings of Sodom and Gomorrah fell and, we may surmise, were never seen again (Gen. 14:10). Therefore, a threefold repetition pushes our understanding to the breaking point and arrests it there: "holy, holy" would differ from all other holinesses, but "holy, holy, holy" differs differently.

Isaiah's inaugural vision of God's glory provides important context to John's vision. Isaiah sees winged seraphim—literally "burning ones"—standing above the Lord sitting on the throne, similar to how some Egyptian art featured winged cobras protecting Pharaoh's throne. However, the differences are unsettling. The winged cobras would protect Pharaoh with their wings, whereas the seraphim use their wings to protect *themselves* from God (Isa. 6:2). God needs no protection, but in his presence all creatures do—even the terrifying seraphim, who stood as a reminder of the danger unclean lips pose to God's people (Num. 21:4–9; Isa. 6:5; 10:17).[13] This same Holy One

---

12. Bengel, *Erklärte Offenbarung Johannes oder vielmehr Jesu Christi*, 232; cf. Exod. 29:43; Lev. 10:3; Isa. 6:3.

13. Leithart, *Revelation 1–11*, 242–45; cf. Roberts, "Isaiah in Old Testament Theology," 131–32, on the Egyptian art in question.

will execute his just wrath as John's prophecy declares (Rev. 16:1–7). Like Isaiah, John beholds God's terrifying majesty and purity, on account of which God not only differs from even the most terrifying creatures but also *differs differently*—that is, uniquely, not in the way that creatures mutually differ from one another.

The character of God's transcendence implied in his holiness is, however, not mere remoteness. It may affirm itself in the utmost intimacy with his chosen people: "For thus says the One who is high and lifted up, who inhabits eternity, whose name is Holy: 'I dwell in the high and holy place, and also with him who is of a contrite and lowly spirit, to revive the spirit of the lowly, and to revive the heart of the contrite'" (Isa. 57:15; Ps. 99). God's presence to his people as the "Holy One of Israel," a designation characteristic of Isaiah, involves communication and communion. God elects and separates a people for himself, declaring that they will be holy, patterned after his holiness (Lev. 11:44–45; 19:2; 20:26; 21:8). When Israel fails to be holy and profanes God's holy name, God acts to vindicate himself (Ezek. 36:20–32; Amos 2:7). Hence, the One who is lofty and transcendent is also near, drawing to himself "all nations" (Rev. 15:4). For all the distinctiveness, purity, and devotion to his own glory that God's holiness implies, none of it is threatened by but rather expressed in the most intimate nearness and communion with his people. God's sublime transcendence thus grounds a startlingly humble immanence. This too is proof of how God differs differently.

### *"Who Was, and Is, and Is to Come"*

Second, we must now consider how John characterizes God's eternality and immutability. In keeping with Jewish custom of the time, John does not use the Tetragrammaton (YHWH) itself. However, he does paraphrase it with a triadic temporal formula here found on the lips of the cherubim: "who was and is and is to come" (Rev. 4:8). The formula's background lies in ancient Jewish theology's dialogue with Greek philosophical claims about Being.[14] Hence, the appropriation of this philosophical terminology says something about God's being, though precisely what is not as clear. What is clear is how John disfigures the Greek, which is suggestive on account of Scripture's exactness.[15] The rules of our mundane grammar, expressing as they do the temporal realm

---

14. McDonough, *YHWH at Patmos*.

15. As many interpreters have argued, the grammatical issues in the text are intended in some way to honor God's absoluteness or immutability. See, inter alia, Marckius, *In Apocalypsin Johannis Commentarium*, 13; Charles, *A Critical and Exegetical Commentary on the Revelation of St. John*, 1:10; Aune, *Revelation 1–5*, 30–32.

of our experience, naturally bend under the staggering weight and surplus significance of God's glorious Name. This is because words tremble when called upon to express God's perfect life. Trembling as they do, what do these words communicate? To grasp the rich meaning of this philosophical paraphrase, we may break down its individual elements.[16]

*Who was.* In the first case, we have here some sort of affirmation of God's absoluteness, constancy, and immutability. The verbs for "him who is" and "who is to come" both employ participles, but in Greek there is no participle for the past tense of "to be" (εἰμί, *eimi*). Without a past participle for "to be," the closest past participle would have been for "to come into being" (γίνομαι, *ginomai*), which would suggest that "having come into being" (ὁ γεγονώς, *ho gegonōs*) was true of God.[17] But since this would imply change and "becoming" in God's life, John bends the Greek language to avoid it. The pithy statement that God is he "who was" (ὁ ἦν, *ho ēn*)—combining an article with a finite verb in the imperfect, a past tense—stresses God's distinction from the realm of things that acquire and can lose their being, which is the realm of creatures (cf. John 1:1–3; Pss. 90:3–6, 9–10; 102:26–27). Creatures come and go, but in God there is no shadow of turning (James 1:17). However, the real force of "who was" derives from its pairing with the following element, "who is" (the two constitute a formula in Rev. 11:17; 16:5).

*Who is.* Just as God is free from becoming, so also God is free from the constraints of time.[18] The description of God as "he who is" (ὁ ὤν, *ho ōn*) draws upon the Septuagint translation of Exodus 3:14. There God glosses his personal, proper name with the phrase "the One who Is," using the present participle (ὁ ὤν, *ho ōn*; cf. Jer. 1:6; 14:13; 39:16–17 LXX).[19] Some implications of this gloss on the divine name are implicit in the first commandment, that Israel should have no gods before God (Exod. 20:3). Namely, that God is "the One who Is" underscores God's difference from idols: unlike false gods, God is real and does not depend on the ministrations of his worshipers for his being or his well-being (Ps. 50:7–15; Isa. 46:1–4; Acts 17:24–25). There are no necessary or sufficient conditions for God's life; he simply *is.* Undergirding these implications, "the One who Is" signifies God's immeasurability in

---

16. For what follows, see McDonough, *YHWH at Patmos*, 195–217; Aune, *Revelation 1–5*, 30–32; Koester, *Revelation*, 210–20.

17. This is how Plato describes the cosmos: "The universe was [γεγονώς] and is and always will be" (*Timaeus* 38c; cf. the contrast with the "eternal" in 37e–38a). Other examples can be found in McDonough, *YHWH at Patmos*, 211; Aune, *Revelation 1–5*, 31–32.

18. Aquinas logically derives God's eternality from his immutability (*STh* I.10.1; cf. Aristotle, *Physics* 4.11). Paul van Imschoot connects these two threads in the OT in his *Theology of the Old Testament*, 1:54–56.

19. McDonough, *YHWH at Patmos*, 205–11; Aune, *Revelation 1–5*, 30–31.

relation to time and its measurements of past and future, before and after.[20] As the psalmist says, "From eternity to eternity you are God" (Ps. 90:2 AT; cf. 93:2; 102:25–27).[21] Jesus can therefore say, "Before Abraham was, I am," because God's life cannot be circumscribed by time's boundaries (John 8:58; Heb. 13:8). The cherubim thus offer their praise to the God who lives "forever and ever" (Rev. 4:9–10; 10:6; 15:7). When "who was" is paired with "who is," it functions like a boundary statement, a horizon that draws our attention beyond itself. God "was" in the sense that God exists "before" creation, though "before" and "after" are words that measure temporal things, rendering them inadequate to express the truth about God.

The unchangeableness and eternality of God are repeated in the Apocalypse with the divine self-declaration, "I am the Alpha and the Omega" (Rev. 1:8), which is also glossed as "the first and the last" (1:17; 22:13) as well as "the beginning and the end" (21:6; 22:13). Against the background of Isaiah's polemic against Babylonian idols and false gods, John's language accentuates God's unmatched sovereignty and singularity: "I am God, and there is no other" (Isa. 45:22; cf. 46:9; 47:8–10; 48:12–13; Deut. 32:39).[22] In Isaiah 40, we read that God has no counselor or teacher, he measures all and is measured by none, he transcends creation and gains nothing from it, he effortlessly reduces the mightiest rulers to nothing, and so he renews the strength of the weary because he never tires. Isaiah further develops this portrait with the formula that John adopts: "I am the first and I am the last; besides me there is no god'" (Isa. 44:6; 48:12). In other words, God alone is God. The truth is important enough in John's Apocalypse that God pronounces these phrases himself seven times, the number of completeness (Gen. 2:2). Cumulatively this suggests that God's uniqueness runs all the way down. There are no rivals to God's throne. God oversees the whole of history because he is the "whole of God," which is to say, there are no other gods alongside God. His divinity is not a category and is thus not measured by other "divinities." God does not belong to a genus. "The Lord is one" and therefore not one of a kind (Deut. 6:4).[23]

*Who is to come.* Despite the emphasis on God's transcendent majesty thus far, the final element of John's paraphrase reaffirms God's intimate involvement

---

20. Swete, *The Apocalypse of St. John*, 5.

21. For an attentive reading of "eternity to eternity" as God's complete otherworldliness and distinction from time and space, rather than a mere endless temporal duration, see Köckert, "Zeit und Ewigkeit in Psalm 90."

22. Koester, *Revelation*, 220.

23. To capture these truths, theologians speak of God's infinitude and simplicity (e.g., Bavinck, *Reformed Dogmatics*, 2:159–77; Maximus, *Two Hundred Chapters on Theology* 1.1–8).

with his creatures in a manner that complements God's loftiness. God "is to come" (ὁ ἐρχόμενος, *ho erchomenos*), which stresses the future advent of Christ (cf. Joel 2:1; Matt. 11:3; Heb. 10:37). Crucially, this element breaks with philosophical formulas for divinity in antiquity. For example, Zeus and Athena are both depicted as ones who "will be" (ἔσσεται/ἐσσόμενον, *essetai/ essomenon*).[24] Without denying that God "is" in the future just as God "is" in the past, the eschatological language of "is to come" focuses our attention on the fact that the thrice-holy, transcendent, eternal God is also near and involved in history and time. This language again manifests the deep compatibility of God's transcendence with God's immanence. In this case, it is a matter of God's eternality and immutability remaining true alongside God's "becoming" man in the "fullness of time" (John 1:14; Gal. 4:4). Indeed, because God is the one who will come, he will consummate his creative purposes in the final showdown with "that ancient serpent, who is called the devil and Satan" (Rev. 12:9). God's "coming" therefore signals in the Apocalypse the same future it does in the Prophets: his return in judgment and mercy and consequent vindication of the saints who persevere (Rev. 11:17–18; 16:5–7; cf. Exod. 34:6–7). God's commitment to his covenant people in time and space is grounded in his transcendence of creation and covenant alike. We may have confidence in the Lord's sovereignty and vindication of his people precisely because God is not subject to the vicissitudes of time.

### *"Worthy Are You . . ."*

Immediately after the living creatures render their confession, the elders take their turn and our narrator moves to the "outer" circle. John tells us that "whenever the living creatures give glory and honor and thanks to him who is seated on the throne," the twenty-four elders cast their golden crowns around the glassy sea and respond: "Worthy are you, our Lord and God, to receive glory and honor and power, for you created all things, and by your will they existed and were created" (Rev. 4:9, 11). Whereas the cherubim confess that God is holy (ἅγιος, *hagios*), the elders confess that God is worthy (ἄξιος, *axios*) because the latter is a response to the former, an antiphony.[25] Similar responses grounded in God's majesty are scattered throughout the Psalms: "Sing to the Lord a new song; sing to the Lord, all the earth! . . . For great is the Lord, and greatly to be praised; he is to be feared above all gods" (Ps. 96:1, 4; cf. Pss. 33; 113; 145). Because this is a response, we must understand that God "receives" glory and honor from the living creatures and

---

24. Aune, *Revelation 1–5*, 31.
25. Jörns, *Das hymnische Evangelium*, 161.

elders in the sense that they acknowledge his holiness (Ps. 29:1–2). God does not acquire anything, which becomes even plainer when the elders ground God's "worthiness" to receive praise in his creation of "all things." What is the significance of this?

"Worthy" carries the sense of "fitting," "proper," or "appropriate," and it is this aspect that is most relevant to our rule.[26] To say something is "worthy" expresses a fit between one thing and another. Fittingness thus describes the relationships that obtain between parts and the larger wholes to which they belong. Pieces of a puzzle "fit" if they are pieces of *this* puzzle; melodies "fit" songs if they share their time signatures, keys, and structures; actions "fit" circumstances when the two belong together and display a sense of decorum. Such a sense is evident in Scripture: bearing fruit fits with repentance (Matt. 3:8; Luke 3:8; Acts 26:20); a just punishment fits the crime (Acts 23:29; 26:31); Christ's ministry is "fitting" (ἔπρεπεν, *eprepen*) on account of both God's plan and our needs (Heb. 2:10; 7:26); John the Baptist is "not fit" (οὐκ . . . ἱκανός, *ouk . . . hikanos*), or "unworthy" (οὐκ . . . ἄξιος, *ouk . . . axios*), to untie Jesus's sandals because Jesus outranks him (Matt. 3:11; John 1:27, 30; 3:31).[27] Judgments about what is fitting therefore presuppose a larger vision of the whole in which the parts are situated.

In our text, the larger vision of God's eternal holiness alongside his creation of all things by his will makes it "fitting" to praise God's honor, glory, and power. Whatever the immediate historical background of the language may be, "worthiness" contrasts God's holiness with any and all would-be usurpers, whether political or demonic.[28] To confess God as "worthy" to be glorified and honored is therefore to observe the first commandment (Exod. 20:1–3; Deut. 5:6–7). Anyone or anything else is unworthy of such praise: "worthy" implies *solus Deus*, which in turn implies *solus Christus* (Rev. 5:12). Here this truth animates the confession that God created "all things," and that their existence is owed only to God's "will" (Rev. 4:11). In Second Temple Jewish literature, the fact that God created all things is one of the chief characteristics that distinguishes him from all other beings, including the so-called gods of the gentiles.[29] Explaining this, Scripture yet again takes us into philosophical territory: various NT authors appropriate Greco-Roman "prepositional

---

26. See Tiedtke, "ἄξιος," in *NIDNTT* 3:348–49. Commentators routinely offer little to no theological reflection on this language.

27. Perhaps like Moses, John feels he should remove his own sandals (Exod. 3:5).

28. Jörns argues convincingly that the "worthy . . . to receive" formula is original to John (*Das hymnische Evangelium*, 56–73). Readings of the "worthy" language as counterimperial and so forth are implications but not the center of the text's emphasis on God's singularity.

29. Bauckham, *Jesus and the God of Israel*, 7–11, 26–30, 176–79.

metaphysics"—formulas such as "from him and through him and to him"—to accent the comprehensive scope of God's creative activity, leaving nothing outside his reach (John 1:3; Rom. 11:36; 1 Cor. 8:6; Col. 1:15–20; Heb. 1:2–3).[30] Especially in light of God's holiness and eternality, the counterpart to these formulas is God's creation of τὰ πάντα (*ta panta*), "all things" (John 1:3; Acts 17:24–25; Rom. 11:36; Eph. 3:9; Col. 1:16; Rev. 4:11; 21:5). The cumulative weight of these affirmations is to stress the universal significance of "all": all means all, not some. Everything besides God is a creature. Since everything other than God has been created, only God deserves the acknowledgment and praise the elders give to the creator.

## The Grammar of the Heavenly Liturgy: Divine Transcendence and Creation *Ex Nihilo*

In our overview of these hymns in Revelation 4, we find a series of affirmations that cumulatively pressure us toward recognizing a deeper coherence or underlying grammar. We may summarize some of our findings in the following points.

First, God is uniquely transcendent. He differs from all other things morally and metaphysically, but he differs "differently," not in the way that creatures mutually differ from one another. Second, God's transcendence and immanence are complementary. God's transcendence from and nearness to creatures is grounded in his perfect life. God is eminently holy and therefore unchanging and eternal, set apart in himself from all that is not God; yet for this very reason he acts on the stage of history to make a people holy unto himself. Third, God alone is truly God; God is the whole of "divinity." Whatever it means for God to be divine both overlaps with and differs from how the philosophers normally think of divinity (Acts 17:22–34). While John adopts certain philosophical formulas for speaking about "the divine," he also modifies these in keeping with Scripture's overarching polemic against false idols, "so-called gods" (1 Cor. 8:5). Particularly, as we saw with the "is coming" language, Christology compels this recognition. Fourth, God alone is worthy to be acknowledged as God because all other things are creatures. In response to the vision of God's eternal holiness and in light of creation, the elders confess that God is worthy to be praised *as God*. Because God is God—the eternal, holy, almighty creator—acknowledgments of genuine divinity "fit" God alone.

---

30. See Sterling, "Prepositional Metaphysics in Jewish Wisdom Speculation and Early Christianity"; Cox, *By the Same Word*, 43–51, 141–275; O. McFarland, "Divine Causation and Prepositional Metaphysics."

With these four elements in view, we may now ask how they hang together on a deeper level. These various affirmations cohere in what Kathryn Tanner calls a "non-contrastive" account of God's transcendence, in which God's distinction from creation is not a distinction between two things within the world.[31] Contrastive accounts of transcendence are the currency of mythological portraits of divinity found in pagan philosophy, and they establish a zero-sum game: the more God, the less creatures, as if God's presence and activity displace the presence and activity of creatures. In this picture, God is the highest part of the God-world whole, but God is still just a part of something larger than himself. This account can operate even where God is considered remote from creation, because the condition of "remoteness" is precisely *not*-nearness. A non-contrastive account of transcendence, on the other hand, refuses these false dichotomies because it understands God as uniquely distinct from creation, not belonging to an order or whole larger than himself. Hence, God can be intimately near to creation and involved in it without in any way compromising himself or his creatures. God's transcendence, the way God differs differently, means that God is beyond mere identification with or opposition to creation. This leads us to our fourth principle: *God, who is the creator of all things* ex nihilo, *is holy, infinite, and unchangeable. Since God is qualitatively distinct from all things, he therefore differs from creatures differently than creatures differ from one another.*

One of the most telling affirmations of God's non-contrastive transcendence is the account of creation we find implicit in the worship of the twenty-four elders. The elders profile God's "Godness" against the background of God's creation of "all things," the weight of which makes it fitting to confess God as God. This makes sense when we understand the character of creation, which distinguishes firmly between God and all else. Here we must insist that "all" in "all things" does not secretly mean "some." If *all* else other than God is created, then only God is uncreated. Consequently, the biblical portrait of God's "creation of all things" (*creatio omnium*), alongside its portrait of God's sovereignty and majesty, leads naturally to the conclusion that God creates "out of nothing" (*creatio ex nihilo*).[32] According to the dominant wisdom of antiquity, the cosmos came from something; it was just a question of what. Perhaps it was forged from the body of a slain god, generated from the chaotic interplay of matter and spirit, or leaked fortuitously from some divine fount. On the contrary, creation *ex nihilo* means there is no preexistent "stuff" with which God works when he creates, nor is creation somehow a chip off the old

---

31. K. Tanner, *God and Creation in Christian Theology*, 37–48.
32. Davison, *Participation in God*, 13–26.

divine block. The preposition "of" does not suggest that "nothing" is actually some kind of material or thing, a "nothingness," something with which God must contend in order to create. Creation is instead a pure, absolute origination: "the introduction of being entirely."[33] Therefore, creation *ex nihilo* denies that there is anything prior to, above, or coexistent with God, which is exactly what the hymns of the cherubim and twenty-four elders affirm.

The consequences of this insight were far-reaching for the trinitarian debates of the fourth century and they remain so today.[34] To see how this is so, we must grasp how creation *ex nihilo* refines our understanding of God and creatures alike. Creation *ex nihilo* distinguishes Christian theology from pagan philosophy and natural religion at a foundational level because its consequences reach farther than claims about world origins (cosmogony). Indeed, they are first and foremost claims about the nature of God. Already in our text we see how creation *ex nihilo* reflects rather than establishes God's eternal holiness and non-contrastive transcendence. As a reflection of more basic truths, the distinction between God and creation lies downstream from the reality of God himself. In other words, God is more basic than the distinction between God and creation. Since creation is *ex nihilo*, it neither adds to nor subtracts from God. This leads to what Robert Sokolowski calls the "Christian distinction" between God and the world: God is more basic than creation such that the latter might not have existed without any loss to God's goodness and majesty.[35]

The importance of this doctrine reaches right to the heart of the gospel because it helps us understand how God became man without ceasing to be God.[36] Creatures mutually condition one another because in many ways they are mutually dependent, existing as they do on the same metaphysical plane. For example, everyone is dependent genealogically on a father and mother, receiving biological traits we do not choose; we are dependent further on those who nurture us. This conditioning runs the other way as well: every parent feels the sorrows and joys of their children, to an extent. On the other hand, as the creator of all things *ex nihilo*, God conditions all things but is not conditioned by anything, because God is not subject to the laws of created

---

33. Aquinas, *STh* I.45.1.*resp.*
34. See, e.g., Anatolios, *Retrieving Nicaea*, 36–39, 80–81, 114–20.
35. Sokolowski, *The God of Faith and Reason*; Sokolowski, "Creation and Christian Understanding."
36. Indeed, the coherence of the incarnation rests upon a non-contrastive account of divine transcendence. See Tertullian, *Against Praxeas* 27 (*ANF* 3:623–24); Athanasius, *Letter* 59.2 (*NPNF²* 4:570); Cyril of Alexandria, *On Orthodoxy to Theodosius* 10–11, in *Three Christological Treatises*. The Nicene Creed concludes with the anathema against those who claim that the Son's divinity changes (Denzinger §126).

being. God is not merely one being among other beings, one truth next to other truths, or one good among other finite goods. Instead, God is the creator of all things *ex nihilo* and therefore is not limited by anything, whether preexistent stuff or some eternal law above his own being. God is the source of all stuff, limits, and laws.

Because of this, God's qualitative, non-contrastive transcendence means that God can be more immanent to creatures than creatures are to themselves without any loss of his divinity.[37] In a mythological or pagan notion of divinity, the gods are only elements within a larger whole, however exalted and lofty they might be within that whole. And if the gods are part of a larger whole, they are subject to its rules. If such a god "became" human it would either merely "appear" to be human or it would "transform" its divinity into humanity, because its being would be negotiated alongside other beings in the same finite order.

At the heart of the good news is the radically contrary claim that Jesus is both God and man in the fullest and truest senses of those terms. Jesus is neither human in mere appearance nor human instead of divine. Our salvation demands nothing less. Confessing Christ as the unchanging and eternal God in a "non-contrastive" sense enables us to affirm fully the mutable and temporal humanity of Jesus of Nazareth. Indeed, one of the chief "pressures" toward the doctrine of God's immutability in the early church was the NT's unequivocal emphasis on the concrete reality of Christ's humanity.

To conclude, the underlying grammar we may discern from our passage is the generative source of Christian teaching about creation: everything that exists is either God or a creature because God is God, the creator of all things *ex nihilo*, and thus worthy to be praised in a manner corresponding to this distinctiveness. It remains for us to formulate this as a rule for biblical reasoning and to put this rule to the test.

## The God-Fittingness Rule

Equipped with the proper understanding of God's qualitative distinction from creation, which is grounded in God's holy name and his creation of all things *ex nihilo*, we may now develop a corresponding rule for reading Scripture with the grain of its own grammar. We may formulate our third rule as follows: *Biblical discourse about God should be understood in a way appropriate to its object, so read Scripture's depictions of God in a manner that fits the canonical portrait of God's holy name and his creation of all things out of*

---

37. Cf. Augustine, *Confessions* 3.6.11.

*nothing*. Sacrificing elegance for clarity, we will call this the "God-fittingness" (θεοπρέπεια, *theoprepeia*) rule because it concerns how our understanding of God, and our reading of scriptural passages, may prove fitting or unfitting in light of who and what God is. In our reading of the heavenly liturgy we saw the twenty-four elders confess God as "worthy" of exclusive divine honors, which was their *response* to God's revelation of his eternally holy character and his creation of all things out of nothing. As we use the God-fittingness rule as a tool of biblical reasoning, we reenact the elders' response to divine teaching by confessing what is "worthy" or "fitting" of God. In this way, our own acts of reading Scripture prove to be worshipful responses to God's revelation of his holy name.

### The Rule's Christian Distinctiveness

Identifying the ways in which the God-fittingness rule is like and unlike its original counterpart in Greek philosophy will help us draw out its Christian distinctiveness. First, the likeness. As we see with Clement of Alexandria, the "God-fittingness" rule articulates an intimate kinship between growth in Christian virtue and truthful perception of God. This is not entirely unlike Xenophanes's concern with the morally deleterious example of the Greek pantheon. God-fittingness thus draws together faith's perception of God and faith's outworking in love.

Paul's description of the gospel as the "mystery of godliness" suggests this intrinsic unity of truthful perception with religious conduct and reverence (1 Tim. 3:15–16). On the one hand, piety or "godliness" (εὐσέβεια [*eusebeia*] or θεοσέβεια [*theosebeia*]) signifies appropriate reverence and fear of the Lord, which serves at crucial moments as an index for whether the truth has been internalized as it should be.[38] Thus Paul characterizes the doctrine and truth that he delivered as "in accordance with" both "godliness" (1 Tim. 6:3; Titus 1:1) and "the gospel of the glory of the blessed God" (1 Tim. 1:11). Apostolic teaching accords with both godliness and the blessed God's glory because, as faith's understanding of the "mystery" deepens, godliness enables greater perception of God's glory, and greater perception of God's glory enables greater lived conformity to that glory.[39]

Paul's depiction of this mystery, once hidden but now revealed, embraces the whole truth of Christ from his incarnation to his ascension and continuing

---

38. See Job 28:28 (LXX); Isa. 11:2 (LXX); 1 Tim. 3:16; 4:7–8; 2 Pet. 1:3. On the importance of such reverence and godliness for the rule of faith, see the suggestive comments by Torrance, *The Trinitarian Faith*, 38–46.

39. Nota bene: "enables" does not mean "guarantees."

reign. All of this is ordered to and finds its ultimate source in "the blessed God." The blessed God's glory radiates backward and forward from its historical epicenter in Christ, casting shadows with OT types and framing with its brilliance the silhouette of the coming Lord to whom we may draw near, for now, only by hearing (Matt. 17:5). Like the disciples on the mount, we may know the Lord in his glory only if we fear him and let that fear guide our pursuit of his face. As we do so, we discern that the whole economy of salvation is suspended from the "blessed God." That God is "blessed" means that he "absolutely delights in himself, absolutely rests in himself, and is absolutely self-sufficient."[40] If the apostolic teaching accords with both godliness and the gospel's display of the glory of God, who is blessed, it is because there is a correspondence between these two realities. Godliness defines true blessedness (Matt. 5:2–11), and God's blessedness is the source and hope of our own (1 Tim. 6:15; Titus 2:13). Because God is blessed, "we shall be like him, because we shall see him as he is" (1 John 3:2). Teaching that promotes godliness is oriented by a vision of God's blessed fullness—his unique, divine "Godliness" we might say—and the gospel's roots in that reality. We argued in chapter 1 that this vision is begun by faith and will be consummated in sight in the beatific vision. Using the God-fittingness rule in biblical reasoning therefore cultivates and is cultivated by godliness, or piety.

Exegesis is "godly" to the extent that it perceives and upholds God's own "Godliness."[41] In other words, exegesis should be a form of worship that conforms us to its Object. Worship, not mere knowledge, is what effects this conformity: to be holy or blessed we must see and worship the one who is thrice holy, "the blessed and only Sovereign, the King of kings and Lord of lords, who alone has immortality, who dwells in unapproachable light, whom no one has ever seen or can see" (1 Tim. 6:15–16). The more God-befitting our own lives become, the more able we are to read Scripture in a God-befitting manner.

The Christian God-fittingness rule also significantly differs from that of Greek and Roman philosophers. Xenophanes's understanding of God's nature served as a tool for critically interpreting anthropomorphic and "mythical" language about the gods in Homeric poetry. Christian theologians appropriated this demythologizing strategy, but for their own reasons, and not because the God of the Bible morally embarrassed them.[42] One of the implicit pressures leading Christians to adopt this strategy is Scripture's own markedly

40. Bavinck, *Reformed Dogmatics*, 2:251.
41. This wordplay between "godly" and "Godliness" is merely heuristic.
42. Briggman, *God and Christ in Irenaeus*, 92–95.

unmythological portrait of God. According to Yehezkel Kaufmann, the basic insight of Israelite religion is that God "is utterly distinct from, and other than, the world; he is subject to no laws, no compulsions, or powers that transcend him. He is, in short, non-mythological."[43] Absent from Scripture are the telltale interests of pagan myths, like theogonies (tales of the deity's origin). In the OT, God has "no pedigree, fathers no generations; he neither inherits nor bequeaths his authority."[44]

Particularly in how the OT depicts God's warfare on behalf of Israel, we see what Kaufmann calls its "non-mythologism" in the fact that God does not need to wrest dominion away from his enemies, who are understood as lifeless idols dependent on frail and foolish creatures (Isa. 44:9–20; 45:14–46:13). For polemical and contrastive purposes, Scripture employs mythological language and concepts from Israel's surrounding cultures— like the "sea" as a malevolent force, or "death" as a god who swallows up the living.[45] But these contenders are understood non-mythologically. They are creatures at best and pose no real threat to God. He alone creates and commands the sea and swallows up death (Exod. 14:29; Ps. 95:5; Prov. 8:29; Isa. 25:8; Rev. 21:1). God has no genuine rivals, may not be manipulated by magic, and is not bound by fate or talismans. In short, while Scripture uses mythological language and forms of expression, it does not use them *mythologically*.[46] Rather, Scripture's insistence on God's oneness and singularity, which resounds in his eternality and holiness as well as in creation *ex nihilo*, necessarily undercuts mythology and its natural habitat in pagan religion. The upshot is that God must not be thought to be like a creature, for he is like himself (Isa. 40:25). Therefore, the God-fittingness rule cannot have anything to do with demythologizing Scripture, because Scripture, so to speak, already comes to us demythologized. Instead, the God-fittingness rule aligns us with Scripture's non-mythological viewpoint and thus helps us to perceive and receive Scripture's language in light of its object, God, as he is disclosed in the whole canon.

---

43. Kaufmann, *The Religion of Israel*, esp. 21–121 (60). The central insight we take away from Kaufmann is that "mythological" accounts of God, humanity, and the cosmos construe everything as ontologically continuous. For an overview of Kaufmann's account of monotheism and a brief defense against his critics, see Sommer, *The Bodies of God and the World of Ancient Israel*, 154–74. It will be clear to readers why we disagree with Sommer's argument for God having a "body."

44. Kaufmann, *The Religion of Israel*, 60–61.

45. For an insightful introductory study of the OT's polemical appropriation of ANE religious imagery and concepts, see Currid, *Against the Gods*.

46. To consider another example, this applies to the cosmologies of NT authors, which serve a variety of theological and rhetorical purposes. See here Pennington and McDonough, *Cosmology and New Testament Theology*.

## Understanding Biblical Discourse in a God-Befitting Manner

We have grounded the God-fittingness rule in God's fullness of life in himself, his non-contrastive transcendence of all things, and his creation of all things *ex nihilo*. Moreover, we have noted the rule's spiritually formative, pedagogical function: it fosters our understanding of God's divinity so that we may be conformed to God as participants in the divine nature (2 Pet. 1:4). In short, the God-fittingness rule prohibits mythological interpretations of Scripture's language, thereby enabling us to better understand God and to worship him accordingly. But what does this look like in practice?

Traditionally, the logic of the God-fittingness rule is grounded in some summary perfection of God's nature, such as his glory, perfection, or blessedness.[47] Now, it is possible to move too quickly here, using an a priori conception of God's perfection to distort the text and miss its own grammar. The notion of God's perfection or blessedness operative in this context must be gathered from the whole witness of Scripture, not imported from a few philosophical syllogisms. God's perfections too are those that befit him.[48] What befits God is something we learn only by considering all of Scripture over a long time, through continual prayer and obedience, and in the company of many saints. That said, the God-fittingness rule requires some notion of God's perfection, even though rereading Scripture often forces us to refine our understanding of his perfection. Reckoning with such a portrait—which includes the Apocalypse's incipient notes of God's holiness, absoluteness, and eternality—enables biblical reasoning to handle different passages differently. So, when Scripture's readers encounter language that seems to impugn God's perfection, how do we understand that language in a way that "fits" its divine referent? A few examples will provide a sense of the rule's function.

Traditionally, the most common instance where the tradition applies the God-fittingness rule is when faced with anthropomorphic or anthropopathic language, which depicts God in the forms of the human body and human passions. For example, Scripture routinely employs anthropomorphic language, attributing to God human characteristics such as eyes (Ezek. 7:4; Amos 9:4; 1 Pet. 3:12), hands (1 Sam. 5:11; Amos 9:2), and arms (Jer. 27:5) just as much as human activities such as sleep and travel (Gen. 11:5; Ps. 44:23; Mic. 1:3). Yet Scripture also denies these on occasion as well (Job 10:4; Ps. 121:4; Isa.

---

47. Implicitly, e.g., Basil, *Against Eunomius* 2.23–24. Among Reformed and Lutheran scholastics, inter alia: Heidegger, *Corpus Theologiae Christianae* 3.3.23; Calov, *Systema Locorum Theologicorum*, 2:230; Owen, *Vindiciae Evangelicae* (*Works* 12:111); Mastricht, *Theoretical-Practical Theology* 1.2.23.7; cf. 1.2.13.11; 1.2.15.19.

48. Gregory of Nyssa, *Catechetical Discourse* 24.5–7 (PPS 60:115–16).

40:28), in keeping with the prohibition against rendering and conceiving God in creaturely forms (Exod. 20:4).[49]

Just as Scripture occasionally uses imagery and language drawn from pagan myths without endorsing the corresponding mythology, so too Scripture uses anthropomorphism without thereby ascribing human limits to God. Cyril of Alexandria is representative when he says that those of "mature judgment" understand these figures of speech in the most plain or unadorned way, which means to understand them in a way "befitting [πρέποι, *prepoi*] God's ineffable nature."[50] For our purposes, this means understanding anthropomorphism metaphorically. The chief characteristic of a theological metaphor is that it can be affirmed *and* denied of God.[51] Consider when we say that "God is our rock." We do not mean "rock" here in the literal sense of a mineral substance but in the sense that the analogy between rocks and strength holds true with regard to God. The same happens with anthropomorphic language. For instance, Adam and Eve "heard the sound of the LORD God walking in the garden" (Gen. 3:8–9), but we hear nothing of what makes the "sound," like grass or feet—a silence that suggests the anthropomorphism is neither the point nor to be taken literally.[52] If we understand this language in a way befitting God, who is everywhere, who cannot be confined by his temple (1 Kings 8:27), and so much less a garden, then it cannot suggest that God's presence is localized in a body.[53] The language, adapted from our experience, paints a vivid picture of two children who attempt to hide from their father, whom they have disobeyed (Gen. 3:10). With reference to Scripture's teaching about God's holiness and blessedness, as well as creation *ex nihilo* and his infinite transcendence of space and time, we can detect metaphor here and so understand this biblical discourse about God in a God-befitting way. Consequently, we hear what these statements

49. Johann Gerhard catalogs many such examples in *Theological Commonplaces* II.8.117–19. The first thing the God-fittingness rule does when faced with this language is to remind us that God is the creator of all things *ex nihilo*, including human creatures that are made in his image. This means God is not so much "anthropomorphic" as creatures are "theomorphic."

50. Cyril, *Commentary on the Twelve Prophets*, on Mic. 1:3–4 (FC 116:185; Pusey 1:605).

51. See, e.g., Clarke, *The One and the Many*, 55.

52. See Cassuto, *A Commentary on the Book of Genesis*, 150–52. The OT is aware of the limitations of anthropomorphic imagery, like the way language of Moses seeing the Lord's "face" and "back" (Exod. 33:20–23) is employed to emphasize God's "qualitative superiority." See Moberly, *At the Mountain of God*, 79–83 (82). Arguably illustrating this point is the reality that despite Scripture's myriad anthropomorphisms and theriomorphisms, archaeologists have yet to find ancient iconography of Yahweh. See T. J. Lewis, *The Origin and Character of God*, 287–333.

53. John Chrysostom, *Homilies on Genesis* 17.3.

have to say: God is indestructible and so worthy of our trust; God is just and omnipresent, and so worthy of our fear.

The God-fittingness rule also helps us understand theological language that is not metaphorical, such as analogy, which bears some likeness to our everyday uses of that language while nevertheless bearing an even greater unlikeness. This is how we must understand the Son as the "only begotten" (John 1:14). To understand this language in a God-befitting manner, we strip away all the "imperfections" or uniquely created characteristics that surround the notion of begetting, such as change and distinctions in time and place, which are incompatible with God's eternality and immutability.[54] The Son's begetting occurs without any separation of the Son from the Father, without any change in God's being, without any before or after—in short, it is an *eternal begetting*. What we are left with is the idea of an intimate "likeness" between Father and Son, grounded in a communication of the Father's whole being, which is what "befits" God in the language of begetting. In this manner the Son's eternal generation, like the Spirit's eternal procession, is "worthy" of the Father's divinity, because it conforms to God's blessed life that abides without change, time, or division.[55]

For one more example, we may consider Jesus's words about the Spirit: "He will take what is mine and declare it to you" (John 16:14). Didymus the Blind says that we should understand the Spirit's taking, or "receiving," all things from the Son "in a way appropriate to the divine nature." This means that "the Spirit did not receive what he did not have before," because losing and gaining characterize finite relations and are therefore unfitting of God.[56] At minimum, therefore, this "taking" discloses an order within the life of the Trinity: the Son receiving from the Father and the Spirit receiving from the Father and the Son.[57]

We shall say much more about these matters in later chapters, particularly in chapter 9. For the moment, it suffices to see that the God-fittingness rule encourages us to discern the divine pedagogy operative in Scripture's most difficult language about God. For this very reason, using this God-fittingness rule in exegesis requires *more* exacting attention to the individual features of any given discourse, not less. The God-fittingness rule is easily misapplied if it takes us away from Scripture's natural properties, such as the semantic domains of its words, how language is used in particular discourses, the way that narrative contexts help us to see these differences, and much else besides.

---

54. Turretin, *Institutes of Elenctic Theology* 3.29.5. On the meaning of this doctrine, see Sanders and Swain, *Retrieving Eternal Generation*.
55. Gregory of Nazianzus, *Oration* 2.38 (NPNF[2] 7:212–13).
56. Didymus the Blind, *On the Holy Spirit* 163–64 (PPS 43:193–94).
57. Aquinas, *Commentary on the Gospel of St. John* 16.4.2107–115. We return to this issue in chap. 9.

Distinguishing between negative and positive aspects of the rule can help us avoid this pitfall. Negatively, God must not be understood in a way that *contradicts* his divine perfection. This aspect of the rule conforms to the "pressure" the text exerts by keeping us attuned to its larger economic context as one part of the canon's unified witness to the triune God. In this respect the God-fittingness rule incorporates the logic of the analogy of faith (rule 1): Scripture's individual parts must be read in light of the whole. But this does not absolve us from careful scrutiny of Scripture's individual parts. Positively, God must be understood in a way that *coheres* with his perfect life. In this regard, as we will see below in conclusion, the rule allows for some flexibility in application since it does not overdetermine one's understanding of divine perfection and therefore one's exegesis of passages that seem to clash with that understanding. As we have already noted, the rule depends on one's acquired understanding of God's perfection. This understanding always remains incomplete this side of the resurrection, so we must continually refine it through contemplative exegesis. While different approaches to God's perfection will thus result in somewhat different readings of particular passages, the God-fittingness rule is applicable all the same.

## Concluding Case Study: Is Regret Suitable to God?

Given the extensive consequences of the God-fittingness rule for theological exegesis, an extensive case study is in order. The proof must be in the pudding. Does this rule lead us further into the biblical text and help resolve potential antinomies? Or does it impose foreign interests on particular texts and lead us away from their native concerns? In conclusion, we test the rule on an exegetical issue that is as commonly debated as it is enlisted to ground wide-ranging conclusions for the character of God's divinity. Perhaps nothing speaks against the traditional understanding of God's perfection as immutable or impassible as much as the pervasive OT theme of God's "regret," "repentance," or "relenting" (all from the Hebrew root נחם, *nḥm*).[58] For many, this is evidence against the biblical support for immutability and impassibility, suggesting on the contrary that God changes in some sense or that God sovereignly opens himself to risk and ignorance.[59]

A paradigmatic example is from Jeremiah's vision of God as a potter shaping Israel, his clay (Jer. 18:1–11). When the clay spoils in the potter's hands, the potter shapes it into another vessel "as it seemed good to the potter to do"

---

58. On the various meanings of the root word, see DCH.
59. Most extensively, Döhling, *Der bewegliche Gott*.

(18:4). God addresses Israel with the image, promising that he will "relent" or "repent" from his planned blessing or judgment of a nation if that nation "turns" or "repents" from its good or evil conduct. Hence, God's activity seems to depend on Israel's activity. The message is echoed elsewhere in the Prophets: "Return to the LORD your God, for he is gracious and merciful, slow to anger, and abounding in steadfast love; and he relents over disaster. Who knows whether he will not turn and relent?" (Joel 2:13–14). God repeatedly "repents" in a sense suggesting a change of mind about a course of action (Hosea 11:8–9; Amos 7:3, 6; Jon. 4:2). Famously, when Saul disobeys God and takes the king of the Amalekites hostage rather than destroying him, God tells Samuel: "I regret that I have made Saul king, for he has turned back from following me and has not performed my commandments" (1 Sam. 15:11; cf. 15:35; Gen. 6:6–7).

However, Scripture also complicates this picture. In the same narrative, Samuel tells Saul that God does *not* regret because he is "not a man, that he should have regret" (1 Sam. 15:29; cf. Num. 23:19). So which is it: Does God regret or not? Does God change his mind? How do we understand the theme of "repentance" or regret in a manner suitable to God?

Applying the God-fittingness rule to these passages leads us away from an impressionistic reading of "relenting" language, which might suggest that God literally changes his mind like creatures change their minds. But how to understand the language depends on the way one wishes to uphold God's immutability or impassibility. Traditionally, when readers encounter this language the result is to uphold divine immutability and impassibility by denying any kind of emotional turmoil or disturbance in God. On this reading, instead of pointing us to some putative emotional life within God, the language points us to God's activity. Turretin is characteristically clear in this regard: "Repentance is attributed to God after the manner of men (*anthropopathos*) but must be understood after the manner of God (*theoprepos*): not with respect to his counsel, but to the event; not in reference to his will, but to the thing willed; not to affection and internal grief, but to the effect and external work because he does what a penitent man usually does . . . it must be understood not pathetically (*pathetikos*), but energetically (*energetikos*)."[60] Hence, the traditional reading of "repentance," "relenting," and "regretting" language refers to God's acts rather than God's feelings. Central to the traditional readings are Scripture's two apparently axiomatic denials of divine repentance: "God is not man, that he should lie, or a son of man, that he should change his mind" (Num. 23:19), and "The Glory

---

60. Turretin, *Institutes of Elenctic Theology* 3.11.11 (Giger, 1:206).

of Israel will not lie or have regret, for he is not a man, that he should have regret" (1 Sam. 15:29).[61]

Contemporary interpreters often suspect traditional readings of running roughshod over the texts (perhaps not entirely without warrant), prompting further critical reflection. Walter Moberly's careful analysis of this theme focuses on the narrative contexts of 1 Samuel 15 and Numbers 23, where the only strong denials of divine repentance occur. According to Moberly, when read in context these axiomatic statements are only apparently so, since both have more local concerns: in one instance, the denial that God changes his mind refers to God's election of Israel (Num. 23:19), and in the other the denial refers to God's election of David (1 Sam. 15:29).[62] Moberly concludes that these relatively rare denials should not occupy center stage, as they do in traditional readings of the divine repentance theme. However, these famous denials do emphasize the "qualitative distinction between divine and human repentance."[63] There is no positive analogy between God's relenting or regret and our own. That said, Moberly argues that the portrait of the potter and clay in Jeremiah 18 should be axiomatic for our interpretation: God's relenting depends on whether the kingdoms relent, whether they turn toward good or ill. This comports with another axiomatic formulation, found in Ezekiel 33:12–16, which depicts God changing in response to individuals and not simply kingdoms.

Crucially, however, in both Jeremiah and Ezekiel there are factors that speak against any mechanical and presumptuous formula, such as, "If you repent, then God *will* relent." In other words, there are grounds for understanding these statements as *general* rather than universal, and thus admitting of exceptions on account of God's freedom. The king of Nineveh articulates this sense of God's freedom: "Who knows? God *may* turn and relent" (Jon. 3:9 CSB; cf. Joel 2:14). This sense of contingency and divine sovereignty fits the overall context of both Jeremiah and Ezekiel. Both prophets speak about a time when repentance may be sought with tears yet not found (Jer. 15:1–4; Ezek. 33:12–16, 21) or when God will act unilaterally to save his people apart from their prior repentance (Jer. 32:1–44; Ezek. 36:16–32).[64] Hence, the axiomatic formula becomes, "If you repent, God *may* relent." At the heart of this theme, Moberly sees an unresolved "creative tension" between God's freedom and human response, along with some degree of mutual conditioning.[65] But he

---

61. For a recent take on the traditional reading, see Duby, "For I Am God, Not a Man."
62. Moberly, *Old Testament Theology*, 132–38; also Döhling, *Der bewegliche Gott*, 223–29.
63. Moberly, *Old Testament Theology*, 131.
64. Moberly, *Old Testament Theology*, 124–25.
65. Moberly, *Old Testament Theology*, 143.

admits that on any reckoning with this theme, "an interpreter's grasp of the subject matter will inevitably influence how one construes the text."[66] This is to say, how we understand the divine repentance texts requires a larger perspective than these texts provide. Our understanding of God, Scripture's ultimate subject matter, inevitably influences our understanding of the texts. This is precisely where the God-fittingness rule can help.

Moberly's analysis is more attentive to the texts' narrative function and syntax than traditional accounts, but his conclusions with respect to the relation between God and creation are not for that reason more compelling. Moberly seems indebted to Karl Barth's account of God's constancy. According to Barth, "There is such a thing as the holy *mutability* of God. . . . His constancy consists in the fact that He is always the same in every change."[67] On Barth's slightly different understanding of divine perfection, God welcomes a degree of reciprocity with creation such that his responses might involve what traditionally has been understood as "change" (*motio*) without losing his essential perfections. According to Barth, God reacts, responds, and *changes* in relation to the creature in ways that are consistent with what and who God is: the "One who Loves in Freedom." It is entirely plausible that an application of the God-fittingness rule might stop at this point and rest content with this alternative, "softer" conception of God's immutability. However, the traditional understanding of God's immutability is preferable, not least for the christological reasons discussed earlier, and is compatible both with Moberly's insight into the axiomatic, general formulas of Jeremiah 18 and Ezekiel 33 and with his emphasis on God's freedom.

First, we must understand divine immutability and impassibility properly. Unease with these doctrines often arises from misunderstanding what they do and do not say about God. It is important to remember that immutability is first of all a denial: there is no change (*mutatio*) in God's being and will. Misunderstanding creeps in where we mistake this denial for a modal affirmation about God's life, as if saying "God does not change" is equivalent to saying, "God is inactive" or "God is active in only one kind of way," like a runaway train or a broken record. The denial of change rests upon the fact that God is infinitely alive and active, adapting his activity and its forms to the circumstances, having genuine moral fellowship with creatures—and all without undergoing any growth, improvement, or loss.[68] Similar misunderstandings plague critiques of God's "impassibility" (*apatheia*), where the

66. Moberly, *Old Testament Theology*, 125.
67. Barth, *CD* II/1, 496.
68. Matthias Joseph Scheeben explains helpfully how the "mutability" of God's external acts toward creatures is compatible with God's intrinsic immutability:

doctrine is mistaken for "indifference" (what we typically mean by apathy).[69] Indeed, how could an indifferent God love the world by sending his only begotten Son to die for our sins? Quite the contrary, impassibility is the strength of God's indestructible love, the strength with which Christ's death destroys sin's unruly passions and its fruit, death. Impassibility affirms God's "love that is stronger than death" (Song 8:6)—infinitely stronger, and thus beyond contest or struggle with suffering. The doctrine thus denies that God is subject to or capable of suffering (*pathos, passio*), maintaining instead that God's being cannot be threatened by evil and that God's love need not—indeed, cannot—be "goaded into being by pain."[70] When properly understood, these doctrines both fit with and emerge from the portrait of God's qualitative distinction from creation as the thrice-holy Creator of all things *ex nihilo*. This God cannot even "open" himself willingly to commerce with pain and change because he is altogether beyond the logic of finite being that characterizes such commerce. Far from compromising God's love, impassibility testifies to its divine depths. The logic of finite being sets boundaries to the love creatures can have for one another, whereas the Lord's love for us is unfettered, sovereign, and wild.

In this light, the creative tension at the heart of God's relenting and human response is contextualized within the "Christian distinction." As the one who has life in and of himself and is therefore truly free, God is beyond all logic of mutual conditioning with creatures. For Peter Martyr Vermigli, the theme of repentance across Scripture emphasizes just these truths.[71] Creatures have nothing that they have not received (1 Cor. 4:7), in keeping with their very being as created *ex nihilo*. We neither create nor recreate ourselves, so God's sovereign will, grace, and mercy are the final consideration in our works and even apart from our works (Rom. 9:16; 1 Cor. 15:10; Phil. 2:13). Hence, even the conditional repentance of creatures is the gift of God (2 Tim. 2:25),

---

God in his work and in his will himself takes into consideration the changes brought about in the creature by itself, and adjusts his conduct and disposition accordingly; and thus it seems that such changes in the creature encroach upon God himself in his inner life, having an affecting and changing influence. However, the considerations which God takes into his will and action are never the real and underlying motive cause of his will and action, which always lies within God himself. The various temperaments [*Stimmungen*] in God towards the good or evil conduct of the creature are not various acts or states, but the same infinite love for the highest Good is at the same time love for good creatures and hatred or wrath against evil. (*Handbuch der katholischen Dogmatik* 2, n. 229)

69. See the examples and discussion in Dodds, *The Unchanging God of Love*, 208.
70. Hart, "No Shadow of Turning," 191. See, further, on divine impassibility, Gavrilyuk, *The Suffering of the Impassible God*.
71. Vermigli, *Loci Communes*, I.15 (83–86).

something for which the Psalms instruct us to pray (Pss. 51:12; 119:36). Vermigli overlays the theme of repentance onto broader considerations of creation and God's grace, which helps us to see that the mysterious relation between God's freedom and human response carries no hint of mutual conditioning.

To conclude: when God relents, this signifies God's will to relate in fitting ways to particular people or circumstances. The standard for what "fits" in these situations is always God's own nature so that he acts in a manner consistent with his holiness and blessedness. That is to say, God acts in a way that is fitting to God, so we must understand his acts accordingly. When people or circumstances change, God and his will remain unchanged, only now his activity toward them varies with the circumstances. Stephen Charnock comments on God sparing Nineveh: "When the threatening was made, they were a fit object for justice; but when they repented, they were a fit object for a merciful respite. To threaten when sins are high, is a part of God's justice; not to execute when sins are revoked by repentance, is a part of God's goodness."[72]

We might state this by drawing a distinction between answers and reactions. God answers his creatures and the question of their moral standing without suffering any change. To react, on the other hand, would signal a change in God hastened by external influences—perhaps even "equal and opposite" influences. A reaction is either automatic and elicited by something that happens to us, or it depends on something else to happen or come to light. Unlike reactions, answers do not necessarily imply such change. Prudent human teachers anticipate questions and answer them without undergoing transformation; how much more the divine Teacher?

God genuinely communicates with his creatures when answering our righteousness or wickedness. David thus confesses, "With the merciful you show yourself merciful; with the blameless man you show yourself blameless; with the purified you show yourself pure; and with the crooked you make yourself seem tortuous" (Ps. 18:25–26). This is the dynamic we see in Jeremiah and Ezekiel, where God warns of how he plans to answer either the evil or obedience of individuals and nations. God promises these kinds of answers in order to put the question to his people: will they repent, now that God is beginning to answer Jerusalem and Judah by shaping disaster against them (Jer. 18:11)? Like certain kinds of answers, this is indeed "response-seeking language."[73] What response is God seeking?

God calls his people to repent from our evil ways, turn toward him, and then endure to the end. We find this in the theme of repentance in the Apocalypse,

---

72. Charnock, *The Existence and Attributes of God*, 403–4.
73. Moberly, *Old Testament Theology*, 120.

where warnings are framed with conditions. Jesus warns the church at Ephe-sus, "I will come to you and remove your lampstand from its place, unless you repent" (Rev. 2:5). This warning is meant to persuade them to persevere: "To the one who conquers I will grant to eat of the tree of life, which is in the paradise of God" (2:7); "Hold fast to what you have, so that no one may seize your crown. The one who conquers, I will make him a pillar in the temple of my God" (3:11–12). Our confidence is that God remains the Holy One in our midst, so his actions toward our repentance or nonrepentance will befit his own mercy and justice. Our actions make a difference for how God acts toward us, but they do so because of a change that happens within us, not within God—a change, moreover, that God works according to his good pleasure (cf. Jer. 18:4).[74] God's holy will is constant in what it approves and what it rejects: "The King in his might loves justice," so he is "not a God who delights in wickedness" (Pss. 99:4; 5:4; cf. Prov. 6:16–19). The Messiah cor-respondingly loves righteousness and hates wickedness (Ps. 45:6–7). He came to enact God's will and reveal God's grace—all of which had been planned and constant since before the foundations of the world (Titus 2:11; Heb. 10:7).

The God who addresses us in Christ is the holy, eternal, and unchanging God who works his grace in us and adjusts his activity toward us accordingly. Part of the grace of his teaching is to elicit within us a sense of what befits his nature so that we may honor him with appropriate praise, ever conscious that we serve a God who is holy and free, a God wholly unlike the tractable deities of pagan myths. Our sense of what is worthy of God must therefore always issue from our fear of God. Thus Cyril: "The Father, then, brings to the Son, through knowledge and God-befitting insights, those to whom he has decreed the divine grace."[75] We must now continue to explore further rules that train our attentions on these sorts of insights, beginning with those rules concerning the unity of the blessed Trinity.

---

74. Maximus, *Ambiguum* 1.4 (Constas, 1:10–11).
75. Cyril, *Commentary on John* 4.1499 (Maxwell, 1:223).

# 5

# The LORD Is One

## The Trinity's Unity and Equality in Scripture's Twofold Discourse

**Principle 5:** The one true and living God is eternally Father, Son, and Holy Spirit, distinct in their relations to one another and the same in substance, power, and glory.

**Rule 4:** Scripture speaks both of what is common to the Father, Son, and Holy Spirit and of what is proper to each person, reflecting the conceptual distinction between the divine nature and the divine persons. Biblical reasoning discerns this distinction, upholds it, and contemplates the Holy Trinity in its light. Therefore, read Scripture's discourse about God in such a way that its twofold discourse—the common and the proper—is recognized and employed, rather than in a way that collapses the two ways into one. In this way, we learn to count persons rather than natures.

The following two chapters add to biblical reasoning's toolkit by developing another principle and three rules that follow from it. These all concern the unity and equality of the Holy Trinity. Readers of the NT encounter this reality early on, as when in the Gospel of Matthew Jesus warns Satan that only God should be worshiped (Matt. 4:10) while nevertheless receiving worship himself (Matt. 2:11; 14:33; 28:17).[1] If the Son receives the worship that only God can receive, then he must be the only God together with the Father. This is not an isolated judgment, as we will see. Further, it obliges readers to begin reckoning with the identity of Jesus and what it means to perceive and confess him as Lord and God. However, this is not the only way that readers must reckon with him. Jesus also teaches us that the Father is greater than he is (John 14:28) and that he has come to submit his own will to the will of the Father (Matt. 26:39; John 6:38). Doing justice to all of Jesus's teaching about himself requires us to think through these various elements, a task that occupies us in the following chapters. But the present consideration comes first because it provides the necessary backdrop: the meaning and significance of Israel's confession of God's oneness for trinitarian theology and thus for biblical reasoning.

As we saw in the previous chapter, only God is God because he alone is "holy, holy, holy," he alone creates all things *ex nihilo*, and so he alone is worthy of all praise. According to Calvin, however, God "so proclaims himself the sole God as to offer himself to be contemplated clearly in three persons."[2] Our pursuit of God's face is not a pursuit of nameless, amorphous, and impersonal divinity. Instead, we are concerned irreducibly with knowledge of God the Father, revealed in his only begotten Son Jesus Christ, through his Holy Spirit. All knowledge of God is ultimately knowledge of these three persons in some respect. And these three are one God. In order to see this clearly, biblical reasoning embraces the truth of the divine Trinity's unity and equality. Without this we lose our focus on Christ's glory, foolishly looking for the "real" God's glory in something other than the ingloriously crucified Nazarene, somewhere other than where God passes before our eyes. Consequently, we end up diminishing the Son and the Spirit or contenting ourselves with abstract accounts of "divinity," failing to see who it is that calls us from darkness into the light.

The present chapter explicates our fifth principle, which concerns the unity and equality of the three divine persons: *The one true and living God is eternally Father, Son, and Holy Spirit, distinct in their relations to one another and the same in substance, power, and glory*. Three rules derive from this principle and help us to perceive its mysterious truth: that "we worship one God in the Trinity, and the Trinity in Unity; without confusing the persons or separating the substance," for which reason we understand that the Father is

---

1. Leim, *Matthew's Theological Grammar*, skillfully draws out the significance of such details for how Matthew construes the identity of YHWH around the Father-Son relationship.
2. Calvin, *Institutes of the Christian Religion* 1.13.2.

glorious, the Son is glorious, and the Spirit is glorious; yet there are not three glories but one glory.[3] God does not give his glory to another (Isa. 42:8). So when we perceive the glory of the crucified Christ, we perceive the glory of God—full stop—which is our hope and joy.

The three rules following from this fifth principle respectively concern the twofold grammar attending the conceptual distinction between person and essence in God, the Trinity's inseparable operations, and the biblical practice of "appropriation." All three rules serve the contemplation of the *persons* with whom we seek to commune when reading Scripture. These three rules serve this end by training us to count persons rather than gods, or actors rather than actions, so that we recognize the one God in three persons rather than in anything else.

Our discussion in particular centers on the first two rules, concerning "redoublement" and inseparable operations. These two rules are part of the same governing grammar and run along parallel tracks, to an extent strengthening and complementing one another. Because these rules touch the very heart of trinitarian theology and deserve careful explication, we have split them up into two chapters. In this chapter we will focus on the rule of redoublement, turning in the next chapter to discuss the rules of inseparable operations and appropriation. In what follows, we begin by analyzing our fifth principle concerning the Lord's oneness against the background of our findings thus far. Then we will proceed to justify and explain the redoublement rule, which opens up space to talk about inseparable operations and appropriation in chapter 6.

## The Lord's Oneness

From our investigation of the heavenly liturgy (Rev. 4) we learned that God is qualitatively distinct from all things, as the one who created everything *ex nihilo*, and is "non-contrastively" transcendent. Among the implications of these realities we discovered God's eternality, impassibility, immutability, and the insight that God is immeasurable (that is, infinite) and thus the whole of divinity, excluding membership in any broader classification of "gods." We now need to relate these discoveries to the OT's persistent witness to God's oneness, which serves as the starting point for reflecting on the Trinity's unity and equality. Within a preliminary grammar of God's oneness, we can perceive the significance of the way the NT attributes the name YHWH to Father, Son, and Holy Spirit.

---

3. From the *Quicumque vult* (Denzinger §75).

## The Basic Grammar of Israel's Confession

That the Lord is one in a singularly exclusive sense finds axiomatic and liturgical expression in the Shema: "Hear, O Israel: The Lord our God, the Lord is one. You shall love the Lord your God with all your heart and with all your soul and with all your might" (Deut. 6:4–5).[4] This confession comes on the heels of the Decalogue, which it echoes, while nevertheless drawing especially on the first commandment: "I am the Lord your God. . . . You shall have no other gods before me" (Exod. 20:2–3; Deut. 5:6–7). Israel's devotion was supposed to be exclusive because there is none other than God who created and redeemed them, who lovingly chose them from among the nations and covenanted with them (Deut. 4:32–40; Ps. 96:4–5; Jer. 10:1–25). God must be loved with one's whole being, corresponding to the fact that the Lord is the whole of God: "You shall love the Lord your God with your whole [ὅλης, holēs] heart and with your whole soul and with your whole mind and with your whole strength" (Mark 12:30 AT). If God is the whole of "divinity," then there are no others.

Consequently, any and all hints of polytheistic devotion are prohibited (Deut. 12:1–4). This is so not least because—especially in light of creation *ex nihilo*—all other gods are false: "See now that I, even I, am he, and there is no god beside me" (Deut. 32:39). Idols are inert, dumb and deaf, mere artifacts, things made of elements that crumble and fall apart: "Behold, they are all a delusion; their works are nothing; their metal images are empty wind" (Isa. 41:29; cf. 2:8, 18–20). Isaiah's polemic against idolatry unequivocally spells out the unreality of all other "gods" (Isa. 44:6–20; 45:5–6, 18, 21–22; 46:5–11). In her idolatry, Israel has "sworn by those who are no gods" (Jer. 5:7). The demonic forces behind idolatry are merely "so-called gods," for they "by nature are not gods" (1 Cor. 8:5; Gal. 4:8). Scripture therefore does not entertain the existence of other gods alongside the Lord in a broader genus of "divinities."[5]

---

4. See Moberly, *Old Testament Theology*, 7–40; Feldmeier and Spieckermann, *God of the Living*, 93–124.

5. Rendtorff, *The Canonical Hebrew Bible*, 634–36. Earlier historians of Israelite religion in the twentieth century (such as Kaufmann, *The Religion of Israel*), saw "monotheism" as an early and definitive trait. More recent historians argue that at least theoretical (as opposed to practical) monotheism is a late development of the postexilic period, due in part to its prominence in Isa. 40–55. For instance, see, e.g., Smith, *The Origins of Biblical Monotheism*; Smith, *The Early History of God*. In many respects, these debates parallel similar shifts in the nineteenth century (cf. Bavinck's discussion in *Reformed Dogmatics*, 2:170–73). A full-scale theological assessment of these debates is needed, but beyond our scope. Suffice to say, regardless of how historians speculatively reconstruct Israelite religious practice, the canon's

When we begin to ask how what Scripture says about God's oneness is true, we can do so only with the grammar of God's qualitative transcendence and creation *ex nihilo* in view. That is to say, we must understand God's "oneness" in a God-befitting way. Biblical pressures we have already considered, and the grammar that lays bare their inner logic, cumulatively focus our interpretation of further testimony across Scripture. Together, it all leads to the insight that God "is one as nothing else is."[6]

We may explain the consequent grammar of God's oneness in two senses that will be informative for us moving forward.[7] First, God is one in number, which theologians often designate as God's uniqueness (*singularitas*). God exhausts the category of "divinity." Indeed, God proves there is no such category at all because God is uncategorizable. There can be no other gods alongside him because then there would be a category into which we would fit God, and he would not be "the first and the last" (Rev. 1:17). Second, God is indissolubly one, which is traditionally formulated as God's "simplicity" (*simplicitas*). God's unity of simplicity entails that God neither is a part nor has parts. God's attributes are not parts of him; God "has" love in the sense that he loves, but even more than that, he *is* love (1 John 4:8). More importantly and decisively, as we shall see below, the Father, Son, and Holy Spirit are not parts of God, but they are each fully God. Neither is God part of something bigger than himself, like a God-world conglomerate. God cannot be mixed in with creation because only finite realities mix together, and when they do so they always involve limitations of intimacy and agency.

God's simplicity is therefore good news: he need not displace creatures in order to be intimately near to them; he need not evacuate his divinity to become fully human. Proximity does not threaten God because it cannot. In the terms of our previous chapter, transcendence and immanence are not mutually exclusive for God. We should underscore that these conclusions do not follow from a simple reading of the Shema, but from the summative pressures of creation *ex nihilo* and the two-testament canon's unified witness to God's oneness. Theological concepts like singularity and simplicity thus help us understand what the Shema itself confesses: that the LORD is one. With that in mind, how does God's oneness structure Scripture's witness to the triune God and our pursuit of the *visio Dei*?

---

overall testimony to creation *ex nihilo* and the unreality of other "gods" consistently attests God's ontological singularity.

6. Bernard of Clairvaux, *On Consideration* 5.7.17 (Evans, 161).

7. For exemplary modern expositions of God's oneness, see Bavinck, *Reformed Dogmatics*, 2:170–77; Barth, *CD* II/1, 440–61; Sonderegger, *Systematic Theology*, 1:3–45. It is difficult to improve on the basics of the grammar provided by Aquinas, *STh* I.3–11.

## Pressures of the Shema in Light of Jesus: One Lord, Not Two (Much Less Three)

The NT takes up the theme of God's oneness and, as it were, fits within it three distinct persons: the Father, the Son, and the Holy Spirit. This fact alone is startling and informative, but to understand its full significance we must also attend to the way that the NT attributes the name YHWH to three persons.[8] For our purposes, brief consideration of a few central texts will suffice to illustrate this fact and the characteristic pattern with which it is set before us. Against the background of the OT's witness to God's oneness, we will then be able to formulate the basic grammar of the Trinity's unity and equality.

The most famous text pressuring its readers toward identifying Israel's one God with all three persons appears in the concluding words of the first Gospel: "Go therefore and make disciples of all nations, baptizing them in the name of the Father and of the Son and of the Holy Spirit" (Matt. 28:19).[9] In the early church, this text became an important guide for structuring catechesis and centering teaching about God on the full divinity of the three persons.[10] Grammatically, we find a singular divine name ("the name") applied to and inclusive of three distinct personal names, each of which is connected to the others with a conjunction ("and") and distinguished with its own article ("the"). These three personal names are thus distinct, joined together, and on equal footing with regard to "the name" that belongs to them all. Baptism is therefore "into the name" (εἰς τὸ ὄνομα, *eis to onoma*), an oblique reference to the name YHWH, and the One whom this singular name signifies is the Son and the Holy Spirit as much as the Father. If no other passages corroborated these conclusions, we might doubt them. But this strange statement illustrates a paradox we encounter throughout the NT: the one God of Israel is indeed one God, but nevertheless also three distinct persons. And this paradox is typically set forth through a pattern of attributing one name singularly to three divine persons, without detracting from their abiding distinction from one another.

---

8. The NT applies the Tetragrammaton to the Father, Son, and Holy Spirit in diverse ways: sometimes by identifying YHWH's speech in the OT with one of the divine persons (e.g., Isa. 6:9 and Acts 28:25–26; Jer. 31:33–34 and Heb. 10:15), other times by highlighting inner-divine conversation (Heb. 1:5 and Ps. 2:7; Mark 12:35–37 and Ps. 110:1), or by showing how the persons commonly possess divine prerogatives that belong to YHWH alone (e.g., worship in Matt. 4:10; Deut. 6:13; cf. Matt. 2:11; 14:33; 28:17), and more.

9. For modern readings of this passage as teaching the Trinity, see Soulen, *The Divine Name(s) and the Holy Trinity*, 182–84; Bauckham, *Jesus and the God of Israel*, 56–57. Rowe, "Biblical Pressure and Trinitarian Hermeneutics," provides a brief account of the pressures leading to the identification of Israel's one God with the Father, Son, and Holy Spirit.

10. Lienhard, "The Baptismal Command (Matthew 28:19–20) and the Doctrine of the Trinity."

### Psalm 110

Jesus illustrates this paradox and pattern explicitly in his use of Psalm 110. Late in the Gospel of Mark, one of the scribes asks Jesus about the greatest commandment, prompting Jesus to begin his response with the Shema: "The most important is, 'Hear, O Israel: The Lord our God, the Lord is one' [κύριος εἷς ἐστιν, *kyrios heis estin*]" (Mark 12:29; cf. Deut. 6:4 LXX).[11] Jesus means to uphold God's oneness, because he has already implicitly testified to his own divinity with recourse to the Shema (Mark 2:7–11). Immediately after this, Jesus is in the temple and reiterates that he in fact is this same Lord. He asks the crowd, "How can the scribes say that the Christ is the son of David? David himself, in the Holy Spirit, declared, 'The Lord said to my Lord, "Sit at my right hand, until I put your enemies under your feet"' [Ps. 110:1]. David himself calls him Lord [κύριος, *kyrios*]. So how is he his son?" (Mark 12:35–37). The net effect of Jesus's teaching is to complicate and deepen our understanding of who he really is. There are two whom David (rightly) calls "Lord," who address one another and are therefore distinct. One might reasonably conclude from this that there are two Lords. However, Mark's placement of these statements right next to one another underscores that Jesus's overall logic functions within the boundaries of God's oneness. Hence, the Father is Lord and the Son is Lord, yet there are not two Lords but one because "the Lord is one." Jesus nowhere denies that he is the Son, nor that the Father is the Father, but he maintains that they are both the one Lord of Israel. We have both identity and distinction. Mark does not solve the riddle for us, but he sets it forth in unembarrassed clarity. The name "Lord" applies to two distinct figures, the Father and the Son, without resulting in two Lords. Why does Scripture speak this way?

### 1 Corinthians 8:4-6

Another example of the same pattern comes from 1 Corinthians, where Paul addresses one of the church's controversies having to do with food offered to idols.[12] The passage is worth quoting in full:

> Therefore, as to the eating of food offered to idols, we know that "an idol has no real existence," and that "there is no God but one [οὐδεὶς θεὸς εἰ μὴ εἷς, *oudeis theos ei mē heis*]." For although there may be so-called gods in heaven or on earth—as indeed there are many "gods" and many "lords"—yet for us there

---

11. The title "Lord" (κύριος, *kyrios*) consistently renders יהוה (YHWH) in the Septuagint.
12. God's oneness functions throughout Paul's letter to underscore the kind of people the church is, being in covenant with the one true and living God, and therefore one as he is one: Macaskill, "The Way the One God Works"; Byers, "The One Body of the Shema in 1 Corinthians."

is one God [εἷς θεὸς, *heis theos*], the Father, from whom are all things and for whom we exist, and one Lord [εἷς κύριος, *heis kyrios*], Jesus Christ, through whom are all things and through whom we exist. (1 Cor. 8:4–6)

In this widely recognized gloss on the Shema, which Paul alludes to at the outset, we find again the pattern of distinguishing two personal subjects from one another while identifying them both as the one God. As concerns identity, the subject of the Shema is "the LORD our God" (Deut. 6:4), which Paul separates grammatically for the sake of making his point. He uses "Lord" of Jesus and "God" of the Father not in order to distinguish between God and Lord but in order to include Jesus and the Father within the single extension of the phrase "the LORD our God." Paul even stresses their oneness by repeating that there is "one God" and "one Lord." Therefore, he identifies both as the one Lord of Israel. If his point were not clear enough, he contrasts the oneness of the Father and Jesus with "many 'gods' and many 'lords'" (1 Cor. 8:4–5). Again, the Father is Lord and the Son is Lord, but there are not two Lords—and "many" is right out.

If we considered this text in isolation we might draw all manner of false inferences—for instance, that Father or Son were only forms, or appearances, of a unipersonal subject known variously as "God" or "Lord." But Paul does not leave matters there. He also firmly distinguishes Father and Son with an instance of the prepositional formula we discussed briefly in the previous chapter. In this instance, the formula has a soteriological twist: the "for whom" directing us to the Father and the "through whom" locating us in Christ are unique to such formulas.[13] One consequence of these prepositions here is firmly to distinguish Father and Son, even though they also attribute to both the cosmic responsibility for creation and salvation that belongs to God alone (cf. Rom. 11:36). Like our passage in Mark, these notes of distinction make the common identification of the Father and the Son as YHWH that much stranger. The pattern in the two texts is therefore similar—namely, the one Lord God is identified with two distinct figures while the reality of many lords or many gods is nevertheless excluded.

### 2 Corinthians 3:17

One final example shows us that the identification of the Lord does not stop with the Father and the Son but extends to the Holy Spirit.[14] In 2 Corinthians 3, the Spirit is a prominent theme: he is "the Spirit of the living God"

---

13. Cox, *By the Same Word*, 147.
14. For what follows see esp. Hill, *Paul and the Trinity*, 143–53, who surveys the major debates and draws out the connection of cloud and Spirit in relation to Exod. 33. See, further,

(2 Cor. 3:3); the Spirit "gives life," unlike the "letter" (3:6); and the glory of the "ministry of the Spirit" exceeds the radiance of Moses (3:8). In this chapter Paul contrasts the fading glory of the old covenant with the greater glory of the new covenant, which we discussed briefly in chapter 1. Continuing this contrast, Paul alludes to the fact that whenever the Israelites read Moses, a veil covers their hearts like the veil covered Moses's luminous face (2 Cor. 3:13–15). Moses would don a veil when he "went in before the LORD [κύριος, *kyrios*] to speak with him" (Exod. 34:34 LXX; cf. 2 Cor. 3:16), and when he spoke with God, the "pillar of cloud would descend" to the tent (Exod. 33:9). With this background in place, Paul continues: "Now the Lord is the Spirit [ὁ δὲ κύριος τὸ πνεῦμά ἐστιν, *ho de kyrios to pneuma estin*], and where the Spirit of the Lord is, there is freedom" (2 Cor. 3:17). Likely drawing figural connections between the "cloud" and the "Spirit" (1 Cor. 6:11; 10:1–2), Paul says the one Lord of Israel is the Holy Spirit.[15] Yet in the same breath Paul distinguishes the Spirit from the Lord, whom he also identifies as Christ (e.g., 2 Cor. 1:2–3, 14; 4:5, 14).

Just as in our previous passages, here we perceive a pattern of both identification and distinction. The Spirit is both the Lord and distinct from the Lord. While in this verse we do not find any commentary on the oneness of Israel's God, we nevertheless find that YHWH is the Spirit of the Father (v. 3) and Jesus Christ (v. 17). While these three are related to and distinct from one another, they are all Israel's one Lord. How is this true, and what should we learn from the pattern itself?

## Grammar of the Common and Proper and the Rule of Redoublement

The basic pattern in the texts we have surveyed is as follows: YHWH, the "Lord," is one *and* at once Father, Son, and Spirit. The OT's basic grammar of God's oneness is nowhere diminished or qualified, neither in its exclusivity nor in its indissolubility. Within the abiding authority of Israel's confession,

---

Rowe, "Biblical Pressure and Trinitarian Hermeneutics," 303–4; Seifrid, *The Second Letter to the Corinthians*, 174–75.

15. Further figural connections might encourage a tight association of "Lord" with the Spirit here, though they are not decisive: the Spirit is the one who writes the Law on hearts (2 Cor. 3:3; Jer. 31:33) because he is the "finger of God" (Luke 11:20; cf. Exod. 8:19; Matt. 12:28) who wrote the law on "two tablets of stone" (Deut. 9:10; cf. Exod. 31:18). See the rudimentary comments in Aquinas, *Commentary on 2 Corinthians* 3.3.111. In any case, even if "Lord" in our text does not refer to the Spirit but to Christ, this is no argument against the Trinity; Basil accepts this meaning and uses it to support his case for the divinity of the Spirit on the basis of common names signifying common being (*Against Eunomius* 3.3).

the NT claims that there are three simultaneously distinct persons who are this one Lord *in the same sense*. Just so, the Lord our God is neither many lords nor many gods. Each person is demarcated from the others by prepositions or personal names, while nevertheless receiving the singular name "Lord," which does not multiply into "Lords." It belongs to Scripture's exactness that it sets forth this paradox within a pattern, for as we shall now see, the pattern normatively discloses the paradox's ultimate coherence. We must now turn to the grammatical "how" behind this pattern and the paradox it communicates.

What draws these various elements together is a grammar that distinguishes between the divine nature and the divine persons. This distinction is found in the way Scripture speaks distinctly about what is *common* to the divine persons and to what is *proper* to each person, requiring of readers a "redoublement" of two corresponding levels of discourse to articulate what is common or essential and what is proper or personal.[16] In short, redoublement functions as follows: whatever Scripture attributes to the divine persons in common signifies and belongs to what all three divine persons possess equally, their singular essence or being; whatever is attributed to one person alone pertains to his unique personal property. As Scott Swain puts it, "*Common predications* are patterns of speech that refer to what the three persons of the Trinity hold in common with each other as the one God. . . . *Proper predications* are patterns of speech that refer to that which distinguishes the three persons of the Trinity from each other within the one God."[17] Speaking about the divine persons requires a twofold form of discourse, a redoublement.

### Ontological and Epistemological Aspects

This distinction between the common and proper is as much ontological as it is epistemological. Indeed, it rests upon some basic ontological affirmations concerning the common divine being and the distinct reality of the persons.[18] Specifically, the Father, Son, and Holy Spirit are one God and not

---

16. Historical background is provided in Halleux, "Personnalisme ou essentialisme trinitaire chez les Pères cappadociens?" An exemplary articulation of this distinction by a contemporary theologian is Emery, "Essentialism or Personalism in the Treatise on God in Saint Thomas Aquinas?"

17. Swain, *The Trinity*, 34–35 (emphasis original).

18. Rowe, "Biblical Pressure and Trinitarian Hermeneutics," 307, recognizes that the above-mentioned pressures necessarily lead us to ontological specification in terms of "being" or "essence." Hahn takes the opposite view: we should express the trinitarian structure of various NT statements *without* concepts like essence or nature because of the "concrete," historical way that God reveals himself (*Theologie des Neuen Testaments*, 2:308). Pitting metaphysical and historical categories against one another is precarious for some of the same reasons that

many gods because they all possess the numerically same being or "essence" (*homoousios*).[19] This is why Scripture observes the pattern of attributing what is common to the three divine persons *in the singular*; there is *one* Lord. Yet there is one Lord *in three persons*. Whereas "Lord" in each of our texts represents what is common among them, their singular and indissoluble being, the personal names of "Father," "Son," and "Holy Spirit" signify what is proper and unique to each person. Nowhere are these personal names shared between the persons like the "essential" names are (like "Lord" in our texts or "God" in others; cf. John 1:1; 20:28; Acts 5:4). What distinguishes the persons, then, is not what is true of them essentially but what is true of them personally. What makes the Father a father is his fatherhood (paternity); what makes the Son a son is his sonship (filiation); and what makes the Spirit or "Breath" (πνεῦμα, *pneuma*) a breath is "breathed-ness" (spiration).[20] These characteristics disclose the relations between the persons and help us understand the divine processions, which we will discuss in chapter 9. From fatherhood and sonship, we discern begetting and begotten, and so forth. Since their divinity is one and the same, the Son has "all" that the Father has (John 16:15) except that which makes him Father—namely, his paternity.[21] The same applies to the Spirit in relation to the Son and the Father. The conceptual distinction in God between essence and person is articulated in the distinction between two kinds of names, common and proper.

As we begin to reflect on how it is that three distinct persons can all have the numerically same being, other biblical pressures constrain our inquiry in salutary ways. God's simplicity is crucial in helping us understand the underlying coherence of these claims while also tempering our expectations about what we can really know. The basic sense of God's simplicity—that God does not have parts—enables us to articulate this numerical identity

---

Barth uses to warn against "untheologically speculative" understandings of God's work *pro nobis* (Barth, *CD* I/1, 420–21; cf. also Emery, *The Trinity*, 91–92). Namely, we must sufficiently confess God's antecedence, his perfect fullness before and apart from his saving outreach. A more extensive response to modern scruples over the conceptuality of "being" is found in Levering, *Scripture and Metaphysics*, 47–74.

19. In affirming this identity of being, various alternatives were excluded by pro-Nicene theologians (cf. Cyril of Alexandria, *Dialogues on the Trinity* 1.405e–410b). For instance, the being of the distinct persons is not that of merely similar essences (*homoiousios*), which would ultimately make them different essences (*heteroousios*) and therefore either different gods or a hierarchy of divine and semi-divine beings. Neither do they have the "same" being in the sense that three human persons have the "same" humanity, which would be a generic sameness.

20. Emery, *The Trinity*, 111–58; Sanders, *The Triune God*, 122–33.

21. See Athanasius, *Letters to Serapion* 3.3.4–3.7.2; Cyril of Alexandria, *Dialogues on the Trinity* 1.409b–d.

by providing us with an essential denial. Because God is indivisibly one, the way each divine person possesses this same being *cannot* be an instance of division in God's being. God is not a block of matter that can be partitioned.

Therefore, each divine person is completely God and not merely part of God. Only if this is the case are all three *one* Lord God: whatever it is to be YHWH belongs fully to the Son, fully to the Father, and fully to the Spirit without any qualitative or quantitative division.[22] As it is applied in trinitarian theology, then, divine simplicity enables us to say that the divine persons are indivisibly one in their common being, while nevertheless *distinct*—not divided—by virtue of their relations to one another.

God's simplicity also reminds us that we have come to the limits of what we can conceive and think, for God is incomprehensible to our finite understanding. However, Scripture's grammar serves an epistemological function by providing guardrails for our contemplation of God's inescapably mysterious life. That is, Scripture's grammar *structures* our thinking about God's unity by giving us two ways of speaking about the same incomprehensible reality so that we avoid contradictions. This is crucial. Distinguishing between person and essence through the practice of redoublement does not give us access to some modality of God's being by which we understand "how" God is one God in three persons. Scripture tells us *that* the three divine persons have the same being and *that* they are distinct (cf. Heb. 11:6) without either confusing these two affirmations or resolving these "that"-statements into a more comprehensive "how"-statement. Any such portrait would require knowledge of *what* God is, which we do not have.[23] In short, Scripture speaks about the Trinity in two distinct, complementary ways. One way speaks to what is common, or essential, and the other speaks to what is proper, or personal. This trains us to recognize and affirm the basic conceptual distinction between essence and person without which we inevitably mistake the sense and referents of Scripture's discourse. The pattern also requires that we employ both levels of discourse to articulate the truth instead of using one, comprehensive level of discourse. The pattern keeps the paradox from dissolving into contradiction.

22. "All that belongs to the Father belongs to the Son except unbegottenness. All that belongs to the Son belongs to the Spirit except begottenness. These things do not divide the essence . . . but they are divided in the [common] essence" (Gregory of Nazianzus, *Oration* 41.9 [PPS 36:152]; cf. *Oration* 31.14).

23. See Basil, *Against Eunomius* 1.14–15. Gregory of Nazianzus: "I am satisfied with the declaration that he is Son and that he is from the Father, and that the one is Father and the other Son; and I refuse to engage in meaningless speculation beyond this point" (*Oration* 20.10 [FC 107:114]). See also Bavinck, *Reformed Dogmatics*, 1:36–38; 2:47–52.

## The Redoublement Rule and Its Significance

These insights give us our fourth rule: *Scripture speaks both of what is common to the Father, Son, and Holy Spirit and of what is proper to each person, reflecting the conceptual distinction between the divine nature and the divine persons. Biblical reasoning discerns this distinction, upholds it, and contemplates the Holy Trinity in its light. Therefore, read Scripture's discourse about God in such a way that its twofold discourse—the common and the proper—is recognized and employed, rather than in a way that collapses the two ways into one. In this way, we learn to count persons rather than natures.*

Drawing out and employing this distinction is arguably the chief contribution of Basil the Great to trinitarian theology. Basil faults Eunomius of Cyzicus for privileging extrabiblical names over the ones given in Scripture and then for not distinguishing between essential and personal names.[24] Reflecting on God's status as the sole creator, Eunomius concludes that "unbegottenness" defines God's essence and so anything that is "begotten," like the Son, cannot be God in the same sense as the Father.[25] Basil acknowledges the truth in this concept—namely, that God's life has no beginning or source—without letting it replace Scripture's primary names, such as "Father" and "Son." After all, unlike unbegottenness, the name Father "has the additional advantage of implying a relation, thereby introducing the notion of the Son."[26] Furthermore, we cannot know what God's essence is, but only what it is *like*.[27] So calling God "unbegotten" merely denies that God comes from something, but in no way exhausts what there is to know about God. Eunomius's chief error is that he operates outside of Scripture's own patterns of discourse, failing to distinguish between essential and personal names.

Basil responds with an eclectic use of available philosophical categories, making a distinction: "Who does not know that some names are expressed absolutely and in respect of themselves, signifying the things which are their referents, but other names are said relative to others, expressing only the relation to the other names relative to which they are said?"[28] Only by using

---

24. For further nuance and context, see Ayres, *Nicaea and Its Legacy*, 191–204; Radde-Gallwitz, *Basil of Caesarea, Gregory of Nyssa, and the Transformation of Divine Simplicity*, 131–37; DelCogliano, *Basil of Caesarea's Anti-Eunomian Theory of Names*.

25. Basil points to Eunomius, *Apology* 7.1–7; 8.1–5.

26. Basil, *Against Eunomius* 1.5 (FC 122:94); cf. Tertullian, *Against Praxeas* 10. Cyril probes at length how "unbegotten" and "Father" do not mean the same thing, how being "unbegotten" is not even particularly unique to God, how it cannot define God's substance, and so forth (*Dialogues on the Trinity* 2.419e–434e).

27. Basil, *Against Eunomius* 1.15.

28. Basil, *Against Eunomius* 2.9 (FC 122:142). The distinction becomes more refined and systematic in Augustine, *The Trinity* 5–7. There, Augustine appropriates Aristotelian categories

both "absolute" and "relative" names, or names designating what is common and what is proper, can we contemplate the mystery: "The divinity is common, whereas fatherhood and sonship are distinguishing marks [ἰδιώματα, *idiōmata*]: from the combination of both, that is, of the common and the unique, we arrive at comprehension of the truth."[29] To understand Scripture's language, we must see that both unbegotten and begotten are true of God, when understood as "proper" or "personal" predicates referring to the Father and the Son, respectively.[30] On the other hand, statements referring to the whole Trinity include those that pertain to all three persons, or those pertaining to "God" when a single divine person (like the Father) is not specifically in view.[31] The redoublement of these distinct ways of speaking keeps us within Scripture's teaching and guards us from error.

The next chapter will explore some of the ways that redoublement is put to use as it is extended into the unity and distinctness of the Trinity's external works. It has sufficed for this chapter to set forth our fifth principle, concerning the unity of the Trinity, and the rule about Scripture's twofold discourse.

## Conclusion

Redoublement is an effect of God's generous pedagogy and therefore a means by which we are led to the vision of Christ's glory. Because God is one and

---

to distinguish between those statements that pertain to God's substance (*ad se* predicates) and those that pertain to the relations between the persons (*ad aliquid* predicates). However, Aristotle categorizes relations as accidents, things that change a substance in some respect, prompting Augustine to adapt the categories to his own purposes. Since God is simple, God has no parts, such as accidents (cf. Cyril, *Dialogues on the Trinity* 2.421c). Therefore, statements about relations internal to God's life belong to the eternal divine "persons." Statements referring to God on the basis of our relation to him in time signify accidents *in us* rather than accidents in God (Augustine, *The Trinity* 5.17). It is a commonplace in the tradition that God's relation to us is not the sort that characterizes finite beings (like our relation to God), for such finite relations always produce or signify change.

29. Basil, *Against Eunomius* 2.28 (FC 122:174). As the translators point out, Basil's terminology is Stoic: "comprehension" (κατάληψις) designates true perception, as opposed to scientific knowledge or mere opinion (see n. 83 of *Against Eunomius* 1 [FC 122:110]). He merely affirms our reliable perception of the truth, all while denying such perception of God's *ousia*, which "transcends not only human beings, but also every rational nature" (*Against Eunomius* 1.14 [FC 122:112]; cf. Gregory of Nazianzus, *Oration* 28.3; 40.5).

30. "Unbegotten" can apply to the Father in the sense that he has no personal source (although, strictly speaking, the Spirit is unbegotten too). There may nevertheless be senses, which require careful articulation, in which "unbegotten" may also apply to the Trinity's common essence because all three persons are eternal and unchanging (cf. Gregory of Nazianzus, *Oration* 39.12; John of Damascus, *On the Orthodox Faith* 1.8).

31. The reason "God" is sometimes predicated of the Father or "Lord" of the Son has to do with appropriations, which we discuss in the following chapter.

three in a unity that transcends our created cognition, God adapts his teaching to us by speaking of himself in two ways: in one way as God is one, and in another way as God is three. God does not give us a singular discourse, perhaps concerning "triunity," but rather two discourses that trace unity and distinction.

Pedagogically, redoublement focuses our attention on personal communion with God. There is a formal parallel here with how we must speak in two ways about the one person of Christ, often called reduplication or partitive exegesis, which chapters 7 and 8 will explore. There we must speak in two ways to acknowledge one person as both God and man. Here, we must speak in two ways to acknowledge three persons as one God. Neither form of twofold speech is, strictly speaking, ultimately concerned with "essences" or "natures" abstractly. Rather, these patterns of speech are concerned with acknowledging persons for what they are: divine, and in only one instance, divine and human. It is impossible for us to plumb the depths of the Father, Son, and Holy Spirit. Instead, only by a continuous cycle of repeating the two manners of speaking may we contemplatively ascend to the truth.

For example, Scripture says that YHWH is robed in light (Ps. 104:2), that the Son is "light" (John 1:9), and that the Father "dwells in unapproachable light" (1 Tim. 6:16). Luminous imagery also characterizes the Father's relation to the Son, who is "the radiance of the glory of God" (Heb. 1:3), and the Spirit's relation to them both (1 Pet. 4:14). An inadequate reading unites these statements without regard for Scripture's twofold pattern, forcing them into a singular pattern. The persons consequently end up being differentiated by their relation to "glory," rather than by their relations to one another. Within Scripture's redoubling or twofold grammar, however, common predicates belong to what the persons have in common: the divine essence. Therefore, Father, Son, and Spirit are all "light" essentially, whereas the Son is "light from light" as the "radiance" of the Father's glory and therefore *homoousios* with the Father.[32] Such judgments help us to see what we saw in chapter 1, that the Father and the Son are *both* invisible.[33] It also instructs us that our hope for the vision of Christ's glory cannot be superseded by hope for some higher glory, for Christ's glory is the same glory that belongs to the Father and the Spirit. If we seek his face, we seek in it the full glory of the Holy Trinity.

---

32. After considering such imagery, Basil concludes that we may even understand such phrases as "begotten light" of the Son and "unbegotten light" of the Father (*Against Eunomius* 2.29; cf. Augustine, *The Trinity* 7.2–3). These compound statements operate simultaneously on both levels, the common and the proper.

33. See pp. 7–11.

# 6

# Varieties of Activities but the Same God

## The Trinity's Inseparable Operations and Scripture's Appropriation

**Principle 5:** The one true and living God is eternally Father, Son, and Holy Spirit, distinct in their relations to one another and the same in substance, power, and glory.

**Rule 5:** The external works of the Trinity are indivisibly one, just as God is one. Whenever Scripture mentions only one or two divine persons, understand that all three are equally present and active, undertaking the same actions in ways that imply their relations to one another. In this way, learn to count persons rather than actions.

**Rule 6:** Scripture sometimes attributes to only one divine person a perfection, action, or name common to all three, because of some contextual fit or analogy between the common attribute and the divine person in question. Read such passages in a way that does not compromise the Trinity's essential oneness and equality.

Our fifth principle concerns the oneness and equality of the three divine persons, which is set before us in Scripture's doubled discourse concerning the Father, Son, and Holy Spirit. There are three persons who are each God, but there are not three gods. The redoublement rule from the previous chapter conforms to Scripture's twofold discourse about the three divine persons, recognizing that everything is one in God except for the relations that distinguish the persons from one another.[1] However, redoublement does not say everything that must be said. There are additional factors in Scripture that pose a challenge to our vision of Christ's glory unless we understand how they cohere with and uphold the Trinity's oneness. What do we do when Scripture says that the Holy Spirit overshadowed Mary, or that the Father elected us in Christ (Luke 1:35; Eph. 1:4)? In such passages, one of the Trinity appears to do something that the other divine persons do not. When it concerns the Trinity's outer works, is God's oneness suddenly that of a common purpose between three independent actors? If so, that seems to conflict with what we have so far discerned concerning God's unity, especially his simplicity. And if not, then why does Scripture speak this way?

To answer these questions, we turn our attention to the indivisibility of the Trinity's external works. The doctrine is traditionally formulated as an axiom: "The external works of the Trinity are undivided" (*opera Trinitatis ad extra indivisa sunt*). This axiom states that the external works of the Father, Son, and Spirit are identical and numerically one. The three persons act as one source of all their external works. Despite being firmly established in the Christian tradition, this doctrine has been as misunderstood as any throughout the last one hundred years.[2] The reasons why this is so mainly have to do with how the doctrine flies in the face of everything we know about three persons acting together. Indeed, it flatly contradicts our intuitions. There are good reasons for this, as we shall see in the conclusion to this chapter. But the doctrine is so well established because it emerges unavoidably from Holy Scripture and the cumulative pressures of Scripture's grammar that we have discussed thus far.

To that end, we must explore the biblical pressures that presuppose the grammar of what we may call the inseparable operations of the Trinity, a doctrine that will require careful exposition because of its counterintuitive nature. We will then proceed to formulate this grammar into our fifth rule, but it is not a rule that stands by itself. The grammar of inseparable operations goes together with the rule of appropriations, which concerns how and why things that are common to the Trinity—like perfections or actions—are sometimes attributed to only one of the persons.[3] We will see how these rules

---

1. Denzinger §1330.

2. For an overview of the doctrine's ancient development and modern decline, see Vidu, *The Same God Who Works All Things*, 52–90.

3. Our discussion of appropriation offers a "mere" account that functions primarily to support our fifth principle concerning the Trinity's unity and equality. Nevertheless, our account is amenable to fuller versions of the practice and so should be useful to all.

complement one another when we apply them to several exegetical examples, preparing the way for our consideration of the person of Christ in the following chapters.

## Pressures of Indivisible Presence and Working

Having just explored the Trinity's oneness of being and distinction of persons, we must see how this oneness coheres with the way that the divine persons act. On occasion in the NT, the Father, Son, and Spirit appear to act distinctly and even disparately. After all, only the Son becomes man, obeys the Father unto death on the cross, dies, and is buried. The Father nowhere obeys the Son, nor does the Spirit die on the cross. The three divine persons therefore seem to have their own jobs and roles. Thus, the NT seems to paint a picture where we can count not only three actors but also three actions. That, however, sits uneasily with the logic of redoublement, in which we may count three persons, but not three gods. How do we proceed?

In fact, one of the chief ways the NT confirms the unity of being belonging to the Father, Son, and Holy Spirit is through the unity of their works. Augustine begins his contemplative pursuit of the Trinity by reflecting on this truth: "Just as Father and Son and Holy Spirit are inseparable, so do they work inseparably."[4] This truth functions regulatively, keeping our attention on the divine persons in their unity and equality rather than parceling out their work independently of one another. Inseparability of working does not abolish the distinctions between the persons, but it reminds Scripture's readers that whenever we perceive one person, the other two divine persons are implicitly present and active. Though we can divide the persons in our thought, they are not and cannot be divided in themselves. This has some structural significance for how we think about and praise the persons of the Holy Trinity: "each one God, if contemplated separately, because the mind can divide the indivisible; the three God, if contemplated collectively, because their activity and nature are the same."[5] Doing justice to Scripture's teaching on the inseparable operations of the Trinity therefore involves an extension of the redoublement rule that recognizes distinct persons acting in one and the same action. As we will see, this doctrine will teach us to count actors without counting actions.

To see how this is so, we must explore how Scripture pressures us to perceive the inseparable presence and working of the Trinity, which in turn confirms their inseparable oneness of being. Four distinct pressures collectively

---

4. Augustine, *The Trinity* 1.7 (WSA I/5:70–71).
5. Gregory of Nazianzus, *Oration* 23.11 (FC 107:139).

encourage us to discern this truth. A brief engagement with representative passages in the Gospel of John, the Gospel of Mark, and 1 Corinthians will bear this out.

### Correlative Presence and Working of Father and Son in John's Gospel

Two conclusions emerge in the following analysis of the Gospel of John. First, God's works disclose his being, so the Trinity's oneness of working confirms their oneness of being. The second point extends this thought: the divine persons' works coincide because the divine persons themselves coincide, being mutually immanent to one another on account of having the same being as God.

Throughout his Gospel, John testifies to the identity of the Father and the Son as the one LORD by confirming this oneness through their works. This shows up explicitly in a wordplay highlighting the depth and mysteriousness of the Son's works. Repeatedly, the Jewish leaders charge Jesus with blasphemy for "making" (ποιεῖν, *poiein*) himself out to be something they believe he is not: "equal" with God (John 5:18; cf. Phil. 2:6), identical to God (John 8:53–59), the Son of God (19:7), and King (19:12).[6] This is precisely how they respond to his claim that he and the Father are one: "You, being a man, make yourself God [ποιεῖς σεαυτὸν θεόν, *poieis seauton theon*]" (10:33). Jesus answers by turning the accusation inside out: "If I am not doing [ποιῶ, *poiō*] the works of my Father, then do not believe me; but if I do [ποιῶ, *poiō*] them, even though you do not believe me, believe the works, that you may know and understand that the Father is in me and I am in the Father" (10:37–38). John toys with the verb ποιέω (*poieō*) to show that Jesus "does" what "makes" his oneness with the Father evident: the "same" works as the Father (John 5:19), works that uniquely befit Israel's God (5:21–27).[7] These many "works" include the "signs" Jesus gives that legitimate his claim to be the Son of God (e.g., 2:1–11; 4:46–54; 6:1–15), sent from the Father (5:36; 9:4).

Jesus's response to the Jewish leaders hints further at the equality of Father and Son: "The Father is in me and I am in the Father" (10:38; cf. 14:9, 20; 16:32; 17:21).[8] This Johannine theme of the Father and the Son's reciprocal existence in one another is linked closely to the love that the Father and the Son share, by which the whole being of each is embraced by the other (15:9–10;

6. On this wordplay, see Baron, "The *Shema* in John's Gospel," 298–300.

7. See Kammler, "Die Theologie des Johannesevangeliums," 93, echoing Schnelle, *Theology of the New Testament*, 663, 669, 711.

8. Schnelle, *Theology of the New Testament*, 665–67. Mutual indwelling also includes the Spirit: see Didymus the Blind, *On the Holy Spirit* 106–9.

17:24, 26). Their mutual immanence is also described as the Son's "abiding" in the Father, which is similar to how the Father and the Son dwell within believers who abide in the Son by keeping his commands (15:5–7, 9–10; cf. 14:23). However, the correlative presence of the Father and the Son transcends anything the disciples have with Jesus.[9] The Son has the *same* life "in himself" that the Father has (5:26), which confirms his words to the Father, "All I have is yours, and all you have is mine" (17:10 NIV; cf. 10:15; 16:15).

The Father and the Son possess everything they have in common, and the mutual immanence theme helps us to see that their works are one of these common possessions. Consider when the Pharisees accuse Jesus of testifying about himself: "You are bearing witness about yourself; your testimony is not true" (John 8:13; cf. 5:31). Jesus responds by pointing out that while he indeed testifies about himself, his testimony is not as independent as appearances may suggest: "In your Law it is written that the testimony of two people is true. I am the one who bears witness about myself, and the Father who sent me bears witness about me" (8:17–18). In so many words, Jesus's self-testimony is simultaneously the Father's testimony. The logic of Jesus's appeal depends on the unity of the Father and the Son and thus of their witness. One of the chief ways the Father testifies about the Son is through the works the Son does: "The works that the Father has given me to accomplish, the very works that I am doing, *bear witness* about me that the Father has sent me. And the Father who sent me has himself *borne witness* about me" (5:36–37 [emphasis added]; cf. 9:4; 10:37–38). The Father's witness to the Son embraces the Son's works and therefore his words: "My teaching is not mine, but his who sent me" (7:16; cf. 5:37–38; 8:26–28; 12:49–50).

Jesus's working and teaching have an irreducible reference to the Father who sent him, so they are inseparable from this relationship. Jesus works, teaches, and testifies, but none of this is isolated or comes merely from himself (John 7:17). Instead, everything the Son is and does is related to his Father. This inseparability of Father and Son surfaces most conspicuously when Jesus speaks to his disciples about revealing the Father: "Do you not believe that I am in the Father and the Father is in me? The words that I say to you I do not speak from myself, *but the Father who abides within me does his works*. Believe me that I am in the Father and the Father is in me, or else believe on account of the works themselves" (14:10–11 AT; cf. 12:44–45).[10] In

---

9. Jesus abides in the Father uniquely, as the "Only-Begotten God who is *in* the bosom of the Father" (John 1:18 AT). This establishes why the Son can reveal the Father: as one who exists in the Father, he has "seen" the Father, whereas no one else has (1:18; 3:11–13; 5:19, 37).

10. Schnelle, *Theology of the New Testament*, 660–69; Aquinas, *Commentary on the Gospel of St. John* 14.3.1887–96. *Pace* Zumstein and his general reticence with ontological judgments,

everything Jesus does and says, the Father also works and speaks. The Son does not merely represent the Father.[11] Instead, the Son and the Father are one such that everything the Son is and does irreducibly refers to the Father as his source who is inseparably present and acting *in* and *with* him. All of this manifests the essential oneness and equality of the Father and the Son.[12] Hence, to believe in Jesus is to believe in the Father and to see Jesus is to see the Father, not because they are indistinct but because they are inseparably one.[13]

### The Indivisibility of Jesus and the Spirit (Mark 3:22-30)

Our second passage concerning inseparable operations indicates that a strong identity and undividedness characterize the work of Jesus and the Spirit. In Mark's Gospel, Jesus teaches about his intimate unity with the Holy Spirit, and therefore with God, in a confrontation with some scribes. By his activity, Jesus has already upset his family, who think "he is out of his mind" (Mark 3:21). Especially in light of Jesus casting out demons, the scribes think matters are worse: "He is possessed by Beelzebul" (3:22). The former accusation rolls off him, but he rebukes the latter as blasphemy, which, as Mark confirms elsewhere, is directed against God (cf. 2:7; 14:62–64; 15:29). In judging his work to be from Satan, Jesus tells them, they have in fact blasphemed the Holy Spirit (3:28–30). Matters may not be quite so obvious to the scribes, but the reader knows that the Spirit is "in"—not merely "upon"—Jesus (1:10). The Spirit and Jesus are so intrinsic to one another that it is difficult to distinguish or demarcate one's work from the other. Somehow, what one says of Jesus's works is also said of the Spirit's works.

The way Jesus responds suggests how we might conceptualize this intimacy of action between the Son and the Spirit. He answers their accusation with a series of parables:

> How can Satan cast out Satan? If a kingdom is divided [μερισθῇ, *meristhē*] against itself, that kingdom cannot be made to stand. And if a house is divided against itself, that house cannot be made to stand. And if Satan has risen up against himself and become divided, he cannot stand, but is coming to an end. But no one can enter a strong man's house and plunder his goods, unless he first binds the strong man. Then indeed he may plunder his house. (Mark 3:23–27 AT)

---

the Son's unity with the Father here is functional only *because* it is first of all an ontological unity of being (*L'Évangile selon Saint Jean*, 2:67–68).

11. Filtvedt, "The Transcendence and Visibility of the Father in the Gospel of John," 109–10.

12. Contra, e.g., Anderson, "Jesus, the Eschatological Prophet in the Fourth Gospel," 280.

13. Rightly noted by Bieringer, "'. . . because the Father Is Greater Than I' (John 14:28)," 196.

Several contrasts are embedded within these parables: Jesus is not part of Satan's "kingdom," but is rather a hostile invader from "the kingdom of God" (1:15); he is not part of Satan's household, but a "mightier" man (1:7) who has bound Satan and begun plundering his house (3:27). But these contrasts smuggle in a comparison that moves from lesser to greater (*a minore ad maius*). If even Satan is not divided against himself, then much more so God is "undivided" (ἀμερής, *amerēs*) or inseparable, because God is "one" (2:7; 12:29). Hence, in a profound sense what Jesus does is undivided from what the Spirit does because Mark has identified their action.

### The Identity of Action between Father and Spirit (1 Cor. 12:4-11)

Our final snapshot is one to which we will return later when applying our rule, but here we must see how it discloses an identity of action between the Father and the Spirit. In 1 Corinthians, Paul points to the deeper unity underneath the diversity of the church's spiritual gifts in ways suggestive for a trinitarian grammar. He begins by laying out the source of the different spiritual gifts: "Now there are varieties of gifts, but the same Spirit; and there are varieties of service, but the same Lord; and there are varieties of activities, but it is the same God who empowers them all in everyone" (1 Cor. 12:4–6). Parallel to three distinct gifts (charisms, service, activities) he names three apparently distinct *sources* that disclose a trinitarian structure: Spirit, Lord, and God.[14] However, he quickly complicates any notion of distinct sources by testifying to their profound unity. The diversity of gifts comes from the "same" (αὐτός, *autos*) Spirit, the "same" Lord, and the "same" God. The repeated use of "same" continues an emphasis found throughout the letter: the oneness of God (8:4–6).[15] Having previously spoken of the "one Lord" and "one God," he now testifies several times about the "one [εἷς, *heis*] Spirit" (12:9, 11, 13). From the one God comes a diversity of gifts that join the members of the one body together, in service of the one God, through one common hope, faith, and baptism (cf. Eph. 4:4–7). Paul's argument moves from unity to diversity and back to unity: the Spirit's diverse "manifestations" are given "for the common good" (1 Cor. 12:7).[16] That

14. In the larger context, one must strain to read this in anything other than trinitarian terms. We may not understand the "Spirit" as other or less than the third person of the Trinity, as if he were a cipher for God's power or a reference to the realm of created spirits, for Paul clearly uses *personal* language: the Spirit works, distributes, and wills (1 Cor. 12:11; *pace* Hahn, *Theologie des Neuen Testaments*, 2:290–91). On the history of these verses in trinitarian disputes, see Radde-Gallwitz, "The Holy Spirit as Agent, Not Activity."

15. Waaler, *The Shema and the First Commandment in First Corinthians*, 391–95.

16. As the immediate context makes clear, not to mention the following chapters, here πρὸς τὸ συμφέρον carries the meaning of a *common* rather than individual "benefit" (cf. 1 Cor. 10:23). So Zeller, *Der erste Brief an die Korinther*, 391.

is to say, from what the Father, Son, and Spirit are in common there proceed gifts that should create an echo of this unity in the church.

In light of Paul's larger rhetorical and thematic interest in how the church's unity reflects God's own oneness, the trinitarian elements become intelligible. While each person of the Trinity is active here, they are not doing different things the way finite, created agents do. Paul blocks any such inference. The activity of the Trinity almost becomes fluid as the passage progresses. We see this most clearly in the overlap or identity of activity between the Father and the Spirit with regard to the activities or "workings" (ἐνέργημα, *energēma*) of the community: "All these are the work [πάντα δὲ ταῦτα ἐνεργεῖ, *panta de tauta energei*] of one and the same Spirit, who apportions to each one individually as he wills" (1 Cor. 12:11 AT). Both the Father and the Spirit distribute the activities (ἐνέργημα, *energēma*) of the church's members, and both empower (ἐνεργεῖ, *energei*) these activities (12:4, 10, 11; cf. Gal. 2:8; 3:5; Eph. 1:11; Phil. 2:13). Neither Father nor Spirit act exclusively, nor do they partition their activity among different parts of the body. Paul's argument is stranger: the Spirit works "all things" *and* the Father "works all things" (1 Cor. 12:6, 11). If the Spirit works all things, then the Father cannot work all things, and vice versa—unless their distinct agencies are compatible with an identity of action.[17] In some sense, then, their working must be the same. If indeed Paul's focus here is on the oneness of God and thus the single source of the church's manifold gifts, then that oneness exerts a pressure on the ways he speaks about the Trinity's working.

## The Grammar of the Trinity's Inseparable Operations

When set alongside one another, we find four distinct pressures in our representative texts, all pushing us to articulate an underlying grammar that draws out their coherence. In John, first, acts reveal being, so that oneness of action manifests oneness of being; second, the Father and the Son dwell within one another, and this mutual immanence characterizes their works as well. Third, Mark identifies Jesus's works as the Spirit's works without suggesting that Jesus withdraws his agency to make room for the Spirit. They are distinct yet undivided. Fourth and finally, Paul argues from the diversity of the church's spiritual gifts to the unity of their source in the Father, Son, and Spirit by explicitly identifying the action of the Father and the Spirit.

17. Augustine, *The Trinity* 1.12, draws similar conclusions vis-à-vis the Father and the Son from 1 Cor. 8:6, Rom. 11:33–36, and John 1:3. Our present text (1 Cor. 12:11) is decisive for others: Didymus the Blind, *On the Holy Spirit* 96–97; Athanasius, *Letters to Serapion* 1.30.4–1.31.1; Basil, *On the Holy Spirit* 16.37; *Against Eunomius* 3.4.

Scripture speaks this way on account of the underlying grammar of the Trinity's inseparable operations: "The Trinity's external works are indivisible, the order and distinction of persons being maintained."[18] According to this traditional element of trinitarian teaching, in any of their acts respecting something other than their intrinsic life, the Father, Son, and Spirit work as one God, but in accord with the structured relations characterizing that life. This doctrine is as notoriously difficult as it is agreed upon, so we must exercise patience and humility if we are to understand it. For our purposes, we need only capture some of the basic grammar emerging from Scripture that feeds the more complex discussions of this doctrine in theological discourse. There are two elements to this grammar that we must briefly unpack.

First, the divine persons' works are inseparable. John gives us a striking example of this sameness: "Truly, truly, I say to you, the Son cannot do anything of himself, but only what he sees the Father doing. For whatever the Father does, these same things [ταῦτα, *tauta*] the Son also does likewise" (John 5:19 AT). In terms of what the Son does, he does not do different things than the Father nor merely similar things to the Father. Rather, he does the same things as the Father. The unity of the Father, Son, and Spirit's working is therefore no mere agreement or harmony of distinct wills or agencies. If matters were otherwise, anyone willing the same thing as God could say "I and the Father are one" (John 10:30).[19] But that is clearly inadmissible. Something uniquely one is in view with the working of the Father, Son, and Holy Spirit. There are three who are working in *one and the same* work, just as there are three who possess one and the same being. For this reason, theologians have often connected the common being of Father, Son, and Spirit to their common working, and vice versa. Didymus the Blind expresses this clearly: "Those who have a single activity also have a single substance. For things of the same substance [ὁμοούσια, *homoousia*] have the same activities, and things of a different substance [ἑτεροούσια, *heteroousia*] have discordant and distinct activities."[20] We may extrapolate some of this logic for the sake of clarity: Because God is one and his power is one, then God's working is

---

18. *Opera trinitatis ad extra indivisa sunt, servato ordine et discrimine personarum.* Along with divine simplicity, this rule is adopted from Scripture early on (see Ayres, *Nicaea and Its Legacy*, 273–301). See, further, Emery, *The Trinity*, 159–97; Beckwith, *The Holy Trinity*, 310–33.

19. Athanasius, *Against the Arians* 3.10.

20. Didymus the Blind, *On the Holy Spirit* 81 (PPS 43:168) (on such inferences to consubstantiality, see Beeley, *Gregory of Nazianzus on the Trinity and the Knowledge of God*, 182–83). Emery summarizes: "The three persons act together, not by the juxtaposition or superimposition of three different actions, but in one and the same action, because the three persons act by the same power and in virtue of their one divine nature" (*The Trinity*, 162).

also one. And since the Trinity's working is one, then their power and being is one. Acts reveal and express being.

Teasing out the relationship between essence, power, and work will help dispel some common misunderstandings about the Trinity's inseparable operations. Insofar as agents act by virtue of their natures, then where there are distinct agents with *distinct sources of power*, there will be distinct works. For instance, three painters could each apply a coat of paint to the same wall using the same bucket of paint, but their actions would still fail to be inseparable and indistinct. We would still have three *separate acts* of painting and therefore three *distinct efficient causalities*, three *different* coats of paint, and so on. It does not matter that their efforts are all coextensive and directed to the same object, for they are fundamentally separate—one painter or one coat of paint could exist without the others. Things are otherwise for the Trinity's inseparable operations. God is one, as is his power, so his working is one. Although there are three divine persons who work (*actiones sunt suppositorum*: actions belong to persons), they all work by virtue of their *one* common divine essence and power, so their working is inseparable and indistinct.[21] This kind of agency is *sui generis*, only like itself. Hence, the Father creates, the Son creates, and the Holy Spirit creates, yet there are neither three creators nor three acts of creation.

Second, although the persons work indivisibly as one God, each person works according to the relations existing between them. We see this as well in John 5:19: "For whatever the Father does, these same things the Son also does likewise [ὁμοίως, *homoiōs*]" (AT). The Son performs the same actions as the Father and does so in a manner that is like (ὁμοίως, *homoiōs*) the Father. This likeness is probably another way of saying that the Son's working

---

21. The metaphysical axiom that "actions belong to persons" (an imprecise rendering of *actiones sunt suppositorum*) is a product of scholastic theologians, though it arguably originates in Aristotle (*Metaphysics* 1.1.981a). Within the distinction between person and nature, this axiom secures a series of vital anthropological, trinitarian, and christological affirmations that we need not address in full. Historically, however, there has been some minor disagreement and confusion about how it intersects with the inseparable operations rule. Without getting too far into the issue, we need only observe the distinction between an active power as *the source by which* (*principium quo*) an actor acts, and the actor as *the source which* (*principium quod*) acts. Michael Gierens summarizes the essential point: "The principle *actiones sunt suppositorum* obtains in the external activity of God, because the three divine persons are actually the actors (*principium quod*) of this activity. However, this principle does not require that in all cases there exist as many actions as there are actors. To wit, if all [the actors] in their property [*Eigenart*] bring forth the action in question by the same *principium proximum quo*, then only one act can result" (Pohle, *Lehrbuch der Dogmatik*, 1:349).

To anticipate the following chapters: the axiom applies in Christology as well. Christ has two natures and therefore two active powers (*principia quo*), but he is only one person because *he*, the Logos incarnate, is the one actor (*principium quod*) of all his acts.

is "from" the Father.[22] There is therefore a distinct order of working between the persons. A relational order is suggested when Jesus speaks of not working "from himself" but from the Father, speaking and doing what he hears and sees from the Father (John 7:17; 14:10). Throughout John's Gospel, the Son does nothing merely from himself (5:30; 8:28); all his actions are "from" the Father (e.g., 5:19, 30; 7:28; 8:42; 12:49).[23] So too the Holy Spirit never acts from himself, but only "from" both Father and Son (14:16–17, 26; 15:26; 16:13–15).[24] These ordered relations receive more careful attention in chapter 9. For now we need only see that the personal properties of the Father, Son, and Holy Spirit clarify their one activity because they tell us about how those three persons work in relation to one another. The three persons all work by virtue of the same divine nature, which they nevertheless possess in relations of giving and receiving.[25] The same therefore holds true for their working: the Father works through the Son and by the Spirit; the Son works from the Father and through the Spirit; and the Spirit works from both Father and Son. Conversely, the Spirit's manner and order of working always refers us back to the Son, who in turn refers us to back the Father.[26] The persons exist and act indivisibly, being and working "from" and "toward" one another. In all

22. Augustine, *The Trinity* 2.3, interprets ὁμοίως as indicating order of working, an interpretation we find plausible in light of the argument we make in chap. 9. Others read ὁμοίως as chiefly another way of stating the unity and equality of the Father and the Son's working: Aquinas, *Commentary on the Gospel of St. John* 5.3.752; Kammler, *Christologie und Eschatologie*, 23–24.

23. Jesus does lay down his life "from himself," but this contrasts with creatures taking it from him (John 10:18).

24. See esp. Gregory of Nyssa, *On Not Three Gods, To Ablabius*: "There is one motion . . . communicated from [ἐκ] the Father through [διά] the Son to [πρός] the Spirit" (NPNF² 5:334; GNO 3/1:48.23–49.1). Because the Spirit's order of working comes last, Gregory goes on to characterize the Spirit as "perfecting" (τελειῶν) the Trinity's external works (NPNF² 5:334; GNO 3/1:50.17).

25. The Trinity's external working "belongs to each person in the same order and interrelation as does the divine nature as the *principium quo* of the activity: passing from the Father to the Son, it arrives at the Holy Spirit through the Son and here stands still. Thus also is the [efficient causality of the Trinity's external works] from the Father through the Son in the Holy Spirit." Scheeben, *Handbuch der katholischen Dogmatik* 2:440n1041; cf. Franzelin, *Tractatus de Deo Trino secundam personas* §12, 213–14. Emery, "The Personal Mode of Trinitarian Action in Saint Thomas Aquinas," argues convincingly that many have overlooked the consequences of this element of Aquinas's trinitarian theology. Namely, by virtue of their *relations to one another* the persons each have a distinct mode of action that follows from their distinct modes of being or subsistence. Hence, on occasion Scripture distinguishes the persons with certain "proper" prepositions that imply their personal properties: the Father really creates *through* the Son (cf. John 1:3) because the Father eternally communicates his being and activity to the Son. But these distinct modes of acting do not yield unique kinds of external activity; the Trinity's external works still have one principle and one effect.

26. Basil, *On the Holy Spirit* 18.47.

these prepositions we find articulated the relations between the persons and therefore the irreducible order intrinsic to their inseparable working, which nevertheless remains hidden to natural reason.

## Rules of Inseparable Operations and Appropriations

To summarize: the distinct divine persons perform one and the same identical works. Parallel to how we must count three persons but not three gods, we may count three actors but not three actions.[27] Just as Scripture's pattern of redoublement pressures us to recognize three persons in one and the same being, so too this pattern of redoublement leads us to recognize distinct persons acting in one and the same action. On this basis, we may therefore formulate our fifth rule as follows: *The external works of the Trinity are indivisibly one, just as God is one. Whenever Scripture mentions only one or two divine persons, understand that all three are equally present and active, undertaking the same actions in ways that imply their relations to one another. In this way, learn to count persons rather than actions.*

This rule is an extension of redoublement into our understanding of the Trinity's economic acts. Rather than seeing distinct actions belonging to each person, or subordinating persons to one another on account of the order within their working, the rule focuses our eyes on the mysterious unity and equality of the Trinity. It trains us to see unity in all the Trinity's external works without denying that these works are intrinsically characterized by the distinct manners of working belonging to the persons. Both aspects emerge in redoublement: for every external work of the Trinity we may speak about and understand it in an essential way as belonging to all three persons indistinctly; we may also speak about and understand these works relatively as belonging to the three persons distinctly, following the order of their relations to one another. When extending redoublement this way into God's outer works, distinctions in manner and order of working concern the persons in relation to one another, whereas the sameness and identity concern the persons in relation to creatures. That said, this rule will soon enough produce frustration without a complementary rule concerning "appropriation," which has already appeared in some of the texts we have considered above. Briefly, we must consider appropriation before applying our rules to some examples in Scripture.

Appropriation describes a phenomenon of biblical discourse when something belonging to all three divine persons in common is attributed to only one

---

27. Marshall, *Trinity and Truth*, 256.

of them, as if it belonged exclusively to that one.[28] Biblical examples include Paul's assertion that Christ is "the power of God and the wisdom of God" (1 Cor. 1:24), and his ascription of particular salvific effects to particular persons: "The grace of the Lord Jesus Christ and the love of God and the fellowship of the Holy Spirit be with you all" (2 Cor. 13:14). In the Apocalypse, the Father is referred to as "the Almighty" (Rev. 1:8; cf. 1:4), which the Apostles' Creed echoes when it also appropriates creation to "God the Father Almighty." Similarly, the Father alone is said to be the one who chose us and predestined us in Christ before the foundation of the world (Eph. 1:4–5). Since these and similar passages speak of actions and perfections that are common to all three divine persons as if they were proper to only one of them, we must treat this phenomenon alongside inseparable operations.

The rule of appropriation may be defined as follows: *Scripture sometimes attributes to only one divine person a perfection, action, or name common to all three, because of some contextual fit or analogy between the common attribute and the divine person in question. Read such passages in a way that does not compromise the Trinity's essential oneness and equality.* Briefly unpacking this rule will suffice to show how it upholds the Trinity's unity.

The key to appropriations is already suggested in and around the word itself. First, if we may play with some connotations in English, appropriations must be *appropriate*, conforming to an objective standard in relation to which their "fit" or suitability becomes apparent. In other words, biblical appropriations function when we see how they befit the reality to which they point us. The Trinity itself is the special object that appropriations seek to manifest. In particular, the personal distinctions between the Father, Son, and Holy Spirit—grasped by us through the properties (*propria*) of paternity, filiation, and spiration—are the basis for determining the appropriateness of an appropriation. Precisely for this reason, then, appropriations draw our minds toward that which is "proper" (*ad proprium*) to the persons. When Scripture attributes to one person something common *as if* it were proper, it is leading us to consider the fit or analogy between the common attribute or action in question and the property of that person. The rule of appropriations thus discerns one small way Scripture focuses our attention on the divine persons.

28. This is admittedly anachronistic, since "appropriation" was developed chiefly in medieval theology. That said, it goes some way toward describing features of biblical language. In our estimation, this doctrine is one of the more complex "rules" historically, in terms of how it has been construed and employed. In keeping with our aim of providing biblical "on-ramps" to these more complicated discussions, our approach to it here is intentionally minimalist in its commitments and entailments. For the medieval background, an analysis of Aquinas's view, and some relevant literature, see Emery, *The Trinitarian Theology of St Thomas Aquinas*, 312–37.

The way we have defined appropriation highlights its regulative function and affords some flexibility in application. What matters most is that the appropriation rule leads us away from compromising what Scripture plainly sets before us: the oneness and equality of the Father, Son, and Spirit in all their irreducible distinctness. The contemplative insights we gather in applying that rule may ultimately be more of an art than a science.

## Putting the Rules to Use

Having seen how our rules concerning the Trinity's inseparable operations and Scripture's appropriation arise from the pressures of biblical discourse, we must now apply them to Scripture. A series of examples will show that these rules help us to avoid improper inferences, focus our attention on the texts in their local and wider contexts, and foster contemplation of Christ's glory that he possesses with the Father and the Spirit.

### God's Power and Wisdom (1 Cor. 1:24)

Our initial example is concentrated on appropriation since we have not given much direct attention to it exegetically. A famous instance of appropriation is when Paul calls Christ "the power of God and the wisdom of God" (1 Cor. 1:24). Because power and wisdom are common possessions of the whole Trinity, not being proper to any one person, we are in the domain of appropriation. How does this rule help unpack Paul's language?

First, the appropriation rule's regulative function reminds us that we must not read this in a way that divides God's substance. The easiest mistake in this regard is to misinterpret this language as functionalizing the persons of the Trinity, making one of them the sole or primary possessor of the perfection or action in question. For instance, if we understood Christ to be the "wisdom" of God in a functional or formal sense, then the Father would not be wise without the Son; Christ would be the wisdom by virtue of which the Father is wise.[29] On account of their perfect unity and equality of being, the Son's existence does not supplement or improve the Father's existence, much less enable the Father's activity like an instrument. The Father does not work "through" the Son like a carpenter works with a hammer or person thinks with their mind. The Father and the Son stand in a mutual relation (Father

---

29. Stated otherwise: the Son would, on this mistaken view, be understood as the "principle by which" (*principium quo*) the Father is wise. Not only would this conflate the Son with the divine essence, it would also begin to suggest that God makes himself. See Augustine, *The Trinity* 6.2.

entails Son, Son presupposes Father), but not a supplementary relation—as if the Father's being somehow lacks something the Son provides. By closing the door on these misinterpretations, biblical reasoning stays on track. Central to our pursuit of Christ's glory is the fact that the Son glorifies the Father by being his perfect representation and image, such that the Son must be everything the Father is, and vice versa, except in the relation of origin that distinguishes them (John 17:10; 16:15). Christ's glory is the Father's glory. If the Son were the wisdom with which God is wise, then the Son *could not* be the perfect image of the Father (Col. 1:15), the "radiance of the glory of God and the exact imprint of his nature" (Heb. 1:3). After all, the perfect image of a Father without wisdom would itself lack wisdom; the radiance of a nature without wisdom would be dim.[30] Because Christ is everything the Father is, in him we see not only Light from Light, but Wisdom from Wisdom.

Second, appropriation bids us to contemplate the Son himself in this passage. In the context of Paul's argument, Christ is the wisdom and power of God in the sense that *in his cross* God has acted with saving wisdom and power, which confounds Greek and Jew alike, and which offers salvation to everyone who believes (1 Cor. 1:24, 30; Rom. 1:16). In order for our minds to be conformed to the realities Paul proclaims, we must first allow this revelation of God's wisdom to confound our usual definitions of wisdom. God's weakness is true power, and the world's power is weak. God's folly is true wisdom, and the world's wisdom is folly. Within these antitheses, why does Paul treat these common nouns, wisdom and power, as if they were proper to the Son? Aquinas answers that Christ is the "power" of God in the sense that God acts "through" him, and that he is the wisdom "of" God in the sense that he is Wisdom from Wisdom, as eternally begotten by the Father (cf. Eph. 3:10; Col. 2:3). As such, Christ transcends all merely human power and wisdom, which is why his cross confounds us.[31] If this is not the immediate concern of Paul's words, it is nevertheless not far from the surface. Because God's wisdom and power are transcendent and incomprehensible, they carve unexpected paths through our midst. Consequently, those who follow Christ cannot do so with a wisdom or power that would lead them away from Christ's cross, perhaps following the wisdom of the world and its "will to power." Such "wisdom" and "power" are all too intuitive because they are all too worldly. The way of a true "son," by contrast, is to take up one's cross and follow Christ, like Paul himself did (1 Cor. 4:9–13). True children of God are those who, like the Son, show forth God's wisdom in the foolishness and shame of living as

---

30. Anatolios, *Deification through the Cross*, 258.
31. Aquinas, *Commentary on 1 Corinthians* 1.3.60–62.

sacrifices, who manifest God's power in their weakness and service of others.[32] As Jesus Christ demonstrates the wisdom and power of God in his humility and service, he shows us what perfect likeness to the Father looks like (cf. Matt. 5:48). Appropriation thus functions in this case to raise our attention to the Son and draw us deeper into his saving economy, showing us what it means to be children of God who live by the Spirit (Rom. 8:14–17).

### Gifts, Ministries, and Activities (1 Cor. 12:4-6)

Our next example takes us back briefly to a passage we have already considered: 1 Corinthians 12:4–6. Here Paul identifies the working of the Father with the working of the Spirit, speaking to their inseparable operations (12:6, 11). There is nevertheless a deep trinitarian structure to the passage.[33] Paul speaks of the Spirit, the Lord (Jesus Christ), and God (the Father) all working to dispense diverse gifts, ministries, and activities, respectively. If the persons work inseparably, then why parcel out these gifts to the distinct persons? It is because there is a fit or analogy between the personal properties of the Father, Son, and Spirit and these diverse gifts. Ernest Bernard Allo explains:

> By appropriation, the "gifts," considered as gratuitous favors, are all related to the Holy Spirit, who is God communicating himself, the great "Gift" of God; considered as "ministries" or "services," they are all appropriated to Christ, the King, the Head who governs the church; and considered as "acts of power" or of energy (not exclusively "miracles"), they all lead back to the Father, the source of all being and all activity, who (through the Word and the Spirit) "works all things in all."[34]

Even though the whole Trinity indivisibly creates and dispenses gifts (for example) to the church, there is a likeness between those gifts and the Spirit's personal property, spiration. In the apostolic preaching, the Spirit is called "gift" or the "gift of God" (e.g., Acts 2:38; 8:20; 10:45; 11:17). God's Spirit is the promised eschatological Gift of the new covenant, poured out abundantly on God's people (Joel 2:28–29). In some way, this shows forth his distinction from the Father and the Son, from whom he is given and from whom he proceeds (which we will discuss in chap. 9). Appropriation thus helps us to

---

32. See here Feldmeier, *Power, Service, Humility.*

33. On which see, e.g., Rowe, "The Trinity in the Letters of St Paul and Hebrews," 49–51.

34. Allo, *Saint Paul: Première Épitre aux Corinthiens,* 323. Traditionally, "Gift" has been understood by many theologians as a proper name of the Holy Spirit, thus signifying his personal property of spiration. For a recent exposition and defense, see Levering, *Engaging the Doctrine of the Holy Spirit,* 51–70.

contemplate the persons in distinction from one another within their inseparable works.

### "The Word Became Flesh" (John 1:14)

The most notorious test of our rules is our Lord's incarnation, which we
will examine in greater depth in the next two chapters. We might think that
surely, here of all places, the Son acts alone. But as Augustine argues, although
the Son alone was born of the Virgin Mary, nevertheless it was the work of
Father, Son, and Holy Spirit inseparably.[35] To explain how, we may employ
redoublement to consider the action essentially with respect to the whole
Trinity and then personally with regard to the mutual relations between the
persons. Doing so employs both inseparable operations and appropriation.

Describing the incarnation calls for two manners of speaking. In one way,
we see the persons acting in accordance with their distinct modes of acting.
The Father sends the Son and prepares a body for him (Gal. 4:4; Heb. 10:5) in
keeping with his paternity: the Father does not receive his being from another,
so he does not act from another. The Son's being-sent is in keeping with his
filiation, as is his self-emptying by taking the "form of a servant," his birth
from the seed of David according to the flesh (Phil. 2:6–7; Rom. 1:3). Being
born as man, the Son displays his filial existence in our flesh. The form his
sonship takes in his human existence is perfect devotion, loving obedience,
and complete dependence. He thus acts "from" the Father and with reference
to him. The Son's incarnation also includes the Holy Spirit, in keeping with
the Spirit's spiration from both Father and Son. The Spirit thus overshadows
Mary and brings her womb to fruition. Just as the Spirit broods over the
waters of creation and over the wilderness until they bring forth fruit (Gen.
1:2; Deut. 32:11; Matt. 1:20; Luke 1:35), so he brings the Father's sending of
the Son to fruition. However, if we left our description of the incarnation
here, we might be in danger of describing three actors and three actions,
thereby transgressing the inseparable operations rule. And while that would
certainly be more intuitive for us, it would not for that reason be more faithful to divine teaching.

A second pass over the incarnation enables us to see the incarnation as
an indivisible act of the whole Trinity. Though it involves all three actors,
the incarnation remains one action rather than three. The Father sent (Rom.
8:3); the Son came (John 6:38); the Spirit effected conception (Luke 1:35)—
yet each verb names the same single act of incarnation. While it is true that

---

35. Augustine, *Sermon* 52.6–8. See, further, Polanus, *Syntagma theologiae christianae* 6.13
(364a–g); Legge, *The Trinitarian Christology of St Thomas Aquinas*, 104–11.

the Father prepares a body for the Son, it is also true that the Son and the Spirit perform this same act. The same is true of the Spirit overshadowing Mary's womb; this act belongs equally to the Father and the Son. All things are made through the Son (John 1:3), and since the body prepared for him and conceived in Mary's womb is a creature, then it is not outside of the singular creative activity belonging to all three divine persons. When Scripture speaks of the *Father* preparing this body, or the *Spirit* bringing to fruition Jesus's conception, these are appropriations.

However, it is not appropriation when Scripture says the "Word became flesh" (John 1:14), or that the Son "emptied himself, by taking the form of a servant" (Phil. 2:7). This is *proper* to the Son, because only the Son is incarnate. A major reason for this is that the incarnation results in the hypostatic union, which we explore in the next chapter. Though the Father, Son, and Holy Spirit all create the humanity of the Son and join it to the Son, only the Son assumes it into his own person. This inseparable act of the Trinity concludes or "terminates" in the person of the Son alone. In a faintly analogous sense, the incarnation of the Son is like a pitch that the whole Trinity throws but only the Son catches. Redoublement captures this twofold aspect of the Son's assumption of human flesh well: the *principle of assumption* is the divine nature that belongs to the whole Trinity, specifically as it exists in the Son, who assumes human nature, but the *terminus of assumption* is the Son alone.[36] Therefore, the Trinity indivisibly creates Christ's humanity and unites it to the Son, but only the Son assumes it as his own.

### Divine Teaching, Again

We may conclude with one final example that sets biblical reasoning within the context of the Trinity's inseparable operations. When we considered the setting for biblical reasoning in chapter 3, we saw that the inseparable Trinity is responsible for John's prophecy in the Apocalypse. The whole book comes to John as "the revelation of Jesus Christ, which God gave him" (Rev. 1:1). And each letter to the seven churches is *simultaneously* spoken by the Holy Spirit (Rev. 2:7, 11, 17, 29; 3:6, 13, 22) and by Jesus (2:1, 8, 12, 18; 3:1, 7, 14). Synthesizing these details with redoublement, we can understand divine teaching as an indivisible work of the whole Trinity (essentially) that allows for an

---

36. Aquinas, *STh* III.3.1–2; Turretin, *Institutes of Elenctic Theology* 13.4. Traditionally, theologians agree that in this one instance, the Trinity's inseparable works terminate on one person (the Son). However, there is disagreement about whether there are other instances in which common works of the Trinity terminate on particular persons (like the Spirit appearing in the form of a dove). See, for instance, Polanus, *Syntagma theologiae christianae* 4.2 (236–37); Turretin, *Institutes of Elenctic Theology* 3.27.20.

order of working between the persons (personally). The message that comes from the Father through Jesus is simultaneously spoken by the Spirit, so that the text gives no hints about where Jesus's activity ends and the Spirit's begins. Nor is there any suggestion that one person's teaching is different in content or extent from the others'; their teaching is numerically one and identical. Yet there is clearly an order between the persons, which is visible especially in John's Gospel. The Holy Spirit testifies to Christ just as the Father does (John 15:26). Jesus says of the Spirit, "He will guide you into all the truth, for he will not speak from himself, but as much as he hears he will speak, and he will declare to you what is to come" (John 16:13 AT). The Spirit takes "all" that the Son has in common with the Father and declares it to us (16:14–15). Because the Father, Son, and Spirit work indivisibly, the Spirit's work "makes it impossible to separate the proclaiming Jesus from the proclaimed Christ. . . . The gap between past and present is abolished."[37] When we read by the Spirit's illumination, we see Light from Light in Light. Yet what we see by faith is one glory, not three. The Trinity's inseparable operations therefore remind us that the God who acts in Scripture is not merely acting in a time long past but performs these same works in the present. Thereby we have fellowship with the apostles through fellowship with the same God: what they have "heard" and "seen," we now hear and will indeed see (1 John 1:3).

## Conclusion

Being drawn by the Spirit into the teaching of Christ, which he has from the Father, requires us to perceive Scripture's patterned discourse and learn how it trains us to contemplate the Lord at ever greater heights. But at times, the heights can be dizzying. The doctrine of inseparable operations in particular scandalizes modern ears, often because people fail to place it within God's larger pedagogical purposes with Scripture. One of the ways we typically distinguish human persons from each other is by distinguishing their actions. For instance, this book is coauthored, but it is a product of two distinct acts of writing. There is no getting around this. Those personally familiar with the authors will be able to pick out one voice in distinction from the other because there are two voices, two writers, and two writings that come together as one book. The "oneness" of the writing activity here is less a unity of agency than a unity of product. Because of common experiences like this, it seems counterintuitive to say we cannot do something similar with the Trinity's external works. And this raises a question: Why does the

---

37. Schnelle, *Theology of the New Testament*, 707.

rule of inseparable operation focus so intently on the divine persons' unity and equality?

The rule's emphasis on unity has nothing to do with privileging God's one essence over the three divine persons. It is not as if when we think of the Trinity working the *same* works we think of the divine persons more truly than when we meditate on their mutual fellowship or distinct modes of agency. As Gregory of Nazianzus reminds us, we must not "honor the unity of God more than is appropriate."[38] The truth is, we must think of Father, Son, and Spirit in *both ways* to think of them in conformity with Scripture. To the extent that this rule accents divine unity, then, it is because of our natural tendency to think of the Father, Son, and Spirit like three human people contributing to the same project. If the rule is counterintuitive, this is because our intuitions about three persons working together mislead us when it comes to the *Trinity's* works. The inseparable operations rule disciplines our understanding and speech in the direction of God's incomprehensibility and mysteriousness so that we do not sacrifice the Trinity's essential oneness and equality. Speaking of the divine persons as working the same works, as each fully God, and as distinct from and unconfused with one another "does not so much lead us to an easy imagining of their diversity and unity as it defers our comprehension and draws our minds to the constantly failing (even as constantly growing), character of our interpretation of what is held in faith."[39] We thus balance ourselves between the limits of our understanding (and imagination) and the patterns of Holy Scripture's discourse.

If we have trouble with this balancing act, Augustine counsels us to purify our minds with faith, to grow in virtue, and pray "with the sighs of holy desire."[40] This is no spiritualized hand-waving. Augustine's counsel suggests that the inseparable operations of the Trinity are perceived contemplatively, from the "inside" of the Trinity's working, as the Spirit draws us into the teaching of Christ and the Father here and now. And this calls us back to where we began: biblical reasoning takes place in the presence of God. It therefore depends on and is answerable to God, whose face we may seek only in faith, humility, and prayer.

---

38. Gregory of Nazianzus, *Oration* 20.7, in Daley, *Gregory of Nazianzus*, 101.
39. Ayres, *Nicaea and Its Legacy*, 297.
40. Augustine, *The Trinity* 4.31 (WSA I/5:184).

# 7

# One and the Same

## The Unity of Christ and Scripture's Communication of Idioms

**Principle 6:** One and the same Lord Jesus Christ, the only begotten Son of the Father, exists as one person in two natures, without confusion or change, without division or separation.

**Rule 7:** The eternal, divine Son is the sole subject of everything Jesus does and suffers. Christ is one person, one agent, one "who." Therefore, in reading Scripture's witness to Christ we must never divide Christ's acts between two acting subjects, attributing some to the divine Son and others to the human Jesus as if there were two different people.

**Rule 8:** Since Christ is a single divine person who subsists in both a divine and a human nature, Scripture sometimes names him according to one nature and predicates of him what belongs to the other nature. Scripture ascribes divine prerogatives to the man Jesus, and human acts and sufferings to the divine Son. So read Scripture in a way that recognizes and reproduces this paradoxical grammar of christological predication.

In the previous chapters we have explored principles and rules that guide our pursuit of God's face in Scripture as we seek the vision of Christ's glory through his commissioned prophets and apostles. We saw in the last two chapters that reckoning with the identity of Jesus leads us to see that he is, with the Father and the Spirit, the one Lord of Israel. The intellectual difficulties this presents are not restricted to "how" the one God can be three persons. As we saw, this is a question Scripture refuses to answer because it transcends our comprehension. Instead, Scripture's regulative grammar of redoublement shows us that this truth, which is incomprehensible, is nevertheless not incoherent. However, the intellectual difficulties are compounded because it is a human being, a Jewish man from Nazareth, who is teaching us all these things and who claims this divine identity without compromising or undermining his humanity. What should we make of the fact that Jesus is both God and man? What sense does God pressure us to make of it in his Word, and how does this truth further nurture faith's understanding and quest for the vision of Christ's glory?

A preliminary answer to this question may be found in the characteristic paradoxes surrounding Christ. These paradoxes are found in Scripture, as we will see, and for this reason they spill over into hymnody. A line in a beloved hymn might stop you short, not because of archaic words or stretched syntax, but because it seems to utter an absurdity or even blasphemy. Consider the following lines from Charles Wesley's classic hymn, "And Can It Be":

> 'Tis myst'ry all: th' Immortal dies:
> Who can explore His strange design?

This couplet claims to set forth a mystery, or "strange design." But is "mystery" or "strange" just a polite word for "contradiction"? How is it not nonsense to sing "th' Immortal dies"?

This chapter and the next are about how it can be that such bracingly paradoxical statements are not nonsense. Instead, such paradoxes combine and crystallize Scripture's central claims about Christ. If all that the Bible says about Christ is true, then Wesley is right: the immortal died.

More than that, these paradoxical statements gesture toward a truth that undergirds our whole pursuit of Christ's glory. According to Henri de Lubac, paradoxes are one way mysteries express themselves: "Paradox is the search or wait for synthesis. It is the provisional expression of a view which remains incomplete, but whose orientation is ever towards fullness."[1] It is part of Scripture's exactness to be full of paradoxes, especially surrounding the incarnate Son of God, who is the paradox of paradoxes. Jesus is God as man, man as God, infinite difference within identity. The fullness toward which Scripture's christological paradoxes orient us is the invisible fullness that dwells in Christ

---

1. De Lubac, *Paradoxes of Faith*, 9.

bodily (Col. 2:9). The pedagogical significance of these paradoxes is disclosed in how they signal ineffable fullness, which the saints will only behold when we behold Christ's glory in the beatific vision. Because Jesus leads us to the transfigured vision of himself, it is imperative to feel the pedagogical pressure of these paradoxes so that our faith is indeed oriented to sight. After all, Jesus is not only the life and the truth but also the *way* (John 14:6). Jesus alone is the way faith travels to vision, and he is the vision faith travels toward. Therefore, to feel the pressures of Scripture's christological paradoxes, we must learn the larger grammar they presuppose—a grammar that discloses how Christ is both the way to beholding God's fullness and the fullness that we will behold. This chapter and the next therefore consider the grammar of the mystery of Christ, attending to his incarnation and the unity of his person. The goal in both chapters, as throughout the book, is to fix our attentions on and seek to understand *the* Way who leads faith to sight.

This chapter sets forth our sixth principle, which concerns the hypostatic union: *One and the same Lord Jesus Christ, the only begotten Son of the Father, exists as one person in two natures, without confusion or change, without division or separation.* This truth is exhibited in two further rules for biblical reasoning, which help fix faith's attention on Jesus: the unity of Christ and the communication of idioms (*communicatio idiomatum*).[2] As we will see, the unity of Christ is a simple, relatively commonsensical observation about Jesus. Yet this simple observation holds major metaphysical entailments as well as far-reaching consequences that shape Scripture's testimony to Christ and therefore our own. One of those consequences is the "communication of idioms," which is a way of speaking about Christ that produces such striking paradoxes as "th' Immortal dies." We explore these two rules together because they complement and imply each other. The communication of idioms works out implications of, and mines theological and linguistic resources afforded by, the ontological unity of Christ.

This chapter will proceed in four steps, each treating the principle and its two accompanying rules in tandem. First, we will explore Scripture's pedagogical pressure that impels us to formulate our sixth principle and both rules that derive from it. Second, we will discuss the theological grammar of the hypostatic union. Third, we will probe the conceptual substance, implications, and coherence of the two rules pertaining to Christ's one-in-two-ness. Fourth, we will demonstrate the exegetical payoff of both rules by discussing a series of Christ's saving acts narrated in the Gospels.

---

2. Translations of the Latin phrase vary. Instead of "idioms," some say "attributes" or "properties."

## New Testament Pressure to Confess Christ's Paradoxical Unity

We will now survey the pressures by which Scripture constrains us to confess the mysterious union of divinity and humanity in the person of Christ. This section will first consider how Hebrews and Paul ascribe a striking diversity of predicates to Christ, which diversity attests his divine unity. We will then examine scriptural passages that explicitly attest Christ's act of becoming incarnate. Finally, we will discuss passages that exemplify the communication of idioms: some that predicate humanity of God the Son and others that ascribe divinity to the man Jesus.

### Hebrews' Opening Witness to the Divinity and Humanity of the Single Son

We begin with the divine unity of Christ. This unity is an ontological reality with a range of grammatical implications. Consider how Hebrews 1:1–4 attributes wildly diverse characteristics, actions, and experiences to one and the same subject, the divine Son incarnate.[3]

> Long ago, at many times and in many ways, God spoke to our fathers by the prophets, but in these last days he has spoken to us by his Son, whom he appointed the heir of all things, through whom also he created the world. He is the radiance of the glory of God and the exact imprint of his nature, and he upholds the universe by the word of his power. After making purification for sins, he sat down at the right hand of the Majesty on high, having become as much superior to angels as the name he has inherited is more excellent than theirs. (Heb. 1:1–4)

The whole paragraph speaks of one and the same Son, not of two different sons. This one Son is the means by which God has spoken to us in these last days. Or we could more literally say "the location": God has now spoken to us "in the Son" (1:2; ἐν υἱῷ, *en huiō*). God's final word comes to us in the person of his Son.[4] Two relative clauses that follow keep our focus pinned to this Son: he is the one whom God appointed heir of all things and also the one through whom he created the world (1:2). Though English translations typically start a new sentence in verse 3, the "He" there is another relative pronoun, continuing

---

3. For a fuller discussion of the seven predicates that Heb. 1:2–4 ascribes to Christ, including warrant for some of the exegetical decisions asserted or presupposed below, see Jamieson, *The Paradox of Sonship*, 51–59.

4. As Webster, "One Who Is Son," 79, observes, "In the case of the prophets, ἐν bore an instrumental sense; here its sense is more local. One might, perhaps, say 'in and as,' to try to catch the sense that God's act of revelation can properly be attributed not only to θεός but also to υἱός, who is, by consequence, not simply its instrumental cause."

the sentence by ascribing uniquely divine traits to this Son. Namely, the Son is the personal effulgence of the Father's intrinsic glory and the full communication of his essence (1:3). Existing as only God does, he does what only God can: he conserves and preserves the existence of all things (1:3). Next, Christ is the one subject of a series of verbs: "After making . . . he sat down . . . having become . . ." (Heb. 1:3–4). The first participle tells us what Christ did before he sat down on God's throne: he made purification for sins, obtaining his people's permanent freedom from sin's defiling consequences. The second participle tells us a consequence of Christ's session on God's throne. By sitting where only God may, he obtained a dignity that infinitely outmatches that of any angel.

Grammatically speaking, God is the subject of verses 1 and 2. He is the one who spoke then and now. And yet, through the relative clauses that follow, Christ becomes the conceptual subject of this paragraph before he becomes its grammatical subject in verse 3, which he remains through verse 4.

Following the initial assertion that God spoke through his Son, this paragraph offers seven further statements about Christ. Some of these depend conceptually on his humanity. For instance, Christ's act of purifying sins encompasses his death, resurrection, and ascension to the Holy of Holies in heaven. And since Christ's acts of sitting and becoming follow his act of purifying, they preserve an implicit reference to his (now-resurrected) humanity. Further, in light of its echo of Psalm 2:8, God's act of appointing Christ the heir of all things took place upon his enthronement in heaven (Heb. 1:2). So, four of these predicates—purifying, sitting, becoming, being appointed—presuppose Christ's incarnation and present possession of a human nature. But what about the other three? As we briefly discussed above, the author also designates Christ as divine (Heb. 1:3). The same one who is the radiance of God's glory made purification for sin by his death, resurrection, and ascension. The same one who created and upholds the universe also received that universe as his messianic inheritance. The upshot of this grammatical and conceptual analysis of Hebrews 1:1–4 is that these all describe the same person—the single divine Son. Underlying and ultimately verifying all seven predicates applied to Christ are not two actors, not two agents or characters, but one.

### Diversity of Predicates and Unity of Subject in Paul and the Gospels

What we perceive in especially concentrated form in the opening of Hebrews is consistently the case throughout the NT. Although the content of the NT's statements about Christ varies wildly, none of its authors divide him into two subjects. As Rowan Williams observes with reference to Paul, "The earliest surviving written sentences to have 'Jesus' or 'Christ'/'the anointed,' or 'the Lord Jesus' as their subject . . . exhibit a bewildering variety of register or idiom within a very brief space." In what does this bewildering variety consist? "We may move rapidly from sentences of a kind that could apply to any member of the human race to other sentences stating or implying things that could not normally be said of a human subject."[5]

To illustrate: Speaking of one and the same person, Jesus, Paul can write that he was "born of woman," like all of us (Gal. 4:4). He can name Jesus's human descent: from David (Rom. 1:3) and, more broadly, from Israel (Rom. 9:5) and therefore Abraham (Gal. 3:16). As a human being, Jesus died for our sins, shedding his blood for us (1 Cor. 11:23–26; 15:3). And yet, as we saw in chapter 5, Paul also calls this same man the "one Lord" whom Israel confesses in the Shema (1 Cor. 8:6; cf. Deut. 6:4). Additionally, Paul frequently applies to Jesus OT passages that explicitly refer to the one true God of Israel (e.g., Joel 2:32 in Rom. 10:13; Isa. 45:23 in Phil. 2:10–11).[6]

In the Gospels too we observe a stunning diversity of predicates ascribed to the same subject. On the one hand, Jesus was born (Luke 2:7), obeyed his parents and learned and grew up (Luke 2:51–52), taught and traveled (Matt. 4:17, 23), grew weary (John 4:6), slept in a boat (Mark 4:38), wept (John 11:35), suffered humiliation and torture (Mark 15:15–24), was crucified, died, and was laid in a tomb (Luke 23:33, 46, 53). On the other hand, he calmed a storm (Matt. 8:26), walked on water (Matt. 14:26), healed the sick (Mark 1:31), raised the dead (John 11:43–44), forgave sins (Matt. 9:1–8), and claimed to preexist the patriarchs (John 8:58).[7]

Regardless of how one assesses or accounts for this diversity of predicates, they all pertain to the same acting subject. The point is so obvious that we might easily miss it. Whatever Paul says about Jesus, there is only one Jesus that he is talking about. This is what we mean by calling the unity of Christ a simple, even commonsensical, observation. Everything the NT says about Jesus Christ, it says about the *one person* who bears that name. Given all that the NT says about Jesus, this is no mere tautology.

### Christ's Unity and the Incarnation

Another important strand of passages that pressure us to confess Christ's unity are those that explicitly narrate the act of incarnation. Famously and

---

5. R. Williams, *Christ the Heart of Creation*, 47.

6. On this see Bauckham, *Jesus and the God of Israel*, 186–91; and Capes, *The Divine Christ*.

7. For a fuller rendering of both lists, and an astute probing of their theological coherence, see Gregory of Nazianzus, *Oration* 29.18–20 (PPS 23:85–88).

among the most explicit is John 1:14: "And the Word became flesh and dwelt among us, and we have seen his glory, glory as of the only begotten from the Father, full of grace and truth" (AT).[8] The one who became flesh is none other than the eternal Word, who was with God in the beginning and is God (John 1:1). The one who came walking toward John the Baptist, such that John could point to him physically as much as verbally, is the one who not only exceeds John but precedes him, and that eternally (John 1:15, 19).

Paul states essentially the same point in a variety of ways. In an economic idiom: "For you know the grace of our Lord Jesus Christ, that though he was rich, yet for your sake he became poor, so that you by his poverty might become rich" (2 Cor. 8:9). It is the one who was eternally, divinely rich who became poor—that is, he became a mortal man—to enrich us.[9] In the language of mission, of sending someone somewhere to accomplish something: "But when the fullness of time had come, God sent forth his Son, born of woman, born under the law, to redeem those who were under the law, so that we might receive adoption as sons" (Gal. 4:4–5).[10] The Son who existed with the Father before he was sent is the one whom the Father sent and who received human life from the mother who bore him. To commend humility, by tracing the arc of the greatest conceivable self-abasement: "Have this mind among yourselves, which is yours in Christ Jesus, who, though he was in the form of God, did not count equality with God as something to be used for his own advantage, but emptied himself, by taking the form of a servant, being born in the likeness of men" (Phil. 2:5–7 AT). The one who has always existed in the form of God, and is God's equal by nature, is the one who took to himself human nature, "the form of a servant."[11] The taking is the emptying. It is by becoming human that he became abased, given the infinite contrast in dignity

---

8. Schnelle, *Theology of the New Testament*, 639, observes that, along with Heb. 2:14, this is the clearest affirmation of the incarnation in the NT.

9. Thrall, *A Critical and Exegetical Commentary on the Second Epistle of Paul to the Corinthians*, 2:532–34, endorses this "traditional interpretation."

10. For Gal. 4:4 as incarnational see, e.g., D. A. Campbell, "The Story of Jesus in Romans and Galatians," 119; Hays, *The Faith of Jesus Christ*, 96–97; Gathercole, *The Preexistent Son*, 28–29; Bates, *The Birth of the Trinity*, 116.

11. In the vast chorus of scholarly commentary on this passage, a majority argue that the two phrases "in the form of God" and "equality with God" describe the Son's preincarnate existence as God, on par with the Father. See, e.g., the concise survey in Martin and Nash, "Philippians 2:6–11 as Subversive *Hymnos*," 114–16. Particularly influential is Wright, *The Climax of the Covenant*, 56–98. Whether the preexistent Son already possesses equality with God must be determined on contextual grounds. In addition to the contextual arguments for Christ's divine preexistence in Phil. 2:6–7 offered by Wright, also worth highlighting are Bockmuehl, *A Commentary on the Epistle to the Philippians*, 126–38; Oakes, *Philippians*, 193–96; Hellerman, *Reconstructing Honor in Roman Philippi*, 129–48; Hill, *Paul and the Trinity*, 89–97; Martin and Nash, "Philippians 2:6–11 as Subversive *Hymnos*," 114–23. The concept of "form"

and glory between the form of God in which he always is and the form of a servant which he took.[12]

To return to Hebrews, the author makes explicit the purpose and fittingness of the Son's incarnation, attributing it to the Son's agency: "Since therefore the children share in flesh and blood, he himself likewise partook of the same things, that through death he might destroy the one who has the power of death, that is, the devil, and deliver all those who through fear of death were subject to lifelong slavery" (Heb. 2:14–15). What we are by nature, he became by will.[13] Note the intensified reference to a single subject: "he himself" and no other. The one of whom all the divine prerogatives of Hebrews 1:3 are fitting, the one who upholds the universe by his powerful word, is the same one who entered our frail and fraught human condition in order to transform it forever.[14]

Employing a variety of metaphors and conceptual idioms, all these passages attest an act or event. Being born into the world is not the kind of event that we mere humans can ascribe to our own agency. To say that the Logos became flesh is to say that the Logos precedes his own human existence and history. Hence, God became a man. Conceptually, if not always grammatically, God the Son is the subject, and "became a human being" is the predicate. These passages all start from and presuppose what the Son is; they all add and assert what he became. Incarnation does not convert what is divine into what is human but instead unites what is human to one who is divine. Whatever other human attributes or acts John, Paul, and the author of Hebrews ascribe to Jesus, these explicit incarnational passages tell us that all those acts and attributes belong to the one who is God and became a man. This one selfsame subject united a human nature to himself in such a way that all its characteristics, capacities, and limits became truly *his*.[15] The incarnation causes new

---

(μορφή) is broader than, but includes, what theology has traditionally intended with the language of "nature."

12. As Barclay, *Paul and the Power of Grace*, 123, concisely comments on Phil. 2:6–11, "Nearly all scholars agree that this passage (alongside Gal 4:4, 2 Cor 8:9, and Rom 8:3) indicates an act of incarnation, whereby Christ takes on the human condition and participates in the limitations and vulnerabilities of human nature."

13. So Bruce, *The Epistle to the Hebrews*, 78n55.

14. For further exegesis of Hebrews' explicit and implicit testimony to the Son's incarnation, see Jamieson, *The Paradox of Sonship*, 77–85.

15. So Athanasius, *Against the Arians* 3.31 (NPNF[2] 4:410): "And on account of this, the properties of the flesh are said to be his, since he was in it, such as to hunger, to thirst, to suffer, to weary, and the like, of which the flesh is capable; while on the other hand the works proper to the Word himself, such as to raise the dead, to restore sight to the blind, and to cure the woman with an issue of blood, he did through his own body. And the Word bore the infirmities of the flesh, as his own, for his was the flesh; and the flesh ministered to the works of the godhead, because the godhead was in it, for the body was God's."

realities to be true of this one subject; it does not add another, human subject alongside the original, divine one.[16] In sum, the NT employs a variety of strategies to emphasize the ontological unity and singularity of Christ's person. Because he receives all sorts of predicates, and he does and suffers all sorts of things, we must recognize that he is one acting subject (and not many).

## Ascribing Humanity to God the Son and Divinity to the Man Jesus

Another way to perceive Scripture's pressure concerning Christ's paradoxical unity is to consider passages that, whether implicitly or explicitly, ascribe humanity to God the Son or ascribe divinity to the man Jesus. To anticipate the conceptual discussion that follows in the next section, we can recognize these two types of passages as articulating "ascending" and "descending" christological paradoxes.[17]

To begin, we can simply glance back at the incarnational passages we just considered. Speaking of the Word who not only was with God in the beginning but is himself God, John 1:14 tells us, "And the Word became flesh and dwelt among us, and we have seen his glory." In this verse, "Word" is an ascription of divinity, a title that names him as God. What we already know about the Word from the preceding context constrains us to consider him divine in the fullest sense. Further, John 1:14 tells us that this divine Word became a human being. Because of this act, all that is true of the human being Jesus of Nazareth is true of God the Son. As Bruce Marshall observes, "John takes the Logos as subject and ascribes 'flesh' to him."[18] Similarly, in Philippians 2:6–7, it is the one who exists in the form of God (ἐν μορφῇ θεοῦ ὑπάρχων, *en morphē theou hyparchōn*) who emptied himself by taking the form of a servant—that is, "being born in the likeness of men." While the subject of the main clause is a bare relative pronoun, the prepositional phrase before the verb characterizes and identifies just who it is that emptied himself by assuming a human nature. Paul identifies Jesus as divine and ascribes to him the act of the incarnation and its logical entailments: self-abasement and servitude.

An even sharper instance of "descending" communication of idioms is found in 1 Corinthians 2:8: "None of the rulers of this age understood this,

---

16. As we argued in chap. 4, this implies no change or mutability in God. As we will explore in the next chapter, the change is true of the Son *with respect to* his human nature. For worthwhile discussions of how the incarnation coheres with divine immutability, see Weinandy, *Does God Change?*; Duby, *Jesus and the God of Classical Theism*.

17. In other words, we will begin with what one scholar calls "descending" communication of idioms and then discuss its "ascending" counterpart. See Strzelczyk, *Communicatio Idiomatum*, 21–23. See also the discussion in McCosker, review of *Communicatio Idiomatum*.

18. Marshall, *Trinity and Truth*, 111.

for if they had, they would not have crucified the Lord of glory."[19] Here, of course, the grammatical subject is "they," the rulers of this age. But if we focus on Christ, as we mean to throughout this book, then we can rephrase the last clause, with no loss or distortion, so as to highlight its christological claim: "The Lord of glory was crucified." What does Paul mean by naming Christ "the Lord of glory"? The biblical phrases "the glory of the LORD" (e.g., Exod. 16:7; Num. 14:10), "God of glory" (Ps. 29:3), and "king of glory" (Ps. 24:7–10) triangulate the phrase's meaning. By calling Christ "the Lord of glory," Paul identifies him as the one who possesses the unique, unshareable divine glory (cf. Isa. 48:11). And Paul asserts that this divinely glorious Christ was crucified. Paul predicates an inescapably human fate of the divine Lord. Paradox? Yes. Contradiction? No. Why? Because it was precisely by becoming incarnate that the Lord of glory became crucifiable.

Two assertions in sermons in Acts likely exemplify this same grammar. First, consider what Peter says in Acts 3:14–15: "But you denied the Holy and Righteous One, and asked for a murderer to be granted to you, and you killed the Author of life, whom God raised from the dead. To this we are witnesses." The key phrase is in verse 15: "You killed the Author of life." We are inclined to take "Author of life" as an ascription of divinity: Peter names Jesus as the divine source of creation, the one who gives life to all. If that is correct, then here we have an explicit instance of the communication of idioms and a paradox as bracing as that in 1 Corinthians 2:8. However, some scholars hold that the title simply describes Christ as, by virtue of his resurrection, the source of eternal life, salvific life, and therefore the sole source of salvation (cf. Acts 4:12).[20] Yet even on this understanding, the question naturally follows: Who can give eternal life? Can it be granted by any creature? Scripture resoundingly declares that God alone can save (Deut. 32:39; Jon. 2:8). In which case, even on this latter reading, Acts 3:15 remains an implicit instance of the communication of idioms. That Christ is one who can grant salvation implies his divinity, yet it was by being killed that he became the source of salvation.

A second instance of this pattern of speech in Acts is less certain, though still worth discussing briefly. In his address at Miletus to the Ephesian elders, Paul urges them, "Pay careful attention to yourselves and to all the flock, in which the Holy Spirit has made you overseers, to care for the church of God, which he obtained with his own blood" (Acts 20:28).[21] How does God have

19. See also Jamieson, "1 Corinthians 15.28 and the Grammar of Paul's Christology," 197–98, on which our discussion draws.

20. See, e.g., Bock, *Acts*, 171; Peterson, *The Acts of the Apostles*, 175–76; Schnabel, *Acts*, 210–11.

21. The Greek phrase behind "with his own blood" is διὰ τοῦ αἵματος τοῦ ἰδίου. The grammatical question here is whether the genitive phrase τοῦ ἰδίου modifies "blood" adjectivally or functions as a possessive genitive. The former understanding is reflected here in the ESV's

blood with which to purchase a people? The blood belongs to his Son, who is himself God, who became incarnate for us and for our salvation. That blood truly belongs to God because it truly belongs to the human nature that truly belongs to God the Son incarnate.

So far, we have considered "descending" paradoxical passages that ascribe human-befitting qualities to God the Son, Jesus Christ. We will now briefly discuss just a few out of many "ascending" paradoxical passages that, explicitly or implicitly, predicate God-befitting qualities of the man Jesus. Consider first one of the most striking, in the Gospel of John. At the climax of a long, contentious debate regarding Jesus's parentage and that of his opponents, Jesus declares, "Truly, truly, I say to you, before Abraham was, I am" (John 8:58). Here, Jesus claims for himself God's unique, personal, proper name and the timeless, eternal self-existence that goes with it.[22] His opponents respond tellingly: "So they picked up stones to throw at him, but Jesus hid himself and went out of the temple" (v. 59). They attempt to stone Jesus because they judge him to be blaspheming. As his opponents say a little later, "It is not for a good work that we are going to stone you but for blasphemy, because you, being a man, make yourself God" (John 10:33; cf. 5:18). Their problem is the evident humanity of the speaking subject who claims for himself God's unique name and existence.[23] In any sentence, the subject is the given to which the predicate is added. In this dialogue, Jesus's humanity is the given and his divinity is what he so provocatively adds.

Another pair of passages that ascribe divinity to the human Jesus can be found in Colossians: "For in him all the fullness of God was pleased to dwell" (Col. 1:19); and "For in him the whole fullness of deity dwells bodily" (Col. 2:9).[24] In the near contexts of both assertions, Jesus's humanity is either as-

---

translation; the latter yields the sense, "the blood of his Own." On this latter understanding, the blood belongs not to God but to the one who himself belongs to God—namely, Jesus. Either construal is grammatically possible. We regard the translation "through his own blood" as the more natural reading of the Greek, and therefore take Acts 20:28 as another explicit NT instance of the communication of idioms. We therefore take issue with Barrett, *A Critical and Exegetical Commentary on the Acts of the Apostles*, 2:977: "*Communicatio idiomatum* will not really serve here because we are dealing not with the two natures of Christ but with two Persons of the Trinity."

22. See, e.g., Neyrey, "Jesus the Judge," 534. For detailed, albeit tentative, support of the conclusion that in John 8:58 Jesus claims the unique divine name, see C. H. Williams, *I Am He*, 279–83. See also Bauckham, "Monotheism and Christology in the Gospel of John," 157–59; Baron, "The *Shema* in John's Gospel," 316–33.

23. Rightly, Macaskill, "Name Christology, Divine Aseity, and the I Am Sayings in the Fourth Gospel," 329n43.

24. The Greek of Col. 1:19 has no phrase corresponding to "of God"; instead, it leaves implicit the answer to the question, "Fullness of what?" However, in light of the explicit answer in 2:9, the interpretive insertion in translating 1:19 is fully justified; rightly, Foster, *Colossians*, 195.

serted or assumed. For instance, 1:18 names Christ "the firstborn from the dead," presupposing his crucified-and-resurrected humanity. The sentence in 1:19 continues by asserting that the blood of Christ's cross reconciled all things to God (1:20). The humanity of Christ is given, and against that backdrop 1:19 spotlights his divinity.

Strictly speaking, Colossians 1:19 and 2:9 furnish implicit instances of the communication of idioms, while John 8:58 offers a conceptual rather than grammatical example. That is, Colossians 1:19 and 2:9 do not go out of their way to highlight Christ's humanity. They do not explicitly name him as a man. Yet his humanity is implicit even in the simple "in him," since the context requires reference to a human being. In John 8:58, by contrast, Jesus's "I" does not explicitly name himself as a human being. However, the unignorable fact of his humanity is a necessary premise in his opponents' response, since he uses his human voice to speak the divine "I am." Hence, even where the linguistic grammar of the sentence does not predicate divinity of a human subject, the theological or conceptual grammar does.

To sum up, then, in this section we have surveyed and analyzed biblical pressure for both the unity of Christ as a single acting subject and the pattern of speech called the communication of idioms. Since Christ is one in a fundamental, ontological sense, that which is divine is true of a human, and this human truly is divine. This man is truly God, and God truly is this man. To put it more schematically, in this section we have measured four pressures from various NT passages. First, Scripture speaks of Christ as a single acting subject. Second, Scripture ascribes to this single Christ a bewildering diversity of attributes, actions, experiences, and sufferings. These wildly diverse predicates proclaim that what is proper to divinity and humanity both pertain to him. Third, Scripture ascribes to the divine Son not only the possession of a human nature but also the act of assuming a human nature. Fourth, whether implicitly or explicitly, the subjects and predicates of Scripture's assertions about Christ cross the line from human to divine and divine to human.

## The Grammar of Christological Paradoxes: The Hypostatic Union

Given the pressures discerned and described above, in this section we must now process these pressures in order to discern their underlying grammar, asking how it is that these various pressures presuppose and display a deeper framework of coherence. In other words, why does Scripture speak about

Jesus in these ways? What is the reality that demands to be spoken of in such paradoxical patterns?

## Preserving Paradox

As we move from Scripture's pressures about Jesus to its underlying grammar, we must state at the outset that the truth these passages teach is irreducibly mysterious. According to Francis Turretin, the most difficult questions in theology are the unity of three persons in one being and "the union of the two natures in the one person in the incarnation."[25] So when discussing the hypostatic union, we are not solving but stating the mystery.

Therefore, we are not setting aside paradox, but vindicating it as paradox and not contradiction. By "paradox" here we mean an apparent contradiction that ultimately is consistent. For Jesus to be both God and man seems contradictory but ultimately is not. Paradox is thus intrinsic to the confession that "Jesus is Lord" (1 Cor. 12:3), and biblical reasoning must preserve this paradox, owning that seemingly contradictory characteristics coalesce in Christ.[26] For this reason, the incarnation is a mystery, something we cannot fully explain. Given the reality of the Word made flesh, we should not shrink from paradox but instead revel in it. Orthodoxy is not about explaining mystery away but maintaining it. Orthodoxy stands upright not because it discards the weight of inconvenient evidence but because it keeps seemingly opposing truths in exact equipoise. So what does Scripture's pressure presuppose about the union in Christ of divinity and humanity?

## The Hypostatic Union

In light of the foregoing, the biblical discourse about the unity of Christ and the diversity of predicates befitting him are reconciled in the underlying grammar of what theologians traditionally call the hypostatic union. This doctrine is clearly articulated by the Chalcedonian creed, which our sixth principle echoes: "One and the same Lord Jesus Christ, the only begotten Son, must be acknowledged in two natures, without confusion or change, without division or separation. The distinction between the natures was never abolished by their union, but rather the character [ἰδιότητος, idiōtētos] proper to each of the two natures was preserved as they came together in one Person and one hypostasis."[27]

Notice first of all that this tells us nothing about *how* the hypostatic union occurs, but only *that* the union occurs in Christ's one person. The Son of

---

25. Turretin, *Institutes of Elenctic Theology* 13.6.1 (Giger, 2:310).
26. See, e.g., Pawl, *In Defense of Conciliar Christology*, 25.
27. Denzinger §302.

God assumed a human nature into union with his person, such that God the Son now truly exists as a man. This remains a mystery because *this* personal union is not "such as could be found in the sphere of created nature at all, but is an absolutely unique, supereminent union."[28] Therefore, we can know more about what this union is not than about what it is. This is not a union in nature, where divinity and humanity become some third thing. Nor is it a mere association or conjunction, where a divine agent and a human one work in close association behind a single external appearance. Further, it is crucial to remember here that the terms "person" and "nature" are metaphysically mere. With regard to Christ, they refer respectively to who he is and what he is: Christ is one "who" who subsists in two "whats."[29]

Against Nestorius's parceling out of Christ into two distinct, conjoined acting subjects, Cyril of Alexandria repeatedly insists that the Son personally or "hypostatically" united human nature to himself.[30] As Cyril puts it in the second anathema in his *Third Letter to Nestorius*, which was endorsed by the Council of Ephesus in AD 431, "If anyone does not confess that the Word of God the Father was hypostatically united to the flesh so as to be One Christ with his own flesh, that is the same one at once God and man, let him be anathema."[31] This understanding underpins Chalcedon's repeated declaration that it is "one and the same" Christ who is both God and man, and that this one and the same Lord Jesus, the Father's only begotten Son, "must be acknowledged in two natures, without confusion or change, without division or separation."[32] Only if the Son personally united a human nature to himself are his two natures neither divided nor separated.

---

28. Scheeben, *The Mysteries of Christianity*, 319.

29. We borrow this language of "one who, two whats" from the discussion of post-Chalcedonian Christology in Yeago, "Jesus of Nazareth and Cosmic Redemption," 167–68. See also I. McFarland, *The Word Made Flesh*, 7: "The upshot of these postconciliar developments can be summarized as follows: nature refers to the *whatness* of an entity, as defined by its constitutive qualities or attributes (e.g. 'immaterial intellect' as the definition of angelic nature). By contrast, hypostasis (or person) applies to entities that have rational and spiritual natures, and which therefore take individualized form as *whos*. In other words, to be a hypostasis is to have a personal identity: to be some*one* in addition to being some*thing*" (emphasis original).

30. See, e.g., Cyril of Alexandria, *Second Letter to Nestorius* 4: "Nonetheless, because the Word hypostatically united human reality to himself, 'for us and for our salvation,' and came forth of a woman, this is why he is said to have been begotten in a fleshly manner." And in *Third Letter to Nestorius* 11: "As we have said before, it means rather that he hypostatically united the human condition to himself and underwent a fleshly birth from her womb." Translations from McGuckin, *Saint Cyril of Alexandria and the Christological Controversy*, 264, 273.

31. Translation in McGuckin, *Saint Cyril of Alexandria and the Christological Controversy*, 273.

32. Denzinger §302.

Thomas Weinandy has helpfully summarized the Cyrillian, conciliar under-standing of the hypostatic union in three statements: It is *truly God* the Son who is man. It is *truly man* that the Son of God is. And the Son of God *truly is* man.[33] That the union is hypostatic particularly safeguards the third claim. As John of Damascus observes, "We do not set each nature apart by itself, but hold them to be united to each other in one composite Person. For we say that the union is substantial; that is to say, true and not imaginary."[34] To say that Christ's human nature is united to him hypostatically is to deny that it is united to him by any lesser or weaker or extrinsic bond.[35]

As we have hinted in previous chapters, the hypostatic union is best grasped with the aid of the grammar cumulatively developed so far. First, invoking the God-fittingness rule, Athanasius says the incarnation "supremely befitted the goodness of God."[36] God becoming man is a God-befitting act because be-coming man does not contradict being God. The grounds for this are not only God's goodness but also his non-contrastive transcendence. Creation *ex nihilo* is crucial at this point because it reminds us that the relation between humanity and divinity is noncompetitive. In the hypostatic union, Christ's two natures are not competing for room. There is no "space" in Christ's human nature that his divine nature takes up; both natures can belong to the Son because his human nature does not displace his divinity.[37] Divinity and humanity are not comparable entities; there is an infinite difference between them.[38] In the person of Christ, di-vinity and humanity are not united by either one being compromised or abridged. Instead, it is precisely because divinity and humanity are not on the same level, not competing with one another in any sense, that they can be united in the person of the incarnate Son. God can become man without ceasing to be God.[39]

Second, as we saw in the previous chapter, the work of the incarnation is an inseparable act of the whole Trinity that nevertheless "terminates" on the

---

33. Weinandy, "Cyril and the Mystery of the Incarnation," 30. See also the instructive dis-cussion of these topics in Weinandy, *Does God Suffer?*, 172–206.

34. John of Damascus, *On the Orthodox Faith* 3.3 (FC 27:273–74).

35. For other clarifying, fruitful discussions of the hypostatic union see, e.g., Thomas Aqui-nas, *STh* III.2; Owen, *Christologia* (*Works* 1:223–35); Turretin, *Institutes of Elenctic Theology* 13.6–7; T. J. White, *The Incarnate Lord*, 73–125. For a helpful overview of Aquinas's doctrine of the hypostatic union see Bauerschmidt, *Thomas Aquinas*, 188–97.

36. Athanasius, *On the Incarnation* 10 (PPS 44a:69).

37. Hence Chalcedon's "without division or separation" (ἀδιαιρέτως, ἀχωρίστως).

38. As Henk Schoot puts it, "God is not different from creatures the way in which creatures mutually differ. God differs differently" (*Christ the "Name" of God*, 144). See also Soskice: "God and creatures are not simply two different kinds of things to be compared and contrasted, with one much bigger—and stronger—than the other. The contrast, to twist Wittgenstein, is too big to be a binary" ("Why *Creatio Ex Nihilo* for Theology Today?," 49).

39. Hence Chalcedon's "without confusion or change" (ἀσυγχύτως, ἀτρέπτως).

Son alone. As the language of "assumption" or "taking" (Phil. 2:7) suggests, only the Son takes human nature into his own person. So what we say of Christ we say of this one divine person. Aquinas succinctly summarizes our discussion here and introduces hermeneutical implications of the hypostatic union that we will develop with our rules in the next section:

> To the hypostasis alone are attributed the operations and the natural properties, and whatever belongs to the nature in the concrete; for we say that this man reasons, and is risible, and is a rational animal. So likewise this man is said to be a suppositum, because he underlies (*supponitur*) whatever belongs to man and receives its predication. Therefore, if there is any hypostasis in Christ besides the hypostasis of the Word, it follows that whatever pertains to man is verified of someone other than the Word, e.g. that He was born of a Virgin, suffered, was crucified, was buried.[40]

Whatever is true of Christ's humanity is true of the person of the Son. All the actions performed by the human Jesus are rightly and necessarily attributed to the divine Son as their agent. Christ's human nature does not act independently of the divine Son, because acts belong to persons, not natures (*actiones sunt suppositorum, non naturarum*).[41] And since persons act, then the action of assuming his human nature belongs to one and the same subject of all that Scripture says about Christ: the only begotten Son. It is now time to explore this logic and consider how it should guide our reading of Scripture.

## Rules Pertaining to Christ's Unity and the Communication of Idioms

We may now formulate the rules corresponding to the grammar of the hypostatic union, and then dig one level deeper to probe their conceptual substance, implications, and coherence. As we have seen, the ontological unity of Christ gives rise to a grammatical unity of reference. In Scripture, characteristics proper to both God and humanity are attributed to one subject, the God-man, Jesus the Messiah. It is crucial to discern that the unity of Christ is not merely grammatical but ontological, and the ontology grounds the grammar. Hence rule 7, which we can call the "single subject" rule: *The eternal, divine Son is the sole subject of everything Jesus does and suffers. Christ is one person, one agent, one "who." Therefore, in reading Scripture's*

---

40. *STh* III.2.3.*corp*; cf. I.39.5.*ad*1.
41. Aquinas, *STh* III.3.1.*corp*. See our discussion of this axiom in the previous chapter.

*witness to Christ we must never divide Christ's acts between two acting subjects, attributing some to the divine Son and others to the human Jesus as if there were two different people.*

This grammatical unity, in turn, makes it both possible and necessary to form two types of sentences about Jesus. It is intuitive and uncontroversial to ascribe divine predicates to one identified as God, and human predicates to one identified as human. What is counterintuitive and seemingly contradictory is to name Christ according to one nature and predicate of him what belongs to the other. This pattern of speech forms our rule 8, which is traditionally called the "communication of idioms": *Since Christ is a single divine person who subsists in both a divine and a human nature, Scripture sometimes names him according to one nature and predicates of him what belongs to the other nature. Scripture ascribes divine prerogatives to the man Jesus, and human acts and sufferings to the divine Son. So read Scripture in a way that recognizes and reproduces this paradoxical grammar of christological predication.* And again, "idiom" here simply means "name" in the sense of "description."

The "single subject" rule follows from the ontology of Christ as a *single subject* who abidingly exists in two natures. The unity of Christ is a hermeneutical rule because it is an ontological reality. Christological grammar is grounded in christological ontology.[42] How Scripture speaks of Christ is rooted in, and therefore reveals, who and what he is. It is because Christ is a single acting subject, the divine Son existing as man, that Scripture always speaks of him as such, and so must we. This is why Cyril infers a crucial hermeneutical rule from the hypostatic union:

> If anyone interprets the sayings in the Gospels and apostolic writings, or the things said about Christ by the saints, or the things he says about himself, as referring to two prosopa or hypostases, attributing some of them to a man conceived of as separate from the Word of God, and attributing others (as divine) exclusively to the Word of God the Father, let him be anathema.[43]

As Aquinas observes, only by confessing that the two natures of Christ are united in one hypostasis or person can we "safeguard the teaching of the Scriptures about the incarnation."[44] The only way to "save" all the phenomena of Scripture's teaching on the incarnation is to confess the hypostatic

---

42. On the importance of ontology for Christology, see T. J. White, *The Incarnate Lord*, 1–21.
43. Cyril of Alexandria, *Third Letter to Nestorius*, anathema 4; translation from McGuckin, *Saint Cyril of Alexandria and the Christological Controversy*, 274.
44. Aquinas, *SCG* 4.39.

union in all its mystery and paradoxicality. In sum, the hypostatic union is a conceptual distillation of Scripture that gives us fresh purchase on Scripture.[45]

The communication of idioms rule follows from the ontology of Christ as a single subject who abidingly exists *in two natures*. This rule is a grammar of christological predication that is descriptive, prescriptive, and generative. First, the communication of idioms is descriptive because it accurately labels biblical patterns of attribution. Materially speaking, the communication of idioms does not add anything to the text but merely discerns and describes the logic of Scripture's paradoxical predications about Christ. It is the authors of Scripture who are speaking of Christ in these ways; as a descriptive grammar, the phrase "communication of idioms" simply points out the ways the words run.

Further, the communication of idioms is prescriptive in that we must not parcel out christological predicates to separate subjects. Fear of apparent contradiction might tempt us to ascribe human traits to "the man Jesus Christ" as one acting subject, and divine qualities to "God the Son" as another, as if there were two persons. But if we do, we void the incarnation and vacate the reality of Christ's saving work, since we are no longer saying that God became man. Instead, the prescriptive aspect of the communication of idioms reminds us that it is not only permissible but necessary to ascribe divine predicates to the man Jesus Christ and to attribute human features and fates to God the Son. Nothing less measures up to the ontological reality of the incarnation.

Finally, the communication of idioms is a generative grammar. It warrants proclamation, prayer, and praise that follows the paradoxical pattern of naming Christ according to one nature and predicating of him what pertains to the other. Since Scripture does this, as we saw above, so may we. And in doing so, we are fully justified in putting the point as paradoxically as possible. Consider, for instance, the declaration of Ignatius of Antioch from around AD 100 that Christians have attained new life "through the blood of God."[46] Or consider the claim of Melito of Sardis in a sermon on the Passover in the early second century: "He who hung the earth is hanging; he who fixed the heavens has been fixed; he who fastened the universe has been fastened to a

---

45. As Schoot, *Christ the "Name" of God*, 151, observes regarding the function of the hypostatic union in Aquinas's theology and exegesis, "With this model of the personal union one is able to account for these texts, whereas conversely, with the model of the accidental union, one is unable to account for texts in which a divine property is predicated of a man, or a human property of God. The rule is a hermeneutical rule." See also Moser, "Tools for Interpreting Christ's Saving Mysteries in Scripture," 287–88.

46. Ignatius of Antioch, *Ephesians* 1.1 (trans. M. W. Holmes, 183).

tree. . . . God has been murdered."[47] Or we could highlight Gregory of Nazianzus's poetic proclamation of Christ's birth: "I shall cry out the meaning of this day: the fleshless one is made flesh, the Word becomes material, the invisible is seen, the intangible is touched, the timeless has a beginning, the Son of God becomes Son of Man—'Jesus Christ, yesterday and today, the same also for all ages!'"[48]

None of these theologians are saying that a divine perfection is changed into its opposite. Instead, the subject-clauses fix the identity of the one who possesses the human trait or endures the human fate that the predicate ascribes to him. Consider, for instance, Cyril of Alexandria's careful discussion of Luke's assertion that Jesus "increased in wisdom and in stature and in favor with God and man" (Luke 2:52):

> He who as God is all perfect, submits to bodily growth; the incorporeal has limbs that advance to the ripeness of manhood; he is filled with wisdom who is himself all wisdom. And what say we to this? Behold by these things him who was in the form of the Father made like unto us; the rich in poverty; the high in humiliation; him said to "receive," whose is the fullness as God. So thoroughly did God the Word empty himself![49]

Cyril is sometimes accused of confusing Christ's divinity and humanity, as if he taught that after the moment of incarnation Christ possessed only one nature, one "what," compounded of divinity and humanity like flour and eggs make dough. Yet Cyril's explicit denial of such teaching is striking, both in the exposition above and in a statement such as the following: "But who would be so misguided and stupid as to think that the divine nature of the Word had changed into something which formerly it was not? or that the flesh was changed by some kind of transformation into the nature of the Word himself? This is impossible."[50]

The Word became flesh: God the Son became a human being. Because God is qualitatively transcendent, being eternal and unchanging, his divinity did not devolve into humanity. Nor was his humanity transformed into divinity. Instead, because of the ontological reality of the hypostatic union, Scripture ascribes divinity to the man and humanity to God. The communication of

---

47. *Peri Pascha* 96.711–15; in Melito of Sardis, *On Pascha and Fragments*, 55. Cf. *Fragment* 13 (in Hall, 80–81).

48. Gregory of Nazianzus, *Oration* 38.2 (in Daley, *Gregory of Nazianzus*, 118).

49. Cyril of Alexandria, *A Commentary upon the Gospel according to S. Luke by S. Cyril, Patriarch of Alexandria*, 29 (trans. Smith; capitalization modernized).

50. Cyril of Alexandria, *On the Unity of Christ* (PPS 13:77). For a useful study of Cyril's teaching on this issue, see Loon, *The Dyophysite Christology of Cyril of Alexandria*.

idioms is a grammar grounded in God the Son's assumption of humanity into personal union with himself. This grammar discerns and deploys the logic of Scripture's speech about the Son incarnate.

Historically and dogmatically speaking, the communication of idioms was not an endpoint of christological reflection but a crucial starting point. We have seen that the communication of idioms is explicitly attested in Scripture and, in a most bracing form, is employed by Christian theologians from the early second century onward. So, the communication of idioms is not a logical conclusion that theologians arrived at by a long chain of deductive reasoning. Instead, beginning with some of the very earliest postapostolic reflection on Scripture, the communication of idioms has been a tool for preserving and proclaiming the paradox of Christ's person in compact, provocative statements. As Thomas Weinandy explains,

> Thus, the whole of orthodox patristic christology, including the conciliar affirmations, can be seen as an attempt to defend the practice and to clarify the use of the communication of idioms. . . . Historically, then, it was not an orthodox or a conciliar account of the Incarnation that gave rise to the communication of idioms, it was the communication of idioms that gave rise to the conciliar and orthodox account of the Incarnation.[51]

The unity of Christ is a facet of Scripture's testimony to the person of our redeemer. Similarly, the linguistic and conceptual move of attributing divine and human qualities to the single person of the Son is both practiced in Scripture and also a necessary way to say of Jesus all that Scripture says of Jesus. The communication of idioms is not merely right reasoning about Scripture; it is a way that Scripture itself reasons.

## Putting the Rules to Use

We now consider how these two rules help us read Scripture rightly. In this section we will briefly engage three well-known snapshots of Jesus's ministry from the Synoptic Gospels: his claim to forgive sins, which elicited the charge of blasphemy (Mark 2:1–12 and par.); his calming the storm and walking on water, which prompted both bewilderment and worship (Mark 4:35–41 and par.; Mark 6:45–52 and par.); and his raising a young girl from death, the advance announcement of which provoked incredulous scorn (Mark 5:21–24, 35–43 and par.). In considering each, we will pay special attention to the divine

51. Weinandy, *Does God Suffer?*, 175.

prerogatives Jesus exercises as a man and the need to perceive the ontological basis of such acts in order to respond to them rightly. In other words, whether right or wrong, fitting or unfitting, the responses to Jesus's actions reveal that the identity he claims for himself is divine in the fullest sense.[52]

## Forgiveness and Blasphemy

First, we consider Jesus's claim to forgive sins. In Mark 2:1–4 we read that a paralytic's friends lower him through the roof of a crammed building to get him near Jesus. Verse 5 tells us Jesus's response: "And when Jesus saw their faith, he said to the paralytic, 'Son, your sins are forgiven.'" This provokes immediate and theologically well-founded opposition: "Now some of the scribes were sitting there, questioning in their hearts, 'Why does this man speak like that? He is blaspheming! Who can forgive sins but God alone?'" (vv. 6–7). Jesus perceives their inward agitation and issues a challenge. Which is easier—to pronounce forgiveness or heal by a word? To Jesus's interlocutors, the answer would be obvious: forgiveness is far harder (vv. 7b–9). Nevertheless, to ground the claim that he can in fact accomplish the more difficult feat, Jesus responds, "But that you may know that the Son of Man has authority on earth to forgive sins'—he said to the paralytic—'I say to you, rise, pick up your bed, and go home'" (vv. 10–11). The man immediately arises and walks out in view of all, so that the whole crowd is "amazed and glorified God, saying, 'We never saw anything like this!'" (v. 12).

Many scholars have understood Jesus's statement in verse 5 as a priestly absolution or prophetic declaration.[53] Yet all efforts to keep Jesus from claiming to effect forgiveness founder on the scribes' response in verse 6. Only if Jesus is claiming the unique divine prerogative of forgiving sins would they accuse him of blasphemy.[54] The problem with the scribes' charge of blasphemy is not the theological presupposition that God alone may forgive sins. "Who is a God like you, pardoning iniquity and passing over transgression for the remnant of his inheritance?" (Mic. 7:18). Nor are they wrong to regard human usurpation of a divine prerogative as blasphemy. But that is just the question. Is Jesus merely human? Is his claim to forgive a usurpation? Thomas Weinandy observes, "Again, what causes consternation . . . is not what is said and done,

---

52. See Gathercole, "The Trinity in the Synoptic Gospels and Acts," 59.
53. We borrow these summary descriptions from Gathercole, "The Trinity in the Synoptic Gospels and Acts," 59.
54. Rightly, Hofius, "Jesu Zuspruch der Sündenvergebung," 40–41: "If Jesus's word had been meant only as an authorized confirmation of forgiveness granted by God, a narrator familiar with the thinking of ancient Judaism could not have described the reaction of the scribes as it occurs in Mark 2:6ff."

but who is alleging authority and power to say and do it—Jesus, the man."[55] The scribes had, inwardly, already rendered their judgment on the question of Jesus's identity—a judgment that, in Matthew 9:4, Jesus characterizes as thinking evil. Weinandy again: "Their thoughts are evil precisely because they have already precluded that Jesus could not possibly be God, and thus were not open to the revelation contained in the ensuing healing that will manifest that he is truly God with the authority and power to forgive."[56] In this the scribes anticipate many modern scholars.

However, even some recent scholars who do not set out to correct or contradict Christ's claim nevertheless seem reluctant to allow its full force. For instance, some argue that Jesus is claiming nothing more than that he is God's authorized agent.[57] Yet, as Kavin Rowe points out regarding Luke's version, the charge of blasphemy "would never have arisen in this precise form on the presupposition of an agent-like christology."[58] The strength of the scribes' response reveals the magnitude of Christ's claim, like a seismograph measuring an earthquake. The prerogative claimed is divine; the one claiming it is human. The disjunction thereby forced is ultimately theological: either Jesus is blaspheming or he is God incarnate. He is either attempting hubristic usurpation or attesting hypostatic union. The scribes bank on the former. The crowd, however, seems to have at least a faint inkling of the latter: they are amazed, they glorify God, and they declare, "We never saw anything like this!" (Mark 2:12). Though their christological judgment is likely not fully formed, their praiseful astonishment points the right way. Astonished praise is the proper response to this singular individual, this man who claims to do what only God can.

How do the present chapter's rules help us read with the grain of this passage? The single subject rule prepares us to measure accurately the theological dimensions of the controversy between Jesus and the scribes. The question is precisely Jesus's identity. Why does this man speak this way? Who does he think he is? Only if this man truly is God is his speech not damnable. To

---

55. Weinandy, *Jesus Becoming Jesus*, 125.
56. Weinandy, *Jesus Becoming Jesus*, 125.
57. For instance, despite many nuanced and helpful observations, the account of Marcus, "Authority to Forgive Sins upon the Earth," ultimately falls short on this point. He concludes, "When he acts on earth in this way, he does not claim to be doing so by his own power but by the power of God; any charge that Christians worship two gods, therefore, is misguided" (204). As our previous chapter suggested and subsequent chapters will show, what is ultimately required to account for the identity of Christ in the Gospels is a dialectic in which something derived from the Father can, nevertheless, be the Son's own proper possession, even when the "something" in question is a properly divine prerogative or perfection.
58. Rowe, *Early Narrative Christology*, 103.

blaspheme is human; to forgive is divine. And the communication of idioms rule reminds us that grammar follows ontology and ontology grounds grammar. The scribes fault Jesus's grammar ("Your sins are forgiven") because they misconstrue his ontology ("this man," as if "man" exhausts who and what Jesus is). Jesus's pronouncement of forgiveness is a narrative instantiation of the communication of idioms in its ascending form: the subject is human, the predicate divine.

### Water Works Prompting Wonder and Worship

Second, we consider Jesus's calming the storm and walking on water. This time the snapshot is actually a diptych. The first panel consists of Mark 4:35–41 and its Synoptic parallels. The setting is the sea of Galilee, which Jesus and his disciples are crossing in a boat by night (vv. 35–36). A storm arises that threatens to sink their small craft. Despite the dousing rain and waves, Jesus sleeps in the stern. Exasperated by Jesus's apparent indifference to their plight, the disciples wake him, saying, "Teacher, do you not care that we are perishing?" (vv. 37–38). Jesus wakes up and rebukes the sea, ordering it to calm down: "Peace! Be still!" Immediately the wind and storm cease (v. 39). Jesus then rebukes his disciples: "Why are you so afraid? Have you still no faith?" (v. 40). The narrative concludes with the disciples' response: astonished incomprehension. "And they were filled with great fear and said to one another, 'Who then is this, that even the wind and the sea obey him?'" (v. 41).

This narrative strikingly evokes Psalm 107.[59] The psalm tells of men doing business in ships on the great sea (Ps. 107:23). When the Lord stirs up a fierce storm, their courage drains away, they cry to the Lord, and he delivers them (vv. 25–28). How? "He made the storm be still, and the waves of the sea were hushed" (v. 29). In responding to the disciples' cries by rebuking the storm, Jesus is enacting the role and manifesting the authority of God himself. Who can bring a storm to heel with a word of command? The one who says to it, "Thus far shall you come, and no farther" (Job 38:11). The one who rules the raging of the sea stills its rising waves (Ps. 89:9; cf. 65:7); the one who rebuked the sea at creation confines it to its bounds (Ps. 104:7, 9); the one who rebuked the Red Sea at the exodus makes its bed a highway for his redeemed (Ps. 106:9).

"Who then is this, that even the wind and the sea obey him?" Good question. Mark does not answer it explicitly, at least not here, but any reader

---

59. As Weinandy, *Jesus Becoming Jesus*, 129, observes, "The entire occurrence is almost a literal enactment of Psalm 107." See also the insightful discussion of this narrative in Hays, *Echoes of Scripture in the Gospels*, 66–69, on which ours draws.

schooled in the OT can (recall the analogy of faith rule). The one who was so tired that he could sleep through a tempest is also the one who rules the raging waves. The human sleeper is also the divine sovereign.

The diptych's second panel is also a sea story. In Mark 6:45–52, Jesus's disciples embark and begin crossing the sea of Galilee to Bethsaida, while Jesus remains behind to dismiss the crowd and pray. At evening, a storm arises that stalls their progress. So Jesus takes the natural, normal, unexceptional step of walking out to them on the surface of the sea (vv. 45–47). He means "to pass by them" (v. 48), but when the disciples see him, they take him for a ghost and cry out in fear. He responds, "Take heart, it is I. Do not be afraid" (v. 50). As soon as Jesus enters the boat, the wind stops, and the disciples are astounded (vv. 51–52). While Mark tells us only of their astonishment, Matthew adds: "And those in the boat worshiped him, saying, 'Truly you are the Son of God'" (Matt. 14:33).

Four features of Jesus's human actions and the disciples' responses disclose his divinity.[60] First, we see his sovereignty over nature. Jesus needs neither boat nor sail to tread the waves and best the wind. Mark's rendering of this action in verse 49 seems designed to evoke the Septuagint translation of Job 9:8, "who alone stretched out the sky, *and walks on the sea as on dry ground.*"[61] Only the Lord of creation can treat the sea as a sidewalk.

Second, this evocation of Job 9 also unlocks the enigmatic phrase that immediately precedes: "He meant to pass by them" (v. 48). For what purpose did Jesus make as if to pass them? To signal that his approach was the approach of the ungraspable God of Israel. As Job confesses, "If he passed over me, I would certainly not see him, and *if he went by me,* I would not even know" (Job 9:11 LXX).[62]

Third, in this context, we should understand Jesus's self-identification not merely as announcing his presence but also as appropriating God's unique self-designation. In Greek, Jesus's heartening greeting features the phrase ἐγώ εἰμι (*egō eimi*, v. 50). In the Greek OT, this phrase frequently appears on God's lips as an assertion of his divine singularity and dominion.[63] These phrases, in turn, echo God's definitive disclosure of himself to Moses as "I AM WHO I AM," or "I am The One Who Is" (ἐγώ εἰμι ὁ ὤν [*egō eimi ho ōn*],

---

60. For fuller discussion of all these points, see Hays, *Echoes of Scripture in the Gospels*, 70–73.

61. Translation from NETS, 675 (emphasis added). Mark's "walking on the sea" (ἐπὶ τῆς θαλάσσης περιπατοῦντα) closely echoes "walks on the sea" in the Greek rendering of Job 9:8 (περιπατῶν . . . ἐπὶ θαλάσσης). See also our earlier discussion of this passage in chap. 1.

62. Translation from NETS, 675 (emphasis added).

63. See LXX Deut. 32:29; Isa. 41:4; 43:10, 25; 45:18, 19; 46:4; 51:12; 52:6. See also the discussion in C. H. Williams, "'I Am' Sayings," 398.

Exod. 3:14).[64] In identifying himself to his disciples, Jesus identifies himself as the God of Abraham, Isaac, and Jacob.[65]

Fourth, we need to reckon with the disciples' worship of Jesus in Matthew 14:33. Given Jesus's actions in context and the content of their confession ("Truly you are the Son of God"), we should understand this action as worship in the full sense.[66] This is an appropriate response only if Jesus is truly divine. And if Jesus is truly divine, then finally this is the only appropriate response. If Jesus is not the "I AM" who appeared to Moses, then his disciples are committing idolatry and blasphemy.

What purchase do this chapter's rules give us on this pair of passages? Chiefly, they enable us to recognize who it is who speaks and the wind obeys. Again, as with Jesus's claim to forgive sins, the single subject rule enables us to recognize that God himself—namely, God the Son—is the divine subject of all the human acts and human words of Jesus. However unprecedented, however category-bursting it may be, perceiving the divine unity of Christ enables us to resist the temptation to try to resolve the paradox by parceling out Christ's acts between two subjects, one human and one divine. And the communication of idioms rule offers rightly formed grammatical tracks on which paraphrase and exposition of these passages may run. The man Jesus is worshiped because this man alone is God. Jesus's divine ontology warrants the ascription of that predicate to this subject. On the other hand, God himself slept in a boat and then awoke to still the storm. Both types of sentences—those that ascribe divinity to the man Jesus and those that ascribe humanity to God the Son—perform not merely legitimate but necessary acts of unfolding the mystery of these narratives.

### Sleep-Waking and Scorn

More briefly, our third and final episode is Jesus's healing of Jairus's daughter (Mark 5:21–24, 35–43). Initially, Jairus, a ruler of the synagogue, implores Jesus to come heal his daughter, who is at the point of death. After Jesus's progress toward Jairus's house is interrupted by his healing of a woman who has a discharge of blood, some come from the ruler's house to tell him there is nothing left for Jesus to do: the girl has already died. Jesus overhears these messengers and counters, "Do not fear, only believe" (v. 36). "Believe

---

64. The latter translation is from NETS, 53.

65. Weinandy, *Jesus Becoming Jesus*, 130, rightly measures the theological freight of this self-identification.

66. For an extensive argument in support of this conclusion, see Leim, *Matthew's Theological Grammar*, 125–66.

in whom?" we might well ask. Taking only three disciples with him into the house, Jesus encounters a loud knot of mourners and says to them, "Why are you making a commotion and weeping? The child is not dead but sleeping" (v. 39). Predictably, they laugh. But he sends them all out and takes the girl's parents and his disciples into the girl's room with him. Then, "taking her by the hand he said to her, 'Talitha cumi,' which means, 'Little girl, I say to you, arise'" (v. 42). Immediately the girl gets up and begins walking, "and they were immediately overcome with amazement" (v. 42).

The most direct testimony to Jesus's divinity in this passage is his power over death. As the Lord proclaims, raising the dead is a uniquely divine pre-rogative: "See now that I, even I, am he, and there is no god beside me; I kill and I make alive; I wound and I heal; and there is none that can deliver out of my hand" (Deut. 32:39). But what about the prophets Elijah and Elisha? Didn't they raise the dead?[67] Not quite. Elijah "cried to the LORD," and "the LORD listened to the voice of Elijah" (1 Kings 17:20, 22). Elisha also "prayed to the Lord" (2 Kings 4:33). The prophets asked God to raise the dead, and he did. By contrast, Jesus simply instructs the girl to rise. It is Jesus's direct address that deprives death of its power. The same one who is sovereign over sea and storms is also able to shut down death by a simple voice command (cf. John 11:43).

Indirect evidence of Jesus's divinity is also seen in the interplay between his command to believe (v. 36) and the crowd's incredulity at his initial di-agnosis: "The child is not dead but sleeping" (v. 39). Believe in whom? The narrative answers: the one who can speak a girl back from death. Yet, taking Jesus's statement of verse 39 literally, the crowds laugh, betraying unbelief. Someone who mistakes death for sleep is more worthy of scorn than trust. Yet the mistake is theirs. For one in the healing hands of the incarnate Lord of life, death is no more a threat to life than sleep is.

Here again, the single subject rule and the communication of idioms help us ask the right questions and discern the text's answers in matters of iden-tity and agency. The man Jesus is the one doing, and what he does is divine. Jesus's human speech accomplishes the divine work of resurrection. Human words manifest divine power. Jesus does divine things humanly.[68] There is no

---

67. As asserted by, e.g., Kirk, *A Man Attested by God*, 92.

68. So Moser, "Tools for Interpreting Christ's Saving Mysteries in Scripture," 289: "And Christ's two energies concur to a single 'theandric action' narrated in scripture, which is a complex state of affairs comprised of a human end-product and a divine end-product. To take one example: when Jesus heals the deceased child, he takes her by the hand humanly and restores her to life divinely, so that she is raised from the dead (Luke 8:54–5). The two end-products of his two energies are the touching and the healing, and these concur to one state of affairs, the resurrection of this girl." See also Weinandy, *Jesus Becoming Jesus*, 123.

hint of another agent at work in distinction from and in conjunction with the man Jesus. What he does shows who he is: the divine acts he humanly accomplishes attest that he is God incarnate. What he does inescapably identifies him as the true God. In verse 39, God calls death sleep and is derided. In verse 41, undeterred, a man's hand lifts a girl from her bed and his word lifts her from death.

## Conclusion: A Pail to a River

This chapter has articulated one rule and two principles, each pertaining to both the unity and duality of Christ. The principle simply declares this scriptural mystery, using language borrowed directly from a time-tested confession of faith. The two rules are both required, complementary ways to maintain the unity of Christ in light of his duality. The single subject rule reminds us that, however bewildering a variety of actions and traits Scripture ascribes to Christ, it ascribes them all to a single acting subject, God the Son incarnate. And the communication of idioms rule discerns how Scripture applies divine predicates to the man Jesus of Nazareth and human traits to God the Son. Because Scripture speaks of Christ in both of these mind-bending ways, we can—and must.

This is certainly a mystery, and clearly a paradox. But is it a contradiction? Not at all, if Jesus is who Scripture says he is: true God and true man in one person. The tensions that arise in affirming all this, at once, of one subject are a sign, not of incoherence, but of this subject's inexhaustible fullness. We bring only a pail to this river.

# 8

# Greater Than Himself and Less Than Himself

## Christ's Two Natures and Scripture's Partitive Discourse

**Principle 6:** One and the same Lord Jesus Christ, the only begotten Son of the Father, exists as one person in two natures, without confusion or change, without division or separation.

**Rule 9:** Scripture speaks of Christ in a twofold manner: some things are said of him as divine, and other things are said of him as human. Biblical reasoning discerns that Scripture speaks of the one Christ in two registers in order to contemplate the whole Christ. Therefore read Scripture in such a way that you discern the different registers in which Scripture speaks of Christ, yet without dividing him.

Our sixth principle, following Chalcedon, seeks to confess that Jesus Christ is one person: the same Son eternally begotten from the Father was made man in these latter days for us and for our salvation. The last chapter upheld the unity of Christ and probed the paradoxical statements by which Scripture directs our attention to the fullness of his glory. In this respect, we sought to maintain that Jesus is *"one person* in two natures." The present chapter continues to consider one and the same Christ, but seeks to maintain that this one Christ is indeed "one person *in two natures."* Why is this element necessary for biblical reasoning, especially as we pursue the vision of Christ's glory?

As we have seen several times already, reckoning with Christ's identity requires us to do justice to the many strange things Scripture says about him—things that seem incompatible with Jesus being the one God of Israel with the Father and Holy Spirit. For instance, Jesus tells his disciples, "If you loved me, you would have rejoiced, because I am going to the Father, for the Father is greater than I" (John 14:28). How can the Father be greater than the Son if the Son and the Father are one, as Jesus himself says (John 10:30)? Elsewhere, Peter proclaims that, upon Jesus's resurrection and ascension to heaven, "God has made him both Lord and Christ" (Acts 2:36). Does this mean that, while the Father is always Lord, the Son only lately became Lord? And wouldn't that make the Son's lordship less than the Father's?

If one takes these passages to speak about Christ's essence as God, one can only conclude that Jesus is not truly God, but is instead something somewhat less than God—a demigod, perhaps. But that plainly clashes with Scripture's testimony to Christ, which we have seen in earlier chapters. So what do these passages teach us, and how do they demand to be read?

In this chapter we will argue that the solution to each of these sorts of conundrums is our ninth rule. A further implication of our sixth principle, that Christ is one person existing in two natures, we can call the "partitive exegesis" rule.[1] The rule is as follows: *Scripture speaks of Christ in a twofold manner: some things are said of him as divine, and other things are said of him as human. Biblical reasoning discerns that Scripture speaks of the one Christ in two registers in order to contemplate the whole Christ. Therefore read Scripture in such a way that you discern the different registers in which*

---

1. See, for instance, Augustine's classic statement of this rule:
   We find scattered through the scriptures, and marked out by learned Catholic expositors of them, a kind of canonical rule, which we hold onto most firmly, about how our Lord Jesus Christ is to be understood to be God's Son, both equal to the Father by the form of God in which he is, and less than the Father by the form of a servant which he took. In this form indeed he is seen to be not only less than the Father, but also less than the Holy Spirit, less, what is more, than himself—and not a self that he was but a self that he is. For when he took the form of a servant he did not lose the form of God. (*The Trinity* 2.2 [WSA I/5:98])
   For an insightful discussion of Augustine's use of this rule and its role in his theology and epistemology, see Ayres, *Augustine and the Trinity,* 142–73. The phrase "partitive exegesis" was coined by Koen, "Partitive Exegesis in Cyril of Alexandria's Commentary on the Gospel according to St. John." The label appears to be gaining wider use, largely through the influence of John Behr. As Behr, *The Nicene Faith,* 14, rightly argues, partitive exegesis is a watershed issue between pro-Nicene trinitarianism and its rivals.

*Scripture speaks of Christ, yet without dividing him.* Scripture ascribes to the one Christ both divine and human attributes and acts, like a duet in which a bass and a soprano line are sung in harmony.

Partitive exegesis considers a scriptural statement about Christ and asks, "In what sense does this apply?"[2] This morning, at about 9:00 a.m., I (Jamieson) set up shop in the Main Reading Room of the Library of Congress in Washington, DC. Imagine that, shortly after sitting down, I received a phone call from my esteemed coauthor, Tyler, asking me what the room was like. After stepping out to answer my silently flashing phone, I might have responded, "It's nearly empty." Tyler could have then replied, "What, are there no books there?" But I was talking about people, not books. As far as I can tell, the Main Reading Room's 70,000-volume general reference collection remains intact. But the number of people present, both readers and tourists, has fluctuated through-out the day. The room can be both full of books and empty of people. Those assertions speak of two dimensions of a single, undivided entity.

Partitive exegesis discerns the precise referent and scope of scriptural state-ments about Christ. Since Scripture proclaims a single Christ who is both divine and human, partitive exegesis recognizes and maintains a distinction between Christ's divine and human natures. As we saw in the previous chap-ter, in Christ himself, divine and human natures unite in a single hypostasis, without division or separation. But in order to think and speak rightly about this undivided Christ, we must recognize that some things Scripture says of him are only true because of and with reference to either his human nature or his divine nature. So long as we presuppose the divine unity of Christ, and therefore that we are speaking of a single acting subject, we can also call partitive exegesis "two-nature exegesis."[3]

To use a common patristic word pair: partitive exegesis distinguishes be-tween "theology" and "economy" with reference to Christ himself.[4] Some passages speak of Christ insofar as he is God. That is, they speak of him with reference to, or according to, "theology." Other passages speak of Christ insofar as he is the divine Son who became man to accomplish our salvation. That is, they speak of him with reference to "the economy." And some passages com-bine those two categories; they speak of him in both ways at once. As we saw in the previous chapter, some passages predicate of the man Jesus what belongs to God alone. Early Christian writers used the terms "theology" and "economy"

---

2. Macdonald, "Pro-Nicene Exegesis in Hilary of Poitiers' *De Trinitate* and Basil of Cae-sarea's *Contra Eunomium*," 14.

3. As does, e.g., Wiles, *The Spiritual Gospel*, 116.

4. For a brief introduction to the patristic theology/economy distinction and an illustration of the purchase it gives on Hebrews' Christology, see Jamieson, *The Paradox of Sonship*, 31–36.

in a broad sense to refer to, respectively, the being of God and God's orderly administration of history and the cosmos. That administration culminates in the salvific plan of God that focuses on, and is fulfilled in, Christ's incarnate mission—this is the sense in which we will use "economy" in what follows.

Similar to the previous chapter, this one proceeds in four steps. First, we will justify this rule, discussing passages of Scripture that offer biblical precedent for practicing partitive exegesis. Second, we will further examine this rule by elaborating its underlying grammar. Third, we will employ this rule in interpreting a range of biblical passages, including the examples introduced above. Fourth, we will draw some conclusions about how partitive exegesis aids in rightly reading Scripture.

## Partitive Pressures in the New Testament

The distinction employed in partitive exegesis emerges from some of the same pressures we evaluated in our last chapter, passages that teach us that Christ is one "who" with two "whats." Scripture teaches that Jesus is the divine Son who became man for our salvation, and that this one Christ is therefore both human and divine. Hence, some passages speak of *him* on account of his divinity and some on account of his humanity.

But to tread a fresh path: given the NT's confession of Christ's humanity and divinity, a second, decisive warrant for partitive exegesis is when NT authors limit the scope of their predications about Christ to what is "in the flesh" or "according to the flesh." We have already seen that partitive exegesis involves delimiting the scope of an assertion about Christ. To do this concisely, one could naturally use some type of adverbial or prepositional qualifier. One might say that Christ is the creator "as God" and is a creature "as man." Or, as the Chalcedonian Definition has it, Christ is "consubstantial with the Father as regards his divinity, and the same consubstantial with us as regards his humanity."[5] In what follows we argue that scriptural writers themselves occasionally employ such partitive qualifiers, or prepositional partitions, though these only face in one direction.

### Christ's Human Birth and Genealogy (Rom. 1:3; 9:5)

For instance, consider two nearly identical assertions of Paul in his letter to the Romans. In the opening of his epistle, Paul asserts that the gospel, which

---

5. Translation from N. P. Tanner, ed., *Decrees of the Ecumenical Councils*, 1:86. The Greek behind "as regards his divinity . . . as regards his humanity" is κατὰ τὴν θεότητα . . . κατὰ τὴν ἀνθρωπότητα, which one might also render "according to his divinity/humanity."

was promised beforehand through the "prophets in the holy Scriptures" (1:2), concerns God's Son, "who was descended from David according to the flesh" (1:3) There is that prepositional partition, "according to the flesh" (κατὰ σάρκα, *kata sarka*). But in order to discern the force of this partitive delimiter, we need to burrow beneath the surface of the ESV's translation. To render the underlying Greek more fully and explicitly, one could translate this phrase as "who as it pertains to the flesh came into existence by means of the seed of David."[6] In this context, the verb Paul uses (γίνομαι, *ginomai*) most naturally means "came into existence." Further, Paul does not merely say that Christ descended from David, but that he came into existence "by means of the seed of David" (ἐκ σπέρματος Δαυίδ, *ek spermatos Dauid*), an implicit reference to the Davidic descent of Jesus's mother, Mary. So Paul names Jesus God's Son and narrates the event of his incarnation—his assumption of human life and lineage derived from his mother.

With this exegetical background sketched in, Paul's partitive qualifier "according to the flesh" should pop off the page. No one speaks of their lineage this way, and for good reason. It would be inelegant and unnecessary—unless, of course, there is more to one's lineage than one's lineage. Why does Paul specify that Jesus's *human lineage* is from the seed of David? Because that is not the only lineage he has. Jesus is not only David's son but also God's Son. So, even though Paul's partitive qualifier only faces in one direction, we can fittingly paraphrase Paul's partition with a Chalcedonian parallelism. In Romans 1:3, Jesus is God's Son as regards his divinity, and David's son as regards his humanity.

In a very similar vein, later in the same letter Paul says of the Jewish people, "To them belong the patriarchs, and from their race, according to the flesh, is the Christ, who is God over all, blessed forever. Amen" (Rom. 9:5). While the syntax of this sentence is difficult, we think Paul does indeed acclaim Christ explicitly as "God."[7] In addition, Paul specifies that, as Messiah, Christ belongs to the Jewish race "according to the flesh" (κατὰ σάρκα, *kata sarka*). As far as his human nature is concerned, Jesus the Messiah is a Jew. Why does Paul include this qualifying partition, this delimiting preposition "according to"? Because, as divine, Jesus's existence utterly transcends ethnic categories. Yet, as human, he can be identified by his ethnicity. Here again, as in Romans

---

6. For a detailed defense of this reading of Rom. 1:3, on which the discussion above depends, see Bates, "A Christology of Incarnation and Enthronement," 114–23. For a briefer discussion, see Jamieson, *The Paradox of Sonship*, 161–67.

7. See esp. M. J. Harris, *Jesus as God*, 143–72; Kammler, "Die Prädikation Jesu Christi als 'Gott' und die paulinische Christologie"; Carraway, *Christ Is God over All*; Gathercole, "Locating Christ and Israel in Romans 9–11," 118–22.

1:3, Paul juxtaposes Jesus's divine nature and human lineage. Paul speaks of the one Christ in two distinct, complementary registers, and he delimits the range of the human register.

### Christ's Manifestation in the Flesh (1 Tim. 3:16)

Another passage in which Paul employs a prepositional phrase that is at least implicitly "partitive" is 1 Timothy 3:16: "Great indeed, we confess, is the mystery of godliness: He was manifested in the flesh [ἐφανερώθη ἐν σαρκί, *ephanerōthē en sarki*], vindicated by the Spirit, seen by angels, proclaimed among the nations, believed on in the world, taken up in glory." Here we focus primarily on the phrase "manifested in the flesh," which declares an action and its location or means. Christ's manifestation in the flesh revealed "the mystery of godliness." In the NT, "mystery" is not an insoluble riddle, but God's plan, which was formerly concealed and has now been revealed (cf. Rom. 16:25; Eph. 3:4–5; Col. 1:26).[8] Christ's manifestation in the flesh brought God's saving plan to light. Further, this verse implicitly identifies Christ as the mystery: he is that which was hidden but has now been revealed. This implies that Christ's existence, strictly speaking, did not begin with his human existence. To employ a needed metaphor, he came to earth from elsewhere.

Frequently in the NT, the verb here translated "was manifested" refers to Christ's incarnation, his end-time appearance on the world stage (e.g., Heb. 9:26; 1 Pet. 1:20; 1 John 3:5, 8). This is a loaded way to speak of a human being. It implies more than mere birth. A faint analogy for this "manifestation" can be glimpsed in one of P. G. Wodehouse's stories about the hapless Bertie Wooster and his butler-savior, Jeeves.

> "Sir?" said Jeeves, kind of manifesting himself. One of the rummy things about Jeeves is that, unless you watch like a hawk, you very seldom see him come into a room. He's like one of those weird chappies . . . who dissolve themselves into thin air and nip through space in a sort of disembodied way and assemble the parts again just where they want them.[9]

In Bertie Wooster's view, Jeeves's manifesting himself attests his near-divine dignity and superhuman capacities. In Paul's confession of the mystery of godliness, Jesus's being manifested is his act of becoming incarnate to save us, thereby bringing to fruition God's eternal purpose of salvation (cf. 2 Tim. 1:9–10).

8. See esp. Lang, *Mystery and the Making of a Christian Historical Consciousness*, 31–129.
9. Wodehouse, "Leave It to Jeeves."

We also need to consider the phrase "in the flesh." This likely refers not merely to Christ's birth as a human but to his entire earthly career that followed.[10] Jesus's whole life on earth was a revelation, a making-known of what had been hidden. This revelation took place "in the flesh": by means of his human nature. There is another reality, beyond and before Jesus's manifestation in the flesh, which his life in the flesh manifests. Here, Paul's qualifier "in the flesh" does not have precisely the same limiting function as the phrase "according to the flesh" in the passages we considered above. Yet it does imply a reality distinct from Christ's humanity, independent of his humanity, and greater than his humanity, which is revealed through his humanity.

### Partitive Prepositions in 1 Peter

Two more partitive prepositional qualifiers appear in 1 Peter. "For Christ also suffered once for sins, the righteous for the unrighteous, that he might bring us to God, being put to death in the flesh but made alive in the Spirit" (1 Pet. 3:18 AT). And, "Since therefore Christ suffered in the flesh, arm yourselves with the same way of thinking, for whoever has suffered in the flesh has ceased from sin" (1 Pet. 4:1). In 1 Peter 3:18, the phrase "in the flesh" specifies that in which Christ suffered: his human nature. Most likely, as in the NIV translation, the phrase "in the Spirit" specifies the agency by which Christ was raised from the dead—the action of the Holy Spirit.[11] And in 1 Peter 4:1, the phrase "in the flesh" again specifies that Christ suffered with respect to his physical, mortal, human existence. This verse affirms Christ's fleshly suffering in order to encourage believers to faithfully endure the same.

Now, unlike the passages from Paul that we have considered, these verses do not refer to or imply Christ's divinity. Nevertheless, the conclusion to the narrative recital of Christ's saving work in 1 Peter 3:18–22 is that he "has gone into heaven and is at the right hand of God, with angels, authorities, and powers having been subjected to him." The same Christ who suffered in the flesh is the one who, after his resurrection, ascended to heaven and sat down on the very throne of God. To sit on God's throne in heaven is to enact the unique divine sovereignty, to rule as only God may.[12] Peter's marking of the flesh as that in which Christ suffered may not have an overtly partitive motivation; he may simply be underscoring Christ's solidarity with those he

---

10. So Gundry, "The Form, Meaning and Background of the Hymn Quoted in 1 Timothy 3:16," 209–10.

11. So, e.g., Schreiner, *1, 2 Peter, Jude*, 184. Cf. 1 Tim. 3:16, where "vindicated by the Spirit" likely describes Christ's resurrection.

12. Bauckham, *Jesus and the God of Israel*, 152–81.

saves. Yet Peter's partitive delimiters here are entirely consistent with, and leave linguistic and conceptual room for, Christ having a more-than-human existence—namely, a divine one. As Peter confesses in 1:3, Jesus is "our Lord," and yet he also suffered for us—in his human nature.

### Christ's Twofold Form (Phil. 2:6-7)

As we mentioned at the outset of this section, in one sense every passage that ascribes to Jesus either a human characteristic or a divine one is, in the broadest sense, warrant for partitive exegesis. However, one passage stands out as applying especially clear pressure to distinguish between scriptural statements that speak of Christ's divinity and those that speak of his humanity. That passage is Philippians 2:6–7, since it does both, in parallel, back-to-back. If we begin at verse 5, we find Paul exhorting the Philippians to have in themselves the mind of Christ Jesus, "who, though he was in the form of God, did not count equality with God as something to be used for his own advantage, but emptied himself, by taking the form of a servant, being born in the likeness of men" (vv. 6–7 AT). The form of God in which Jesus existed prior to his incarnation and in which he continues to exist renders him God's equal.[13] Therefore, whatever nuances lie on the conceptual surface of the phrase "form of God" (μορφῇ θεοῦ, *morphē theou*), Paul uses the phrase to render the judgment that Jesus is one with the Father, that he shares with the Father all that it means to be the one true God.[14] But Jesus does not only exist in the form of God; he also took to himself "the form of a servant" (μορφὴν δούλου, *morphēn doulou*). What is this servant form? It is "the likeness of men." In these two verses Paul teaches that Jesus *is* God and that he *became* human. What does it mean that Jesus "emptied himself"? It is not that he denuded himself of divinity; that would not be God-befitting. Instead, being and remaining God and God the Father's equal, he entered into a state drastically inferior to that which is intrinsically his. Emptying acquires its meaning within the same verse: "by taking" (λαβών, *labōn*). Jesus "emptied himself" in the incarnation not by subtracting divinity, but by adding humanity.[15] He

13. The phrase "though he was in the form of God" renders a present participle in the Greek (ὑπάρχων). The text gives no indication that Jesus gave up the form of God when he took on the form of a servant. Anti-trinitarians (like the Socinians) have always contested interpreting "form of God" as including what theologians mean by "divine essence." The work of Holloway, *Philippians*, 117–29, is a modern, similar example of missing the theological force of this passage by extracting it from the broader canon (neglecting the *analogia fidei*) and the divine economy.

14. On the distinction between judgments and concepts, with particular reference to this passage, see esp. Yeago, "The New Testament and the Nicene Dogma."

15. Hence, we must understand verbs predicated of God the Son's incarnating action—"emptied himself," "became"—in a God-befitting way, and thus not as a displacement or trans-

thereby abased himself in order to serve others, the very vocation Paul presses on the Philippians (cf. Phil. 2:3–4).

So, in these verses, Paul uses the same word, "form," in two different registers, to identify both the divinity Christ eternally possesses and the humanity he assumed in his incarnation. There is only one agent here, one acting subject, Jesus the Messiah. But to this single Jesus Paul ascribes two "forms," two "whats." The "whats" of both God and humanity are his. These two "whats" do not contradict or compete with each other. These two realities do not jostle for space with each other. Since they coalesce in one person, one acting subject, it is possible to refer to that one person with a view to either reality, or both at once. And as we will see in the next two sections, Scripture speaks in all three ways.

## The Grammar of Christ's Two Natures

Thus far we have seen that Scripture pressures us to speak of the one Jesus Christ in two ways: one way insofar as he is God, another way insofar as he is man. If we ask how Scripture can do this, we must fall back upon the grammar we explored in the previous chapter. There, we saw that Christ is the single divine Son who assumes human nature into a unity with his person, thereby possessing two "natures." What might we say briefly about these natures as the "grammar" for our partitive exegesis rule?

### The Double Homoousion

Christ's divine nature ("the form of God") includes all that we have seen in previous chapters of Scripture's portrait of God. Everything that is God-befitting is true of Christ because he possesses the same being (*homoousios*) as the Father and the Spirit. To Christ belong unique divine prerogatives, such as creation and salvation, as well as divine perfections such as holiness, eternality, and immutability. He performs the same inseparable operations as the Father and the Spirit and possesses the same dignity, power, and glory as they do. Therefore, as we saw in the previous chapter, he genuinely possesses divine perfections and is subject of genuinely, uniquely divine actions.

When the Son assumed our human nature in the fullness of time, the one who is eternally *homoousios* with the Father and the Spirit became *homoousios* also with us (Matt. 1:18–25; Luke 1:31–32; Gal. 4:4; Heb. 2:10–16).

---

formation of his divinity. If Christ's divinity were thus negotiated with creaturely being, Paul would be talking about the gods of myths who are ontologically continuous with creation (and would effectively contradict himself; cf. 1 Cor. 8:4–6).

His humanity was thereby drawn into the closest possible communion with God. It is not merely that God the Son is present to his human nature in a special way, but that this human nature is his very own. In this personal union, Christ's two natures remain distinct, and the divine nature remains qualitatively different from and superior to his human nature. Christ's divine nature fills and permeates his humanity without displacing that nature's human integrity. The hypostatic union does not turn Christ's humanity into something more than human. Because the Son is God and therefore qualitatively transcendent as the creator of all things *ex nihilo*, his divinity is not set in a zero-sum game with his humanity. There is a deep compatibility between his divinity and humanity. The Son's human nature therefore is and remains in every way what ours is, only without sin (Heb. 2:17; 4:15). Turretin expresses this conciliar judgment: "The consubstantiality (*homoousion*) of Christ with us consists in identity of nature and essential properties."[16] The Son took as his own a truly human body and soul, complete with a human mind, will, and passions. He also assumed "its guiltless (*adiablētois*) infirmities," such as mortality, the need to learn, and susceptibility to sorrows.[17] Being fully and truly human, then, the Son bears genuinely human properties and is the subject of genuinely human actions and passions.

It has been important, traditionally, to emphasize that the Son's humanity lacked its own personality prior to the Son assuming it into his own person. Thus again Turretin: "Therefore, the singular human nature of Christ was complete physically in its substantial being as to its integral parts, but not metaphysically as to the mode of subsistence."[18] This means that the Son's assumed humanity gains nothing as a nature by the hypostatic union, though it does gain actual existence in his person. If the Son's humanity had its own personality, then the Son would have assumed a man rather than a human nature, which is incompatible with what we saw in the last chapter concerning Christ's unity. Considered apart from the hypostatic union, the Son's humanity would lack nothing *as a nature*, even though it would not exist in a person (it would be *anhypostatic*, impersonal).[19] But inasmuch as it belongs to the Son—and there is never a moment when it does not so belong, being created at the moment it was assumed—it belongs to his person (it is *enhypostatic*). Since it belongs to Christ, then, his humanity remains intimately united to

---

16. Turretin, *Institutes of Elenctic Theology* 13.5.13 (Giger, 2:309). Sinfulness is not an essential property of human nature because humans were not created sinful.

17. Turretin, *Institutes of Elenctic Theology* 13.13.10 (Giger, 2:351).

18. Turretin, *Institutes of Elenctic Theology* 13.5.13 (Giger, 2:309). On the larger significance and context of this clarification, see Riches, *Ecce Homo*, 107–27.

19. See Aquinas, *STh* III.4.2.*ad2*; Turretin, *Institutes of Elenctic Theology* 13.6.8.

and dependent on him for its personal existence. In all of this existence-in and dependence, though, Christ's divine and human natures remain distinct from each another: hence Chalcedon's adverbs, "without confusion or change, without division or separation."[20] The biblical teaching that pressures us to undertake a partitive exegesis also warrants the use of these adverbs in confessing how Christ's two natures unite in one person. And this abiding distinctness, which is a feature of the grammar of biblical discourse about the Trinity and Christ, warrants partitive exegesis.

### The "Partitive Exegesis" Rule

Partitive exegesis is therefore a strategy for reading scriptural statements about Christ that follows necessarily from the reality of Christ. Since any passage of Scripture might refer to Christ in view of either nature or both, partitive exegesis asks, "Which dimension of Christ's existence is the author talking about?" We may delve deeper into partitive exegesis, or the "form of a servant" rule, by unpacking three relevant aspects of this rule, illustrating each one with programmatic statements of partitive exegesis from some of its most exemplary practitioners.

First, partitive exegesis is a legitimate, warranted, exegetically necessary means of blocking faulty inferences from Christ's humanity or divinity that would undermine the integrity of the other. As our God-fittingness rule has shown, such inferences would be inconsistent with the noncompetitive relation between Christ's divinity and his humanity. These two natures can exist in one person without displacing one another. Moreover, those properties of Christ that are not God-befitting—like learning, growing tired, and dying—have a real foundation in Christ's humanity. In this way, partitive exegesis abides by the rule of God-befitting speech with regard to the incarnate Christ. It recognizes elements of biblical discourse about Christ that are uniquely God-befitting, which in turn helps identify those elements that are befitting the "economy" of his flesh. Distinguishing these elements furnishes a greater understanding not only of his divinity and humanity but also of our Lord's salvific economy.

To illustrate some of this, we can consider how Athanasius picks up the partitive qualifier "in the flesh" from 1 Peter 4:1 and applies it to when Jesus "is said to hunger and thirst and to toil and not to know, and to sleep, and to

---

20. Technically, on account of the Son's divine simplicity, there is a merely conceptual distinction between his person and his divinity, whereas there remains a real distinction between his person and his human nature. This is but one way of stating the Son's antecedence to his own human existence.

weep, and to ask, and to flee, and to be born, and to deprecate the cup, and in a word to undergo all that belongs to the flesh." Athanasius takes Peter's partitive qualifier to indicate "that these affections may be acknowledged as, not proper to the very Word by nature, but proper by nature to the very flesh." To anyone who would conclude that such declarations imperil a confession of Christ's true divinity, Athanasius responds, "Let no one then stumble at what belongs to man, but rather let a man know that in nature the Word himself is impassible, and yet because of that flesh which he put on, these things are ascribed to him, since they are proper to the flesh, and the body itself is proper to the Savior."[21] And on the same theme in a different work, Athanasius observes,

> And just as when we hear that he is Lord and God and true light, we perceive him as being from the Father, so it is right that when we hear "created" and "servant" and "suffered" not to refer these to the divinity, for they are out of place there, but rather to measure these statements in reference to the flesh which he bore for us. For these things properly belong to the flesh and the flesh is not another's but is the Word's.[22]

To be created and a servant and to have suffered are true of Christ, but not because of his divine nature. As Athanasius observes, "they are out of place" with regard to Christ's divinity. That is why we must measure—delimit, observe the proper scope and boundaries of—these statements with respect to Christ's assumed humanity. These creaturely realities really belong to the divine Word because that human nature really belongs to the divine Word.

Augustine also highlights the power of partitive exegesis to resolve apparent contradictions:

> Provided then that we know this rule for understanding the scriptures about God's Son and can thus distinguish the two resonances in them, one tuned to the form of God in which he is, and is equal to the Father, the other tuned to the form of a servant which he took and is less than the Father, we will not be upset by statements in the holy books that appear to be in flat contradiction with each other.[23]

The two distinct resonances are there in the scriptural passages, like a soprano and an alto line in a choral score.[24] But we must train our ears, so to speak,

---

21. Athanasius, *Against the Arians* 3.34 (NPNF[2] 4:412). Cf. Athanasius, *On the Incarnation* 18 (PPS 44a:88–91).

22. Athanasius, *Defense of the Nicene Creed* 3.14 (in Anatolios, *Athanasius*, 191). Cf. *On the Thought of Dionysius* 9; *Letters to Serapion* 2.8.1, 3.

23. Augustine, *The Trinity* 1.22 (WSA I/5:86).

24. As Ayres, *Augustine and the Trinity*, 146, comments, "Scripture itself sets out a *regula* or rule for our reading, speaking sometimes of Christ insofar as he was a human being, sometimes

to distinguish the two lines. Once we do, we will not be upset by apparent contradiction because we will know that, and know why, the contradiction is only apparent.

Second, partitive exegesis is concerned not merely with an abstract distinction between Christ's two natures but with the movement by which the one who *is* the eternal Son *became* a man for us and for our salvation. As we heard Augustine say just above, partitive exegesis enables us to distinguish "two resonances" in Scripture, "one tuned to the form of God in which he is . . . the other tuned to the form of a servant which he took." And all that Christ took in his incarnate economy—the human nature he took to himself and the saving ministry he undertook—he took for us. Hence, partitive exegesis is ultimately a matter of not only ontology but also soteriology. Partitive exegesis enables us to distinguish between Christ's preexistent divinity and "proexistent" humanity: all that Christ assumed in the incarnation, he assumed *pro nobis*, for us and for our salvation. As Gregory of Nazianzus proclaims,

> He assumed the worse that he might give us the better; he became poor that we through his poverty might become rich; he took upon him the form of a servant that we might receive back our liberty; he came down that we might be exalted; he was tempted that we might conquer; he was dishonored that he might glorify us; he died that he might save us; he ascended that he might draw to himself us, who were lying low in the fall of sin.[25]

Further, consider how Gregory incorporates ontology, soteriology, and even epistemology in this crisp statement of the rule of partitive exegesis:

> In sum: you must predicate the more sublime expressions of the Godhead, of the nature which transcends bodily experiences, and the lowlier ones of the compound, of him who because of you was emptied, became incarnate and (to use equally valid language) was "made man." Then next he was exalted, in order that you might have done with the earthbound carnality of your opinions and might learn to be nobler, to ascend with the Godhead and not linger on in things visible but rise up to spiritual realities, and that you might know what belongs to his nature and what to God's plan of salvation.[26]

---

with reference to his *substantia*, to his status as eternal. The division, it should be noted, is not simply between the two 'natures' of Christ, but relies on an understanding of Christ as one subject who may be spoken of as he is eternally and as he is having assumed flesh."

25. Gregory of Nazianzus, *Oration* 1.5 (*NPNF*² 7:203). See also Turretin, *Institutes of Elenctic Theology* 13.3.19.

26. Gregory of Nazianzus, *Oration* 29.18 (PPS 23:86). Cf. *Oration* 30.1.

In that final sentence, Gregory urges us to distinguish between two categories of legitimate predications about Christ. The first is "what belongs to his nature": his divine nature, the nature he has by nature, so to speak. The second is "what [belongs] to God's plan of salvation": the nature Christ took on to save us. The Greek here translated "God's plan of salvation" is actually a single word, οἰκονομία (*oikonomia*), "economy." Partitive exegesis marks the distinction between theology and economy as these concepts pertain to Christ's being and acts. Since Christ is God by nature, "theology" describes him as God. Since he became man for our sake, the "economy" details what belongs to that voluntarily entered state.[27]

Third and finally, in its parallel, reduplicative form, partitive exegesis articulates the respect in which, and basis on which, divine and human predicates pertain to Christ.[28] As God, Christ is the Creator; as man, he is also a creature. As man, Christ died; as God, he raised himself to life three days later (John 10:17–18). Reduplicative propositions such as these specify the reason why these predicates apply to this subject—namely, Jesus.[29] Partitive exegesis depends on the prior distinction between theology and economy. It clarifies the target and amplitude of scriptural statements that refer to each. The reduplicative mode of partitive exegesis sets this scriptural material in parallel columns and names the ontological ground of each.[30] Such reduplicative predication distinguishes, without separating, the two sources of the single incarnate Christ's saving actions. For an illustration of this technique, we can consider how Gregory of Nazianzus employs the reduplicative idiom in a lapidary, paradox-laden litany of what Christ did and suffered:

> As man he was baptized, but he absolved sins as God; he needed no purifying rites himself—his purpose was to hallow water. As man he was put to the test, but as God he came through victorious—yes, bids us be of good cheer, because he has conquered the world. He hungered—yet he fed thousands. He is indeed "living, heavenly bread." He thirsted—yet he exclaimed: "Whosoever thirsts, let him come to me and drink." Indeed he promised that believers would become fountains. He was tired—yet he is the "rest" of the weary and the burdened. . . . He is stoned, yet not hit; he prays, yet he hears prayer. He weeps, yet he puts an end to weeping. He asks where Lazarus is laid—he was man; yet he

27. On Gregory of Nazianzus's use of the theology and economy distinction, see Beeley, *Gregory of Nazianzus on the Trinity and the Knowledge of God*, 194–201.
28. For a helpful recent discussion of reduplicative propositions in Christology, see Moser, "Tools for Interpreting Christ's Saving Mysteries in Scripture," 291–93.
29. Moser, "Tools for Interpreting Christ's Saving Mysteries in Scripture," 292.
30. The four preceding sentences closely echo, and slightly revise, Jamieson, *The Paradox of Sonship*, 36–37.

raises Lazarus—he was God. He is sold, and cheap was the price—thirty pieces of silver; yet he buys back the world at the mighty cost of his own blood. . . . If the first set of expressions starts you going astray, the second set takes your error away.[31]

We can fittingly conclude this section and link our discussion to the previous chapter by considering Augustine's partitive exegesis of 1 Corinthians 2:8. Note the ease with which Augustine pivots between the single "who," the "Lord of glory," and his twofold manner of existence, the two "whats" in which he subsists.

> However, if it were not one and the same person who is Son of God in virtue of the form in which he is, and Son of man in virtue of the form of a servant which he took, the apostle Paul would not have said, *If they had known, they would never have crucified the Lord of glory* (1 Cor 2:8). It was in the form of a servant that he was crucified, and yet it was the Lord of glory who was crucified. For that "take-over" was such as to make God a man and a man God. Yet the careful and serious and devout reader will understand what is said of him for the sake of which, and what in virtue of which.[32]

## Partitive Exegesis in Action: Three Exegetical Case Studies

Now for some exegesis of our own. In this section, we will employ partitive exegesis to interpret passages that pose various theological or conceptual challenges. First, we will consider Jesus's assertion that the Father is greater than he is (John 14:28). Second, we will engage Paul's declaration that, at the end, Jesus submits to the Father, which some interpreters take to indicate an ontological difference (1 Cor. 15:24–28). Third, we will reckon with a series of passages in which Jesus is granted a new dignity or status at his enthronement in heaven (Acts 2:36; Rom. 1:3–4; Phil. 2:9–11; Heb. 1:3b–4). If Jesus became Lord or Son or obtained the divine name at his exaltation, does this mean that none of those dignities were his before that moment?

### The Father Greater Than the Son

Our first challenge is a passage that presents the Father as superior to the Son, and thus apparently presents a theological problem. Addressing his disciples on the eve of his crucifixion, Jesus says, "You heard me say to you,

---

31. Gregory of Nazianzus, *Oration* 29.20 (PPS 23:87–88).
32. Augustine, *The Trinity* 1.28 (WSA I/5:91).

'I am going away, and I will come to you.' If you loved me, you would have rejoiced, because I am going to the Father, for the Father is greater than I" (John 14:28). If the Father is greater than the Son, does that imply that the Son is somehow eternally, intrinsically inferior, and therefore not "God" in the fullest sense of the word? Not at all. Jesus, a human being addressing his disciples face-to-face, is speaking with reference to his human nature.[33]

But is partitive exegesis merely a desperate expedient, pulling a theological rabbit out of the exegetical hat? Not in light of the broader context. Consider that throughout John 14–17, Jesus's "farewell discourse," he describes his imminent crucifixion, resurrection, and ascension as his departure from the world and his return to the Father. "And if I go and prepare a place for you" (John 14:3); "You know the way to where I am going" (14:4); "Greater works than these will he do, because I am going to the Father" (14:12; cf. 14:19, 25, 27; 16:5, 7, 16, 28; 17:5, 11, 13). In the disciples' grief over the looming loss of Jesus's personal presence, they fail to see that Jesus's departure is better for them and better for him.

Jesus's departure is better *for them* because it is only by giving his life on the cross, rising from death, and ascending to heaven that Jesus will prepare a place for the disciples with the Father (14:2–3), bequeath to them an unassailable peace (14:27), defeat Satan (14:30–31), and overcome the world (16:33). It is only after suffering, rising again, and being enthroned in power in heaven that Jesus will send the disciples his Spirit, who will empower them for witness and convict the world (16:7–15; cf. 14:25–26). Only when Jesus is granted limitless power in heaven can he enable us to do "greater works" than even he did, as he acts from heaven to answer our prayers and transform people's lives throughout the world (14:12–14). Jesus's "going to the Father" in John 14:28 implies and entails all of this.

And Jesus's departure is not only better for us but also better *for Jesus*. It is only by dying, defeating death, and returning to his Father in heaven that Jesus, now a glorified human being, the first of the new creation, can be enthroned in power and accorded universal dominion. Jesus, speaking on the basis of his humanity, says that it is better for him to ascend to the Father, because only then will God answer Jesus's prayer, "And now, Father, glorify me in your own presence with the glory that I had with you before the world existed" (17:5). As Cyril comments, "What was profitable for him was his ascension to the Father and his now-manifest return to his own glory and

---

33. Some patristic interpreters argued that the Father's superiority to the Son in this verse refers to the Son's eternal generation. So, e.g., Gregory of Nazianzus, *Oration* 30.7 (PPS 23:98). While this is a biblical doctrine, we are not convinced that this is the right text for it. We will discuss the hermeneutics of eternal generation, and related trinitarian teaching, in the next chapter.

authority and God-befitting honor, no longer hidden in shadows."[34] Like in his transfiguration, in Jesus's ascension his humanity becomes more transparent to his divinity, thereby securing our own glorification. Hence, what is "better for Jesus" as man turns out again to be "better for us" because his whole human existence is a "proexistence": for us and for our salvation. As Augustine writes in a similar vein:

> For this reason therefore he said, "If you loved me, you would indeed be glad because I go to the Father"—because congratulations should be extended to human nature precisely because it has been so taken up by the only-begotten Word that it was established immortal in heaven, and earth was made so sublime that dust incorruptible sat at the right hand of the Father. For in this way he said that he would go to the Father. For in truth he who was with him was going to him. But to go to him and to withdraw from us was this: to change and make immortal the mortal that he took from us and to lift into heaven that by which he was on earth for our sake.[35]

Augustine's partitive exegesis of this verse alerts us to another crucial detail in the text. When Jesus says, "I am going to the Father," that statement only makes sense with reference to his human nature. It is only in his human nature that he can be in any sense distant from the Father; it is only in his human nature that he can "go" to the Father. In his divine nature, he is always "with" his Father, in the indissoluble unity of the one divine nature. So it is not arbitrary or forced to limit the referent of "the Father is greater than I" to Jesus's human nature, since Jesus's immediately prior statement moves within precisely that limit. Hence, Augustine is on the mark to conclude, "Insofar as, therefore, the Son is not equal to the Father, he was going to the Father, from whom he will come to judge the living and the dead; but insofar as the Only-Begotten is equal to the Begetter, he never withdraws from the Father, but is with him everywhere, wholly, with equal divinity, which no place confines."[36] Far from being an ill-fitting cover-up of a theologically awkward

---

34. Cyril of Alexandria, *Commentary on John* 10.1 (Maxwell, 2:202).

35. Augustine, *Tractates on the Gospel of John* 78.3 (FC 90:109–10). See also Cyril of Alexandria, *Commentary on John* 10.1 (Maxwell, 2:204).

36. Augustine, *Tractates on the Gospel of John* 78.3 (FC 90:107). Elsewhere, Augustine takes John 14:28 as a crucial test case for the deity of Christ. His solution is that Scripture affirms the Son as both equal to the Father by virtue of the form of God (e.g., John 10:30) and as less than the Father by virtue of the form of a servant (John 14:28). He writes,

> For he did not so take the form of a servant that he lost the form of God in which he was equal to the Father. So if the form of a servant was taken on in such a way that the form of God was not lost—since it is the same only begotten Son of the Father who is both in the form of a servant and in the form of God, equal to the Father in the form of God,

text, partitive exegesis helps us discern the mystery of the economy that pulses through John 14:28. Jesus returns to the Father who is greater than him, as man, in order to obtain what is better for him and better for us.

## The Son Subjected to the Father

Another passage that seems to challenge Jesus's complete unity and equality with the Father is 1 Corinthians 15:24–28, where Paul writes,

> Then comes the end, when he delivers the kingdom to God the Father after destroying every rule and every authority and power. For he must reign until he has put all his enemies under his feet. The last enemy to be destroyed is death. For "God has put all things in subjection under his feet." But when it says, "all things are put in subjection," it is plain that he is excepted who put all things in subjection under him. When all things are subjected to him, then the Son himself will also be subjected to him who put all things in subjection under him, that God may be all in all.

For many scholars, an intrinsic, ontological inferiority of the Son to the Father seems implied when Jesus "delivers the kingdom to God the Father" (1 Cor. 15:24), at which point he "will also be subjected" to God the Father (1 Cor. 15:28).[37] If so, it would seem a natural inference to take these verses to weigh against Christ's divine equality with the Father. But that would of course be to read this passage in something other than a God-befitting manner, transgressing also our fifth principle concerning the Trinity's ontological unity and equality. Indeed, there are at least three strong signs within this passage that Paul is speaking of Christ as human, on the basis of his humanity.[38]

First, the passage plainly presupposes Christ's continued, postresurrection embodiment, and Christ's humanity is a central theme of the passage's context. Within the passage, the one who will destroy every power, who must

---

in the form of a servant the mediator of God and men the man Christ Jesus—who can fail to see that in the form of God he too is greater than himself and in the form of a servant he is less than himself? And so it is not without reason that scripture says both; that the Son is equal to the Father and that the Father is greater than the Son. The one is to be understood in virtue of the form of God, the other in virtue of the form of a servant, without any confusion. (*The Trinity* 1.14 [WSA I/5:77])

37. So, with varying nuances and emphases, Kreitzer, *Jesus and God in Paul's Eschatology*, 159; Ziesler, *Pauline Christianity*, 39–40; Dunn, *The Theology of Paul the Apostle*, 248–49; McGrath, *The Only True God*, 50.

38. For a fuller version of this argument, see Jamieson, "1 Corinthians 15.28 and the Grammar of Paul's Christology," from which these arguments, including a few verbatim sentences here and there, are drawn.

reign until death is defeated, is the resurrected Christ. Though his resurrection renders him a new kind of human being, it is precisely as a human being that Christ now reigns in heaven (vv. 25–26). In the broader context: verse 21 says, "For as by a man came death, by a man has come also the resurrection of the dead." And verses 45–49 continue the comparison between Adam and "the last Adam" (v. 45), the "man of heaven" whose image his people will one day bear (vv. 47–49).

Second, Paul cites and alludes to Scripture in a manner that portrays the Son's submission to the Father as a climactic act of required human obedience. In other words, Christ's final act of submission to the Father (1 Cor. 15:28) completes his representative fulfillment of the human vocation of being God's "ruled rulers," or vicegerents.[39] We see this in three places in our passage and its context where Paul either cites or alludes to Scripture. First, in verse 27, Paul cites Psalm 8:6, which celebrates the dominion God granted humanity at creation, in order to present Christ's rule in heaven as the fulfillment of this ruled rule. By his resurrection, Christ brings Adam's commission to fruition.[40] And a necessary component of this commission is obedience. Second, in verse 21 Paul alludes to the whole creation and fall narrative of Genesis 1–3 with his phrase, "by a man came death." The problem that Christ's resurrection and death-destroying reign addresses is the legacy of Adam's ruinous disobedience. Third, in verse 24, when Paul says that Christ will destroy "every rule and every authority and power," he echoes language from the Old Greek translation of Daniel 7:13–14, 26–27, about one "like a son of man" whom "all dominions shall serve and obey." These citations and allusions add up to a portrait of Christ as the Messiah, the Son of Man, who rules as a representative human being, restoring humanity to their place as ruled rulers of creation. Since humanity's deviance from our appointed destiny was instigated by Adam's sin, it is fitting for the final feat of the last Adam's redemptive reign to be an act of obedience.

Third, 1 Corinthians 15:28 narrates the end of the Son's messianic mediation, the completion of the redemptive rule which the Father delegated to him. Jesus holds the office of Messiah as a human, for humans. And the sequence in 1 Corinthians 15:20–28, especially verses 24–28, forecasts the final tasks of this redemptive rule. Christ's resurrection renders him "the firstfruits of those who have fallen asleep," guaranteeing the resurrection,

---

39. We borrow the phrase "ruled rulers" from Leeman, *Political Church*, 154.

40. Paraphrasing Meyer, *Adam's Dust and Adam's Glory in the Hodayot and the Letters of Paul*, 168.

at his coming, of those who belong to him (v. 23). Then and only then will death, the last enemy, be defeated (vv. 25–26). When at last Christ has subdued all his enemies, death included, there will be no need for him to reign in a manner distinguishable from that of God the Father. At the successful completion of his messianic mission, Christ will return to the Father the keys to his office. Mission accomplished. Once all enemies have been subdued, the general will return to the king who commissioned him and will render fitting submission to that king.[41] As we will consider below, Christ's distinctly redemptive, mediating, messianic reign began at his enthronement in heaven (Acts 2:32–36; Rom. 1:3–4; 14:9; Phil. 2:9–11; Heb. 1:3–4) and will conclude with his return.

Hence, the scope and significance of the Son's subjection to the Father in 1 Corinthians 15:28 are conditioned by his humanity. As Augustine puts it, "Inasmuch as he is God he will jointly with the Father have us as subjects; inasmuch as he is priest he will jointly with us be subject to him."[42] This submission is not eternal, but rather is enacted at the consummation of all things. The Son's submission to the Father is not something true by virtue of his "naked" divinity, but something he does as a human, in and through his humanity.[43]

### Jesus Becoming Lord and Son

The third challenge consists of a network of four passages in which Jesus is granted a new dignity or status at his enthronement in heaven, following his resurrection and ascension.

> This Jesus God raised up, and of that we all are witnesses. Being therefore exalted at the right hand of God, and having received from the Father the promise of the Holy Spirit, he has poured out this that you yourselves are seeing and hearing. For David did not ascend into the heavens, but he himself says,
>
> > "The Lord said to my Lord,
> > 'Sit at my right hand,
> >     until I make your enemies your footstool.'"

---

41. Ciampa and Rosner, *The First Letter to the Corinthians*, 767–68, 776–77, deploy this analogy in detail. If one keeps the analogy within its proper scope, as they do, it is entirely fitting.

42. Augustine, *The Trinity* 1.20 (WSA I/5:84).

43. We borrow the term "naked" (γυμνός) from Cyril of Alexandria to refer to the Son in his divinity alone, apart from his assumed humanity. See Cyril, *On the Unity of Christ* (PPS 13:103; PG 75:1324); discussion in McGuckin, *Saint Cyril of Alexandria and the Christological Controversy*, 221–22.

Let all the house of Israel therefore know for certain that God has made him both Lord and Christ, this Jesus whom you crucified. (Acts 2:32–36)

. . . concerning his Son, who was descended from David according to the flesh and was appointed the Son of God in power according to the Spirit of holiness by his resurrection from the dead, Jesus Christ our Lord . . . (Rom. 1:3–4 AT)[44]

Therefore God has highly exalted him and bestowed on him the name that is above every name, so that at the name of Jesus every knee should bow, in heaven and on earth and under the earth, and every tongue confess that Jesus Christ is Lord, to the glory of God the Father. (Phil. 2:9–11)

He is the radiance of the glory of God and the exact imprint of his nature, and he upholds the universe by the word of his power. After making purification for sins, he sat down at the right hand of the Majesty on high, becoming as much superior to angels as the name he has inherited is more excellent than theirs. (Heb. 1:3–4 AT)[45]

These passages have a great deal in common.[46] Each proclaims or presupposes Christ's resurrection and ascent to heaven. Each announces what took place next, at Christ's enthronement in heaven. Each asserts that, at that time, Christ was given something, or became something: "God has made him Lord and Christ" (Acts 2:36); he "was appointed the Son of God in power" (Rom. 1:4); God "bestowed on him the name that is above every name"—namely, the unique divine name (Phil. 2:9);[47] Jesus became "as much superior to angels as the name he has inherited is more excellent than theirs" (Heb. 1:4). Finally, each passage has elicited two opposite errors.

One error is to infer that whatever Jesus became at his enthronement, he must not in any sense have been before. If it was only at his enthronement that Jesus became Lord, was appointed Son, received the name above every name, and became superior to the angels, then prior to that enthronement he must not have been Lord or Son or possessed the name or been superior to angels.

---

44. We have changed the ESV's "declared to be" to "appointed," since basic senses of the Greek verb used here (ὁρίζω) are "determine, fix, set, appoint," and the verb never means "declare" in the NT or other Hellenistic Greek literature. For discussion of the one usage that BDAG 723 §2b, in our opinion, erroneously glosses as "declare," see Jamieson, *The Paradox of Sonship*, 162n58.

45. We have altered the ESV's "having become" to "becoming," since the aorist participle (γενόμενος) reports an action that happened at the same time as, and is a logical consequence of, Jesus's enthronement.

46. See Jamieson, *The Paradox of Sonship*, esp. 156–68.

47. On "the name above every name" in Phil. 2:9 as YHWH, the unique divine name, see, e.g., Bauckham, *Jesus and the God of Israel*, 199–200.

A second error is to assert that all the phrases cited above must only reveal, or openly declare, something that was already the case. This second error is especially appealing. After all, we know from these same authors that Jesus is by nature Lord and Son (Luke 1:43; 2:11; Rom. 1:3; 8:32; 10:13; Gal. 4:4). He always possesses God's nature and therefore his name (Phil. 2:6). He is intrinsically superior to angels as their creator and sustainer (Heb. 1:3, 10–12).

The first error runs aground on all these texts, since they teach that Jesus is God by nature. The second error collides with the verbs in the four passages we are considering: "made" (Acts 2:36); "appointed" (Rom. 1:4); "exalted" and "bestowed" (Phil. 2:9); "becoming" and "inherited" (Heb. 1:4). None of these can be adequately glossed as "revealed" or "made known as." To treat each of these actions as simply showing something that was already true is to screen out the primary assertion of each passage. So, how do we resolve this interpretive dilemma?

We can begin to unravel these threads by asking, What are these passages about? The simplest summary answer is "Jesus's enthronement as Messiah." Among other things, the Messiah is a king. He is the descendent of David, heir to David's throne (2 Sam. 7:12–14). This means that if Jesus is the Messiah, he needs a throne to reign on. Where is that throne? And when did he begin to reign? Our four-voice chorus of NT passages answers in unison, "His throne is in heaven, and he began to reign when he ascended there after rising from the dead."

How did Peter (speaking at Pentecost in Acts 2), Paul, and the author of Hebrews know this? Because Scripture told them. Two OT passages are especially critical for understanding our NT passages and indeed for understanding Scripture's entire witness to the person and work of Christ: Psalm 2:7 and 110:1. In Psalm 2, God laughs in the face of the raging, rebelling nations (vv. 1–4). Why will the peoples' plots prove vain (v. 1)? Because God will pronounce these fearsome words: "As for me, I have set my King on Zion, my holy hill" (v. 6). It is this royal enthronement, this setting a king in office, that the next verse proclaims: "I will tell of the decree: The LORD said to me, 'You are my Son; today I have begotten you'" (v. 7). This Son will reign over not only Israel but all nations, to the ends of the earth, and those who refuse his rule will be ruined (vv. 8–9).

Psalm 110:1 also announces the enthronement of the Messiah. In the opening verse of this Psalm of David, we read, "The LORD says to my Lord: 'Sit at my right hand, until I make your enemies your footstool.'" The throne on which God invites the Messiah to sit is his own throne, the only throne in heaven. The conversation David was granted to overhear was a prophetic preview of Christ's installation on the throne of heaven.

Both Psalm 2:7 and Psalm 110:1 are decisive background for our four passages.[48] Paul's assertion in Romans 1:4 that Jesus "was appointed Son of God in power" clearly alludes to Psalm 2:7. Further, Hebrews 1:5 cites Psalm 2:7 to clarify that the "name" Jesus inherited is "Son," in the sense of "Messiah reigning in power," and that it is by inheriting this name and the heavenly rule to which it entitles him that Jesus, "who for a little while was made lower than the angels" (Heb. 2:9), is now superior to angels. Further, Acts 2:34–35 cites Psalm 110:1 in full, and Hebrews 1:3 alludes to it and then cites it in verse 13.

The change in Christ's status that all these passages announce is analogous to the change that takes place when a US president is sworn in. After receiving a majority of electoral college votes, he or she becomes president-elect, entitled to the office but not yet exercising it. Only after being sworn in on January 20 does the president's term of office begin. During his earthly ministry, Christ was rightly identified as Messiah, as the Son of David (e.g., Matt.16:16; 20:30; 21:9). But it was only when he was enthroned in heaven that he began to exercise the full prerogatives of the office.

How does partitive exegesis play into all this? In a sense, we have been doing it all along. But we can summarize this whole discussion by saying that the change in all these passages pertains to Christ's human nature, not his divine one. When Jesus rose from the dead, God the Father granted him all authority in heaven and on earth (Matt. 28:18). He already possessed that authority as God, but he received it as man. That same principle—"already" as God, "newly" as man—holds for many details in these verses. According to Luke, Jesus is Lord even before his birth (Luke 1:43; 2:11), but according to Acts 2:36, at his resurrection and exaltation God "made" him Lord: God conferred on him the right to fully exercise the Lordship that is his by natural divine right. In Romans 1:3–4, Jesus is already God's Son according to his divinity, and at his enthronement he enters into the powerful office of messianic sonship. In Philippians 2:9–11, that Jesus is "given" the divine name likely means that he is now, as a human being, granted to exercise the authority intrinsic to, and receive the worship due to, the bearer of that name. In Hebrews 1:3–4, as the divine Son by nature, Jesus is "the radiance of the glory of God and the exact imprint of his nature," and at his enthronement he obtained the office of universal lordship to which only he, as God incarnate, was entitled. In other words, none of these assertions imply either lack or change in Christ's

48. For studies of these two verses' relevance to these NT passages, see esp. L. C. Allen, "The Old Testament Background of (Προ)'Οριζειν in the New Testament"; Hay, *Glory at the Right Hand*; Hengel, "'Sit at My Right Hand!'"; Whitsett, "Son of God, Seed of David"; Jipp, *Christ Is King*, 174–75, 201–2, 207–8; Jipp, "'For David Did Not Ascend into Heaven . . .' (Acts 2:34a)."

divine nature. They all apply to Jesus exclusively on the basis of the human nature with which he clothed himself to become our redeemer.

In reading all four passages, it is crucial for us to keep in mind the shocking, category-collapsing novelty of the ascension. A flesh-and-blood human being is now present in heaven, and not just present but seated on the throne. Patristic interpreters often grasp this nettle more acutely than modern ones.[49] At his ascension and enthronement, Jesus received as man what he always possessed as God. Jesus began to do as man what he had always done as God: reign over all. Along these lines, Athanasius's treatment of Philippians 2:9 is clarifying and illuminating.

> And the term in question, "highly exalted," does not signify that the essence of the Word was exalted, for he was ever and is "equal to God," but the exaltation is of the manhood. Accordingly this is not said before the Word became flesh; that it might be plain that "humbled" and "exalted" are spoken of his human nature; for where there is humble estate, there too may be exaltation; and if because of his taking flesh "humbled" is written, it is clear that "highly exalted" is also said because of it. For of this was man's nature in want, because of the humble estate of the flesh and of death. . . . But if now for us the Christ is entered into heaven itself, though he was even before and always Lord and framer of the heavens, for us therefore is that present exaltation written.[50]

"For us": he did this all on our account. All this he endured and achieved for our sake. He was exalted in order to glorify us (1 Cor. 2:7); he was enriched with spoils of victory over death in order to give gifts to us (Eph. 4:7–8). All that he became in the economy, he became for us. He became incarnate, not because he lacked anything, but because we lacked everything.[51]

## Conclusion: All That Christ Did and Suffered and Became

We close this chapter by drawing two complementary conclusions regarding how partitive exegesis helps us to rightly perceive Scripture and the Christ to whom Scripture bears witness. First, regarding Scripture, partitive exegesis helps us perceive how pervasive and coherent is its witness to Christ's divinity. The most natural, forceful objection to partitive exegesis is that it assumes

---

49. So, e.g., the fourth-century Latin theologian Rufinus's perceptive partitive comments on Christ's ascension in *A Commentary on the Apostles' Creed*, 65–66.

50. Athanasius, *Against the Arians* 1.41; translation adapted from *NPNF*[2] 4:330, with the Scripture citation modernized, roughly following the ESV.

51. For a rich exposition of this theme, see Athanasius, *Against the Arians* 3.37–40 (*NPNF*[2] 4:414–16).

what it needs to prove. This objection holds that partitive exegesis projects a "two-nature" Christology onto the biblical authors and tidies up in exegesis what is actually messier in the texts. In response, we would flip the objection on its head. Frequent modern scholarly objections notwithstanding, every author in the NT bears witness to Christ's divine identity.[52] And as we have discussed in previous chapters, it is only by committing the critical error of thinking of "divinity" and "humanity" as kinds of being that can be classed and compared together that one can see the ascription of both to Christ as creating any kind of conceptual or exegetical "mess." As every parent knows, clothes and toys heaped on a floor make a mess. They can only make a mess because they take up space and therefore compete for space. By contrast, in this narrow respect, Christ's divinity and humanity are more like color and sound. More of one does not mean less of another.

Further, as our exegetical case studies have shown, coming to the text with ears attuned to hear both frequencies, divine and human, ascribed to the one Christ has helped us to hear what is there in the text. When it suits their arguments against Christ's full divinity, modern scholars sometimes seem to forget that the Christ of whom a passage speaks is human. The Christ who submits to the Father at the consummation of all things still is, and forever will be, human (1 Cor. 15:28). The one who confesses that the Father is greater than him is the one who, as human, is away from the Father and will soon close that gap (John 14:28).

Finally, having our ears tuned to both resonances helps us to discern the order and harmony of Scripture's two-part song about Christ's person. Christ is both equal to God as God and less than God as man. He is both timeless and born in time, both limitless and subject to the limits of the flesh. As Gregory of Nazianzus says—or, one might say, sings—"I shall cry out the meaning of this day: the fleshless one is made flesh, the Word becomes material, the invisible is seen, the intangible is touched, the timeless has a beginning, the Son of God becomes Son of Man—'Jesus Christ, yesterday and today, the same also for all ages!'"[53]

Second, embedded as it is in Scripture as an aspect of God's pedagogy, the form of a servant rule helps us rightly behold Christ, and in him our salvation. Partitive exegesis enables us to perceive that everything Christ did, he did for us. Partitive exegesis is not merely about distinguishing between divinity and

---

52. See, e.g., Rowe, "Luke and the Trinity"; Gathercole, *The Preexistent Son*; Bauckham, *Jesus and the God of Israel*; Rowe, *Early Narrative Christology*; Gathercole, "Paul's Christology"; Tilling, *Paul's Divine Christology*; Hays, "Faithful Witness, Alpha and Omega"; Hays, *Echoes of Scripture in the Gospels*.

53. *Oration* 38.2 (in Daley, *Gregory of Nazianzus*, 118).

humanity in Christ; it is about perceiving the unified thread of the incarnate economy he undertook for our sakes. This rule helps us perceive the scope and substance of Christ's journey into our "far country." Everything Jesus is and does as man aims at our salvation. As Rowan Williams has put it, "The Son needs nothing and so is free to give everything."[54] From the economy's inception to its consummation, from the virginal conception to Christ's enthronement in heaven, all that Christ did and suffered and became, he did and suffered and became for us.[55] In other words, partitive exegesis directs us not to Christ's humanity considered in abstraction from his person but as he subsists in it while reconciling the world to himself. When the exegetical question of "What?" or "In what sense?" directs us to Christ's humanity, the next question is "Why?" And the heart of the answer is always: "For us and for our salvation."

---

54. R. Williams, *Christ the Heart of Creation*, 163.
55. This point is well made by Wiles, *The Spiritual Gospel*, 150, summarizing Cyril's account of Christ's incarnate economy as proclaimed in John's Gospel.

# 9

# God from God

## From Missions to Processions

**Principle 7:** Within their unity and equality, the three persons exist in relations of origin: the Son is eternally generated from the Father, and the Spirit eternally proceeds from the Father and the Son.

**Rule 10:** Scripture often attributes to the divine persons ordered relations and actions that do not compromise their unity and equality, but only signify that one person eternally exists from another: the Son from the Father, the Spirit from the Father and the Son. Read Scripture in a way that recognizes and upholds these ordered relations of origin.

One of the main goals of this book is to provide categories in which everything Scripture says about Christ can find a fitting place. Think of a tidy, well-stocked kitchen, where every dish and ingredient and tool has an ample, orderly, intuitively located home. Discerning the theological grammar of Scripture gives us drawers of the right size, shape, and location in which to store up knowledge of God in Christ. Reading Scripture is often like learning where things belong in someone else's kitchen. In previous chapters, we have been discovering where the drawers are, what goes in them, and why.

Pursuing the vision of Christ's glory, we have seen that he is one and equal with the Father. Together with the Father and the Holy Spirit, the Son is the one true God of Israel. Because he is one God together with the Father and the Spirit, the Son's works are identical to those of the Father and the Spirit and may not be divided from them. This same Son who is and remains God also became a man to accomplish our salvation. Since the Son took human nature into personal union with himself, all kinds of paradoxical predications follow. For example, it was the Lord of glory who was crucified for us. And finally, because he has both divine and human natures, Scripture speaks of the Son in ways befitting God and in ways befitting the economy of his flesh. He is less than the Father as man while remaining equal to the Father as God.[1]

But there are many scriptural statements about Christ that do not fit into one of the drawers we have so far discovered. For instance, consider John 5:19, which this chapter will treat in detail: "Truly, truly, I say to you, the Son can do nothing of himself, but only what he sees the Father doing. For whatever the Father does, that the Son does likewise" (AT). At first blush, the phrase "can do nothing of himself" might lead us to think Christ is speaking with reference to his human nature. But the following sentence rules that out. If the Son does everything the Father does, then the activity Jesus speaks of exceeds what he accomplishes as a human being. So how is it that Jesus can perform divine acts in a manner that is not "of himself"? And what role do such enigmatic statements play in the movement by which God draws our hearts and minds upward to behold his glory?

This chapter introduces our final principle and rule. Both concern the eternal relations of origin within the Trinity. As we will see, some passages of Scripture teach that one divine person eternally exists from another, which means that we need to read all related passages in light of this eternal "fromness." This is what we will call the "from another" rule. Here we arrive at both the limit of what we can say and the pinnacle of what we must see.

In somewhat of a departure from the norm, instead of featuring an extended exegetical case study, this chapter will largely consist of examining a series of three sets of biblical pressures: first, the names "Father," "Son," and "Holy Spirit" and their scriptural amplification; second, that the divine persons' distinct modes of action reveal their distinct modes of being; third, that the Son and the Spirit's missions in time reveal their eternal processions. After this, we will briefly discuss the grammar of the principle concerning

---

1. Following Augustine: "The Catholic rule of faith: Christ equal to the Father as Word, less than the Father as man" (*Homilies on the Gospel of John* 18.1 [WSA III/12:321]).

relations of origin and the conceptual dimensions of its derivative rule. We then conclude by reflecting on how the divine missions savingly draw us into the mystery of the Trinity.

## First Pressure: The Names "Father," "Son," and "Holy Spirit" and Their Scriptural Amplification

In this section and the two that follow, we measure the biblical pressure by which Scripture teaches us to contemplate the distinctions and order between the Father, Son, and Holy Spirit. In chapter 5, we took an initial pass at this material and saw *that* the Father, Son, and Holy Spirit are distinct in their relations to one another; now we see something more of *how*. Further, the discussion of the Trinity's inseparable operation in chapter 6 both anticipated and, in a sense, borrowed from the fuller discussion of the divine persons' eternal relations that this chapter undertakes.

Our first set of pressures consists of the biblical names "Father," "Son," and "Holy Spirit" and the manner in which Scripture expounds those names. We will begin with how "Father" and "Son" are evidently relative designations, then consider how Scripture discloses more fully the Son's relation to the Father, and finally conclude with Scripture's amplification of the name "Holy Spirit."[2]

### "Father" and "Son" as Relative Names

In its everyday usage, the word "son" names a relation, as does "father." A son is always the son *of* someone. To say, "Simon is the son of John" is to say, "John is the father of Simon." The terms "father" and "son" imply one another. They are reciprocal or correlative. Ordinarily, they pertain to the relation in which a man is the progenitor of a male child (though there are extraordinary uses, as in adoption). We call these terms "relative" because the reality they signify is a relation.[3] And this relation is one of origin: a son

---

2. Our approach to the personal names of the Trinity in this section is particularly indebted to Swain, "Divine Trinity," esp. 87–90, 92–102.

3. For a discussion that was widely influential in antiquity of "relation" or "relative things" as a philosophical category, see Aristotle, *Categories* 7, 6a36–37: "We call *relatives* all such things as are said to be just what they are, *of* or *than* other things, or in some way *in relation to* something else" (trans. Ackrill, 17). Aristotle extends his discussion to cover relative terms in *Categories* 7, 6b6–8, and offers a second definition of relatives as things for which "*being is the same as being somehow related to something*" in *Categories* 8, a31–32 (trans. Ackrill, 22 [emphasis original]). On these two definitions of Aristotle, see the discussion in Sorabji, *The Philosophy of the Commentators, 200–600 AD*, 3:79–81. See also Plato's distinction between absolute and relative entities and terms in, e.g., *Sophist* 255c; *Republic* 438ab; and *Parmenides* 133d.

is *from* his father. The terms "father" and "son" refer to a subject not simply as that subject is in itself but only as that subject exists in relation to another.

Similarly, in Scripture, when used as titles that identify who Jesus and his heavenly Father are intrinsically, the terms "Father" and "Son" are not absolute but relative.[4] Specifically, these two names are correlative: they name a mutually implicating relation. Cyril of Alexandria explains, "Relative names mutually signify one another, and each grants knowledge of the other. . . . Accordingly, 'Father' is a relative name and equally so also is 'Son.'"[5] This is why, he goes on to reason, if one knows the Son, one knows the Father (John 8:19), and, "No one who denies the Son has the Father. Whoever confesses the Son has the Father also" (1 John 2:23).[6] Throughout the NT, the personal identities of the Father and the Son are defined with reference to each other.[7] This is evident both in the simple, unqualified use of the titles "the Father" and "the Son" (Matt. 28:19; John 3:35; 1 Cor. 15:24, 28) and in Jesus's frequent references to "my Father" (Matt. 7:21; 12:50; John 10:29). Jesus claims a categorically unique relationship with God when he calls him "my Father"—that is, "his own father" (John 5:18). Similarly, the Son is the Father's "own" (Rom. 8:32). In all these instances, "Father" names one divine person as the source of another; "Son" names one as begotten from the other. We will need to explore this biological metaphor of "begetting" more below, but for the moment it suffices to see that these kinship names are reciprocal and point us to a relation of origin.[8]

Further, the mutual relation these names signify is unique, characterized by the singularity of God himself. Consider Jesus's words in Matthew 11:27: "All things have been handed over to me by my Father, and no one knows the Son except the Father, and no one knows the Father except the Son and anyone

---

4. All scriptural uses of "Father" and "Son" to name God are relative in some sense, but they do not always name the same relation. God is named "Father" in Scripture by virtue of his role as creator of all (Isa. 45:9–13) and as the redeemer of Israel (Exod. 4:22; Deut. 32:4–6, 18). When used to describe God's relation to all things as their creator, "Father" signifies God's essence and refers to all three persons in common. And as Carson, "John 5:26," 86, observes, "Son" can refer to Jesus "as the Son of God by virtue of his role as the ultimate Davidic, messianic king, without any necessary eternal and 'Trinitarian' association." Hence our qualification above: it is when they are used to identify the divine persons that the terms are relative to each other.

5. Cyril of Alexandria, *Dialogues on the Trinity* 4.509c–d (SC 237:154 [AT]); see also Origen, *On First Principles* 1.2.10.

6. Cyril of Alexandria, *Dialogues on the Trinity* 4.510a (SC 237:156 [AT]).

7. For an in-depth study of a few key instances of this phenomenon in Paul, see Hill, *Paul and the Trinity*. See also Watson, "The Triune Divine Identity."

8. As Soulen, "*Generatio, Processio Verbi, Donum Nominis*," 137, observes, "Unlike most common nouns, kinship terms are inherently reciprocal in character."

to whom the Son chooses to reveal him."[9] The mutual, exclusive knowledge that the Father and the Son have of each other attests their divine unity and equality. Notice also how the two titles are used without further specification: "the Father" and "the Son." In this sense, there is only one Father and one Son: their relationship is categorically unique. The Father is not "a" father, or like a father; instead he is *the* Father of *this* Son. "Father" names who God the Father uniquely is.

When we perceive the correlativity of these names against the background of God's oneness, we can see how the relations signified by "Father" and "Son" are intrinsic to God's life. This mutual relation is thus characterized by all of God's perfections, such as eternality and immutability. That is, we must understand the relation itself in a God-befitting manner. "Father" is not something that God becomes, something he might not have been. Instead, "Father" signifies the "first" person of the Trinity's unique identity in relation to his Son. The Father is always Father of his Son. All the same, *mutatis mutandis*, can and must be said of the Son. "Father" and "Son" name a relation within God, not a relation between God and what is not God. Again, "Father" and "Son" do not refer in an absolute or undifferentiated fashion to the single divine essence. Instead, they name a relation in which that essence subsists.[10]

### Scriptural Amplification of "Son"

This understanding of "Father" and "Son" as correlative, relational terms that indicate an eternal relation of origin is confirmed by the way that the NT amplifies—that is, expounds or unfolds—what it means for Jesus to be God's Son. We will consider two ways in which Scripture amplifies the title of "Son."

The first is taken from John's Gospel and concerns what it means to say the Son is "begotten" of the Father. In the prologue, John uses the title "only begotten" for the Son: "And the Word became flesh, and dwelt among us, and we beheld his glory, glory as of the only begotten from the Father, full of grace and truth" (John 1:14 AT). In contrast to the earliest English translations from the Greek (Tyndale, KJV, Geneva Bible), most modern translations

---

9. For a concise, illuminating exegesis of Matt. 11:25–27 that traces its trinitarian implications, see Swain, "The Mystery of the Trinity." For a careful study of the mutually constituting identities of Father and Son in Matthew's Gospel, see Leim, *Matthew's Theological Grammar*.

10. This is a common observation among early theologians. See, e.g., Athanasius, *Against the Arians* 1.33, 34; 3.6 (NPNF² 4:325–26, 397); Basil, *Against Eunomius* 1.5, 2.9 (cf. 2.4, 22, 28–29); Gregory of Nazianzus, *Oration* 30.19–20; Gregory of Nyssa, *To Peter* 7g; *Against Eunomius* 3.1.133–34; 3.2.107–8, 143. On the role of relation and the relative divine names in Gregory of Nyssa's trinitarian theology, see Maspero, "Life from Life," esp. 415–25; Maspero, "Trinitarian Theology in Gregory of Nyssa's *Contra Eunomium* I," 472, 491.

take the Greek word μονογενής (*monogenēs*) to mean "unique, only" or "one and only," with no necessary implication of begetting.[11] However, Lee Irons has recently made a detailed, compelling case that *monogenēs*, when applied to the Son in John's Gospel and first epistle (John 1:14, 18; 3:16, 18; 1 John 4:9), is always used in a metaphorical biological sense meaning "only begotten."[12] Note that in John 1:14, Jesus is the "only begotten *from the Father*." Not only that, but the character of his "glory" is that of "the only begotten from the Father."[13] That Jesus is the "only begotten" is why he manifests his Father's glory; being the "only begotten" also inflects the manner in which he manifests that glory: like Father, like Son. The term μονογενής (*monogenēs*) indicates that the Son exists *from* the Father as begotten or generated by the Father.[14]

However, everything depends on understanding this "begetting" in a God-befitting manner. John's Gospel offers us further guidance here with other ways he amplifies the title "Son." In a series of statements throughout the Fourth Gospel, Jesus uses the language of "giving" and "having" the unique divine life, glory, and name in ways that can only imply that the Father eternally communicates the divine nature to the Son. Consider:

> For just as the Father has [ἔχει, *echei*] life in himself, so he gave [ἔδωκεν, *edōken*] to the Son also to have life in himself. (John 5:26 NASB)

> And now, Father, glorify me in your own presence with the glory that I had [εἶχον, *eichon*] with you before the world existed. (John 17:5)

> Holy Father, keep them in your name, which you have given [δέδωκάς, *dedōkas*] me, that they may be one, even as we are one. While I was with them, I kept them in your name, which you have given me. (John 17:11–12)

> Father, I desire that they also, whom you have given me, may be with me where I am, to see my glory that you have given [δέδωκάς, *dedōkas*] me because you loved me before the foundation of the world. (John 17:24)

11. E.g., CSB, ESV, NET, NIV, NLT, NRSV.

12. See Irons, "A Lexical Defense of the Johannine 'Only Begotten'"; for this wording of his main claim, see 112. The following discussion is heavily indebted to Irons.

13. As indicated by the Greek particle ὡς: "glory *as* of the only begotten from the Father." As John Chrysostom observes, "The word 'as' in this context does not express likeness or comparison, but affirms and unmistakably defines" (*Homilies on John* 12 [FC 33:112]).

14. Consider also, especially, John 1:18: "No one has ever seen God. The only-begotten God, who is at the Father's side, he has made him known" (AT). On which see, e.g., Rainbow, *Johannine Theology*, 104; de la Potterie, "The Truth in Saint John," 71; Dahms, "The Johannine Use of Monogenēs Reconsidered."

For our purposes, it suffices to examine only John 5:26.[15] Here, Jesus proclaims that he possesses the kind of life that only God has: "life in himself."[16] God is the one who alone has immortality (1 Tim. 6:16). God alone needs nothing and gives everything (Acts 17:24–25). All things depend on him and he depends on nothing (Rom. 11:36). God alone is the fountain of life (Ps. 36:9), because God alone eternally is fullness of life in himself. In sum, the same life that belongs to the Father belongs to the Son. But Jesus also tells us *the manner in which* he has this divine life: "so he has given the Son also to have life in himself." If Jesus's possession of this life ever had a beginning, such that there was a time when he did not have it, then the life in question could not be the same "life in himself" that the Father has. As D. A. Carson observes, the "just as . . . so also" construction "ensures that whatever 'life in himself' means in the Father's existence, it means the same thing in the Son's existence."[17] Therefore, this giving of "life in himself" from the Father to the Son can only be eternal—without before or after, beginning or end—and thus unlike any ordinary giving. John 5:26 thereby reveals the mode or manner of Jesus's divine life. He eternally possesses life in himself, and that life in himself is from the Father.

With "giving" and "having," John amplifies "Son" and "begetting" in the same breath. As a father begets a son who shares his nature, so the Father eternally gives or communicates his own nature to the Son. Given the prominent use of the title "the Son" in John 5:26 and its near context, we should understand this eternal communication of the divine nature from the Father as a commentary on the title "Son." This is what it means for this Son to be the Son of this Father. And since the life communicated is the same in the Son as in the Father, we must understand it in a God-befitting way: without gender or genetics, matter or maturation, space or schism, womb or war.[18] Neither

15. On John 17:5, 11–12, and 24, see, e.g., Kammler, *Christologie und Eschatologie*, 181; Kammler, "Die Theologie des Johannesevangeliums," 89n41; Hengel, "The Prologue of the Gospel of John as the Gateway to Christological Truth," 272; Gieschen, "The Divine Name in Ante-Nicene Christology," 136–37. See also Gieschen, "The Divine Name That the Son Shares with the Father in the Gospel of John."

16. For fruitful reflections on the Bible's teaching on God's aseity, see Webster, "Life in and of Himself"; Webster, "Eternal Generation"; Bavinck, *Reformed Dogmatics*, 2:150–52. For the conceptual fit of divine aseity with John's Christology of the divine name and its "I am" sayings, see Macaskill, "Name Christology, Divine Aseity, and the I Am Sayings in the Fourth Gospel." Finally, for contemporary readings of John 5:26 that see the verse as attesting the eternal grant of the divine life from the Father to the Son, on which our discussion draws, see, e.g., Kammler, *Christologie und Eschatologie*, 170–83; Rainbow, *Johannine Theology*, 104; Carson, "John 5:26," esp. 79–87; Blumhofer, *The Gospel of John and the Future of Israel*, 109.

17. Carson, "John 5:26," 85.

18. On the absence of gender in God, see, e.g., Gregory of Nazianzus, *Oration* 31.7 (PPS 23:121–22). On the abiding normativity and validity of masculine names like "Father" and "Son" in trinitarian theology, see esp. DiNoia, "Knowing and Naming the Triune God."

theogony nor creation is in view but simply a supernatural communication befitting God's perfect life in which one person is distinguished from another.

A second manner in which Scripture amplifies the personal name "Son" is through a series of images or analogies that characterize the Son as both possessing the divine nature and deriving that nature from the Father. These images or analogies do not give us any kind of exhaustive grasp of the mystery of the intradivine relations. Instead, the light they shed on this reality is oblique and partial but nonetheless reliable and sufficient. Consider three such passages, all speaking about the Son:

> He is the image of the invisible God, the firstborn of all creation. (Col. 1:15)

> He is the radiance of the glory of God and the exact imprint of his nature, and he upholds the universe by the word of his power. (Heb. 1:3)

> In the beginning was the Word, and the Word was with God, and the Word was God. (John 1:1)

Each of these passages explicitly discusses the "Son" (cf. Col. 1:13–14; Heb. 1:2) or the "only begotten" (cf. John 1:14), and each amplifies this one subject with analogies drawn from created realities: image, radiance and imprint, and word. Each of these analogies speaks to the incomprehensible relation of origin the Son bears to the Father. In Colossians, the Son is the "image" reflecting the fullness that God is. In Hebrews, the Son is the "radiance" and "imprint" of the Father, which draws an analogy between a likeness and its source. Both terms indicate that God the Father is the origin of the Son, as the sun is the origin of the light that radiates from it and a seal is the origin of its impress in wax. And just as a "word" is conceived by and expresses the mind of the speaker, so too does the Son intrinsically express the Father. As Augustine puts it, "We cannot speak of a word without understanding it as the word of someone and of that one from whom it originates."[19] All these symbols show how the Son is from the Father as his likeness, though in the context of a clear affirmation of the Son's full divinity and thus equality with the Father.

Athanasius calls biblical illustrations such as these "*paradeigmata*" (παραδείγματα). Among other things, this Greek term can mean "pattern" or "model."[20] Each illustration, each *paradeigma*, treats an element of creaturely

---

19. Augustine, *Answer to an Arian Sermon* 17 (WSA I/18:154). See also Gregory of Nazianzus, *Oration* 30.20 (PPS 23:109–11).

20. See, e.g., Athanasius, *Against the Arians* 2.32 (NPNF² 4:365); *Letters to Serapion* 1.19–20 (PPS 43:82–85). For instructive studies of Athanasius's reading of these scriptural *paradeigmata*,

existence as an analogy for the Son's relation to the Father. That relation is somewhat like—though also unlike—the way an image represents its original, the way light radiates from the sun, the way a form is stamped by a mold, the way a word expresses its speaker. While these images highlight different aspects of the Son's relation to the Father, their common thread is "from-ness."

Similar to the names "Father" and "Son," all four of these illustrations—image, radiance, imprint, and word—feature relative terms. An image is "of" something or someone; radiance is "of" its light source; an imprint is "of" its original; a word is "of" its speaker. Hence, we should understand the relative names "Father" and "Son" on the one hand, and this cluster of relative predicates on the other, to be mutually informing. Aquinas explains: "For he has the name 'Son' in order to show that he is of one nature with the Father; 'Splendour,' to show that he is coeternal; 'Image,' to show that he is entirely alike; 'Word,' to show that he is not begotten carnally. No one name could be devised to bring out all of these."[21] So all these scriptural *paradeigmata* both illumine the name "Son" and mutually illumine each other. They are like reflections, from different angles and off different surfaces, of something much too bright for us to behold directly. But we need all of them together so that we do not conceive the Son's relation to the Father in ways that bear any trace of creaturely limits. As Peter Leithart observes, each of these symbols "assists in the apophatic purgation of our thoughts about God as Father and Son. One paradigm cleanses another."[22] What is the Son's sonship like? It has no beginning, because it is like the radiance of light from its source: as soon as you have light, you have radiance. It implies no diminution of the Son's being compared to that of the Father, because the Son is the Father's image in such a way that he fully shares the Father's nature. It implies no material derivation, because it is like a speaker's word emerging from within. While the eternal, personal, mutually constitutive relation of Father and Son necessarily eludes our exhaustive grasp or complete comprehension, these names and analogies shed on it true and reliable light.[23] They give us real, though limited, means of "rational wrestling with the mystery."[24]

---

see Anatolios, *Athanasius*, 79–80; Anatolios, *Retrieving Nicaea*, 110–14; Ernest, *The Bible in Athanasius of Alexandria*, 151–59; Leithart, *Athanasius*, 42–46.

21. Aquinas, *STh* III.34.2.*ad*3 (trans. O'Brien, 37).

22. Leithart, *Athanasius*, 46.

23. So Athanasius, *Against the Arians* 2.32: "Since human nature is not capable of the comprehension of God, Scripture has placed before us such symbols (*paradeigmata*) and such images (*eikonas*), so that we may understand from them, however slightly and obscurely, as much as is accessible to us" (in Anatolios, *Athanasius*, 127).

24. Barth, *CD* 1/1:368. Scheeben helpfully reminds us what a mystery is: "Two elements are essential to a mystery: first, that the existence of the proposed truth is attainable by no

We have emphasized the relations of origin here, but it remains true that for this reason these titles disclose the unity and equality of Father and Son. Each of these *paradeigmata*, when read in its scriptural context and coordinated with the personal titles "Father" and "Son," asserts two complementary realities about the Son: he possesses the divine nature, and he exists in an irreversible relation to the Father.[25] That is, each *paradeigma* attests both what he holds in common with the Father and the Spirit (their one divine being) and what is proper to him as the Son (his eternal generation from the Father). As the Father's Word (John 1:1), the Son is God and from God. As the Father's radiance and ontological impress (Heb. 1:3), the Son is God and from God. As the Father's perfect image, co-creator and sustainer of all (Col. 1:15–17), the Son is God and from God. In other words, each *paradeigma* speaks in two registers at once: the essential and the relative, the common and the proper, albeit differently. Each *paradeigma* directly attests the personal, irreversible relation in which the Father and the Son exist, the Father begetting the Son and the Son being begotten by the Father. Just so, each image also indirectly signifies the divine essence they possess in common, which the Father communicates to the Son.[26]

## The Name "Holy Spirit" and Its Scriptural Amplification

How does Scripture amplify the title "Holy Spirit" to attest his relation of origin? This is a little harder. Two reasons why will suffice to set up the problem for our purposes. First, the name "Holy Spirit" is itself not quite unique to the Holy Spirit. Since God is "spirit" (John 4:24), and all three persons of the Trinity are "holy" (Mark 1:24; John 17:11; Rom. 1:4), the surface meaning of the title "Holy Spirit" does not convey, intrinsically, what distinguishes the third person of the Trinity from the other two. Indeed, it seems an unlikely candidate for a personal name at all.[27] Chiefly we understand "Holy Spirit" to signify a distinct person by how it is used in biblical discourse.[28] Second, the Spirit's identity as a distinct divine person is revealed "last," as it were, in the divine economy. Gregory of Nazianzus notes that

---

natural means of cognition, that it lies beyond the range of the created intellect; secondly, that its content is capable of apprehension only by analogous concepts" (Scheeben, *The Mysteries of Christianity*, 11).

25. Commenting on Athanasius's treatment of John 14:6, 1 Cor. 1:24, and Heb. 1:3, Anatolios writes, "All these relations are non-reversible, even while they designate equality" (*Athanasius*, 79).

26. See the related discussions in Aquinas, *STh* I.29.4; I.34.1.

27. The name's oddity in this regard might be understood as a pedagogical means of holding us back from relying too much on social metaphors for the Trinity.

28. Aquinas, *STh* I.36.1.*corp.*

the divinity of the Spirit becomes clear to us at the right time in the economy, "after our Savior's return to heaven," when the Spirit personally indwells and teaches us about the relation between the Father and the Son.[29] Since we are situated on the other side of Easter and Pentecost, biblical reasoning occurs as the Spirit is at work within us and in our midst: "No one can say 'Jesus is Lord,' except in the Holy Spirit" (1 Cor. 12:3). If we see that the Light (Son) is indeed from Light (Father), it is only because we see this *in* Light (Spirit). The light in which we see something—a loved one, a painting, words on a page—does not usually assert a direct claim on our attention. In this regard, speaking about the Spirit is much like a fish learning about what it is to be wet. Naturally, then, discerning the Spirit's relation of origin from his name and its scriptural amplification is going to be trickier.

While the name "Holy Spirit" is not intrinsically relative like "Father" and "Son," it is relative in its use. In a manner analogous to that in which a person's spirit belongs to him or her, the Holy Spirit belongs to both the Father and the Son. When we speak of a human being's spirit, we use "of" to signify possession. "For who knows a person's thoughts except the spirit of that person, which is in him?" (1 Cor. 2:11). Scripture does something similar with its use of "Spirit" in genitive constructions. The Holy Spirit is not only *of* God (e.g., Matt. 12:28) but also *of* the Father and *of* the Son: "For it is not you who speak, but the Spirit of your Father speaking through you" (Matt. 10:20); "And because you are sons, God has sent the Spirit of his Son into our hearts, crying, 'Abba! Father!'" (Gal. 4:6; cf. Acts 16:7; Phil. 1:19; 1 Pet. 1:11). Similarly, Paul names the Spirit in all three ways when he writes, "You, however, are not in the flesh but in the Spirit, if in fact the Spirit of God dwells in you. Anyone who does not have the Spirit of Christ does not belong to him. . . . If the Spirit of him who raised Jesus from the dead dwells in you, he who raised Christ Jesus from the dead will also give life to your mortal bodies through his Spirit who dwells in you" (Rom. 8:9, 11). Notably, Paul here appeals to believers who are *in the Spirit* and thus learning about this Light by the light he sheds on their own adopted sonship (Rom. 8:15).

Scripture's relative use of "Holy Spirit" shows that he belongs to both the Father and the Son. The Spirit's very identity—who he is the Spirit *of*—relates to both the Father and the Son. But in what sense should we understand the name "Spirit" itself? Both the Hebrew word (רוּחַ, *rûaḥ*) and the Greek word (πνεῦμα, *pneuma*) used in Scripture for the Spirit derive etymologically from "breath." Jesus provides an object lesson when he "breathes" the Spirit on

---

29. Gregory of Nazianzus, *Oration* 31.27 (PPS 23:138).

the disciples (John 20:22).[30] Breath within a living being is spirit, life (cf. John 6:68; James 2:26). As we will discuss further below, the trinitarian revelation of the new covenant discloses that the Spirit is not merely a manner of speaking about God, but is eternally *breathed forth*, so to speak, by the Father and, as we will see, the Son. Stretching the imagery to its limits, we might say the Spirit is somewhat like—in a God-befitting sense—the Breath that the Father and the Son breathe: not something they depend on for their life, as a human depends on air as the vehicle of life, nor as a mere expression of life, because in humans the breath they breathe is not itself their life but only its manifestation. Within God, the Breath of the Father and the Son is interior to and proceeds from them both as possessor of that life in himself.[31] Ranked alongside them, the Spirit is fully God and thus "breathed" as the "Breath" that is *homoousios* with the Father and the Son.[32]

The most direct amplification of the Spirit's name and the sense in which he is "breathed" is also the most explicit scriptural attestation of the Spirit's relation of origin. In John 15:26, Jesus promises, "But when the Helper comes, whom I will send to you from the Father, the Spirit of truth, who proceeds [ἐκπορεύεται, *ekporeuetai*] from the Father, he will bear witness about me."[33] The phrase "who proceeds from the Father" might refer only to the Spirit's mission in time, his coming to Jesus's disciples to illumine and indwell them. However, on our view it is more likely that this phrase refers to the Spirit's eternal procession from the Father, his immanent, ontological "going forth." One reason is that if the phrase referred to the Spirit's mission in time, it would be somewhat redundant and a poor fit in the context. Further, the present tense "proceeds" suggests an ongoing reality, not a one-off event. The Holy Spirit eternally proceeds, emanates, comes forth from the Father (παρὰ τοῦ πατρός, *para tou patros*)—and, as we will see, also from the Son. What exactly "proceeds" means, however, is beyond our grasp. Gregory of Nazianzus sums up the difficulty: "Insofar as he proceeds from the Father, he is no creature; inasmuch as he is not begotten, he is no Son; and to the extent that procession is the mean between ingeneracy and

---

30. *Pneuma* can also mean "wind," carrying material connotations from the natural world. Jesus also appeals to this sense explicitly (John 3:8).

31. See, e.g., Gregory of Nyssa, *Catechetical Oration* 2–4 (PPS 60:68–71); Owen, *Pneumatologia* 1.ii (*Works* 3:55).

32. Thomas Aquinas, in *STh* I.36.1.*ad*2, concludes that, taking the compound expression "Holy Spirit" as a single name, if we keep in mind the Spirit's procession as "the one who is spirated"—that is, by analogy with a person's breath—then "we can understand a relation even in the name."

33. Especially in the Latin tradition, the name "Spirit" has also been amplified by the names "Gift" and "Love." See Levering, *Engaging the Doctrine of the Holy Spirit*, 51–70.

generacy, he is God. . . . What, then, is 'proceeding'? You explain the in-generacy of the Father and I will give you a biological account of the Son's begetting and the Spirit's proceeding—and let us go mad the pair of us for prying into God's secrets."[34] Proceeding, like breathing, must be understood in a God-befitting sense to mean a supernatural communication of life within God that is not generation and that distinguishes the Spirit hypostatically from the Father and the Son. To say much more than this courts disaster.

Scripture frequently uses genitive constructions, with or without a proposition, to name the Spirit in relation to another divine person (Matt. 10:20; John 15:26; 1 Cor. 2:11–12; Gal. 4:6). Whether they emphasize possession or origin, these genitive constructions all point to relations of "from-ness" or origin.[35] Although it takes a bit of work to see it, since the name "Holy Spirit" is used relatively it refers the Spirit's existence to the Father and the Son to whom he belongs and from whom he originates. Hence the Holy Spirit, like the Son, is both God and *from God.*

In this section we have seen that the titles "Son" and "Holy Spirit," as used and expanded on in Scripture, are relative terms. They name relations of origin or "from-ness" within the single undivided divine essence. The Son and Holy Spirit each are God, and each are eternally from God.

## Second Pressure: Mode of Action Reveals Mode of Being

The second set of passages that pressure us to confess relations of origin within the Trinity are those that show us ordered modes of action within the Trinity. Since actions disclose being, as we saw in chapter 6, these modes of operation disclose ordered modes of subsistence. We will first examine how the Son and the Spirit operate in the economy, then consider the order of operation and subsistence between the persons that is manifested in passages where one person works "through" another.

### The Son and the Spirit's Action in the Economy

We turn now to the manner in which the Son and the Spirit each operate in the economy of salvation, which discloses their eternal relations of origin. Three passages in John's Gospel testify especially clearly to the Son's mode of acting from the Father and are worth quoting in full:

---

34. Gregory of Nazianzus, *Oration* 31.8 (PPS 23:122).
35. According to Scheeben, *Handbuch der katholischen Dogmatik*, vol. 2, n. 1017, the Greek theologians tended to emphasize the genitive of origin, the Latins the genitive of possession.

Truly, truly, I say to you, the Son can do nothing of himself [ἀφ' ἑαυτοῦ, *aph' heautou*], but only what he sees the Father doing. For whatever the Father does, that the Son does likewise. For the Father loves the Son and shows him all that he himself is doing. (John 5:19–20 AT)

My teaching is not mine, but his who sent me. If anyone's will is to do God's will, he will know whether the teaching is from God or whether I am speaking from myself [ἀπ' ἐμαυτοῦ, *ap' emautou*]. The one who speaks from himself [ἀφ' ἑαυτοῦ, *aph' heautou*] seeks his own glory; but the one who seeks the glory of him who sent him is true, and in him there is no falsehood. (John 7:16–18 AT)

Jesus said to him, "Have I been with you so long, and you still do not know me, Philip? Whoever has seen me has seen the Father. How can you say, 'Show us the Father'? Do you not believe that I am in the Father and the Father is in me? The words that I say to you I do not speak from myself [ἀπ' ἐμαυτοῦ, *ap' emautou*], but the Father who dwells in me does his works. Believe me that I am in the Father and the Father is in me, or else believe on account of the works themselves." (John 14:9–11 AT)

Though each passage has different nuances and contextual implications, they all bear upon the questions of the Son's agency and his origin. Delving into each would require more space than we have, so we must content ourselves with a deeper look at John 5:19–20.[36]

In order to understand the first half of verse 19, it is crucial to read it in light of the second half. First, the denial: "Truly, truly, I say to you, the Son can do nothing of his own accord, but only what he sees the Father doing." Then, the reason: "For whatever the Father does, that the Son does likewise." This verse is equal parts denial and affirmation. In the first half, Jesus denies that he does anything "of" or from himself. In the second half, he affirms that he does everything that his Father does. The affirmation is as categorical and comprehensive as the denial. And we can only understand the denial in light of the affirmation. It is not just that the Son does *only* what he sees the Father doing, but that the Father shows him *everything* that he is doing, which means that everything the Father does, the Son does. As Jesus reiterates in verse 20, "For the Father loves the Son and shows him all that he himself is doing." Therefore, as we saw in chapter 6, the Father and the Son act inseparably.

For one thing, the affirmation in verse 19 rules out using partitive exegesis to understand Christ's whole statement on account of his human nature. If

---

36. Among modern scholarly treatments of these verses that we have been able to consult, by far the most exegetically perceptive and theologically insightful is that of Kammler, *Christologie und Eschatologie*, 20–40.

the Son does everything the Father does—including, say, creating and sustaining the universe[37]—then he is speaking of works that he does as God, not as man. In other words, Jesus's frame of reference here is not restricted to his incarnate activity. So, in saying that he does nothing "of himself," Jesus's words give us some purchase on the manner in which he exists and acts as God the Son. He is speaking about himself in a divine key, not a human one.[38]

Further, Jesus's denial cannot mean that the Father acts temporally prior to and independently of the Son, such that the Son acts subsequently to and in imitation of the Father. This would plainly contradict what Scripture more broadly and the Gospel of John more locally say about creation. John's prologue tells us, "All things were made through him, and without him was not any thing made that was made" (John 1:3). The Father created nothing apart from the Son. Everything he created, he created through the Son, with the Son. If we conceive of the action of the Father and the Son as a temporal sequence in which the Father first creates and shows, and the Son subsequently consults and imitates the Father, then we end up having to say that the Son created himself. Not only is this nonsense, but it violates the God-befitting rule.[39] Also, if we think that every act Jesus performed as a human corresponded to a discrete, prior act of the Father, we run into absurdities. Did the Father walk on water before Jesus or raise Lazarus from the dead before Jesus did? Did the Father first make the world, so that the Son made a different world using the first as a model?[40]

So we can neither explain Jesus's words with reference to his human nature, nor conceive of the Son and the Father's acts on the model of two creaturely agents working independently, one after the other. We must not import any creaturely conception into the action of the Son and the Father of which Jesus speaks. What then does Jesus's denial that he can do nothing of his own

37. Rightly noted by Neyrey, *An Ideology of Revolt*, 21, 22, 24.

38. As Aquinas observes, if this referred to his human nature, "then one would be forced to say that whatever the Son of God did in his assumed nature, the Father had done before him. For example, that the Father had walked upon the water as Christ did: otherwise, he would not have said, *but only what he sees the Father doing*" (*Commentary on the Gospel of St. John* 5.3.746 [boldface original]).

39. Cf. Augustine, *Homilies on the Gospel of John* 19.1 (WSA III/12:334): "If everything said here, in fact, is understood in relation to human senses or in a literal-minded way, the soul, stuffed with fancies, only comes up with some images of Father and Son or as two human beings, one showing something, the other seeing it; one talking, the other listening; all of that provides idols for the heart."

40. So Gregory of Nazianzus, *Oration* 30.11: "He cleanses lepers, releases men from demons and diseases, he restores dead men to life, walks on the sea, does all the other things he did—how or when did the Father anticipate these actions of the Son?" (PPS 23:102). Similarly Augustine, *Homilies on the Gospel of John* 20.5–6 (WSA III/12:362–63).

accord, or from himself, mean? It means that he acts from the Father because he exists from the Father. He does not act from himself because he does not exist from himself.[41] As he is eternally, so he acts in time.

Our passage implies the Son's eternal generation from the Father with the verbs of "seeing," "loving," and "showing." All of these are metaphorical descriptions of the Son's eternal relation of origin. First, consider the Son "seeing" all the Father does. In John's Gospel, the theme of the Father's invisibility is prominent, so the "seeing" in question cannot be a human sight with human eyes (1:18; 6:46; cf. 3:11, 13). The statement concerns the Son's divinity. But in his transcendent divinity, the Son does not have eyes with which to "see." Hence, we must interpret this expression in a God-befitting way.[42] To see is to receive knowledge. Jesus receives knowledge, being, power, wisdom, and all that he is as God in the Father's eternal act of begetting him.[43] Second, the same thing is suggested in verse 20: "For the Father loves the Son and shows him all that he himself is doing." Note the present tense of "loves" and "shows." These should be taken not as temporally successive acts, but as a single, eternal act.[44] This is effectively the converse of the second half of verse 19. The Son "sees" all because the Father "shows" all. When understood in a God-befitting sense: the Son eternally receives all because the Father eternally gives all.[45] The Son acts as he exists: *from* the Father.[46] He receives from the

41. As Hilary of Poitiers, *The Trinity* 7.21 (FC 25:247), observes, aptly framing the theological contribution of both halves of our verse, "He is the Son because He can do nothing of Himself; He is God because He Himself does the same things that the Father does." Cf. Augustine, *The Trinity* 2.3.

42. As Cyril of Alexandria, *Commentary on John* 2.6 (Maxwell, 1:148), rightly observes.

43. So Aquinas, *Commentary on the Gospel of St. John* 5.3.750: "And so, because the act of seeing indicates the derivation of knowledge and wisdom from another, it is proper for the generation of the Son from the Father to be indicated by an act of seeing." Note how Aquinas earlier rules out any sense of the Son's ontological inferiority by appealing to the appropriate category of "relation": "Further, in saying, the Son cannot do anything of himself, no inequality is implied, because this refers to a relation; while equality and inequality refer to quantity" (5.3.749).

44. Rightly, Kammler, *Christologie und Eschatologie*, 35–36, 38.

45. See Cyril of Alexandria, *Commentary on John*, 2.6 (Maxwell, 1:148).

46. Rightly, Watson, "Trinity and Community," 179, commenting on John 17: "Everything that Jesus is, has and does is a gift from the Father, and must be recognized as such if Jesus himself is to be understood." Cf. Keck, "Derivation as Destiny," 283, on how in John's Gospel, concerning both Jesus and his opponents, derivation discloses identity:

> To begin with, "of-ness" implies that what is decisive about a person is neither self-generated nor self-defined; to the contrary, one is wholly contingent at the center where the self is constituted. An anthropology based on an autonomous self is precluded. In John, speaking of derivation is itself a way of making an anthropological statement. Indeed, Jesus' repeated insistence that he does not act or speak on his own (5:19, 30; 7:16–18; 8:28, 42) shows that exactly the same holds true of "of" language in Christology as well. This is why Jesus' dictum, "The one who hears the words of God is of God" (8:47), applies to him as well as to those of his hearers who accept his word.

Father the power and knowledge to do what the Father does because he receives from the Father the divine essence they possess in common.[47]

Jesus therefore denies that he acts of himself precisely in order to justify the claim that he acts as God, that he does what only God can, giving life on the Sabbath: "My Father is working until now, and I am working" (5:17; cf. 14:9–11). Jesus's denial that he acts from himself is precisely what verifies his properly divine identity. In other words, Jesus's opponents are right in hearing Jesus's words as a claim to divinity but wrong in concluding that Jesus's claim goes beyond the evidence (5:18). John 5:19–20 does not merely assert that Jesus acts with divine power and that he receives that power from the Father—that he is both God and *from* God. Jesus's teaching here goes a crucial step further: it is precisely his being *from God* that makes him God. Jesus does all that the Father does because Jesus does nothing of himself: all that Jesus is and does is *from* the Father.[48]

Much the same line of thought is present in both John 7:16–18 and 14:9–11. In each, Jesus speaks of himself as "from another"—namely, from the Father. And these statements do not refer to what is true by virtue of his human nature. Nor does he merely assert his unity and equality with the Father, though those are implied in each statement. Instead, he says something else, something that both complements and grounds his unity and equality with the Father. In each passage Jesus teaches that he is God from God. He acts from the Father because he exists from the Father.

We turn now to the Holy Spirit's mode of action, which is clear in another passage from John's Gospel. Speaking of the Spirit's unique mode of action in relation to himself and the Father, Jesus instructs the disciples:

> I still have many things to say to you, but you cannot bear them now. When the Spirit of truth comes, he will guide you into all the truth, for he will not speak from himself [ἀφ' ἑαυτοῦ, *aph' heautou*], but whatever he hears he will speak, and he will declare to you the things that are to come. He will glorify

---

While Keck does not make the point as explicitly or doctrinally as we do, he nevertheless grasps that Jesus's "of-ness" or "from-ness" in relation to the Father constitutes his identity. In one sense we are simply drawing out the necessary ontological, theological implications of Keck's insight.

47. See Augustine, *Homilies on the Gospel of John* 18.10; 20.4, 8; 23.11. See also Ayres, *Augustine and the Trinity*, 243, on Augustine's appeal here to divine simplicity.

48. For a few decades after AD 360, John 5:19 was the subject of intense discussion in pro-Nicene and anti-Nicene polemics. For an overview of these exegetical debates, and a detailed analysis of Augustine's exegesis of the verse, see Ayres, *Augustine and the Trinity*, 233–51. Cf. also the briefer overview of pro-Nicene interpretation of the verse in Barnes, *The Power of God*, 163–65. For a sampling of Nicene and pro-Nicene readings see, e.g., Athanasius, *Against the Pagans* 46; Ambrose, *On the Faith* 4.39–72; Basil, *Against Eunomius* 1.23; Didymus the Blind, *On the Holy Spirit* 158–62, 165; Cyril of Alexandria, *Commentary on John* 2.6.

me, for he will take what is mine and declare it to you. All that the Father has
is mine; therefore I said that he will take what is mine and declare it to you.
(John 16:12–15 AT)

Like the Son, the Spirit does not send himself. Neither does he speak "from
himself." Like the Son, the Spirit's teaching is wholly unoriginal: "Whatever
he hears he will speak"; "He will take what is mine and declare it to you."
Because the Spirit takes his teaching from the Son, he glorifies the Son. But
what the Spirit takes from the Son belongs originally to the Father: "All that
the Father has is mine."

The Spirit extends and completes a chain of "transmission" from the Father
to the Son and through the Son to the Spirit. The Father sent the Son; the
Father and the Son send the Spirit (John 14:26; 15:26). The Son did and said
what he saw and heard from the Father; the Spirit speaks what he hears from
the Son and declares what he takes from the Son. All that belongs originally
to the Father is the Son's too and is available to the Spirit for him to take and
tell. The Son's sending is the source, his name the authority, his teaching the
content, and his glory the goal of the Spirit's indwelling mission.

In light of all this, what does it mean that the Spirit does not speak from
himself but speaks only what he hears (v. 13)? It means that the Spirit speaks
only what he receives from the Son, which belongs originally to the Father,
because he exists from the Son, who, with and from the Father, is the eternal
principle or origin of the Spirit. The Spirit is God. He needs no ears with which
to hear. He needs no instruction to remedy ignorance. He has no lack that he
would fill by "taking" what belongs to the Son. If we took such expressions
literally, we would imagine the Creator Spirit mythologically as some kind of
finite creature. Instead, as we saw in chapter 4, we must interpret the verbs
"hear" and "take" in a God-befitting sense.[49] All of these obviously human
ways of speaking are deliberately anthropomorphic, complementary metaphors for one ineffable, incomprehensible reality: the Spirit's eternal procession from the Father and the Son. The Spirit speaks from the Son because he
exists from the Son. The Spirit is God from God.

This section has only briefly canvassed some of the ways the Son's and
Spirit's relative modes of action imply their relative modes of subsistence.
Why do the Son's actions reveal the Father? Because the Son exists from the
Father. Why does the Spirit's ministry glorify Christ? Because the Spirit exists
from Christ. As one is, so one acts. Everything that is from something else

---

49. See p. 83. See also Cyril of Alexandria, *Commentary on John* 11.1–2 (Maxwell, 2:258–59).
Cf. also Didymus the Blind, *On the Holy Spirit* 153 (PPS 43:191); Augustine, *Tractates on the
Gospel of John* 99.4 (FC 90:223–24).

manifests that from which it is. The way in which the Spirit reveals the Son reveals that he is from the Son; the way in which the Son reveals the Father reveals that he is from the Father.[50]

## One Person Working "through" Another

We turn now to a series of passages in which one divine person works through another. In the light shed on the divine persons' eternal relations of origin by the relative divine names (with their scriptural amplification), and the passages considered above in which one divine person explicitly works "from another," we will discern in these passages an order of action that indirectly discloses an order of being. The Father works through his Son and Spirit, and the Son also works through his Spirit. Here we will very briefly consider the divine missions before treating them more fully in the following section. As we will see, one crucial clue to the revelatory link between action and being is that the order we will perceive in these passages is not reversible.

First, let us consider how the Father works through the Son.[51] Several representative passages speak of the creative act in terms that disclose a personal order of working within the Trinity:

All things were made through him [δι' αὐτοῦ, *di' autou*]. (John 1:3; cf. 1:10)

Yet for us there is one God, the Father, from whom are all things and for whom we exist, and one Lord, Jesus Christ, through whom are all things [δι' οὗ τὰ πάντα, *di' hou ta panta*] and through whom we exist. (1 Cor. 8:6)

For by him [ἐν αὐτῷ, *en autō*] all things were created, in heaven and on earth, visible and invisible, whether thrones or dominions or rulers or authorities—all things were created through him [δι' αὐτοῦ, *di' autou*] and for him. (Col. 1:16)

But in these last days he has spoken to us by his Son, whom he appointed the heir of all things, through whom also he created the world [δι' οὗ καὶ ἐποίησεν τοὺς αἰῶνας, *di' hou kai epoiēsen tous aiōnas*]. (Heb. 1:2)

---

50. See Aquinas, *Commentary on the Gospel of St. John* 16.4.2017; 17.2.2185. See also the discussion in Emery, "Biblical Exegesis and the Speculative Doctrine of the Trinity in St. Thomas Aquinas's *Commentary on St. John*," 40. For an instructive discussion of Aquinas's (biblical!) principle that the divine persons' modes of acting reveal their modes of being, see Emery, "The Personal Mode of Trinitarian Action in Saint Thomas Aquinas," 54–59.

51. While we look at creation here, we could just as easily and fruitfully consider redemption (cf. John 3:17; Acts 2:22; Col. 1:19–20). The world was saved the same way it was made: through him.

In each of these passages, God the Father is the initiator of the creative act, and a prepositional phrase equivalent to "through him" identifies the Son as the mediator of that same creative act.[52] Whether through an active verb, as in Hebrews 1:2, or a passive, such as "were made" or "were created," each passage ascribes initiating agency to the Father and intermediary agency to the Son. There is only a single divine act of creation in view, that by which God brought the entire universe into existence without the aid of nondivine assistants or preexistent material.[53] And yet within this single divine act, the persons relate to one another distinctly and in an irreversible order. As we saw in chapter 6, the Father created all things "through" the Son "not because the Son is an instrumental cause, but because he is a principle from a principle."[54] This "from another" agency does not diminish the Son's divine dignity: together with the Father, he is the one Creator. Passages in the near context of these assertions also appropriate the act of creation singly and directly to the Son (Heb. 1:10–12) and attribute to him the uniquely divine act of conserving creation (Col. 1:17; Heb. 1:3). In other words, the Son's act of creating *from the Father* does not render him anything less than or other than the Creator; instead, it means he creates in a Sonly manner. The Father creates as one not from another, whereas the Son creates as one from another. The work is inseparably one, but the order of working between the persons maintains the order of their mutual relations.

Further, in the grand sweep of his saving economy, the Father works not only through his Son but through his Spirit. Under the old covenant, the Father sent his law and his words "by his Spirit" (ἐν πνεύματι αὐτοῦ, *en pneumati autou*) through the prophets (Zech. 7:12 LXX; cf. Neh. 9:30 LXX). When that revelation failed to achieve its intended end, God promised to go a drastic step further: instead of merely speaking to his people by his Spirit from without, he would transform his people by his Spirit from within. "And it shall come to pass afterward, that I will pour out my Spirit on all flesh" (Joel 2:28; cf. Isa. 32:15; Ezek. 36:27; 37:14; 39:29). And in the end, the Father will impart a new life to his people that is not only spiritual but physical. How? By his

52. For a variety of broadly complementary perspectives on the NT's appropriation of such prepositional formulae, see Grant, "Causation and 'The Ancient World View'"; Hurtado, *Lord Jesus Christ*, 124–25; Cox, *By the Same Word*, 141–275; Bauckham, *Jesus and the God of Israel*, 214–15; Romanov, "Through One Lord Only"; O. McFarland, "Divine Causation and Prepositional Metaphysics"; Kugler, "Judaism/Hellenism in Early Christology."

53. As Hill, *Paul and the Trinity*, 114–15, notes, in 1 Cor. 8:6 Paul seems to adapt a monotheistic formula that he also uses in Rom. 11:36: "From him and through him and to him are all things" (ἐξ αὐτοῦ καὶ δι' αὐτοῦ καὶ εἰς αὐτὸν τὰ πάντα). By dividing these prepositions between "one God" and "one Lord, Jesus Christ," Paul ascribes to both the single, uniquely divine act of creating all things.

54. Aquinas, *STh* I.39.8.*corp* (trans. O'Brien, 137).

Spirit: "If the Spirit of him who raised Jesus from the dead dwells in you, he who raised Christ Jesus from the dead will also give life to your mortal bodies through his Spirit [διὰ τοῦ . . . αὐτοῦ πνεύματος, *dia tou . . . autou pneumatos*] who dwells in you" (Rom. 8:11). In each of these acts—prophetic inspiration, transformative infusion, and end-time resurrection—the Father works by the Spirit. We could equally say the Spirit works from the Father. Now why would he do that?

Consider again that each of these acts—revelation, transformation, and resurrection—are properly divine. That the Spirit is depicted like the medium of the Father's activity in each of these does not indicate any ontological inferiority. Prepositions like "by" or "through" do not mean that one person is the instrument or medium of another's agency.[55] These prepositions need only signify "from-ness." Again, we must remember the inseparable operations rule. We must also remember that, when applied to God, these agential prepositions must be understood in God-befitting ways. After all, Paul uses them to speak of the Father himself: "God is faithful, by whom [δι᾽ οὗ, *di' hou*] you were called into the fellowship of his Son" (1 Cor. 1:9). So if the Father works "by" or "through" the Spirit, it suggests mere order: the Spirit works from the Father because he is from the Father.

Finally, consider how, in his incarnate economy, the Son acts by the Spirit. He exorcises evil spirits by the Holy Spirit: "But if it is by the Spirit of God that I cast out demons, then the kingdom of God has come upon you" (Matt. 12:28). After his resurrection, he instructs his apostles by the Spirit: "He had given commands through the Holy Spirit to the apostles whom he had chosen" (Acts 1:1–2). He offers himself to God through the Spirit to cleanse us inwardly: "How much more will the blood of Christ, who through the eternal Spirit offered himself without blemish to God, purify our conscience from dead works to serve the living God" (Heb. 9:14). Finally, after undergoing his

---

55. Granted, when used to characterize creaturely agency, the construction "διά + genitive" frequently identifies an instrument used by an agent. However, it is a common observation that, in Hellenistic Greek, prepositions' semantic range overlapped much more than in classical usage. So, for instance, in the NT, διά with the genitive can indicate agency in passive constructions (e.g., Matt. 26:24 and par.), a role paradigmatically played by ὑπό plus the genitive. Further, we must remember that, in 1 Cor. 8:6, for instance, Paul uses the preposition διά not only to distinguish the Son from the Father but also to identify the Son as the one Creator God. Hence, the preposition alone cannot imply any ontological inferiority. Instead, given its role in the context, it (indirectly) signals the Son's unity of essence with the Father, and (directly) signals his personal differentiation from the Father. Kammler, "Die Prädikation Jesu Christi als 'Gott' und die paulinische Christologie," 174–75, rightly notes that the different prepositions Paul uses with God and Christ here "do not erect an *ontological* difference between Father and Son, but they mark—in the sense of an *inner-divine distinction*—the irreversibility of the relationship of Father and Son" (emphasis original). See also Basil, *On the Holy Spirit* 3.5–5.12.

own fiery baptism, he baptizes believers with the fire of his Spirit: "He will baptize you with the Holy Spirit and fire" (Matt. 3:11; cf. Mark 1:8; Luke 3:16; John 1:33; cf. Acts 2:1–4, 33). How does Jesus heal and cleanse and transform his people? He works by his Spirit. Not only do the Son and the Spirit act from the Father, but the Spirit also acts from the Son.

Nowhere are these patterns reversed. No scriptural text tells us that the Son or the Spirit works through the Father, or that the Spirit works through the Son. Never does the Son send the Father, nor does the Spirit send the Father or the Son.[56] These patterns of ordered trinitarian action are not reversible. As we have seen, that one divine person works through another argues no inferiority in the one worked through. Yet this ordered action tells us something different about the Son than it does about the Father; it says something different about the Spirit than about the Father and the Son. Just as the arrow of action points from the Father to the Son, and through the Son to the Spirit, so also the arrow of being. The Father works through the Son and not vice versa because the Father begets the Son and not vice versa; the Father and the Son work through the Spirit and not vice versa because the Father and the Son spirate the Spirit and not vice versa. As they are, so they work: the Son from the Father, and the Spirit from the Father and the Son.

## Third Pressure: The Divine Missions

The third biblical pressure that pushes us to formulate the "from another" rule is the divine missions themselves. This is where the argument comes home to roost. In fact, it is only in light of the entire rule-kit we have assembled throughout the book that the missions of the Son and the Spirit are seen to reveal their eternal processions—nothing more, nothing less. Each of the doctrinal principles and exegetical rules we have discerned brings the revelatory link between mission and procession into clearer view. Each helps us recognize the relevant data on the table and to put it all in its right place. Accordingly, in what follows we will draw, either implicitly or explicitly, on each of the principles and rules in our biblical reasoning rule-kit in order to

56. Matt. 4:1 offers an apparent exception: "Then Jesus was led up by the Spirit [ὑπὸ τοῦ πνεύματος] into the wilderness to be tempted by the devil." Here it seems the Spirit initiates the action and the Son responds. Is the Son working from the Spirit? Does the Spirit send the Son into the wilderness? In one sense, yes. However, this initiative of the Spirit is a feature of the Son's anointing with the Spirit as a human being. It is not the case that the Spirit initiates an action that the Son mediates as God; instead, as the truly obedient human being, Jesus is here following the Spirit's leading in order to obey where Adam and Israel failed. See the illuminating discussion in Marshall, "*Ex Occidente Lux?*," 39.

answer the question, What does it reveal about God that God sends God?[57] What we will see, again, is that the Son and the Spirit each are not only God but also from God. The missions reveal the processions.

Now then, we would do well to lay out some of the key passages before working on them. First, that the Father sent the Son:

> Whoever receives you receives me, and whoever receives me receives him who sent me. (Matt. 10:40; cf. Mark 9:37; Luke 9:48; 10:16)

> I was sent only to the lost sheep of the house of Israel. (Matt. 15:24)

> I must preach the good news of the kingdom of God to the other towns as well; for I was sent for this purpose. (Luke 4:43)

> Then the owner of the vineyard said, "What shall I do? I will send my beloved son; perhaps they will respect him." (Luke 20:13; cf. Matt. 21:37; Mark 12:6)

> For God did not send his Son into the world to condemn the world, but in order that the world might be saved through him. (John 3:17)[58]

> God, having raised up his servant, sent him to you first, to bless you by turning every one of you from your wickedness. (Acts 3:26)

> But when the fullness of time had come, God sent forth his Son, born of woman, born under the law, to redeem those who were under the law, so that we might receive adoption as sons. (Gal. 4:4–5; cf. Rom. 8:3)

Then, after the Son died for our sins, rose from the dead, ascended to heaven, and sat down at God's right hand, the Father sent the Spirit by granting the Son to pour him out:

> And behold, I am sending the promise of my Father upon you. But stay in the city until you are clothed with power from on high. (Luke 24:49)

> But the Helper, the Holy Spirit, whom the Father will send in my name, he will teach you all things and bring to your remembrance all that I have said to you. (John 14:26)

---

57. What follows is especially informed by Augustine, *The Trinity* 2.7–11. See also the insightful discussion in Sanders, *The Triune God*, 93–119.

58. The Father's act of sending the Son is especially prominent in John's Gospel. See also John 3:34; 4:34; 5:23, 24, 36, 38; 6:29, 38, 39, 44, 57; 7:16, 29, 33; 8:29, 42; 9:4; 10:36; 11:42; 12:44, 45, 49; 13:20; 14:24; 15:21; 16:5; 17:3, 8, 18, 21, 23, 25; 20:21. Cf. 1 John 4:9, 10, 14.

But when the Helper comes, whom I will send to you from the Father, the Spirit of truth, who proceeds from the Father, he will bear witness about me. (John 15:26)

Nevertheless, I tell you the truth: it is to your advantage that I go away, for if I do not go away, the Helper will not come to you. But if I go, I will send him to you. (John 16:7)

Being therefore exalted at the right hand of God, and having received from the Father the promise of the Holy Spirit, he has poured out this that you yourselves are seeing and hearing. (Acts 2:33)

And because you are sons, God has sent the Spirit of his Son into our hearts, crying, "Abba! Father!" (Gal. 4:6)

In what follows we will generally consider these passages in terms of what they attest in common: that the Father sent the Son, and the Father and the Son sent the Spirit. As we noted above, our primary exegetical question is what these passages all reveal about God—specifically, about the relation between the divine persons. What kind of a God can send God?

### Ruled Reading of the Missions

Our first two rules—regarding the analogy of faith and Scripture's pedagogical pressure—remind us to read these passages in such a way that they cohere with each other and the rest of Scripture, and in a way that both presupposes and pursues a larger theological vision. So we should be alert to the possibility that the intuitions we naturally bring to these passages may mislead us into reading them in a way that clashes with Scripture's overall witness to the Father, Son, and Spirit.

We must also read passages about God "sending" God in a God-befitting way. This is not like one creature sending another or like God sending a creature. This is a sending like no other. So when God sends God, sending is not commanding, and going is not obeying. Why not? Because commanding belongs to a superior, and obeying belongs to an inferior.[59] But there is no superiority or inferiority within the single, undivided, consubstantial divinity of the Trinity. Further, when God sends God, God is not sent to somewhere he was not before, because God is not a finite being circumscribed by space,

---

59. So Aquinas, commenting on John 5:30: "Now to obey belongs to one who receives a command, while to command pertains to one who is superior" (*Commentary on the Gospel of St. John* 5.5.795). See, further, Wittman, "*Dominium Naturale et Oeconomicum*," 151–60.

being present in some places and not at others. So if one divine person is "sent," it can only mean that he begins to be present to creatures in a new mode. What is that new mode? For the Son, it is incarnation; for the Spirit, it is indwelling believers. We will reflect on this more momentarily.

Here the unity of Christ is also a crucial exegetical guardrail. It is the Son who is sent, not a human Jesus who is somehow personally distinct from the Son. The same Son who is always in the world as God newly enters the world as a man (John 1:10; 8:42; 16:28). The Son's sending pressures us to speak of him in two parallel, complementary registers, as we just have. In other words, passages that teach the Son's sending call for partitive exegesis. They require us to speak of the Son both as the God he is and as the man he became. Many of the passages that teach us the Son's sending tell us not only that he was sent but also for what end and what he took to himself in order to undertake his saving mission. For instance, consider John 6:37–38, especially the latter verse: "All that the Father gives me will come to me, and whoever comes to me I will never cast out. For I have come down from heaven, not to do my own will but the will of him who sent me." Jesus goes on to say that the Father's will is that the Son grant eschatological, resurrection life to all who believe in him (vv. 39–40). As the sent, incarnate Son, Jesus entirely submits and completely devotes himself to the Father's saving purpose. The Son did not become incarnate in obedience to the Father, but in order to become obedient to the Father as the second Adam.[60] It is soteriologically necessary that the will the Son submits to the Father is human. That the Son is able to subordinate his will to the Father is therefore a feature not of his divinity, nor of his eternal, divine sonship, but of the human nature he assumed for our salvation. As God, the Son commands all creation together with the Father and the Spirit; as man, the Son obeys the Father's saving will. This obedience that aims at salvation is the form his sonship takes in his incarnate state.[61] Hence, the warrant for scriptural statements that imply any inequality between the Father and the Son is not the bare fact that the Son was sent but the form of a servant the Son took to himself in the sending.[62] After all, the sending of the Spirit does not imply any inequality or inferiority on the Spirit's part.[63]

60. See Bavinck, *Reformed Dogmatics*, 3:377–81.

61. See esp. Sanders, "What Trinitarian Theology Is For," 31, 35.

62. This weighs against an influential stream of contemporary scholarship on John that sees sending as evidence of subordination. See, e.g., Barrett, "Christocentric or Theocentric?," 13; Ashton, *Understanding the Fourth Gospel*, 218–19; Borgen, "God's Agent in the Fourth Gospel," 167–73; Loader, *Jesus in John's Gospel*, 22, 360–61; Anderson, "Jesus, the Eschatological Prophet in the Fourth Gospel," 280–81.

63. As Augustine demonstrates in *The Trinity* 2.11.

At this point, our rules enable us to refine our understanding of the missions and what they reveal.[64] Missions are like a double-sided arrow, pointing us at once to their source and destination. A divine mission thus consists of two elements: a relation of the person sent to the sender (*terminus a quo*; source), and a relation of the person sent to the goal of their sending (*terminus ad quem*; destination), which includes a created effect.[65] As Scott Swain observes, "A mission has an eternal depth (in a divine person's relation of origin) and a temporal shore (in a divine person's coming to dwell among creatures)."[66] Applying this distinction to the decisive missions of the Son and the Spirit that reveal them as distinct persons—Christmas and Pentecost—will illustrate its utility and descriptive power. In the Son's mission, his source is the Father and his destination is his whole incarnate economy. The created effect of this destination is the human nature he united to himself hypostatically. In the Spirit's mission at Pentecost, his source is the Father and the Son, and his destination is the believer's inner person, where he pours out the eschatological blessings of the new covenant. The created effects disclosing his destination are the tongues of fire that descended on those whom the Spirit first filled (Acts 2:3). This visible sign of the Spirit's presence attested that the entire series of old covenant promises concerning God pouring out his Spirit had been fulfilled, including the prophecies of John the Baptist. Not only that, but the visible sign of the Spirit's presence attested that Christ had kept his own promise to send his Spirit to his disciples (John 15:26; 16:7; Acts 1:4–5; 2:33).[67] In other words, the tongues of fire visibly manifest the invisible Spirit's sending into the hearts of believers, who become temples of the Holy Spirit.

But if the Father sends the Son, then this seems to divide the works of the Trinity. So how does the inseparable operations rule help us understand the missions? As we saw in chapter 6, Christ's incarnation is a single, indivisible work of the undivided Trinity. Therefore, we must not conceive of the Son's becoming incarnate, or the Spirit being sent to indwell believers, on the model of three creaturely agents completing separate aspects of a shared project. However, if the incarnation of the Son is accomplished by the whole Trinity, then is his sending accomplished by the whole Trinity? And if so, how can missions reveal anything at all about the relations of the divine person sent?

---

64. Theologians have often distinguished between "visible" and "invisible" missions, the former disclosing an invisible person through a created effect that is visible and the latter through a created effect that is invisible. See, e.g., Emery, *The Trinitarian Theology of St Thomas Aquinas*, 178–94; Legge, *The Trinitarian Christology of St Thomas Aquinas*, 24–58. Our discussion focuses mainly on so-called visible missions.

65. Aquinas, *STh* I.43.1.

66. Swain, *The Trinity*, 114.

67. See, further, Bavinck, *Reformed Dogmatics*, 3:499–503.

Here we must distinguish between different senses of "sender." If by "sender" we mean the principle of the created effect that discloses the sent person's new mode of presence in the world, then in an improper, technical sense the "sender" could be considered the undivided Trinity.[68] But if by "sender" we mean the source or principle of the person who is sent, then the sender is not every divine person, but properly speaking only one person (in the Son's case, the Father) or two persons (in the Spirit's case, the Father and the Son).[69] What purchase does this distinction give us on the "sending" passages we are discussing? Simply this: insofar as each divine person is God, that person is the cause of the created effect that manifests a divine person's sending. But it is only insofar as the divine persons are related to one another that one is explicitly said in the NT to send another. Relations of sending obtain only where relations of origin do. This is why the Father is never said to be sent: he is the origin of the Son and the Spirit, not they of him.[70]

To recapitulate: the God-fittingness rule reminds us that divine missions are not like creaturely missions. They imply no temporal sequence, local commute, or chain of command. Partitive exegesis reminds us that Christ possesses both the form of God and the form of a servant, and it is only by virtue of the latter that he is in any way less than the Father. The Son therefore obeys *because* he is sent, not in his sending. Finally, the inseparable operations rule reminds us that all three divine persons are present and active in each of the missions, while preserving their distinct, ordered modes of subsistence and acting relative to one another. The Father does not send the Son like any human being sends another because no human beings share a single essence and power.

### What the Missions Reveal

When we have cleared the table and sorted the relevant data into their proper places, what is left? What do the divine missions disclose about the divine persons and their relations to one another? To home in on our answer,

68. While this shows us the narrow sense in which statements like "the Trinity sent the Son" or the "Son sent himself" are true, it is ordinarily neither advisable nor useful to make these kinds of statements.

69. Aquinas, *STh* I.43.8.*corp*: "If the sender be designated as the principle of the person sent, in this sense not each person sends, but that person only Who is the principle of that person who is sent; and thus the Son is sent only by the Father; and the Holy Spirit by the Father and the Son. If, however, the person sending is understood as the principle of the effect implied in the mission, in that sense the whole Trinity sends the person sent." Aquinas has in mind Isa. 48:16.

70. Augustine, *The Trinity* 4.28 (WSA I/5:181): "But when the Father is known by someone in time he is not said to have been sent. For he has not got anyone else to be from or to proceed from."

we may return yet again to John's Gospel. Throughout John, the question of Jesus's identity is inextricably intertwined with that of his origin. Ultimately, in the context of the whole Gospel, the two questions are seen to have a single answer. Where is Jesus from? And who is he? John answers both: "from God." Consider this exchange between Jesus and his opponents: "'But we know where this man comes from, and when the Christ appears, no one will know where he comes from.' So Jesus proclaimed, as he taught in the temple, 'You know me, and you know where I come from. But I have not come of myself. He who sent me is true, and him you do not know. I know him, for I am from him, and he sent me'" (John 7:27–29 AT). Here Jesus claims not only to be sent from the Father but to exist from the Father. In verse 29, the second assertion grounds the first. How can Jesus know the Father? Because he originates from the Father. Jesus knows him because he exists from him. Jesus's answer to "Where are you from?" is not a "where" but a "who." The kind of origin Jesus thereby indicates is not merely geographical; instead, it is a relation that accounts for his very existence. Hence, the second and third assertions of verse 29, "I am from him, and he sent me," are not synonymous repetition. Instead, Jesus's prior, eternal existence from the Father is the antecedent ontological basis of his being sent by the Father to become incarnate for our salvation. In professing to know Jesus's origins, his opponents plunge in over their heads. If Jesus comes from a place, heaven, that is only because he comes more fundamentally from a person, the Father. As Harold Attridge summarizes these verses, "His truest homeland is the Father's bosom."[71]

Later, in an extension of this debate, Jesus claims the divine prerogative of self-attestation on the basis of his knowledge of his own origins: "Even if I do bear witness about myself, my testimony is true, for I know where I came from and where I am going, but you do not know where I come from or where I am going" (8:14). In other words, Jesus's unique origin warrants the exercise of uniquely divine prerogatives such as bearing self-authenticating witness to himself. If Jesus's opponents knew where he came from, they would know why he can act in a manner that befits only God.[72] Further, at the climax of the trial of Jesus that runs throughout John's Gospel, following the Jews' accusation that Jesus made himself the Son of God, Pilate asks him, "'Where are you from?' But Jesus gave him no answer" (John 19:9; cf.

---

71. Attridge, "Ambiguous Signs, an Anonymous Character, Unanswerable Riddles," 284. Cf. Dodd, *The Interpretation of the Fourth Gospel*, 89.

72. On bearing testimony to oneself as Jesus's human exercise of a divine prerogative in John 8:14, see, e.g., Lincoln, *Truth on Trial*, 30–31, 67; Borgen, "Observations on God's Agent and Agency in John's Gospel Chapters 5–10," 210; Bekken, *The Lawsuit Motif in John's Gospel from New Perspectives*, 147–49.

v. 7). Without knowing it, here Pilate asks precisely the right question. With almost everyone, where someone is from tells you something about him or her; with Jesus, it tells you everything.[73]

Thus the Gospel of John explicitly makes the point that Jesus is sent from the Father because he exists from the Father. Jesus not only comes from the Father but also exists from the Father, and he comes from the Father precisely because he exists from the Father. Hence, when Jesus says, "I came from God" (8:42; 16:28), he is referring to the origin not only of his mission but of his very existence. Hence, in the Gospel of John's account of the Son's identity, his sending by the Father reveals his existence from the Father.[74] The necessary, ontological ground of the Son's "going forth" from the Father in time, to become incarnate, is his eternal, immanent "going forth" as Son. As C. H. Dodd observes, "The relation of Father and Son is an eternal relation, not attained in time, nor ceasing with this life, or with the history of this world. The human career of Jesus is, as it were, a projection of this eternal relation (which is the divine ἀγάπη) upon the field of time."[75]

To zoom out from John and consider again these "sending" passages as a unit, how is it that Jesus's being sent from the Father discloses that he exists from the Father? Jesus's saving mission reveals his eternal procession in that "sending" indicates a relation of "from-ness." The one sent acts from the one who sends him or her. Sending is an action that involves distinct persons. It is an action that originates with one and is received by another. Among creatures, sending can create or activate a relation that only exists while the mission does, or sending can reveal a relation between a superior and a subordinate. But these aspects of "sending" are not necessary to all instances of sending. As it concerns God sending God, "sending" need only imply "from-ness." Sending is an action that manifests a relation with a certain direction, from sender to sent. But the relation itself does not depend on what manifests it, so it exists prior to the sending. Take away the mission, take away the temporality of this revelatory action, and what you have left is the relation itself—one that does not depend on time. In other words, what you have is an eternal relation of origin. The external act of sending corresponds to the

73. As de Jonge, *Jesus, Stranger from Heaven and Son of God*, 143, observes, "Thus the question as to 'whence?' is the question of the source and authorization of what Jesus says and does" (cf. also 150). See also the insightful broader discussion of John's use of "where" and "whence," including the glimpse of Christ's relation to the Father that they disclose, in Pollard, "The Father-Son and God-Believer Relationships According to St John," 363–66; Kieffer, "L'Espace et Le Temps dans l'Évangile de Jean," 400–404; Dewailly, "'D'où es-tu?' (Jean 19,9)," 489–93.
74. Rightly, Dodd, *The Interpretation of the Fourth Gospel*, 259–60.
75. Dodd, *The Interpretation of the Fourth Gospel*, 262.

internal acts of proceeding, which are begetting and spirating. And since these eternal relations of origin are manifested in the missions, they are intrinsic to the missions. The divine missions are not some other relation added to the processions, but the processions themselves extended into time, stretched down into creation, where they can scoop us up into their saving embrace.[76]

Having focused intently on the Son throughout this section, we should belatedly say at least something about the Holy Spirit. ("And we believe in the Holy Spirit.") Here we may simply note, as we noted above in discussing mode of action, that the same reasoning that obtains for the Son holds for the Spirit. That the Father and the Son sent the Spirit (John 14:26; 15:26; 16:7) implies a relation between the joint senders and the one sent. The only such relation that Scripture attests, the only relation there can be between coequal divine persons who subsist in a singular essence, is an eternal relation of origin.

In this chapter so far, we have considered three sets of biblical pressures that press us up into the divine life. These three sets of pressures provide complementary, overlapping angles on relations that obtain not between God and creation but between the divine persons. To review: first we considered the names "Father," "Son," and "Holy Spirit" and the way Scripture unpacks the relational significance of each name. Second, we discerned that the divine persons' mode of action in the economy of salvation, specifically how they act in relation to the other divine persons, discloses their antecedent, eternal mode of existence. Third, in this final section we examined passages in which the Father is said to send the Son, and the Father and the Son to send the Spirit, asking, What does it show about God that God sends God? By employing the toolkit we have assembled so far, we concluded that, in light of all that these passages cannot mean about the intrinsic relations between Father, Son, and Spirit, the only thing they can mean is that the persons exist in eternal relations of origin: the Son from the Father, and the Spirit from the Father and the Son. In order for God to send God, it must be the case that God is from God.

We have seen that the missions of the Son and the Spirit reveal their eternal processions. These eternal processions are also revealed by the triune manner in which Scripture names the one God as Father, Son, and Spirit. These two means of discerning the eternal relations of origin among the Father, Son, and Spirit are mutually dependent and mutually illuminating. The missions have priority in revelation; the names have priority in interpretation.[77] We

---

76. For a concise review of the ground we have covered in this section, see Augustine, *The Trinity* 4.25–28.

77. For the former point, see Sanders, *The Triune God*, 40: "In the fullness of time, God did not give us facts about himself, but gave us himself in the person of the Father who sent, the

only have the names because, in their missions, the Son and the Spirit name themselves in relation to each other and the Father. And yet we only come to a full understanding of the missions, as they are rooted in and extend the divine processions, because the names and their amplification open a window onto the eternal processions.

## The Grammar of Relations of Origin and the "From Another" Rule

We may now articulate the grammar of these relations in the form of our seventh principle: *Within their unity and equality, the three persons exist in relations of origin: the Son is eternally generated from the Father, and the Spirit eternally proceeds from the Father and the Son.* In keeping with our goal of merely offering exegetically constructed on-ramps to these doctrines, here we leave innumerable pressing questions to the side and offer only the barest grammar of these relations. These relations name the mode in which the Father, the Son, and the Spirit eternally exist as one God.[78] The Father possesses his divine nature from no other; the Son eternally receives the divine nature from the Father who begets him; the Spirit eternally receives the divine nature from the Father and the Son who, as one principle, spirate him. These eternal relations of origin are the manner in which the Father, Son, and Spirit eternally are one God.

We can "operationalize" this grammar into an exegetical rule, our tenth: *Scripture often attributes to the divine persons ordered relations and actions that do not compromise their unity and equality, but only signify that one person eternally exists from another: the Son from the Father, the Spirit from the Father and the Son. Read Scripture in a way that recognizes and upholds these ordered relations of origin.* As Augustine puts it, "This then is the rule which governs many scriptural texts, intended to show not that one person is less than the other, but only that one is from the other."[79] This rule develops and specifies the "common and proper" rule, or "redoublement." That rule recognizes a conceptual distinction between the divine essence and the divine

---

Son who was sent, and the Holy Spirit who was poured out. These events were accompanied by verbally inspired explanatory words; but the latter depend on the former." Similarly, see Marshall, *Trinity and Truth*, 39.

78. As Emery notes, "Each person exists in a distinct manner according to a relation" ("The Personal Mode of Trinitarian Action in Saint Thomas Aquinas," 55). For the idea that a distinct "mode of existence" characterizes the three divine persons in their relations to each other, see, e.g., Basil, *On the Holy Spirit*, 18.46; *Letter* 235.2.

79. Augustine, *The Trinity* 2.3 (WSA I/5:99).

persons. This chapter's rule, the "from another" rule, teaches that the relations which distinguish the divine persons are eternal relations of origin: that the Son exists from the Father, and the Spirit from the Father and the Son. The "common and proper" rule observes a conceptual distinction between nature and person; the "from another" rule discerns a real distinction between the persons, grounded in their relations of origin.[80]

The primary exegetical application of this rule consists in treating the types of passages we have examined. Where we see the divine persons named in relation to one another, where Scripture amplifies those relations by providing creaturely analogates, where one divine person works from or through another, and where one divine person sends another, in all these cases we should infer, not that one divine person is less than or subordinate to another, but simply that one divine person exists from another.

By discerning and distilling the "from another" rule, there is a certain, narrowly qualified sense in which we have attained to a kind of completion in our survey of how Scripture speaks of our Lord Jesus Christ. With this drawer assembled and installed, our biblical reasoning workshop now has a place for everything Scripture says about Christ. As God, Christ is one with and equal to the Father. As God, Christ's actions are indivisible from those of the Father. As a man, he is like us in every way except sin, and is less than the Father. Since he is both God and man, in him we meet the paradox of a man doing divine things and God doing human things. Since he is both God and man, we must discern whether his divine or his human nature is the truth-making property for any scriptural assertion about him. All these angles of insight on Christ's being and action, which recapitulate our fourth through ninth rules, consider Christ primarily in an essential manner, discerning implications of his twofold substance as both God and man. By contrast, the "from another" rule considers Christ exclusively under the aspect of relation—namely, his relation to the Father and, with the Father, to the Spirit.

The move from these preceding rules to the "from another" rule is faintly analogous to moving from a two-dimensional view to a three-dimensional one. When we look into the depths of the Son's person, we see that he eternally exists from the Father, and, with the Father, he eternally breathes forth the Spirit. When we gaze into the depths of the Son's eternal identity, we discover the Father and the Spirit too.

The "from another" rule discerns that the Son's very existence is directional: he exists from the Father, and the Spirit exists from him and from the Father. In other words, the other rules primarily consider Christ in terms of

80. Aquinas, *STh* I.39.1.

what he holds in common with the Father and the Spirit or what is proper to the human nature that only he assumed. Here at last we have considered what is unique to the Son not as man, but as Son.

## Conclusion: To See In and Come In

And yet, for all its uniqueness, for all its exclusive, eternal singularity, neither uniqueness nor exclusion is the last word Scripture utters about Christ's eternal Sonship. Consider again Paul's proclamation of the missions of the Son and the Spirit in Galatians 4:4–7:

> But when the fullness of time had come, God sent forth his Son, born of woman, born under the law, to redeem those who were under the law, so that we might receive adoption as sons. And because you are sons, God has sent the Spirit of his Son into our hearts, crying, "Abba! Father!" So you are no longer a slave, but a son, and if a son, then an heir through God.

What was the Son sent to do?[81] He came to make us sons. He came to make his Father our Father. He came to give us by grace what belongs to him by nature. He came to grant us participation in what he is. God revealed his Son, and thereby revealed himself as Father, so that we would come to share in the Son's relationship to the Father. In the fullness of time, God revealed that he had a Son by sending his Son to make us sons. The Son's mission not only arises from and extends his procession but also brings us into it by his Spirit. Jesus's eternal existence from the Father is not only the source of our salvation but also its goal.[82] By sending his Son and Spirit, God the Father not only came to where we live but also drew us into his own life. As Jesus prays on the night before his death, "I made known to them your name, and I will continue to make it known, that the love with which you have loved me may be in them, and I in them" (John 17:26).

How is this sonship granted to us? By the Father sending the Spirit to dwell in our hearts, enabling us to call on Jesus's Father as our Father. The Spirit who eternally exists in and as the communion of the Father and the Son grafts

---

81. For a rich discussion of this passage's trinitarian dimensions, see Swain, "'Heirs through God.'"

82. See Sanders, "Eternal Generation and Soteriology," 265–66: "The relation of Father to Son is a relation in God, which is brought down to, or given over to, us; or to say the same thing, into which we are exalted and incorporated." So also Davidson: "At the heart of the *beneficia Christi* of which the gospel speaks lies a specific blessing: the opening up of the eternal Son's native sphere to others, the drawing of contingent beings into the realm of his intimate, eternally secure relation to his Father" ("Salvation's Destiny," 161).

us into that communion.[83] The Spirit sent into our hearts enables us to call God now what the Son has always called him: Abba! Father! By sending his Son and Spirit, the Father did not merely reveal the intradivine fellowship—he extended it to include us.

At one and the same time, through one and the same sweeping, twofold act of salvific sending, the missions of the Son and the Spirit both reveal the Trinity and accomplish our salvation by drawing us into the Trinity. As Dominic Legge observes, "These dimensions are interrelated: the visible missions *manifest* the mystery of the Triune God, and *save* us as they draw us into that mystery."[84] In the missions of the Son and the Spirit, salvation and revelation coincide. These missions reveal the Trinity by savingly sweeping us up into the fellowship of the Trinity, and they save us precisely by granting us to know God as Father through the redeeming work of his Son and the renewing work of his Spirit. The divine missions save as they reveal and reveal as they save.[85] The missions of the Son and the Spirit open a door into the eternal processions within God. By opening this door, they let us not only see in but also come in.

Why do all the "from another" passages we have considered matter to faith's quest for the vision of God in Christ? Because they guide our hearts and minds to the unique glory of the Son that will be our eternally satisfying sight. "Father, I desire that they also, whom you have given me, may be with me where I am, to see my glory that you have given me because you loved me before the foundation of the world" (John 17:24).

---

83. So Fairbairn, *Life in the Trinity*, 24.
84. Legge, *The Trinitarian Christology of St Thomas Aquinas*, 55 (emphasis original).
85. See here Augustine, *The Trinity* 4.27–29; Gioia, *The Theological Epistemology of Augustine's* De Trinitate, esp. 17, 32–34, 114, 143, 145.

# 10

# Putting the Rule-Kit to Work

## Reading John 5:17-30

Our goal throughout this book has been to do exegesis in order to distill exegetical rules and then use them. Most of the chapters have included exegetical case studies in which we demonstrate each rule's value by reading Scripture with it. These rules emerge from the text and guide us by the hand back into the text. In this chapter we return to the text with our full rule-kit in hand. Specifically, this chapter will use all ten rules we have developed throughout the book to read John 5:17–30.

Why this passage? Because it is one of the most richly trinitarian texts in the most richly trinitarian book of the Bible.[1] If the kit of gear we have assembled can help us scale this summit, surely it can handle other, lesser peaks. Our goal in this chapter is to show not only the worth of this rule-kit but also that it is in fact a kit, a set of tools that complement each other. To do this, we will expound John 5:17–30 by seeing what each rule contributes to understanding the passage. Where multiple verses find a home under a single rule, we will generally work through them in order. We will have much more

---

1. It is true that the Spirit is not explicitly mentioned in this passage. However, as we saw in the previous chapter, John expounds the Son's relationship to the Father and the Spirit's relationship to the Father and the Son in suggestively parallel ways. Given this dynamic, it is far better to fit a passage such as this into a more capacious trinitarian framework than to employ a construct such as "binitarian" that fails to do justice to John as a whole, much less to the whole canon.

to say under the headings of some rules than others because some rules find more to bite into in the passage.

The best reading of any passage is one that can "save" all the phenomena. If a reading makes sense of the first and fourth sentences but not the second and third, it is not a good reading. Our goal in this chapter is to show how our biblical reasoning toolkit enables us to save all the christological and trinitarian phenomena of John 5:17–30, and not only save them but also integrate them into a coherent account of who the Son is and how he reveals the Father who sent him.[2] We will begin by introducing the passage, and then we will use each of the rules to delve into it.

## Introduction to a Double Accusation

John 5:17–30 is nearly a monologue. From verse 19 on, Jesus alone speaks. But this discourse is prompted by both the healing narrated in verses 1–16 and the exchange of words and actions between Jesus and his opponents in verses 17–18.[3] The opening verses of the chapter inform us that, while Jesus is in Jerusalem for "a feast of the Jews" (v. 1), he heals a man who had been lame for thirty-eight years (v. 5). How? Simply by speaking a word of command: "Get up, take up your bed, and walk" (v. 8). Only after Jesus has spoken this effectual, transformative word do we learn when he spoke it: on the Sabbath (v. 9). This timing touches off the controversy that follows (vv. 10–16). "The Jews" see the newly healed man carrying his mat, question him, and eventually discover that it was Jesus who healed him. "And this was why the Jews were persecuting Jesus, because he was doing these things on the Sabbath" (v. 16).

This persecution prompts Jesus to offer his initial answer to the charge that he is doing something unlawful on the Sabbath: "My Father is working until now, and I am working" (v. 17). This terse defense elicits heightened opposition: "This was why the Jews were seeking all the more to kill him, because not only was he breaking the Sabbath, but he was even calling God his own Father, making himself equal with God" (v. 18). As we will see in more detail below, in the eyes of Jesus's opponents, his initial defense only makes things worse. Now, in addition to breaking the Sabbath, he is guilty of blasphemy.

---

2. That is, we make no claim to offer a comprehensive exegesis of the passage in this chapter, but instead focus on what it reveals about God in Christ. For instance, we leave to the side the vexed questions about the events and timing in view in vv. 24–25 and 28–29.

3. For recent discussions of John 5:1–16, see, e.g., Mealand, "John 5 and the Limits of Rhetorical Criticism," 259–61; Bryan, "Power in the Pool"; Swart, "Aristobulus' Interpretation of LXX Sabbath Texts as an Interpretive Key to John 5:1–18," 576–81; Myers, "'Jesus Said to Them . . . ,'" 416–18; R. Thompson, "Healing at the Pool of Bethesda."

Jesus's self-defense that follows in verses 19–30 is the first half of a long speech whose latter half considers witnesses to Jesus (vv. 31–47). But the half we will focus on, in light of the inciting thesis and initial response of verses 17–18, presents Jesus's substantive defense against the double accusation of Sabbath-breaking and blasphemy.[4]

## The Larger Picture

### Rule 1: The Analogy of Faith

To rightly respond to God's pedagogical pressures in his Word, read Scripture as a unity, interpreting its parts in light of the whole and understanding the whole as a harmonious testimony to God and his works.

### Rule 2: Pedagogical Pressure

To understand the theological grammar and syntax of Scripture, read Scripture in such a way that you learn how its various discourses both form and presuppose a larger theological vision.

Rather than giving us detailed directions for explaining specific assertions, these first two rules orient us to the larger picture of what God is doing in and through Scripture. In one sense, in our passage the larger picture is precisely what is in dispute. The problem Jesus's opponents have with him is that his words and actions seem not to chime in harmony with Scripture's testimony to God and his words, but instead create clanging discord. If Jesus is from God, shouldn't he keep the Sabbath? Don't his audacious claims about himself clash with Scripture's testimony to God's uniqueness? The actions and words of Jesus find no place in his opponents' larger theological vision. But have they read Scripture's theological grammar and syntax rightly? Is their big picture big enough?

Both Scripture as a whole and Jesus's actions and words in this passage pressure their audiences to render a verdict. God in Scripture and Jesus in this passage lead their audiences to discern and ultimately declare theological judgments. Jesus's initiating act and interpretive discourse pedagogically pressure his hearers toward a true judgment about his identity. Further, in response to his opponents' double charge of Sabbath-breaking and blasphemy, Jesus's speech for the defense is meant to enable his listeners to discern how his actions

4. On the lawsuit motif that threads through the entire narrative of John's Gospel, and this passage's place within it, see Harvey, *Jesus on Trial*; Lincoln, *Truth on Trial*, esp. 21–29, 73–77.

and words do in fact fit with God's self-attestation in Scripture. A crucial test of Jesus's testimony to himself is whether it coheres with the whole of God's testimony to himself. One key element of this judgment that Jesus's testimony enables is the recognition that, together with the Father, Jesus deserves the worship that rightly belongs only to God. Jesus declares that the Father has entrusted eschatological judgment to him "that all may honor the Son, just as they honor the Father" (v. 23).

## The Logic of Blasphemy and the Warrant for God-Fitting Claims

### Rule 3: God-Fittingness

Biblical discourse about God should be understood in a way appropriate to its object, so read Scripture's depictions of God in a manner that fits the canonical portrait of God's holy name and his creation of all things out of nothing.

This section has three parts. First, we will consider how Jesus's initial answer in verse 17 employs, and locates himself in relation to, the Creator-creature distinction. Second, we will consider how the principle of God-fittingness emerges from the passage, specifically how blasphemy mirrors the God-fittingness rule. Third, we will examine a series of six uniquely God-fitting perfections and prerogatives that Jesus claims for himself. This section will be by far the longest, since so much of the passage turns on whether Jesus is right to speak of himself in such strikingly God-befitting ways.

### The Creator-Creature Distinction and the Sabbath Command (John 5:17)

First, we will see that creation *ex nihilo* and the qualitative distinction between Creator and creatures are crucial conceptual equipment for understanding the conflict over the Sabbath that opens and permeates our passage. Consider again Jesus's assertion that raises the stakes and stokes the opposition: "My Father is working until now, and I am working" (v. 17). The claim implied is, "I am permitted to work on the Sabbath for the same reasons my Father is."[5]

This dispute over the OT's Sabbath command is intricately entangled with the Creator-creature distinction. On the one hand, the Sabbath command rests on an analogy between Creator and creature. God created in six days and

---

5. Cf. Carson, *The Gospel according to John*, 248: "Instead, Jesus insists that whatever factors justify God's continuous work from creation on also justify his."

rested on the seventh (Gen. 2:2–3; Exod. 31:17), and so should humankind (Exod. 20:11). On the other hand, these references to the pattern of God's creating work remind those obligated to keep the Sabbath that they are creatures, not the Creator. Further, that God rested on the seventh day does not tell us the whole story. As Jesus asserts, "My Father is working until now" (John 5:17). On that original seventh day, and every Sabbath, and every other day thereafter, God has continued to preserve and uphold the world that he made. Does God work on the Sabbath? Yes, in the sense that he continues to do what only he can. He sustains all created beings. He gives life and takes it. Of course, unlike our labor, God's providential, conserving activity is restful. He upholds all things by the same effortlessly effective word by which he created all things (Gen. 1:3; Ps. 33:6; cf. Heb. 1:3). Nevertheless, Jesus appeals to the jurisdictional point that, as the Creator, God is exempt from the Sabbath regulation that binds his human creatures.[6] Jesus insists that this exemption covers him too. In other disputes over the Sabbath, Jesus appeals to human precedent for his actions (e.g., Luke 14:5); here he appeals to divine precedent.[7] In John 5:17, Jesus invokes a rationale for his activity that holds only for the Creator of all.

### God-Fittingness and Blasphemy (John 5:17–18)

Second, there is a sense in which the principle of God-fittingness is a necessary inference from the theological grammar of this passage, specifically the logic of the dispute between Jesus and his opponents. Again, after Jesus claims the divine prerogative of working on the Sabbath in verse 17, in verse 18 we read, "This was why the Jews were seeking all the more to kill him, because not only was he breaking the Sabbath, but he was even calling God his own Father, making himself equal with God." Jesus's opponents seek to kill him because they understand his words to constitute the capital offense

6. For a brief survey of early Jewish discussions of God's work on the Sabbath, see Keener, *The Gospel of John,* 1:646. See esp. Philo, *On the Cherubim* 87; *Allegorical Interpretation* 1.5, 18. Cf. also Aristobulus, *Fragment 5;* discussion in Swart, "Aristobulus' Interpretation of LXX Sabbath Texts as an Interpretative Key to John 5:1–18," 572–74.

7. On the basis of Philo, *On the Cherubim* 87, Bekken, *The Lawsuit Motif in John's Gospel from New Perspectives,* 151, concludes, "Thus, according to Philo, God has his own 'Sabbath halakhah' and his own divine way of observing the rest on the Sabbath, which does not stand in tension with the idea that God is continually at work on the Sabbath." And Bekken argues that, in John 5:17, Jesus applies just such a divine "Sabbath halakhah" to himself (149). Bekken's analysis confirms that Jesus's opponents were right to hear Jesus's words in 5:17 as a claim to a uniquely divine warrant for his actions. Cf. Aquinas, *Commentary on the Gospel of St. John* 5.2.738, who anticipates Bekken's basic point and distinguishes Jesus's different self-justifications in multiple Sabbath disputes by employing partitive exegesis.

of blasphemy, an utterance that affronts God by denigrating or impinging on his transcendent uniqueness.[8]

That Jesus's opponents understand his words to be blasphemy is especially evident in light of close parallels elsewhere in John (8:53, 59; 10:33). In all these passages, Jesus's opponents are not wrong to oppose blasphemy; the Bible itself prohibits it (Exod. 22:28; Lev. 24:16). Nor are they wrong in concluding that a creature speaking of himself in ways that only befit the Creator constitutes blasphemy. Nor again are they mistaken in hearing Jesus's words as a claim to divinity.[9] Their only error is in failing to recognize that the one uttering these words is indeed the Creator.

The concept of blasphemy itself rests on a principle of God-fittingness. One species of blasphemy is arrogating to oneself what is only fitting for God. Hence the biblical proscription of blasphemy is a mirror image of the principle of God-fittingness. Only God-befitting claims rightly pertain to God, and God-befitting claims rightly pertain only to God.

### Six God-Befitting Claims

But is Jesus's assertion in 5:17 an isolated outlier? Does his speech as a whole mitigate or qualify this claim of a divine warrant for his work? Far from it. Instead, at least six elements of Jesus's discourse attest his uniquely divine dignity and perfection and thus confirm that, in verse 17 as in the rest of the passage, Jesus intentionally speaks of himself in God-befitting ways. Hence, our third and final task in this section is to consider these six God-befitting claims.

The first springs from an aspect of verse 17 that we have not yet considered in detail: Jesus calls God his own Father. Again, we should recall what Jesus's opponents hear in this statement. They understand him to be blaspheming because "he was even calling God his own Father, making himself equal with God" (v. 18). By calling God "my Father," Jesus is making a scandalous claim. He is not naming God as the creator of all things or the redeemer of all his

---

8. See Bock, "Blasphemy," 84. See also the discussion of Jesus's opponents' response to his citation of Ps. 110:1 in his trial (Mark 14:62) in Bock, "Blasphemy and the Jewish Examination of Jesus," 78. In first-century Jewish sources, the closest parallels to the sense of "blasphemy" evident in John 5:18 can be found in Philo, *On the Embassy to Gaius* 353–68; and *Dreams* 2.130–32. See discussion in Bekken, *The Lawsuit Motif in John's Gospel from New Perspectives*, 58–60. On the charge of blasphemy in John see, further, Söding, "'Ich und der Vater sind eins' (Joh, 10,30)," 177–83.

9. Rightly, Kammler, *Christologie und Eschatologie*, 16; cf. 17–19 for his critique of scholars who see the blasphemy charge as a misunderstanding of Jesus's claims. Similarly, Frey, *Die johanneische Eschatologie*, 3:345: "That they hear the claim of ἰσότης τῷ θεῷ [*isotēs tō theō*, "equality with God"] in his statement in v. 17 is not fended off, but, through vv. 19ff. and in John 10:30ff., precisely confirmed." Contra, e.g., Loader, *Jesus in John's Gospel*, 337.

people. Instead, he is claiming a unique, unparalleled relationship with God that constitutes him as the Father's equal.[10] As the Father's Son, when it is permitted for God to work, it is permitted for him to work. That can only be because, as the Father's Son, the Son continually conserves all creation together with the Father. In other words, given its use in the sentence he speaks, Jesus's naming God as his Father entails the claim of his irreducibly ontological unity with and equality to the Father.[11]

Second, as we will consider further under the "inseparable operations" rule below, the second half of verse 19 attests the Son and the Father's inseparable action: "For whatever the Father does, that the Son does likewise." Only one who is one with the Father can do all that the Father does.[12] The Father and the Son's unity of act reveals their unity of being. Only one who possesses the unique divine nature can perform the uniquely divine works of creating and conserving all things.

Third, in verse 21, Jesus asserts that he has the uniquely divine power of raising the dead: "For as the Father raises the dead and gives them life, so also the Son gives life to whom he will" (cf. vv. 25, 28–29). Scripture teaches that, since he is the sole life-giver, only God can give life to the dead: "See now that I, even I, am he, and there is no god beside me; I kill and I make alive; I wound and I heal; and there is none that can deliver out of my hand" (Deut. 32:39).[13] This conviction is frequently affirmed in extrabiblical early Jewish literature.[14] Note that Jesus does not merely claim to be able to serve as God's creaturely instrument in raising the dead. Elijah and Elisha prayed, and in answer to their prayers God gave the dead life (1 Kings 17:20–22; 2 Kings 4:32–35). Unlike

10. So Bengel, *Gnomon of the New Testament*, 2:305: "The Only-begotten alone can say, *My Father*: of the Only-begotten alone the Father saith, *My Son*" (emphasis original). See also Frey, *Die johanneische Eschatologie*, 3:344.

11. See Augustine, *Homilies on the Gospel of John* 17.16; Aquinas, *Commentary on the Gospel of St. John* 5.4.742. See also, with reference to John as a whole, Frey, "Between Jewish Monotheism and Proto-Trinitarian Relations," 201–2: "In its Johannine use, the traditional title 'Son of God' clearly implies more than mere messiahship: It distinguishes Jesus from all other humans and assigns him to the side of God. . . . Thus, in the Johannine use of the traditional term 'Son of God' and his application of it to Jesus as 'the Son,' the term has now become an expression of his unique unity with the Father (10:30) and his divinity." Similarly, M. M. Thompson, "The Living Father," 29.

12. On how the unity of the Father's and the Son's action in John 5:19 reveals the unity of their being, see Gregory of Nyssa, *Against Eunomius* 1.395–96 (GNO 1:142.8–23); also Hilary of Poitiers, *The Trinity* 7.18 (FC 25:242); Cyril of Alexandria, *Commentary on John* 2.6 (Maxwell, 1:146).

13. Cf. 1 Sam. 2:6; 2 Kings 5:7; Hosea 6:2; Acts 26:8; Rom. 4:17, 8:11; 1 Cor. 6:14; 2 Cor. 1:9; 4:14. As Kammler observes, "Raising the dead and imparting life belong strictly and exclusively to the divine sovereignty" (*Christologie und Eschatologie*, 76).

14. See Tob. 13:2; 2 Macc. 7:9, 22–23; 14:46; 4 Macc. 18:19; Wis. 16:13.

those two prophets, Jesus says to the dead, "Arise" (Mark 5:41; Luke 7:14), to Lazarus in his tomb, "Come out" (John 11:43). Unlike those prophets, Jesus himself gives the dead new life, and he grants this gift "to whom he will." The Son freely, sovereignly exercises this divine prerogative.[15] The Son's unconstrained ability to raise the dead demonstrates his unity and equality with the Father. Further, since the Son does whatever the Father does (v. 19), we should not understand that the Father raises some and the Son others, but that in raising the dead the Father and the Son act inseparably.[16]

Fourth, in verse 26, as we will consider further under the "from another" rule below, Jesus grounds his claim to give resurrection life by asserting that he possesses the unique divine life, life in himself: "For as the Father has life in himself, so he has granted the Son also to have life in himself." In the previous chapter we argued that "life in himself" is a uniquely divine attribute, so "granted" refers to the Father's eternal gift of the divine essence to the Son. In order to understand this verse's conceptual contribution to Jesus's discourse, we need to notice the word it begins with: "for." Verse 26 grounds verse 25, where Jesus asserts his power to raise the dead: "The dead will hear the voice of the Son of God, and those who hear will live." Jesus can give life to those who have lost theirs because he possesses a life that cannot be lost. Jesus can do what only God does because he has what only God has.[17] Verse 26 thereby offers one of the clearest sights of the deep conceptual structure of our whole passage. Jesus shares what he has; he gives what he is. Jesus's words give eternal life because he himself possesses limitless, unbounded life (vv. 24–25).[18] By ascribing to Jesus the kind of life that only God has, John 5:26 asserts that the Son is one and equal with the Father.

Fifth, in verse 22 Christ claims the divine prerogative of judgment: "For the Father judges no one, but has given all judgment to the Son." That the Father has given all judgment to the Son presumes that judgment is God's exclusive right. Similarly in verse 27, "And he has given him authority to execute judgment, because he is the Son of Man." Then, after asserting in verses 28–29 that he will raise all the dead, thereby summoning the wicked to judgment, Jesus declares, "I can do nothing on my own. As I hear, I judge, and my judgment is just, because I seek not my own will but the will of him who sent me"

---

15. See Aquinas, *Commentary on the Gospel of St. John* 5.4.761.

16. Gregory of Nyssa recognizes the Father and the Son's inseparable action—and, based on John 6:63, the Spirit's—of raising the dead in *Letter* 24.14–15 (Silvas, *Gregory of Nyssa*, 195–96).

17. See Kammler, *Christologie und Eschatologie*, 170, 173.

18. Consider the parallel logic in 11:25–26 and 14:1–6, in which Jesus also names himself "life." See Kammler, *Christologie und Eschatologie*, 173–75; also Blank, *Krisis*, 155: "The giver himself is the objective ground of the gift. *He is, in one, the one who gives, and that which he gives*" (emphasis original).

(v. 30). In dozens of places, Scripture teaches that God will judge all people.[19] Certainly, God sometimes delegates limited, earthly, temporal judgments to human agents, whether the people of Israel as a whole (Gen. 15:16), or the Davidic king (Ps. 72:2). Still, it is God alone who is the judge of all the earth (Gen. 18:25; cf. Ps. 94:1). Yet there is one passage in which God delegates final, comprehensive judgment to a human agent: Daniel 7, especially verses 13–14 and 26–27. We will consider this passage under the "partitive exegesis" rule below. For now, as a placeholder, we can simply note that Jesus himself appeals to the language about "one like a son of man" from Daniel 7:13–14 in John 5:22, 27. This biblical prophecy is fulfilled in the only human being who could rightly exercise the divine prerogative of judgment because he is God incarnate. Daniel's depiction of God authorizing a human agent to execute universal judgment does not make judgment any less a divine prerogative; instead, it attests the divine identity of the Son of Man.[20]

Sixth and finally, Jesus receives worship. For what purpose has the Father given all judgment to the Son? "That all may honor the Son, just as they honor the Father. Whoever does not honor the Son does not honor the Father who sent him" (John 5:23). One day, when Christ returns to execute judgment, those who dishonor him now will honor him (cf. 8:49).[21] In Scripture, "honor" is the right recognition of someone's worth or dignity. Father and mother deserve it (Exod. 20:12), as do the church's true widows and the Roman emperor (1 Tim. 5:3; 1 Pet. 2:17). But there is a kind of honor that is due to God alone—namely, worship. And the Greek translation of the OT, as well as other Jewish literature from Greek antiquity, uses the verb "honor" (τιμάω, timaō) with reference to God to name the worship that is a right response to him alone.[22] In verse 23 Jesus claims precisely the honor that is due to the Father. All are to honor the Son "just as" they honor the Father: in the same manner and to the same degree.[23] Only one who is one with and equal to the Father may be worshiped as the Father is worshiped.

19. E.g., Gen. 18:25; 1 Sam. 2:10; 1 Chron. 16:33; Pss. 7:8, 11; 50:4, 6; 67:4; 75:2; 82:8; 94:2; 96:10, 13; 98:9; Eccl. 3:17; Isa. 2:4; 51:5; Joel 3:12; Matt. 10:15; 11:22–24; Rom. 2:1–11, 16; 3:6; 14:10, 12; 2 Thess. 1:5–6; James 4:12; 1 Pet. 1:17; 2:23; Rev. 11:16–18.

20. Hence Cyril of Alexandria, *Commentary on John* 2.8 (Maxwell, 1:156), is right to observe about vv. 26–27, "The Only Begotten . . . has clothed himself with the brightness of two God-befitting deeds. He distinctly maintains that he will both raise the dead and summon them to be judged at his own judgment seat."

21. So Aquinas, *Commentary on the Gospel of St. John* 5.4b.765, who cites Luke 21:17 and Rev. 7:11 as parallels.

22. See LXX Prov. 3:9 and Isa. 29:13; also *Sibylline Oracles* 2:60; *Letter of Aristeas* 234. Noted by Fletcher-Louis, "John 5:19–30," 419.

23. As Augustine observes, the qualifier "just as" indicates that the Son is the Father's equal (*Homilies on the Gospel of John* 19.6 [WSA III/12:338–39]).

Further, Jesus makes worshiping him the criterion of whether someone worships the Father. One cannot truly worship the Father if one does not worship Jesus. These are stunning statements, and they fully answer the charge of verse 18 that Jesus is making himself equal to God, which implies that he is dishonoring God. It is not Jesus who dishonors God but all who refuse to honor Jesus as God.[24]

These divine prerogatives—upholding creation, doing all that the Father does, raising the dead, possessing life in himself, judging all people, and receiving worship—are points on a closed circle. Only one who possesses life in himself can give life to all and sustain all life. Only one who gives and takes life in the first place can give life after it has been taken. Only one who does all that the Father does, because he is all that the Father is, may receive the worship that only God deserves. Throughout our passage, Jesus claims to possess a series of God-fitting perfections and prerogatives in order to confirm his divine identity by a cumulative case. Each claim illumines and supports the others. Each claim implies the others. He who has one has them all; he who lacks one has none.[25]

To summarize: the principle of God-fittingness, and the Creator-creature distinction it linguistically marks, are necessary intellectual equipment both for discerning the sense of these divine prerogatives and for understanding why Jesus's claiming of them prompts outraged opposition.[26] Jesus speaks of himself in all these God-befitting ways because he possesses the unique divine essence which alone warrants such claims.

## A Distinct, Complementary Register

### Rule 4: Common and Proper

Scripture speaks both of what is common to the Father, Son, and Holy Spirit and of what is proper to each person, reflecting the conceptual distinction between the divine nature and the divine persons. Biblical reasoning discerns this distinction, upholds

---

24. Rightly, Kammler, *Christologie und Eschatologie*, 99–100; cf. Bauckham, "Monotheism and Christology in the Gospel of John," 153.

25. Cf. Radde-Gallwitz, *Basil of Caesarea, Gregory of Nyssa, and the Transformation of Divine Simplicity*, 17, on Gregory of Nyssa's perception of the "inter-entailing" character of the divine perfections.

26. Another way to make this point is to say that John's Christology presupposes the unique, exclusive monotheism of the OT and early Judaism, and that Christ's divine identity is always located within and coordinated with this strict monotheism, not in tension with it. On this see esp. Bauckham, "Monotheism and Christology in the Gospel of John." On biblical monotheism more broadly, see Bauckham, *Jesus and the God of Israel*, 60–106.

it, and contemplates the Holy Trinity in its light. Therefore, read Scripture's discourse about God in such a way that its twofold discourse–the common and the proper–is recognized and employed, rather than in a way that collapses the two ways into one. In this way, we learn to count persons rather than natures.

All the God-fitting perfections and prerogatives that Jesus claims for himself in our passage, which we considered in the previous section, pertain to common predication. That Jesus upholds creation on the Sabbath, has life in himself, rightly receives worship, and so on—all this he has and does in common with the Father and the Spirit. All this pertains to what it means for the Son to be God, just as the Father is God and the Spirit is God.

But this passage also speaks of the Son in a distinct, complementary register. In addition to naming what he has in common with the Father and the Spirit, it also speaks of what distinguishes him from the Father and the Spirit. Like the Father, the Son has life in himself (John 5:26). Unlike the Father, who has life in himself from no one besides himself, the Son has life in himself from the Father.[27] "Life in himself" is common to Father and Son; the mode of having it, whether from no one else or from another, distinguishes the Son from the Father. The life is one; the mode of living is distinct.

Consider verse 19 again. The Son does everything the Father does: common. The Son does all this as seeing and the Father as showing: proper. The acts are common; the modes are proper. The action is one; the mode of action is distinct.

Some modern scholars of John who are perceptive in many other important respects fail to discern and distinguish these two complementary modes of predication. For instance, C. K. Barrett writes, with our passage in view, "It is further to be observed that those notable Johannine passages that seem at first sight to proclaim most unambiguously the unity and equality of the Son with the Father are often set in contexts which if they do not deny at least qualify this theme, and place alongside it the theme of dependence, and indeed of subordination."[28] What Barrett sees as evidence of subordination would more accurately be glossed simply as relation, specifically relation of origin.[29] Jesus's eternal generation from the Father does not qualify or compete with

---

27. Though he speaks with less than full conviction, the following quip from Mealand, "John 5 and the Limits of Rhetorical Criticism," 264, hits the mark: "The paradox is ancient, but it could be dragged to the surface and made all too explicit by translating: 'has granted to the Son to have ungranted life.'"

28. Barrett, "'The Father Is Greater Than I' John 14:28," 23.

29. Hence, provided the term is properly unpacked, "dependence" hits the mark and need not imply "subordination."

his unity and equality with the Father.[30] Instead, as we saw in the previous chapter, his generation from the Father is what proves his unity and equality with the Father (cf. John 14:9–11).

We should also recall from the previous chapter that "Father" and "Son" are relative names. As titles that pick out distinct divine persons, "Father" and "Son" name them in a way that is proper to each. It is no accident that our passage's point of departure is Jesus's peculiar relational moniker for God: "my Father" (v. 17). Nor is it mere coincidence that Jesus's absolute use of the titles "the Son" and "the Father" is a leitmotif of our passage.[31] Jesus repeatedly names himself and the Father in relation to each other because one of the prime subjects of his discourse is his relation to the Father.[32] The names "Father" and "Son" signal the subject of the discourse, and assertions about the intrinsic relation of Son to Father comprise a large portion of its predicate. In other words, the dense concentration of relative names should prime us to hear at least a portion of Jesus's speech as falling in the register of what is proper to him as the Son.

## Whatever the Father Does

### Rule 5: Inseparable Operations

The external works of the Trinity are indivisibly one, just as God is one. Whenever Scripture mentions only one or two divine persons, understand that all three are equally present and active, undertaking the same actions in ways that imply their

---

30. Modern scholars' frequent failure to distinguish between common and proper modes of christological predication is especially evident in treatments of John 1:1 and 1:18. See, e.g., Engberg-Pedersen, *John and Philosophy*, 51, on John 1:1: "Here John clearly wishes to connect the *logos* as closely as possible with God—but also to maintain a distinction. The *logos* is not just identical with God. Still, it is as closely connected with God as is possible when the two entities are *not* identical" (emphasis original). Similarly Loader, *Jesus in John's Gospel*, 319–21, 326, 330–31; Forger, "Jesus as God's Word(s)," 276n6. These scholars and many others would do well to heed the salutary reminder of I. McFarland, *The Word Made Flesh*, 117: "For although in the New Testament the title 'Son' clearly distinguishes Jesus from the *Father*, it does not thereby necessarily distinguish him from *God*" (emphasis original). A notable recent exception to this trend is Byers, *Ecclesiology and Theosis in the Gospel of John*, 34–36, 48, who concludes regarding John 1:18, "These dual dynamics of both unity and plurality are jointly articulated in the compound title μονογενὴς θεός" (34). See also the fruitful appeal to paradox in John 1:1 in Estes, "Dualism or Paradox?," 103–5. For a sophisticated application of the "common and proper" rule to a different NT corpus, see Hill, *Paul and the Trinity*, esp. 112–20.

31. See vv. 19 (2× each), 20, 21, 22, 23 (2× each), 26.

32. The comments of Fletcher-Louis, "John 5:19–30," 430, are on the right track: "As the Son, he already has a peculiar divine identity and position of intimacy with the Father, out of which he works wonders (vv. 19–21) and in virtue of which he deserves to be worshiped (v. 23)."

relations to one another. In this way, learn to count persons rather than actions.

### Rule 6: Appropriation

Scripture sometimes attributes to only one divine person a perfection, action, or name common to all three, because of some contextual fit or analogy between the common attribute and the divine person in question. Read such passages in a way that does not compromise the Trinity's essential oneness and equality.

While many features of our passage warrant and are in turn illumined by the "inseparable operations" rule, we will focus on just one verse: "So Jesus said to them, 'Truly, truly, I say to you, the Son can do nothing of himself, but only what he sees the Father doing. For whatever the Father does, that the Son does likewise'" (John 5:19 AT). We considered the verse in detail in the previous chapter's exposition of the "from another" rule. We now focus on the last sentence, "For whatever the Father does, that the Son does likewise." Jesus here responds to the charge of blasphemy by unpacking his assertion from verse 17.[33] As the Father works until now, so does the Son, because the Son does everything the Father does. Does the Father raise the dead? So too the Son (vv. 21, 25). Does the Father judge all? Not without the Son (vv. 22, 27). Every action of the Father is also an action of the Son; there is no action of the Son that is not also an action of the Father.[34]

In his comments on this phrase in verse 19, Aquinas notes that it "excludes three things in the power of Christ: limitation, difference, and imperfection."[35] First, in case anyone supposed that, since the Son does not exist of himself, his power must be limited to certain existing things rather than being universal as the Father's is, Jesus says that he does "whatever the Father does" (cf. John 1:3). Second, Jesus's words exclude all difference between the acts of the Father and of the Son. Their activity is not like two fires that burn separate pieces of wood. Instead, the "whatever" indicates that they do the very same things. Third, Jesus's words exclude imperfection. The Son is no mere instrument through whom the Father acts as principal agent. Instead, "With the same power by which the Father acts, the Son also acts; because

33. As Bengel, *Gnomon of the New Testament*, 2:305, observes, v. 17 is a thesis that the rest of Jesus's speech in vv. 19–30 expounds.

34. We adapt this formulation from that of Vidu, *The Same God Who Works All Things*, 39. Vidu's discussion of this verse (37–42) is insightful, concise, and rightly discerns several common errors in modern scholarly treatments.

35. Aquinas, *Commentary on the Gospel of St. John* 5.5.752.

the same power and the same perfection are in the Father and the Son."[36] The Father and the Son act inseparably because they exist inseparably. The action of the Father and the Son is one because their divine power is one. As they are, so they act: one God, undivided and indivisible, distinct only in their eternal relations of origin.

Regarding the sixth rule, appropriation: our passage offers no explicit, positive instance of the phenomenon. Nevertheless, the rule offers us indirect aid in reading verse 22: "For the Father judges no one, but has given all judgment to the Son." As we saw above, Jesus's act of executing judgment reveals his unity and equality with the Father. Also, as we will see under the "partitive exegesis" rule below, the Father's act of giving judgment to the Son pertains to the Son's assumed human nature. Yet here we need to consider this passage from still another angle. In order to block the false inference that the Father is inactive in judgment, we can fruitfully appeal to the rule of appropriation. There is a sense in which Jesus's assertion in verse 22 "appropriates" judgment exclusively to himself, yet without intending to deny that the Father too will exercise judgment. In light of the inseparable operations of the Trinity, we should understand Jesus's negation here as denying that the Father *alone* judges and as asserting that the Father will not be the visible agent who executes judgment.[37] Instead, the Father has appointed the incarnate Son, the Son of Man, as his eschatological delegate (cf. v. 27). That the Son will visibly execute eschatological judgment does not exclude the Father from an active role in this judgment. Instead, employing a common Hebrew idiom, Jesus uses absolute language to make a relative point.[38] The invisible Father will execute final judgment through the action of his visible, incarnate Son.

36. Aquinas, *Commentary on the Gospel of St. John* 5.2.752. The most perceptive comments we have found on this phrase among modern biblical scholars are those of Kammler: "Thereby it is said, in principle and without any restriction, that between the action of the Father and the action of the Son there is always and everywhere a perfect parallelism and conformity. Indeed, one may even speak of a *unity and identity* of the action of the two. Namely, the uniformity of the actions of Father and Son is emphasized here (ὁμοίως), and these refer comprehensively to one and the same 'object' (ταῦτα). This can only mean: the action of the Son is itself the action of the Father" (*Christologie und Eschatologie*, 23 [emphasis original]). Cf. Dodd, *The Interpretation of the Fourth Gospel*, 257: "Father and Son are subjects of the same activity" (cf. 327).

37. For the former point, see Kammler, *Christologie und Eschatologie*, 90, who adduces John 5:30; 6:38; 7:16; 12:44; and 14:24 as parallels. The same logic is at work in statements in which Jesus denies that something he is or does is his own, because it belongs to the Father (which implies that the Father has given it to him), and in which, as here, Jesus denies that the Father performs some action, because he has granted the Son to perform it.

38. Cyril seems to understand Jesus's denial in relative terms, in light of the inseparable operations of the Trinity, when he writes, "So listen to how giving must then be understood. Just

## Human Subject, Divine Predicates

### Rule 7: The Unity of Christ

The eternal, divine Son is the sole subject of everything Jesus does and suffers. Christ is one person, one agent, one "who." Therefore, in reading Scripture's witness to Christ we must never divide Christ's acts between two acting subjects, attributing some to the divine Son and others to the human Jesus as if there were two different people.

### Rule 8: The Communication of Idioms

Since Christ is a single divine person who subsists in both a divine and a human nature, Scripture sometimes names him according to one nature and predicates of him what belongs to the other nature. Scripture ascribes divine prerogatives to the man Jesus, and human acts and sufferings to the divine Son. So read Scripture in a way that recognizes and reproduces this paradoxical grammar of christological predication.

The singularity of Christ's personhood is evident throughout our passage. There is no evidence whatsoever that Jesus conceals within himself two agents, a divine one and a human one. It is because he is a man asserting God-befitting things of himself that his opponents are so incensed (John 5:18). The problem with Jesus's opponents is their refusal to accept the reality that warrants Jesus's own use of the communication of idioms, so to speak. The one standing before them is plainly a man (cf. 4:29; 6:42; 8:40), yet he asserts of himself what can only be true of God.[39]

From the standpoint of Jesus's hearers, much of his discourse consists of a kind of "ascending" communication of idioms: a human subject claims divine predicates. This man works on the Sabbath to sustain creation, as only God does (v. 17). He does everything that God his Father does (v. 19). He raises the dead and gives them life (v. 21) because he himself possesses the unique divine life (v. 26). He will judge all people (vv. 22, 27), and therefore

---

as God the Father has the ability to create and creates all things through the Son as through his own power and strength, so also he has the power to judge, and he will exercise that power through the Son as through his own righteousness" (*Commentary on John* 2.7 [Maxwell, 1:150]).

39. Though he is speaking of John 8:25, the comment of Söding, "Ich und der Vater sind eins (Joh, 10,30)," 179, is equally apt of our passage: "Between the work and the person of Jesus his opponents see an unbridgeable gulf." See also the similar observations of Sproston, "'Is Not This Jesus, the Son of Joseph . . . ?' (John 6.42)," 89–91; Myers, "Prosopopoetics and Conflict," 580, 588, 592–95.

he must be worshiped as God the Father is worshiped (v. 23).[40] All these divine attributes and acts are rightly predicated of this man because he is God the Son incarnate, the only begotten God become flesh for our salvation (1:14, 18).

## Every Eye Will See Him

### Rule 9: Partitive Exegesis

Scripture speaks of Christ in a twofold manner: some things are said of him as divine, and other things are said of him as human. Biblical reasoning discerns that Scripture speaks of the one Christ in two registers in order to contemplate the whole Christ. Therefore read Scripture in such a way that you discern the different registers in which Scripture speaks of Christ, yet without dividing him.

Partitive exegesis helps us recognize the human sense and scope of several assertions Christ makes about himself in our passage. First, after stating that the Son does everything the Father does, in verse 20 Jesus says, "For the Father loves the Son and shows him all that he himself is doing. And greater works than these will he show him, so that you may marvel." In the previous chapter we saw that the Son's and the Spirit's modes of action reveal their modes of being. We also argued in the previous chapter that the Father "showing" the Son all that he does is a metaphorical description of the Father's eternal act of begetting the Son. Here, we will focus first on the second half of verse 20, specifically the future tense of "greater works than these *will he show him.*" Why the future tense? Because here Jesus is not speaking about his relation to the Father simply as it is in itself, but as his human actions on earth reveal that relation. He speaks of his own future acts as works the Father will show him in time because he is referring to a future time in which he will perform them.[41]

What works will Jesus do that are greater than healing a man who had been an invalid for thirty-eight years (John 5:5)? Most likely, Jesus is referring to how he will first raise Lazarus from the dead and then raise himself from the dead (11:1–46, esp. 11:40; cf. 10:18). Hence, after he has just ascribed to

---

40. Commenting on v. 27, Bengel, *Gnomon of the New Testament*, 2:309, marks the paradox: "He, a man, saves men: He, a man, judges men."

41. So Augustine, *Homilies on the Gospel of John* 23.12 (WSA III/12:419): "*Will show him,* as if in time, so as if to a man in time, because God the Word, through whom all times were made, was not made; but Christ was made man in time" (emphasis original).

himself the God-befitting dignity of doing all that the Father does, Jesus shifts his speech "downward" to a human register.[42]

Further, in verse 27 Jesus returns to the theme of judgment that he introduced in verse 22: "And he has given him authority to execute judgment, because he is the Son of Man." Here Jesus appeals explicitly to the chief scriptural paradigm of the Father's grant to the Son of this authority to judge—namely, Daniel 7:13–14. We read:

> I saw in the night visions,
>
>> and behold, with the clouds of heaven
>>> there came one like a son of man,
>> and he came to the Ancient of Days
>>> and was presented before him.
>> And to him was given dominion
>>> and glory and a kingdom,
>> that all peoples, nations, and languages
>>> should serve him;
>> his dominion is an everlasting dominion,
>>> which shall not pass away,
>> and his kingdom one
>>> that shall not be destroyed.

John 5:27 is an expanded citation of two phrases from the Old Greek translation of these verses: "he gave him authority" and "son of man."[43] This is an obvious point, but the literal meaning of the phrase "one like a son of man" is "one like a human being." This office that Jesus executes presupposes his incarnation. The Son had to become a man in order to become the Son of Man. And in our verse, Jesus gives "because he is the Son of Man" as the reason why the Father has given all judgment into his hands. Sometimes scholars rightly recognize that judgment is a divine prerogative, and so they downplay the conceptual contribution of Jesus's humanity to this verse.[44] But this is a false dilemma. The text neither forces nor permits a choice between the two. Instead, it is precisely in his capacity as Son of Man that Jesus will

---

42. As noted by John Chrysostom, *Homilies on John* 39 (FC 33:384–99); also Augustine, *Homilies on the Gospel of John* 21.7.

43. For details see Reynolds, *The Apocalyptic Son of Man in the Gospel of John*, 137–38; Fletcher-Louis, "John 5:19–30," 417–18.

44. As does Reynolds, *The Apocalyptic Son of Man in the Gospel of John*, 136, when he says of vv. 26–27, "It is Jesus's relationship with the Father and not his humanity that make these divine activities possible." For recent arguments that Dan. 7:13–14 presents the Son of Man as divine, see Boyarin, "Daniel 7, Intertextuality, and the History of Israel's Cult"; Zehnder, "Why the Danielic 'Son of Man' Is a Divine Being."

visibly return to earth and judge all people. Verse 27 teaches us that "Son of Man" is a "theandric" office: as Son of Man, Jesus exercises divine prerogatives as a human being.

Why did Jesus need to *receive* this authority? In order that, as man, he would execute the office of judge in plain view of all.[45] As man, Jesus will do what only God may: judge all people. As Augustine concludes, employing both partitive exegesis and the communication of idioms, "So it is the Son of man who is going to judge, not though by his human authority but by his authority as Son of God. And again it is the Son of God who is going to judge, though he will not be manifested in the form by which he is equal to the Father, but in that by which he is the Son of man."[46]

In light of Jesus's introduction of the title "Son of Man" in verse 27, we can profitably return to his statement in verses 22–23: "For the Father judges no one, but has given all judgment to the Son, that all may honor the Son, just as they honor the Father." Two features of this verse indicate that Christ is speaking of himself on the basis of his assumed human nature. First, Jesus's denial that the Father judges anyone only makes sense in view of his own incarnation. Specifically, Jesus here refers obliquely to his visible, bodily second advent, when he will come with the clouds and every eye will see him (Rev. 1:7). As Augustine observes, "His reason for saying *The Father judges no one, but has given all judgement to the Son* (Jn 5:22) was that he will be manifested as judge in the form of the Son of man, which is not the Father's form but the Son's only; and not the Son's form either in which he is equal to the Father, but the one in which he is less than the Father."[47] Further, we should understand the Father's act of "giving" all judgment to the Son as an element of this commissioning of the Son's incarnate execution of final judgment.[48] As God, and therefore the Father's equal, the Son intrinsically possesses the authority to judge, but he also receives this authority as man.[49]

45. Rightly, Augustine, *The Trinity* 1.30 (WSA I/5:94): "This then is why he had to receive that authority as Son of man; it is in order that all, as they rise again, may see him in the form in which he can be seen by all—by some however to their undoing, by others to eternal life." Commenting on the parallel "has given" in v. 22, Cyril writes, "In that he is Word and God, he inherently has authority over all things, but in that he has become human, to whom it says somewhere, 'What do you have that you did not receive?' he confesses that it was fitting for him to receive that authority" (*Commentary on John* 2.7 [Maxwell, 1:149]).

46. Augustine, *The Trinity* 1.28 (WSA I/5:92).

47. Augustine, *The Trinity* 1.30 (WSA I/5:93).

48. Again Augustine is helpful: "As the Son of God and equal to the Father, he simply is, together with the Father, the hidden source of this authority, he does not receive it. But he does receive it, in order that both good and bad may see him judging, as Son of man" (*The Trinity* 1.30 [WSA I/5:93]).

49. Cf. Cyril of Alexandria, *Commentary on John* 2.7 (Maxwell, 1:149): "He says, however, that 'judgment' has been given to him by the Father not on the grounds that he lies outside this

Finally, we can consider one more teaching of Jesus about his coming act of judgment: "I can do nothing on my own. As I hear, I judge, and my judgment is just, because I seek not my own will but the will of him who sent me" (v. 30). Here we are concerned only with "I seek not my own will but the will of him who sent me." If we considered the Son simply as God, this statement would make no theological sense. The Father, Son, and Holy Spirit subsist in the one divine essence and therefore possess one will. It is only as a human being that Jesus can distinguish, in principle, between his own will and the will of the Father who sent him. And of course, Jesus distinguishes his (human) will from the Father's will only in order to declare their unity. What Jesus wills is not anything other than what his heavenly Father wills. His judgment will be neither partial nor unjust because he will judge precisely as the Father would.[50] In this statement, as in each of those we have considered in this section, Jesus speaks of himself in a human register. He speaks of himself not in view of the form of God in which he always exists but in view of the form of a servant which he took for our salvation.

## A Signal Instance

### Rule 10: From Another

Scripture often attributes to the divine persons ordered relations and actions that do not compromise their unity and equality, but only signify that one person eternally exists from another: the Son from the Father, the Spirit from the Father and the Son. Read Scripture in a way that recognizes and upholds these ordered relations of origin.

Since we drew heavily on John 5:17–30 in treating this rule in the previous chapter, here we offer only brief comments on two verses—namely, 17 and 19. First, we have repeatedly considered that in verse 17 Jesus declares, "My Father is working until now, and I am working." In verse 18 his opponents take this as a blasphemous claim to equality with God, and a primary goal of Jesus's defense in verses 19–30 is to rebut the charge. Here we note simply that Jesus's use of "my Father" in verse 17, which does indeed imply equality

---

authority but on the grounds that he is a man according to the *oikonomia*, thereby teaching that 'all things' are more fittingly ascribed to the divine nature, which he has as he enters the world."

50. Cf. Aquinas, *Commentary on the Gospel of St. John* 5.5.796: "For there are two wills in our Lord Jesus Christ: one is a divine will, which is the same as the will of the Father; the other is a human will, which is proper to himself, just as it is proper to him to be a man. A human will is borne to its own good; but in Christ it was ruled and regulated by right reason, so that it would always be conformed in all things to the divine will."

with the Father, asserts a relation: the Son claims God as his own Father. In other words, in this verse Jesus does not merely assert his equality with the Father but proclaims a relation, a from-ness, that constitutes him as the Father's equal. The Son is equal to God because he is God from God. Verse 17 teaches not only that Jesus is equal to God but also that he eternally exists from God.

Second, in light of all we have seen in this chapter, it emerges even more clearly that verse 19 attests Jesus's eternal existence from the Father: "Truly, truly, I say to you, the Son can do nothing of himself, but only what he sees the Father doing. For whatever the Father does, that the Son does likewise" (AT). We considered above that the God-fittingness rule is warranted by Jesus's own teaching in this passage against the stark backdrop of the charge of blasphemy. Hence it is entirely appropriate to invoke the God-fittingness rule to understand Jesus's statement that "the Son can do nothing of himself, but only what he sees the Father doing." Given that what the Son does in this derivative, dependent manner is in fact everything that the Father does, this is divine doing, and it must be understood in a God-fitting way. God is spirit, not body, and so has no eyes; applied to God, "seeing" can only be a metaphor.[51] This metaphor conveys that the Son does divine deeds *in a receptive mode.*[52] As eyes receive sensory impressions that enable action, so the Son eternally receives from the Father the single, unique divine essence, enabling his divine action. Hence Augustine rightly regards John 5:19 as a signal instance of the "from another" rule: "This then is the rule which governs many scriptural texts, intended to show not that one person is less than the other, but only that one is from the other."[53]

## Conclusion: Makes Them Spacious so as to Fill Them

This chapter has recapitulated and applied the argument of the whole book. We have tried to show not only that these tools work, but that they work together. Some tools found much more work to do in this passage than others. However, they all have work to do, and we need the work that each does to read the passage rightly. We now offer two concluding reflections on the point of the whole project in light of this completed case study.

---

51. Rightly noted by Vidu, *The Same God Who Works All Things*, 39.
52. As R. Williams, "Trinity and Revelation," 140, observes, "So Jesus shares the creativity of God, yet not as a 'second God,' a separate *individual*: he is God *as* dependent—for whom the metaphors of Word, Image, and Son are appropriate" (emphasis original).
53. Augustine, *The Trinity* 2.3 (WSA I/5:99).

First, theology is exegesis, and exegesis is inescapably theological. The truth of the first half of this axiom has been supported by the demonstration above that a series of mutually reinforcing theological judgments are either presupposed or explicitly articulated in John 5:17–30. In order to perceive the truth of the second half of this axiom, one needs a thick-enough concept of what exegesis is. Exegesis is not merely the analysis of historical background and cultural encyclopedia, the situations of writer and recipients, word meanings, grammar, flow of thought, intracanonical connections, and the unfolding of redemptive history. Exegesis is also, inescapably, reasoning about the subject matter of the text: God and all things in relation to God. While we can distinguish exegetical from dogmatic reasoning, we must not exclude the latter from the former. Exegetical reasoning accounts for an individual passage; dogmatic reasoning accounts for what a passage teaches us about its ultimate subject matter and what the whole Bible teaches us about its ultimate subject matter. Exegetical reasoning aims to save the phenomena of a passage; dogmatic reasoning aims to save the phenomena of the whole canon. Proper dogmatic reasoning moves not away from Scripture to a final resting place in theological construction but stays within Scripture, moves within Scripture, and delves deeper into the inexhaustible riches of the mysteries declared in Scripture.[54] In order to do exegesis, we must explain and give the sense of the text. And in order to give the sense of the text, we need to use words that are different from those in the text. Dogmatic concepts and judgments need not dominate exegesis; instead, they can and must serve it.

Second, as we have argued throughout the book, exegesis requires intellectual ascesis. Rightly reading Scripture demands that we purify our minds, purging our conceptions of God from all intellectual idolatry, however unintentional. In John 5:19–20, when Jesus says that the Son sees the Father working, his language might tempt us to think that the Father works without the Son. Only a couple of sentences later, in verse 22, Jesus says virtually the opposite: "For the Father judges no one, but has given all judgment to the Son." Does the Father work without the Son? Does the Son judge without the Father? How are we supposed to theologically negotiate such a high-speed hairpin turn? As a fitting conclusion to the chapter, we can contemplate

---

54. As Emery, "*Theologia* and *Dispensatio*," 549, observes of Aquinas's trinitarian theology, "The doctrine of the action of the Trinity (third step) is achieved when a speculative reflection on the divine persons (second step) is applied to the agency of the persons discovered in the reading of Scripture (first step). In this way, Trinitarian theology moves not only from Scripture to Scripture, but all three steps move within Scripture itself." Similarly, Emery, "Biblical Exegesis and the Speculative Doctrine of the Trinity in St. Thomas Aquinas's *Commentary on St. John*," 61.

Augustine's comments on this provocative pivot: "How he twists us around and juggles with our minds, leading them hither and thither! He will not let them stay in any single place favored by the flesh, but he twists them about to exercise them, exercises them to clean them up, cleans them up to make them spacious, makes them spacious so as to fill them."[55]

---

55. Augustine, *Homilies on the Gospel of John* 21.12 (WSA III/12:382).

# Conclusion

## From Glory to Glory

Father, I desire that they also, whom you have given me, may be
with me where I am, to see my glory that you have given me because
you loved me before the foundation of the world.

—John 17:24

The vision of which Jesus speaks is, as we have seen, the face-to-face sight
of God that is our ultimate blessedness and peace. This vision is the
culmination of knowing the only true God and Jesus Christ whom he
has sent (John 17:3). Why have we pursued this vision through so much talk
about christological and trinitarian doctrine? Because doctrine is "teaching,"
something done to us before it is something we do. The church hears before
it speaks. Doctrine is therefore chiefly divine teaching: being taught by God,
about God, to lead us to God. Discourse about God—theology—is thus
poorly conceived if it is divorced from the presence and activity of the God
who discourses about himself. And he speaks above all "in his Son" (Heb. 1:2).

Though it has taken twists and turns through waters of different turbulence
and depth, the argument of this book is simple: Beholding Christ by faith requires that we hear and obey Christ's teaching. In order to understand Christ's
teaching, we must reason both exegetically and dogmatically.[1] And we pursue

---

1. Of course, those who are not professionally trained biblical exegetes or systematic theologians also hear and obey Christ. The oral literacy of Scripture acquired through faithful

this project of biblical reasoning in service to biblical living, in the confident hope that one day faith will give way to sight. Christ the teacher concentrates our attention on himself and his earthly life, death, and resurrection so that we may be purified by faith in him. At the heart of this process is the mystery that the Son is not only true man but also true God. Augustine comments: "The Son of God came in order to become Son of man and to capture our faith and draw it to himself, and by means of it to lead us on to his truth; for he took our mortality in such a way that he did not lose his own eternity."[2] Christ mediates eternal life to us because he never loses it, even when taking to himself our temporal limitations and the vicissitudes of mortality. "At one and the same time he was both the way of life here below and life itself in heaven above."[3] Understanding this truth requires us to see how the Son is "holy, holy, holy" in himself, the eternal, immortal, invisible and blessed God (1 Tim. 1:17; 6:16). As the transcendent and immutable God, he became what we are without ceasing to be what he is. So we must acknowledge that the one Son who is *homoousios* with the Father and the Spirit in his divinity became also *homoousios* with us in his humanity. And this was for our sake, that we might be adopted into the life he eternally enjoys with the Father and the Holy Spirit.

These are truths Christ teaches us, truths we must hear and obey. But for this reason, these doctrines are not lifeless propositions; rather, Christ's teachings are an instrument of our sanctification. Not only does Christ redeem us, but Christ teaching about Christ—the mystery of his incarnation and his relations to the Father and the Spirit—leads us to understand the fullness of his person and work. Our own confession of Christ's person and work, ordered to the praise of the Father's glorious grace, is part of the blessing we have received in Christ: "We are drawn into the power of that grace precisely by realizing and acknowledging who Christ really is—by accepting for ourselves, in faith, the lowly narrative, the humiliating paradox, of a humble God."[4] Jesus concentrates our attention on himself so that we might become what we behold, humble and merciful. Only by beholding and being conformed to Christ's glory now do we progress toward our final destination of being glorified with him in his presence (2 Cor. 3:18; 1 John 3:2–3).

This progress toward glorification does not require that we merely learn truths about Christ or become ever more technically proficient trinitarian

submission to the ministry of the Word is one way most Christians throughout history have made use of exegetical and dogmatic reasoning to give them a clearer apprehension of the gospel of the glory of the blessed God.

2. Augustine, *The Trinity* 4.24 (WSA I/5:177).
3. Augustine, *The City of God* 9.15 (WSA I/6:295).
4. Daley, *God Visible*, 173.

theologians. It lays obligations on our loves, as every friendship does. "No longer do I call you servants, for the servant does not know what his master is doing; but I have called you friends, for all that I have heard from my Father I have made known to you. . . . I chose you and appointed you that you should go and bear fruit and that your fruit should abide" (John 15:15–16). Clinging to Christ by faith, we must also cling to him in love and observe his commands (John 14:15). This is no mere homiletical flourish; it is intrinsic to how we apprehend the exegetical rules we have discovered throughout the book and how they clear our eyes. The glory to which Christ draws our gaze is one with the love that drives him to the cross.[5]

The path to contemplating Christ's glory is marked by the humility of Christ's cross, the highest and most paradoxical expression of that glory. For the cross not only humbles us but also embraces us and draws us into Christ's glory. But how does the cross tinge the glory that Christ prays for us to see?

God's glory glorifies us because it is the majesty of God's eternal love, which is full and fruitful in itself and which is also, on that basis, extended toward us in Christ. Petrus van Mastricht describes the glory of God as "nothing other than the brightness, so to speak, of his infinite eminence."[6] In itself, this brightness is too much for us to bear. We long to see the God who "dwells in unapproachable light, whom no one has ever seen or can see" (1 Tim. 6:16). But the Son has seen the Father, and the Spirit has searched their depths (John 1:18; 1 Cor. 2:11). The light of God's glory shines most intensely where it finds its fullest reflection, in the Father's eternal begetting of his Radiance (Heb. 1:3) and the Father and the Son's eternal breathing forth of "the Spirit of glory and of God" (1 Pet. 4:14). God is Light from Light from Light. The brilliance of the divine processions extended toward us in the missions of the Son and the Spirit chases away the nightfall of sin because the missions extend to sinners the beating heart of the divine processions: God's love (John 15:9; 17:23–26). Thus, the Light shines in the darkness without being overcome by it (John 1:5). The Son declares the glory of the Father, and the Father glorifies the Son in himself in the darkest place possible. Why? To demonstrate definitively that this Light cannot be occluded and that it will irradiate and glorify God's wayward, darkened creatures.

---

5. In this, we differ only slightly from Dodd, *The Interpretation of the Fourth Gospel*, 207–8: "If the actions of Christ are to be taken as equivalents for the radiance in which the power and presence of God are brought within human experience, or in other words, in which the eternal light is apprehended by means of itself, φωτὶ φῶς ["light by light"], then the action in which He most fully expressed Himself, namely His self-devotion to death in love for mankind, is the conclusive manifestation of the divine glory . . . the eternal majesty of God."

6. Mastricht, *Theoretical-Practical Theology* 1.2.22.v.

The revelation of God's glory in the cross of Christ enables us to glorify him. But glorification occurs first of all within God's triune life, and it is on this basis that the divine persons glorify one another in the economy: the Father glorifies the Son (John 17:1), the Son the Father (17:4), and the Holy Spirit the Son (16:14) and, by extension, the Father (16:15).[7] This revelation of the eternal glory of the Trinity makes known to us the infinite object of our beatific enjoyment and glorification. Matthias Scheeben explains:

> The supernatural beatitude which the creature enjoys in the vision of God is thus inaugurated and anticipated by the revelation of the Trinity. Belief in the Trinity is a foretaste of the beatific vision of God; it builds a bridge to heaven for our souls, it lifts them up to God while they tarry still on earth; it introduces them into the joy of their Lord. If the supreme delight of God's own beatitude is the fellowship and mutual relationship of the persons, our very faith in the Trinity enables us in some slight way to savor the innermost sweetness and loveliness of God.[8]

To behold the glory of the crucified Christ is to know now by faith what we will one day see in truth, with unveiled face: the glory that embraces us, purifies us, and raises us further up and further in to the radiant beauty of God. This is the end of Christian exegesis because it is the end of the Christian life. In making this end known, God grants us a token of our future blessedness and glory and implants in us a confident longing to see him face-to-face. In the power of the Spirit, we cultivate this knowledge and longing by enacting in our lives the pattern of the Lord's cruciform glory. We grow more glorious here and now by taking up our cross and following Christ so that our light shines before others to the glory of the Father (Matt. 5:16). We read God's glorious self-testimony in order to behold a glory that makes us glorious. This is the way Christians read Scripture because it is the way Christians live.

---

7. Khaled Anatolios provides a rich exploration of this theme in *Deification through the Cross*.

8. Scheeben, *The Mysteries of Christianity*, 129.

# Table of Principles and Rules

**Principle 1**: Holy Scripture presupposes and fosters readers whose end is the vision of Christ's glory, and therein eternal life. Biblical reasoning must be ordered to this same end.

**Principle 2**: Everything Scripture says about God is part of God's meticulous and wise pedagogy, by which God adapts the form of his wisdom to educate finite and fallen creatures so that we might see his glory. Biblical reasoning fits within this larger context of divine teaching.

**Principle 3:** Scripture is the inspired, textual form of Christ's teaching in which he is present to his people across time and space, leading us toward wisdom.

**Rule 1: The Analogy of Faith**
To rightly respond to God's pedagogical pressures in his Word, read Scripture as a unity, interpreting its parts in light of the whole and understanding the whole as a harmonious testimony to God and his works.

**Rule 2: Pedagogical Pressure**
To understand the theological grammar and syntax of Scripture, read Scripture in such a way that you learn how its various discourses both form and presuppose a larger theological vision.

**Principle 4:** God, who is the creator of all things *ex nihilo*, is holy, infinite, and unchangeable. Since God is qualitatively distinct from all things, he therefore differs from creatures differently than creatures differ from one another.

**Rule 3: God-Fittingness**
Biblical discourse about God should be understood in a way appropriate to its object, so read Scripture's depictions of God in a manner that fits the canonical portrait of God's holy name and his creation of all things out of nothing.

**Principle 5**: The one true and living God is eternally Father, Son, and Holy Spirit, distinct in their relations to one another and the same in substance, power, and glory.

**Rule 4: Common and Proper**

Scripture speaks both of what is common to the Father, Son, and Holy Spirit and of what is proper to each person, reflecting the conceptual distinction between the divine nature and the divine persons. Biblical reasoning discerns this distinction, upholds it, and contemplates the Holy Trinity in its light. Therefore, read Scripture's discourse about God in such a way that its twofold discourse—the common and the proper—is recognized and employed, rather than in a way that collapses the two ways into one. In this way, we learn to count persons rather than natures.

**Rule 5: Inseparable Operations**

The external works of the Trinity are indivisibly one, just as God is one. Whenever Scripture mentions only one or two divine persons, understand that all three are equally present and active, undertaking the same actions in ways that imply their relations to one another. In this way, learn to count persons rather than actions.

**Rule 6: Appropriation**

Scripture sometimes attributes to only one divine person a perfection, action, or name common to all three, because of some contextual fit or analogy between the common attribute and the divine person in question. Read such passages in a way that does not compromise the Trinity's essential oneness and equality.

**Principle 6:** One and the same Lord Jesus Christ, the only begotten Son of the Father, exists as one person in two natures, without confusion or change, without division or separation.

**Rule 7: The Unity of Christ**

The eternal, divine Son is the sole subject of everything Jesus does and suffers. Christ is one person, one agent, one "who." Therefore, in reading Scripture's witness to Christ we must never divide Christ's acts between two acting subjects, attributing some to the divine Son and others to the human Jesus as if there were two different people.

**Rule 8: The Communication of Idioms**

Since Christ is a single divine person who subsists in both a divine and a human nature, Scripture sometimes names him according to one nature and predicates of him what belongs to the other nature. Scripture ascribes divine prerogatives to the man Jesus, and human acts and sufferings to the divine Son. So read Scripture in a way that recognizes and reproduces this paradoxical grammar of christological predication.

### Rule 9: Partitive Exegesis

Scripture speaks of Christ in a twofold manner: some things are said of him as divine, and other things are said of him as human. Biblical reasoning discerns that Scripture speaks of the one Christ in two registers in order to contemplate the whole Christ. Therefore read Scripture in such a way that you discern the different registers in which Scripture speaks of Christ, yet without dividing him.

**Principle 7:** Within their unity and equality, the three persons exist in relations of origin: the Son is eternally generated from the Father, and the Spirit eternally proceeds from the Father and the Son.

### Rule 10: From Another

Scripture often attributes to the divine persons ordered relations and actions that do not compromise their unity and equality, but only signify that one person eternally exists from another: the Son from the Father, the Spirit from the Father and the Son. Read Scripture in a way that recognizes and upholds these ordered relations of origin.

# Bibliography

Alexander of Hales. *Summa theologica seu sic ab origine dicta "Summa fratris Alexandri."* Edited by Bernardini Klumper, Victorin Doucet, and the Quarracchi Fathers. 4 vols. Rome: Collegium S. Bonaventurae, 1924–48.

Allen, Leslie C. "The Old Testament Background of (Προ)Ὁρίζειν in the New Testament." *NTS* 17 (1970): 104–8.

Allen, Michael. *Grounded in Heaven: Recentering Christian Hope and Life on God.* Grand Rapids: Eerdmans, 2018.

———. "Systematic Theology and Biblical Theology—Part Two." *JRT* 14 (2020): 344–57.

Allison, Dale C., Jr. "The Eye Is the Lamp of the Body (Matthew 6.22–23=Luke 11.34–36)." *NTS* 33, no. 1 (1987): 61–83.

———. *The New Moses: A Matthean Typology.* Minneapolis: Fortress, 1993.

———. "Seeing God (Matt. 5:8)." In *Studies in Matthew: Interpretation Past and Present,* 43–63. Grand Rapids: Baker Academic, 2005.

Allo, E.-B. *Saint Paul: Première Épitre aux Corinthiens.* 2nd ed. Études Bibliques. Paris: J. Gabalda, 1956.

Anatolios, Khaled. *Athanasius.* The Early Church Fathers. London: Routledge, 2004.

———. *Deification through the Cross: An Eastern Christian Theology of Salvation.* Grand Rapids: Eerdmans, 2020.

———. *Retrieving Nicaea: The Development and Meaning of Trinitarian Doctrine.* Grand Rapids: Baker Academic, 2011.

Anderson, Paul N. "Jesus, the Eschatological Prophet in the Fourth Gospel: A Case Study in Dialectical Tensions." In *Reading the Gospel of John's Christology as Jewish Messianism: Royal, Prophetic, and Divine Messiahs,* edited by Benjamin E. Reynolds and Gabriele Boccaccini, 271–99. AJEC 106. Leiden: Brill, 2018.

Aquinas, Thomas. *See* Thomas Aquinas

Aristotle. *Categories and De Interpretatione*. Translated by J. L. Ackrill. Clarendon Aristotle Series. Oxford: Clarendon, 1963.

———. *Metaphysics, Books I–IX*. Translated by Hugh Tredennick. LCL 271. Cambridge, MA: Harvard University Press, 1933.

Ashton, John. *Understanding the Fourth Gospel*. 2nd ed. Oxford: Oxford University Press, 2007.

Athanasius. *On the Incarnation*. Translated by John Behr. PPS 44a. Yonkers, NY: St. Vladimir's Seminary Press, 2011.

Athanasius the Great and Didymus the Blind. *Works on the Spirit*. Translated by Mark DelCogliano, Andrew Radde-Gallwitz, and Lewis Ayres. PPS 43. Yonkers, NY: St. Vladimir's Seminary Press, 2011.

Attridge, Harold W. "Ambiguous Signs, an Anonymous Character, Unanswerable Riddles: The Role of the Unknown in Johannine Epistemology." *NTS* 65 (2019): 267–88.

Augustine. *Arianism and Other Heresies*. Edited by John E. Rotelle. Translated by Roland J. Teske. WSA I/18. Hyde Park, NY: New City, 1995.

———. *The City of God (De Civitate Dei), I–X*. Translated by William Babcock. WSA I/6. Hyde Park, NY: New City, 2012.

———. *Homilies on the First Epistle of John*. Translated by Boniface Ramsey. Edited by Daniel E. Doyle and Thomas Martin. WSA III/14. Hyde Park, NY: New City, 2008.

———. *Homilies on the Gospel of John 1–40*. Edited by Allan D. Fitzgerald. Translated by Edmund Hill. WSA III/12. Hyde Park, NY: New City, 2009.

———. *Letters 100–155*. Translated by Roland Teske. Edited by Boniface Ramsey. WSA II/2. Hyde Park, NY: New City, 2002.

———. *On Christian Teaching*. Translated by R. P. H. Green. Oxford: Oxford University Press, 2008.

———. *Sermons 20–50*. Translated by Edmund Hill. WSA III/2. Hyde Park, NY: New City, 1991.

———. *Sermons 51–94*. Translated by Edmund Hill. WSA III/3. Hyde Park, NY: New City, 1992.

———. *Sermons 94A–147A*. Translated by Edmund Hill. WSA III/4. Hyde Park, NY: New City, 1992.

———. *Tractates on the Gospel of John, 55–111*. Translated by John W. Rettig. FC 90. Washington, DC: Catholic University of America Press, 1994.

———. *The Trinity*. Edited by John E. Rotelle. Translated by Edmund Hill. WSA I/5. 2nd ed. Hyde Park, NY: New City, 2010.

Aune, David. *Revelation 1–5*. WBC 52A. Nashville: Nelson, 1997.

Ayres, Lewis. *Augustine and the Trinity*. Cambridge: Cambridge University Press, 2010.

———. *Nicaea and Its Legacy: An Approach to Fourth-Century Trinitarian Theology.* Oxford: Oxford University Press, 2004.

Barclay, John M. G. *Paul and the Power of Grace.* Grand Rapids: Eerdmans, 2020.

Barnes, Michel René. *The Power of God: Δύναμις in Gregory of Nyssa's Trinitarian Theology.* Washington, DC: Catholic University of America Press, 2001.

Baron, Lori. "The *Shema* in John's Gospel against Its Background in Second Temple Judaism." PhD diss., Duke University, 2015.

Barrett, C. K. "Christocentric or Theocentric? Observations on the Theological Method of the Fourth Gospel." In *Essays on John*, 1–18. Philadelphia: Westminster, 1982.

———. *A Critical and Exegetical Commentary on the Acts of the Apostles.* Vol. 2, *Acts XV–XXVIII.* ICC. Edinburgh: T&T Clark, 1998.

———. "'The Father Is Greater Than I' John 14:28: Subordinationist Christology in the New Testament." In *Essays on John*, 19–36. Philadelphia: Westminster, 1982.

Basil of Caesarea. *Against Eunomius.* Translated by Mark DelCogliano and Andrew Radde-Gallwitz. FC 122. Washington, DC: Catholic University of America Press, 2011.

———. *On the Holy Spirit.* Translated by Stephen Hildebrand. PPS 42. Yonkers, NY: St. Vladimir's Seminary Press, 2011.

Bates, Matthew W. *The Birth of the Trinity: Jesus, God, and Spirit in New Testament and Early Christian Interpretations of the Old Testament.* Oxford: Oxford University Press, 2015.

———. "A Christology of Incarnation and Enthronement: Romans 1:3–4 as Unified, Nonadoptionist, and Nonconciliatory." *CBQ* 77 (2015): 107–27.

Bauckham, Richard. *Jesus and the God of Israel: "God Crucified" and Other Studies on the New Testament's Christology of Divine Identity.* Grand Rapids: Eerdmans, 2008.

———. "Monotheism and Christology in the Gospel of John." In *Contours of Christology in the New Testament*, edited by Richard N. Longenecker, 148–66. McMaster New Testament Studies. Grand Rapids: Eerdmans, 2005.

———. *The Theology of the Book of Revelation.* Cambridge: Cambridge University Press, 1993.

Bauerschmidt, Frederick Christian. *Thomas Aquinas: Faith, Reason, and Following Christ.* CTC. Oxford: Oxford University Press, 2013.

Bavinck, Herman. *Reformed Dogmatics.* Vol. 2, *God and Creation.* Edited by John Bolt. Translated by John Vriend. Grand Rapids: Baker Academic, 2004.

Bayer, Oswald. *Theology the Lutheran Way.* Translated by Jeffrey G. Silcock and Mark C. Mattes. Grand Rapids: Eerdmans, 2007.

Beale, G. K. *The Book of Revelation.* NIGTC. Grand Rapids: Eerdmans, 1999.

————. *We Become What We Worship: A Biblical Theology of Idolatry*. Downers Grove, IL: IVP Academic, 2008.

Beckwith, Carl L. *The Holy Trinity*. Confessional Lutheran Dogmatics 3. Fort Wayne, IN: The Luther Academy, 2016.

Beeley, Christopher A. *Gregory of Nazianzus on the Trinity and the Knowledge of God: In Your Light We Shall See Light*. OSHT. Oxford: Oxford University Press, 2008.

Behr, John. *The Nicene Faith*. Part 1, *True God of True God*. Formation of Christian Theology 2. Crestwood, NY: St. Vladimir's Seminary Press, 2004.

Bekken, Per Jarle. *The Lawsuit Motif in John's Gospel from New Perspectives: Jesus Christ, Crucified Criminal and Emperor of the World*. NovTSup 158. Leiden: Brill, 2014.

Bengel, Johan Albrecht. *Erklärte Offenbarung Johannes oder vielmehr Jesu Christi*. Stuttgart: Fr. Brodhag, 1834.

————. *Gnomon of the New Testament*. Edited and translated by Andrew R. Fausset. 5 vols. Edinburgh: T&T Clark, 1877.

Benin, Stephen D. *The Footprints of God: Divine Accommodation in Jewish and Christian Thought*. Albany: SUNY Press, 1993.

Bernard of Clairvaux. *On Consideration*. In *Bernard of Clairvaux: Selected Works*. Translated by G. R. Evans, 145–72. CWS. New York: Paulist Press, 1987.

Bieringer, Reimund. "'. . . because the Father Is Greater Than I' (John 14:28): Johannine Christology in Light of the Relationship between the Father and the Son." In *Gospel Images of Jesus Christ in Church Tradition and in Biblical Scholarship*, edited by Christos Karakolis, Karl-Wilhelm Niebuhr, and Sviatoslav Rogalsky, 181–204. WUNT 288. Tübingen: Mohr Siebeck, 2012.

Blacketer, Raymond A. *The School of God: Pedagogy and Rhetoric in Calvin's Interpretation of Deuteronomy*. Dordrecht: Springer, 2006.

Blank, Joseph. *Krisis: Untersuchungen zur johanneischen Christologie und Eschatologie*. Freiburg im Breisgau: Lambertus, 1964.

Blumhofer, Christopher M. *The Gospel of John and the Future of Israel*. SNTSMS 177. Cambridge: Cambridge University Press, 2020.

Bock, Darrell L. *Acts*. BECNT. Grand Rapids: Baker Academic, 2007.

————. "Blasphemy." In *Dictionary of Jesus and the Gospels*, edited by Joel B. Green, Jeannine K. Brown, and Nicholas Perrin, 84–87. 2nd ed. Downers Grove, IL: InterVarsity, 2013.

————. "Blasphemy and the Jewish Examination of Jesus." *BBR* 17 (2007): 53–114.

Bockmuehl, Markus. *A Commentary on the Epistle to the Philippians*. BNTC. London: A & C Black, 1997.

Bonaventure. *Collations on the Six Days*. Translated by José de Vinck. The Works of Saint Bonaventure 5. Paterson, NJ: St. Anthony Guild Press, 1970.

Borgen, Peder. "God's Agent in the Fourth Gospel." In *The Gospel of John: More Light from Philo, Paul and Archaeology; The Scriptures, Tradition, Exposition, Settings, Meaning*, 167–78. NovTSup 154. Leiden: Brill, 2014.

———. "Observations on God's Agent and Agency in John's Gospel Chapters 5–10: Agency and the Quest for the Historical Jesus." In *The Gospel of John: More Light from Philo, Paul and Archaeology; The Scriptures, Tradition, Exposition, Settings, Meaning*, 193–218. NovTSup 154. Leiden: Brill, 2014.

Boyarin, Daniel. "Daniel 7, Intertextuality, and the History of Israel's Cult." *HTR* 105 (2012): 139–62.

Brakel, Wilhelmus à. *The Christian's Reasonable Service*. Translated by Bartel Elshout. Edited by Joel R. Beeke. 4 vols. Grand Rapids: Reformation Heritage, 1992–95.

Brendsel, Daniel J. *"Isaiah Saw His Glory": The Use of Isaiah 52–53 in John 12*. BZNW 208. Berlin: de Gruyter, 2014.

Briggman, Anthony. *God and Christ in Irenaeus*. Oxford: Oxford University Press, 2019.

Brown, Alexandra R. *The Cross and Human Transformation: Paul's Apocalyptic Word in 1 Corinthians*. Minneapolis: Fortress, 1995.

Bruce, F. F. *The Epistle to the Hebrews*. Rev. ed. NICNT. Grand Rapids: Eerdmans, 1990.

Bryan, Steven M. "Power in the Pool: The Healing of the Man at Bethesda and Jesus' Violation of the Sabbath (Jn. 5:1–18)." *TynBul* 54 (2003): 7–22.

Byers, Andrew J. *Ecclesiology and Theosis in the Gospel of John*. SNTSMS 166. Cambridge: Cambridge University Press, 2017.

———. "The One Body of the Shema in 1 Corinthians: An Ecclesiology of Christological Monotheism." *NTS* 62 (2016): 517–32.

Caird, G. B. *The Revelation of Saint John*. London: A&C Black, 1966. Reprint, Peabody, MA: Hendrickson, 1999.

Calov, Abraham. *Systema Locorum Theologicorum*. Vol. 2, *De Cognitione, Nominibus, Natura & Attributis Dei*. Wittenberg: Andreae Hartmanni, 1655.

Calvin, John. *The Commentaries of John Calvin*. Various translators. 46 vols. Edinburgh: The Calvin Translation Society, 1843–55. Reprint, Bellingham, WA: Logos Bible Software, 2010.

———. *Institutes of the Christian Religion*. Translated by Ford Lewis Battles. Edited by John T. McNeill. Philadelphia: Westminster, 1960.

———. *Ioannis Calvini opera quae supersunt omnia*. Edited by G. Baum, E. Cunitz, E. Reuss et al. 59 vols. Volumes 29–87 of *Corpus Reformatorum*. Brunswick: Schwetschke, 1863–1900.

Campbell, Douglas A. "The Story of Jesus in Romans and Galatians." In *Narrative Dynamics in Paul: A Critical Assessment*, edited by Bruce W. Longenecker, 97–124. Louisville: Westminster John Knox, 2002.

Campbell, W. Gordon. "Apocalypse johannique et adoratuer implicite." *RTL* 47, no. 3 (2016): 338–52.

Capes, David B. *The Divine Christ: Paul, the Lord Jesus, and the Scriptures of Israel.* Acadia Studies in Bible and Theology. Grand Rapids: Baker Academic, 2018.

Carraway, George. *Christ Is God over All: Romans 9:5 in the Context of Romans 9–11.* LNTS 489. London: Bloomsbury T&T Clark, 2013.

Carson, D. A. *The Gospel according to John.* PNTC. Grand Rapids: Eerdmans, 1991.

————. "John 5:26: *Crux Interpretum* for Eternal Generation." In *Retrieving Eternal Generation*, edited by Fred Sanders and Scott R. Swain, 79–97. Grand Rapids: Zondervan, 2017.

Cassuto, Umberto. *A Commentary on the Book of Genesis.* Part 1, *From Adam to Noah (Genesis I–VI 8).* Translated by Israel Abrahams. Jerusalem: The Magnes Press, 1961.

Charles, Robert Henry. *A Critical and Exegetical Commentary on the Revelation of St. John.* 2 vols. ICC. New York: Scribner's Sons, 1920.

Charnock, Stephen. *The Existence and Attributes of God.* The Complete Works of Stephen Charnock 1. Edinburgh: James Nichol, 1864.

Chibici-Revneanu, Nicole. *Die Herrlichkeit des Verherrlichten: Das Verständis der* δόξα *im Johannesevangelium.* WUNT 2/231. Tübingen: Mohr Siebeck, 2007.

Ciampa, Roy E., and Brian S. Rosner. *The First Letter to the Corinthians.* PNTC. Grand Rapids: Eerdmans, 2010.

Clarke, W. Norris, Jr. *The One and the Many: A Contemporary Thomistic Metaphysics.* Notre Dame, IN: University of Notre Dame Press, 2001.

Clement of Alexandria. *Christ the Educator.* Translated by Simon P. Wood. FC 23. Washington, DC: Catholic University of America Press, 1954.

————. *Miscellanies Book VII: The Greek Text with Introduction, Translation, Notes, Dissertations and Indices.* Edited and translated by Fenton John Anthony Hort and Joseph B. Mayor. New York: Macmillan, 1902.

Cox, Ronald. *By the Same Word: Creation and Salvation in Hellenistic Judaism and Early Christianity.* BZNW 145. Berlin: de Gruyter, 2007.

Cranfield, C. E. B. *Romans 9–16.* ICC. London: T&T Clark, 2004.

Croy, N. Clayton. *Endurance in Suffering: Hebrews 12:1–13 in Its Rhetorical, Religious, and Philosophical Context.* Cambridge: Cambridge University Press, 2005.

Currid, John D. *Against the Gods: The Polemical Theology of the Old Testament.* Wheaton: Crossway, 2013.

Cyril of Alexandria. *Commentary on John.* Vol. 1. Edited by Joel C. Elowsky. Translated by David R. Maxwell. ACT. Downers Grove, IL: IVP Academic, 2013.

————. *Commentary on John.* Vol. 2. Edited by Joel C. Elowsky. Translated by David R. Maxwell. ACT. Downers Grove, IL: IVP Academic, 2015.

————. *Commentary on the Twelve Prophets.* Vol. 2. Translated by Robert C. Hill. FC 116. Washington, DC: Catholic University of America Press, 2008.

————. *A Commentary upon the Gospel according to S. Luke by S. Cyril, Patriarch of Alexandria.* Translated by Robert Payne Smith. Piscataway, NJ: Gorgias, 2009.

————. *Dialogues sur la Trinité* [Dialogues on the Trinity]. 3 vols. SC 231, 237, 246. Edited and translated by Georges Matthieu de Durand. Paris: Cerf, 1976, 1977, 1978.

————. *On the Unity of Christ*. Translated by John Anthony McGuckin. PPS 13. Crestwood, NY: St. Vladimir's Seminary Press, 1995.

————. *Sancti patris nostri Cyrilli archiepiscopi Alexandrini in xii prophetas*. 2 vols. Edited by P. E. Pusey. Oxford: Oxford University Press, 1868.

————. *Three Christological Treatises*. Translated by Daniel King. FC 129. Washington, DC: Catholic University of America Press, 2014.

Dahms, John V. "The Johannine Use of Monogenēs Reconsidered." *NTS* 29 (1983): 222–32.

Daley, Brian E. *God Visible: Patristic Christology Reconsidered*. Changing Paradigms in Historical and Systematic Theology. Oxford: Oxford University Press, 2018.

————. *Gregory of Nazianzus*. The Early Church Fathers. London: Routledge, 2006.

Davidson, Ivor. "Salvation's Destiny: Heirs of God." In *God of Salvation: Soteriology in Theological Perspective*, edited by Ivor Davidson and Murray Rae, 155–75. London: Routledge, 2010.

Davis, Phillip A., Jr. *The Place of Paideia in Hebrews' Moral Thought*. WUNT 2/475. Tübingen: Mohr Siebeck, 2018.

Davison, Andrew. *Participation in God: A Study in Christian Doctrine and Metaphysics*. Cambridge: Cambridge University Press, 2019.

de Jonge, Marinus. *Jesus, Stranger from Heaven and Son of God: Jesus Christ and the Christians in Johannine Perspective*. SBLSBS 11. Missoula, MT: Scholars Press, 1977.

de la Potterie, Ignace. "The Truth in Saint John." In *The Interpretation of John*, edited by John Ashton, 67–82. 2nd ed. Edinburgh: T&T Clark, 1997.

DeLapp, Nevada Levi. *Theophanic "Type-Scenes" in the Pentateuch: Visions of YHWH*. LHBOTS 660. London: Bloomsbury T&T Clark, 2018.

DelCogliano, Mark. *Basil of Caesarea's Anti-Eunomian Theory of Names: Christian Theology and Late-Antique Philosophy in the Fourth Century Trinitarian Controversy*. VCSup 103. Leiden: Brill, 2010.

de Lubac, Henri. *Paradoxes of Faith*. San Francisco: Ignatius, 1987.

Dewailly, Louis-Marie. "'D'où es-tu?' (Jean 19,9)." *RB* 92 (1985): 481–96.

DiNoia, J. Augustine. "Knowing and Naming the Triune God: The Grammar of Christian Confession." In *Speaking the Christian God: The Holy Trinity and the Challenge of Feminism*, edited by Alvin Kimel Jr., 162–87. Grand Rapids: Eerdmans, 1992.

Dodd, C. H. *The Interpretation of the Fourth Gospel*. Cambridge: Cambridge University Press, 1953.

Dodds, Michael J. *The Unchanging God of Love: Thomas Aquinas and Contemporary Theology on Divine Immutability*. 2nd ed. Washington, DC: Catholic University of America Press, 2008.

Döhling, Jan-Dirk. *Der bewegliche Gott: Eine Untersuchung des Motivs der Reue Gottes in der Hebräischen Bibel.* Herders biblische Studien 61. Freiburg: Herder, 2009.

Duby, Steven J. "'For I Am God, Not a Man': Divine Repentance and the Creator-Creature Distinction." *JTI* 12, no. 2 (2018):149–69.

———. *Jesus and the God of Classical Theism: Biblical Christology in Light of the Doctrine of God.* Grand Rapids: Baker Academic, 2022.

Dunn, James D. G. *The Theology of Paul the Apostle.* Grand Rapids: Eerdmans, 1998.

East, Brad. "What Are the Standards of Excellence for Theological Interpretation of Scripture?" *JTI* 14, no. 2 (2020): 149–79.

Emery, Gilles. "Biblical Exegesis and the Speculative Doctrine of the Trinity in St. Thomas Aquinas's *Commentary on St. John.*" In *Reading John with St. Thomas Aquinas: Theological Exegesis and Speculative Theology,* edited by Michael Dauphinais and Matthew Levering, 23–61. Washington, DC: Catholic University of America Press, 2005.

———. "Essentialism or Personalism in the Treatise on God in Saint Thomas Aquinas?" *The Thomist* 64 (2000): 521–63.

———. "The Personal Mode of Trinitarian Action in Saint Thomas Aquinas." *The Thomist* 69 (2005): 31–77.

———. "*Theologia* and *Dispensatio*: The Centrality of the Divine Missions in St. Thomas's Trinitarian Theology." *The Thomist* 74 (2010): 515–61.

———. *The Trinitarian Theology of St Thomas Aquinas.* Translated by Francesca Aran Murphy. Oxford: Oxford University Press, 2007.

———. *The Trinity: An Introduction to Catholic Teaching on the Triune God.* Translated by Matthew Levering. Thomistic Ressourcement Series 1. Washington, DC: Catholic University of America Press, 2011.

Engberg-Pedersen, Troels. *John and Philosophy: A New Reading of the Fourth Gospel.* Oxford: Oxford University Press, 2017.

Ernest, James D. *The Bible in Athanasius of Alexandria.* BAC 2. Boston: Brill, 2004.

Estes, Douglas. "Dualism or Paradox? A New 'Light' on the Gospel of John." *JTS* 71 (2020): 90–118.

Fairbairn, Donald. *Life in the Trinity: An Introduction to Theology with the Help of the Church Fathers.* Downers Grove, IL: InterVarsity, 2009.

Fee, Gordon D. "Paul and the Trinity: The Experience of Christ and the Spirit for Paul's Understanding of God." In *The Incarnation: An Interdisciplinary Symposium on the Incarnation of the Son of God,* edited by Stephen T. Davis, Daniel Kendall, and Gerald O'Collins, 49–72. Oxford: Oxford University Press, 2002.

Feldmeier, Reinhard. *Power, Service, Humility: A New Testament Ethic.* Translated by Brian McNeil. Waco: Baylor University Press, 2014.

Feldmeier, Reinhard, and Hermann Spieckermann. *God of the Living: A Biblical Theology.* Translated by Mark E. Biddle. Waco: Baylor University Press, 2013.

Ferguson, Everett. *The Rule of Faith: A Guide.* Eugene, OR: Cascade Books, 2015.

Filtvedt, Ole Jakob. "The Transcendence and Visibility of the Father in the Gospel of John." *ZNW* 108, no. 1 (2017): 90–118.

Fitzmyer, Joseph A. *First Corinthians: A New Translation with Introduction and Commentary.* AB 32. New Haven: Yale University Press, 2008.

Fletcher-Louis, Crispin. "John 5:19–30: The Son of God Is the Apocalyptic Son of Man." In *Reading the Gospel of John's Christology as Jewish Messianism: Royal, Prophetic, and Divine Messiahs,* edited by Benjamin E. Reynolds and Gabriele Boccaccini, 411–34. AJEC 106. Leiden: Brill, 2018.

Forger, Deborah. "Jesus as God's Word(s): Aurality, Epistemology and Embodiment in the Gospel of John." *JSNT* 42 (2020): 274–302.

Foster, Paul. *Colossians.* BNTC. London: Bloomsbury T&T Clark, 2016.

Franzelin, Johann Baptist. *Tractatus de Deo Trino secundam personas.* Revised ed. Rome: Sacra Congregatio de Propaganda Fidei, 1874.

Frey, Jörg. "Between Jewish Monotheism and Proto-Trinitarian Relations: The Making and Character of Johannine Christology." In *Monotheism and Christology in Greco-Roman Antiquity,* edited by Matthew V. Novenson, 189–221. NovTSup 180. Leiden: Brill, 2020.

———. *Die johanneische Eschatologie.* Vol. 3, *Die eschatologische Verkündigung in den johanneischen Texten.* WUNT 117. Tübingen: Mohr Siebeck, 2000.

———. *The Glory of the Crucified One: Christology and Theology in the Gospel of John.* Translated by Wayne Coppins and Christoph Heilig. BMSEC. Waco: Baylor University Press, 2018.

Froehlich, Karlfried. *Sensing the Scriptures: Amminadab's Chariot and the Predicament of Biblical Interpretation.* Grand Rapids: Eerdmans, 2014.

Gathercole, Simon J. "Locating Christ and Israel in Romans 9–11." In *God and Israel: Providence and Purpose in Romans 9–11,* edited by Todd D. Still, 115–39. Waco: Baylor University Press, 2017.

———. "Paul's Christology." In *The Blackwell Companion to Paul,* edited by Stephen Westerholm, 172–87. Oxford: Blackwell, 2011.

———. *The Preexistent Son: Recovering the Christologies of Matthew, Mark, and Luke.* Grand Rapids: Eerdmans, 2006.

———. "The Trinity in the Synoptic Gospels and Acts." In *The Oxford Handbook of the Trinity,* edited by Gilles Emery and Matthew Levering, 55–67. Oxford: Oxford University Press, 2011.

Gavrilyuk, Paul L. *The Suffering of the Impassible God: The Dialectics of Patristic Thought.* Oxford: Oxford University Press, 2004.

Gerhard, Johann. *Theological Commonplaces: On the Nature of God and on the Trinity.* Translated by Richard J. Dinda. Edited by Benjamin T. G. Mayes. St. Louis: Concordia, 2007.

Gieschen, Charles A. "The Divine Name in Ante-Nicene Christology." *VC* 57 (2003): 115–58.

———. "The Divine Name That the Son Shares with the Father in the Gospel of John." In *Reading the Gospel of John's Christology as Jewish Messianism: Royal, Prophetic, and Divine Messiahs*, edited by Benjamin E. Reynolds and Gabriele Boccaccini, 387–410. AJEC 106. Leiden: Brill, 2018.

Gill, John. *A Complete Body of Doctrinal and Practical Divinity; or, A System of Evangelical Truths, Deduced from the Sacred Scriptures*. 1839. Reprint, Paris, AR: The Baptist Standard Bearer, 1989.

Gioia, Luigi. *The Theological Epistemology of Augustine's* De Trinitate. OTM. Oxford: Oxford University Press, 2008.

Glad, Clarence E. *Paul and Philodemus: Adaptability in Epicurean and Early Christian Psychagogy*. NovTSup 81. Leiden: Brill, 1995.

Gladd, Benjamin. *Revealing the* Mysterion: *The Use of Mystery in Daniel and Second Temple Judaism with Its Bearing on First Corinthians*. BZNW 160. Berlin: de Gruyter, 2008.

Grant, Robert M. "Causation and 'The Ancient World View.'" *JBL* 83 (1964): 34–40.

Gregory of Nazianzus. *Festal Orations*. Translated by Nonna Verna Harrison. PPS 36. Yonkers, NY: St. Vladimir's Seminary Press, 2008.

———. *On God and Christ: The Five Theological Orations and Two Letters to Cledonius*. Translated by Frederick Williams and Lionel R. Wickham. PPS 23. Crestwood, NY: St. Vladimir's Seminary Press, 2002.

———. *Select Orations*. Translated by Martha Vinson. FC 107. Washington, DC: Catholic University of America Press, 2017.

Gregory of Nyssa. *Catechetical Discourse*. Translated by Ignatius Green. PPS 60. Yonkers, NY: St. Vladimir's Seminary Press, 2019.

———. *The Life of Moses*. Translated by Abraham Malherbe and Everett Ferguson. CWS. New York: Paulist Press, 1978.

Griffiths, Paul. *Decreation: The Last Things of All Creatures*. Waco: Baylor University Press, 2014.

Gundry, Robert H. "The Form, Meaning and Background of the Hymn Quoted in 1 Timothy 3:16." In *Apostolic History and the Gospel: Biblical and Historical Essays Presented to F. F. Bruce on His 60th Birthday*, edited by W. Ward Gasque and Ralph P. Martin, 203–22. Exeter: Paternoster, 1970.

Hahn, Ferdinand. "Die Schöpfungsthematik in der Johannesoffenbarung." In *Studien zum Neuen Testament*, vol. 2, *Bekenntnisbildung und Theologie in urchristlicher Zeit*, edited by Jörg Frey and Juliane Schlegel, 603–11. WUNT 192. Tübingen: Mohr Siebeck, 2006.

———. *Theologie des Neuen Testaments*. Vol. 2, *Die Einheit des Neuen Testaments*. Tübingen: Mohr Siebeck, 2002.

Halleux, André de. "Personnalisme ou essentialisme trinitaire chez les Pères cappadociens? Une mauvaise controverse." *RTL* 17 (1986): 129–55, 265–92.

Harris, Murray J. *Jesus as God: The New Testament Use of Theos in Reference to Jesus.* Grand Rapids: Baker, 1992.

Harris, Steven Edward. *God and the Teaching of Theology: Divine Pedagogy in 1 Corinthians 1–4.* Notre Dame, IN: University of Notre Dame Press, 2019.

Hart, David Bentley. "No Shadow of Turning: On Divine Impassibility." *Pro Ecclesia* 11, no. 2 (Spring 2002): 184–206.

Harvey, A. E. *Jesus on Trial.* London: SPCK, 1976.

Hay, David M. *Glory at the Right Hand: Psalm 110 in Early Christianity.* SBLMS 18. Nashville: Abingdon, 1973.

Hays, Richard B. *Echoes of Scripture in the Gospels.* Waco: Baylor University Press, 2016.

———. "Faithful Witness, Alpha and Omega: The Identity of Jesus in the Apocalypse of John." In *Revelation and the Politics of Apocalyptic Interpretation,* edited by Richard B. Hays and Stefan Alkier, 69–83. Waco: Baylor University Press, 2015.

———. *The Faith of Jesus Christ: The Narrative Substructure of Galatians 3:1–4:11.* 2nd ed. Grand Rapids: Eerdmans, 2002.

Heidegger, Johann Heinrich. *The Concise Marrow of Theology.* Translated by Casey Carmichael. Grand Rapids: Reformation Heritage, 2018.

———. *Corpus Theologiae Christianae.* Zürich: Johann Henrici Bodmeri, 1700.

Hellerman, Joseph H. *Reconstructing Honor in Roman Philippi: Carmen Christi as Cursus Pudorum.* SNTSMS 132. Cambridge: Cambridge University Press, 2005.

Hengel, Martin. "The Prologue of the Gospel of John as the Gateway to Christological Truth." In *The Gospel of John and Christian Theology,* edited by Richard Bauckham and Carl Mosser, 265–94. Grand Rapids: Eerdmans, 2008.

———. "'Sit at My Right Hand!' The Enthronement of Christ at the Right Hand of God and Psalm 110:1." In *Studies in Early Christology,* 119–225. Edinburgh: T&T Clark, 1995.

Hilary of Poitiers. *The Trinity.* Translated by Stephen McKenna. FC 25. Washington, DC: Catholic University of America Press, 1954.

Hill, Wesley. "In Defense of 'Doctrinal Exegesis': A Proposal, with Reference to Trinitarian Theology and the Fourth Gospel." *JTI* 14 (2020): 20–35.

———. *Paul and the Trinity: Persons, Relations, and the Pauline Letters.* Grand Rapids: Eerdmans, 2015.

Hofius, Otfried. "Jesu Zuspruch der Sündenvergebung: Exegetische Erwägungen zu Mk 2,5b." In *Neutestamentliche Studien,* 38–56. WUNT 1/132. Tübingen: Mohr Siebeck, 2000.

Holloway, Paul. *Philippians: A Commentary.* Hermeneia. Minneapolis: Fortress, 2017.

Holmes, Michael W., trans. *The Apostolic Fathers: Greek Texts and English Translations.* 3rd ed. Grand Rapids: Baker Academic, 2007.

Holmes, Stephen R. "Scripture in Liturgy and Theology." In *Theologians on Scripture*, edited by Angus Paddison, 105–18. London: Bloomsbury T&T Clark, 2016.

Hurtado, Larry W. *Lord Jesus Christ: Devotion to Jesus in Earliest Christianity*. Grand Rapids: Eerdmans, 2003.

Imschoot, Paul van. *Theology of the Old Testament*. Vol. 1, *God*. Translated by Kathryn Sullivan and Fidelis Buck. New York: Desclee, 1965.

Irons, Charles Lee. "A Lexical Defense of the Johannine 'Only Begotten.'" In *Retrieving Eternal Generation*, edited by Fred Sanders and Scott R. Swain, 98–116. Grand Rapids: Zondervan, 2017.

Jaeger, Werner. *The Theology of the Greek Philosophers: The Gifford Lectures, 1936*. Oxford: Oxford University Press, 1967.

Jamieson, R. B. "1 Corinthians 15.28 and the Grammar of Paul's Christology." *NTS* 66 (2020): 187–207.

———. *The Paradox of Sonship: Christology in the Epistle to the Hebrews*. SCDS. Downers Grove, IL: IVP Academic, 2021.

Jipp, Joshua W. *Christ Is King: Paul's Royal Ideology*. Minneapolis: Fortress, 2015.

———. "'For David Did Not Ascend into Heaven . . .' (Acts 2:34a): Reprogramming Royal Psalms to Proclaim the Enthroned-in-Heaven King." In *Ascent into Heaven in Luke–Acts: New Explorations of Luke's Narrative Hinge*, edited by David K. Bryan and David W. Pao, 41–59. Minneapolis: Fortress, 2016.

John Chrysostom. *Commentary on Saint John the Apostle and Evangelist: Homilies 1–47*. Translated by Sister Thomas Aquinas Goggin, SCH. FC 33. Washington, DC: Catholic University of America Press, 1957.

———. *Homilies on Genesis 1–17*. Translated by Robert C. Hill. FC 74. Washington, DC: Catholic University of America Press, 1986.

John of Damascus. *On the Orthodox Faith*. In *Saint John of Damascus: Writings*, translated by Frederic H. Chase Jr., 165–406. FC 37. Washington, DC: Catholic University of America Press, 1958.

Jörns, Klaus-Peter. *Das hymnische Evangelium: Untersuchungen zu Aufblau, Funktion und Herkunft der hymnischen Stücke in der Johannesoffenbarung*. Gütersloh: Mohn, 1971.

Kammler, Hans-Christian. *Christologie und Eschatologie: Joh 5,17–30 als Schlüsseltext johanneischer Theologie*. WUNT 126. Tübingen: Mohr Siebeck, 2000.

———. "Die Prädikation Jesu Christi als 'Gott' und die paulinische Christologie: Erwägungen zur Exegese von Röm 9,5b." *ZNW* 95 (2003): 164–80.

———. "Die Theologie des Johannesevangeliums: Eine exegetische Skizze." *KD* 63 (2017): 79–101.

Kant, Immanuel. *Critique of Pure Reason*. The Cambridge Edition of the Works of Immanuel Kant. Translated and edited by Paul Guyer and Allen W. Wood. Cambridge: Cambridge University Press, 1998.

Kaufmann, Yehezkel. *The Religion of Israel: From Its Beginnings to the Babylonian Exile*. Translated by Moshe Greenberg. Chicago: University of Chicago Press, 1960.

Keck, Leander E. "Derivation as Destiny: 'Of-ness' in Johannine Christology, Anthropology, and Soteriology." In *Exploring the Gospel of John: Essays in Honor of D. Moody Smith*, edited by R. Alan Culpepper and C. Clifton Black, 274–88. Louisville: Westminster John Knox, 1996.

Keener, Craig S. *The Gospel of John: A Commentary*. 2 vols. Peabody, MA: Hendrickson, 2003.

Kieffer, René. "L'Espace et Le Temps dans l'Évangile de Jean." *NTS* 31 (1985): 393–409.

Kirk, J. R. Daniel. *A Man Attested by God: The Human Jesus of the Synoptic Gospels*. Grand Rapids: Eerdmans, 2016.

Köckert, Matthias. "Zeit und Ewigkeit in Psalm 90." In *Zeit und Ewigkeit als Raum göttlichen Handelns: Religionsgeschichtliche, theologische und philosophische Perspektiven*, edited by Reinhard G. Kratz and Hermann Spieckermann, 155–86. BZAW 390. Berlin: de Gruyter, 2009.

Koen, Lars. "Partitive Exegesis in Cyril of Alexandria's Commentary on the Gospel according to St. John." *StPatr* 25 (1993): 116–21.

Koester, Craig R. *Revelation: A New Translation with Introduction and Commentary*. AB 38A. New Haven: Yale University Press, 2014.

Kraus, Hans-Joachim. *Theology of the Psalms*. Translated by Keith Crim. Minneapolis: Fortress, 1992.

Kreitzer, L. Joseph. *Jesus and God in Paul's Eschatology*. JSNTSup 19. Sheffield: Sheffield Academic, 1987.

Kugler, Chris. "Judaism/Hellenism in Early Christology: Prepositional Metaphysics and Middle Platonic Intermediary Doctrine." *JSNT* 43 (2020): 214–25.

Lang, T. J. *Mystery and the Making of a Christian Historical Consciousness: From Paul to the Second Century*. BZNW 219. Berlin: de Gruyter, 2015.

Leeman, Jonathan. *Political Church: The Local Assembly as Embassy of Christ's Rule*. SCDS. Downers Grove, IL: IVP Academic, 2016.

Legaspi, Michael C. *The Death of Scripture and the Rise of Biblical Studies*. OSHT. Oxford: Oxford University Press, 2010.

Legge, Dominic. *The Trinitarian Christology of St Thomas Aquinas*. Oxford: Oxford University Press, 2017.

Leim, Joshua E. *Matthew's Theological Grammar: The Father and the Son*. WUNT 2/402. Tübingen: Mohr Siebeck, 2015.

Leithart, Peter J. *Athanasius*. FTECS. Grand Rapids: Baker Academic, 2011.

———. *Revelation 1–11*. ITC. London: Bloomsbury, 2018.

Levering, Matthew. *Engaging the Doctrine of the Holy Spirit: Love and Gift in the Trinity and the Church*. Grand Rapids: Baker Academic, 2016.

————. *Scripture and Metaphysics: Aquinas and the Renewal of Trinitarian Theology.* Oxford: Blackwell, 2004.

Lewis, C. S. *Mere Christianity.* New York: HarperCollins, 2001.

Lewis, Theodore J. *The Origin and Character of God: Ancient Israelite Religion through the Lens of Divinity.* New York: Oxford University Press, 2020.

Lienhard, Joseph T. "The Baptismal Command (Matthew 28:19–20) and the Doctrine of the Trinity." In *The Holy Trinity in the Life of the Church*, edited by Khaled Anatolios, 3–14. Grand Rapids: Baker Academic, 2014.

Lincoln, Andrew T. *Truth on Trial: The Lawsuit Motif in the Fourth Gospel.* Peabody, MA: Hendrickson, 2000.

Lints, Richard. *Identity and Idolatry: The Image of God and Its Inversion.* Downers Grove, IL: InterVarsity, 2015.

Loader, William. *Jesus in John's Gospel: Structure and Issues in Johannine Christology.* 3rd ed. Grand Rapids: Eerdmans, 2017.

Loon, Hans van. *The Dyophysite Christology of Cyril of Alexandria.* VCSup 96. Leiden: Brill, 2009.

Luther, Martin. *Luther's Works.* Vol. 41, *Church and Ministry III.* Edited by Eric W. Gritsch. Philadelphia: Fortress, 1966.

Macaskill, Grant. "Name Christology, Divine Aseity, and the I Am Sayings in the Fourth Gospel." *JTI* 12 (2018): 217–41.

————. "The Way the One God Works: Covenant and Ethics in 1 Corinthians." In *One God, One People, One Future: Essays in Honor of N. T. Wright*, edited by John Anthony Dunne and Eric Lewellen, 112–25. Minneapolis: Fortress, 2018.

Macdonald, Seumas Jeltzz Clayton. "Pro-Nicene Exegesis in Hilary of Poitiers' *De Trinitate* and Basil of Caesarea's *Contra Eunomium*: A Comparative Study." PhD diss., Macquarie University, 2016.

Marckius, Johannes. *In Apocalypsin Johannis Commentarium.* Utrecht: T. Appels, 1699.

Marcus, Joel. "Authority to Forgive Sins upon the Earth: The Shema in the Gospel of Mark." In *The Gospels and the Scriptures of Israel*, edited by Craig A. Evans, 196–211. JSNTSup 104. Sheffield: Sheffield Academic, 1994.

————. *Mark 1–8: A New Translation with Introduction and Commentary.* AB 27. New Haven: Yale University Press, 2002.

————. *Mark 8–16: A New Translation with Introduction and Commentary.* AB 27A. New Haven: Yale University Press, 2009.

Margerie, Bertrand de. *The Greek Fathers.* Vol. 1 of *An Introduction to the History of Exegesis.* Translated by Leonard Maluf. Petersham: Saint Bede's Publications, 1993.

Marshall, Bruce D. "*Ex Occidente Lux*? Aquinas and Eastern Orthodox Theology." *Modern Theology* 20 (2004): 23–50.

————. *Trinity and Truth.* CSCD. Cambridge: Cambridge University Press, 2000.

Martens, Peter. *Origen and Scripture: The Contours of the Exegetical Life*. Oxford: Oxford University Press, 2012.

Martin, Michael Wade, and Bryan A. Nash. "Philippians 2:6–11 as Subversive *Hymnos*: A Study in the Light of Ancient Rhetorical Theory." *JTS* 66 (2015): 90–138.

Maspero, Giulio. "Life from Life: The Procession of the Son and the Divine Attributes in Book VIII of Gregory of Nyssa's *Contra Eunomium*." In *Gregory of Nyssa: Contra Eunomium III; An English Translation with Commentary and Supporting Studies*, edited by Johan Leemans and Matthieu Cassin, 401–28. VCSup 124. Leiden: Brill, 2014.

———. "Trinitarian Theology in Gregory of Nyssa's *Contra Eunomium* I: The Interplay between Ontology and Scripture." In *Gregory of Nyssa:* Contra Eunomium *I; An English Translation with Supporting Studies*, edited by Miguel Brugarolas, 441–93. VCSup 148. Leiden: Brill, 2018.

Mastricht, Petrus van. *Theoretical-Practical Theology*. Vol. 2, *Faith in the Triune God*. Grand Rapids: Reformation Heritage, 2019.

Maximus the Confessor. *On Difficulties in the Church Fathers: The* Ambigua. Edited and translated by Nicholas Constas. 2 vols. Cambridge, MA: Harvard University Press, 2014.

———. *Two Hundred Chapters on Theology*. Translated by Luis Joshua Salés. PPS 53. Yonkers, NY: St. Vladimir's Seminary Press, 2015.

McCosker, Philip. Review of *Communicatio Idiomatum: Lo scambio delle proprietà; Storia, status quaestionis e prospettive*, by Grzegorz Strzelczyk. *Modern Theology* 24 (2007): 298–301.

McDonough, Sean M. *YHWH at Patmos: Rev. 1:4 in Its Hellenistic and Early Jewish Setting*. WUNT 2/107. Tübingen: Mohr Siebeck, 1999.

McElrath, Damian, ed. *Franciscan Christology: Selected Texts, Translations and Introductory Essays*. St. Bonaventure, NY: Franciscan Institute Publications, 1994.

McFarland, Ian A. *The Word Made Flesh: A Theology of the Incarnation*. Louisville: Westminster John Knox, 2019.

McFarland, Orrey. "Divine Causation and Prepositional Metaphysics in Philo of Alexandria and the Apostle Paul." In *Paul and the Greco-Roman Philosophical Tradition*, edited by Joseph R. Dodson and Andrew W. Pitts, 117–34. LNTS 527. London: T&T Clark, 2017.

McGrath, James F. *The Only True God: Early Christian Monotheism in Its Jewish Context*. Urbana: University of Illinois Press, 2009.

McGuckin, John Anthony. *Saint Cyril of Alexandria and the Christological Controversy: Its History, Theology, and Texts*. Crestwood, NY: St. Vladimir's Seminary Press, 2004.

Mealand, D. L. "John 5 and the Limits of Rhetorical Criticism." In *Understanding Poets and Prophets: Essays in Honour of George Wishart Anderson*, edited by A. Graeme Auld, 258–72. JSOTSup 152. Sheffield: Sheffield Academic Press, 1993.

Melito of Sardis. *On Pascha and Fragments*. Translated by Stuart George Hall. OECT. Oxford: Clarendon, 1979.

Meyer, Nicholas A. *Adam's Dust and Adam's Glory in the Hodayot and the Letters of Paul: Rethinking Anthropogony and Theology*. NovTSup 168. Leiden: Brill, 2016.

Miller, Patrick D. *The Lord of the Psalms*. Louisville: Westminster John Knox, 2013.

Mitchell, Margaret M. "Pauline Accommodation and 'Condescension' (συγκατάβασις): 1 Cor. 9:19–23 and the History of Influence." In *Paul beyond the Judaism/Hellenism Divine*, edited by Troels Engberg-Pederson, 197–214. Louisville: Westminster John Knox, 2001.

Moberly, R. W. L. *At the Mountain of God: Story and Theology in Exodus 32–34*. JSOTSup 99. Sheffield: JSOT Press, 1983.

———. *The Bible, Theology, and Faith: A Study of Abraham and Jesus*. CSCD 5. Cambridge: Cambridge University Press, 2000.

———. *Old Testament Theology: Reading the Hebrew Bible as Christian Scripture*. Grand Rapids: Baker Academic, 2013.

Moloney, Francis. *Love in the Gospel of John: An Exegetical, Theological, and Literary Study*. Grand Rapids: Baker Academic, 2013.

Morales, L. Michael. *Who Shall Ascend the Mountain of the Lord? A Biblical Theology of the Book of Leviticus*. Downers Grove, IL: IVP Academic, 2015.

Moser, J. David. "Tools for Interpreting Christ's Saving Mysteries in Scripture: Aquinas on Reduplicative Propositions in Christology." *SJT* 73 (2020): 285–94.

Myers, Alicia D. "'Jesus Said to Them . . .': The Adaptation of Juridical Rhetoric in John 5:19–47." *JBL* 132 (2013): 415–30.

———. "Prosopopoetics and Conflict: Speech and Expectations in John 8." *Biblica* 92 (2011): 580–96.

Neyrey, Jerome H. *An Ideology of Revolt: John's Christology in Social-Science Perspective*. Philadelphia: Fortress, 1988.

———. "Jesus the Judge: Forensic Process in John 8,21–59." *Biblica* 68 (1987): 509–42.

Nielsen, Jesper Tang. "The Narrative Structures of Glory and Glorification in the Fourth Gospel." *NTS* 56 (2010): 343–66.

Oakes, Peter. *Philippians: From People to Letter*. SNTSMS 110. Cambridge: Cambridge University Press, 2001.

Owen, John. *The Works of John Owen*. Edited by William H. Goold. 16 vols. Edinburgh: Banner of Truth, 1965.

Pawl, Timothy. *In Defense of Conciliar Christology: A Philosophical Essay*. OSAT. Oxford: Oxford University Press, 2016.

Pennington, Jonathan T. *The Sermon on the Mount and Human Flourishing: A Theological Commentary*. Grand Rapids: Baker Academic, 2017.

Pennington, Jonathan T., and Sean M. McDonough, eds. *Cosmology and New Testament Theology*. LNTS 355. London: T&T Clark, 2008.

Peterson, David G. *The Acts of the Apostles*. PNTC. Grand Rapids: Eerdmans, 2009.

Plato. *"Timaeus" and "Critias."* Translated by Robin Waterfield. Oxford World's Classics. Oxford: Oxford University Press, 2008.

Pohle, Joseph. *Lehrbuch der Dogmatik*, vol. 1. Edited by Michael Gierens. 8th ed. Paderborn: Schöningh, 1931.

Polanus, Amandus. *Syntagma theologiae christianae*. Hanau, 1615.

Pollard, T. E. "The Father-Son and God-Believer Relationships according to St John: A Brief Study of John's Use of Prepositions." In *L'Évangile de Jean: Sources, Rédaction, Théologie*, edited by Marinus de Jonge, 363–69. BETL 44. Leuven: Peeters, 1977.

Prigent, Pierre. *Commentary on the Apocalypse of St. John*. Translated by Wendy Pradels. Tübingen: Mohr Siebeck, 2004.

Radde-Gallwitz, Andrew. *Basil of Caesarea, Gregory of Nyssa, and the Transformation of Divine Simplicity*. OECS. Oxford: Oxford University Press, 2009.

———. "The Holy Spirit as Agent, Not Activity: Origen's Argument with Modalism and Its Afterlife in Didymus, Eunomius, and Gregory of Nazianzus." *VC* 65 (2011): 227–48.

Rainbow, Paul A. *Johannine Theology: The Gospel, the Epistles, and the Apocalypse*. Downers Grove, IL: IVP Academic, 2014.

Rendtorff, Rolf. *The Canonical Hebrew Bible: A Theology of the Old Testament*. Translated by David Orton. Leiden: Deo Publishing, 2005.

Reynolds, Benjamin E. *The Apocalyptic Son of Man in the Gospel of John*. WUNT 2/249. Tübingen: Mohr Siebeck, 2008.

Riches, Aaron. *Ecce Homo: On the Divine Unity of Christ*. Grand Rapids: Eerdmans, 2016.

Richter, Gerhard. *Oikonomia: Der Gebrauch des Wortes Oikonomia im Neuen Testament, bei den en Kirchenvätern und in der theologischen Literatur bis ins 20. Jahrhundert*. Arbeiten zur Kirchengeschichte 90. Berlin: de Gruyter, 2005.

Roberts, J. J. M. "Isaiah in Old Testament Theology." *Interpretation* 36 (1982): 130–43.

Romanov, Andrey. "Through One Lord Only." *Biblica* 96 (2015): 391–415.

Rowe, C. Kavin. "Biblical Pressure and Trinitarian Hermeneutics." *Pro Ecclesia* 11 (2002): 295–312.

———. *Early Narrative Christology: The Lord in the Gospel of Luke*. Grand Rapids: Baker Academic, 2009.

———. "For Future Generations: Worshipping Jesus and the Integration of the Theological Disciplines." *Pro Ecclesia* 17 (2008): 186–209.

———. "Luke and the Trinity: An Essay in Ecclesial Biblical Theology." *SJT* 56 (2003): 1–26.

———. "The Trinity in the Letters of St Paul and Hebrews." In *The Oxford Handbook of the Trinity*, edited by Gilles Emery and Matthew Levering, 41–54. Oxford: Oxford University Press, 2011.

Rufinus. *A Commentary on the Apostles' Creed*. ACW 20. New York: Newman, 1954.

Rylaarsdam, David. *John Chrysostom on Divine Pedagogy: The Coherence of His Theology and Preaching*. Oxford: Oxford University Press, 2014.

Sanders, Fred. "Eternal Generation and Soteriology." In *Retrieving Eternal Generation*, edited by Fred Sanders and Scott R. Swain, 260–70. Grand Rapids: Zondervan, 2017.

———. *The Triune God*. NSD. Grand Rapids: Zondervan, 2016.

———. "What Trinitarian Theology Is For: Placing the Doctrine of the Trinity in Christian Theology and Life." In *Advancing Trinitarian Theology: Explorations in Constructive Dogmatics*, edited by Oliver D. Crisp and Fred Sanders, 21–41. Grand Rapids: Zondervan, 2014.

Sanders, Fred, and Scott R. Swain, eds. *Retrieving Eternal Generation*. Grand Rapids: Zondervan, 2017.

Sarisky, Darren. "Judgements in Scripture and the Creed: Reflections on Identity and Difference." *Modern Theology* 37, no. 3 (July 2021): 703–20.

———. *Reading the Bible Theologically*. CIT 13. Cambridge: Cambridge University Press, 2020.

Scheeben, Matthias Joseph. *Handbuch der katholischen Dogmatik*. Vol. 2, *Gotteslehre oder die Theologie im engeren Sinne*. Edited by Michael Schmaus. Vol. 4 of *Gesammelte Schriften*. 3rd ed. Freiburg: Herder, 1948.

———. *The Mysteries of Christianity*. Translated by Cyril Vollert. London: Herder, 1946.

Schnabel, Eckhard J. *Acts*. ZECNT. Grand Rapids: Zondervan, 2012.

Schnelle, Udo. "Cross and Resurrection in the Gospel of John." In *The Resurrection of Jesus in the Gospel of John*, edited by Craig R. Koester and Reimund Bieringer, 127–51. WUNT 1/222. Tübingen: Mohr Siebeck, 2008.

———. *Theology of the New Testament*. Translated by M. Eugene Boring. Grand Rapids: Baker Academic, 2009.

Schoot, Henk J. M. *Christ the "Name" of God: Thomas Aquinas on Naming Christ*. Publications of the Thomas Instituut Te Utrecht 1. Leuven: Peeters, 1993.

Schreiner, Thomas R. *1, 2 Peter, Jude*. NAC 37. Nashville: B&H, 2003.

———. *Romans*. BECNT. Grand Rapids: Baker Academic, 1998.

Seifrid, Mark A. *The Second Letter to the Corinthians*. PNTC. Grand Rapids: Eerdmans, 2014.

Servetus, Michael. *De Trinitatis erroribus, libri septem*. Hagenau: Johann Setzer, 1531.

Shead, Andrew G. *A Mouth Full of Fire: The Word of God in the Words of Jeremiah*. Downers Grove, IL: InterVarsity, 2012.

Sheridan, Mark. *Language for God in Patristic Tradition: Wrestling with Biblical Anthropomorphism*. Downers Grove, IL: IVP Academic, 2014.

Silvas, Anna M. *Gregory of Nyssa: The Letters; Introduction, Translation, and Commentary*. VCSup 83. Leiden: Brill, 2007.

Smith, Mark S. *The Early History of God: Yahweh and the Other Deities in Ancient Israel*. 2nd ed. Grand Rapids: Eerdmans, 2002.

———. *The Origins of Biblical Monotheism: Israel's Polytheistic Background and the Ugaritic Texts*. Oxford: Oxford University Press, 2001.

Söding, Thomas. "'Ich und der Vater sind eins' (Joh, 10,30): Die johanneische Christologie vor dem Anspruch des Hauptgebotes (Dtn 6,4f)." *ZNW* 93 (2002): 177–99.

Sokolowski, Robert. "Creation and Christian Understanding." In *God and Creation: An Ecumenical Symposium*, edited by David B. Burrell and Bernard McGinn, 179–92. Notre Dame, IN: University of Notre Dame, 1990.

———. *The God of Faith and Reason: Foundations of Christian Theology*. Notre Dame, IN: University of Notre Dame Press, 1982; Washington, DC: Catholic University of America Press, 1995.

Sommer, Benjamin D. *The Bodies of God and the World of Ancient Israel*. Cambridge: Cambridge University Press, 2008.

Sonderegger, Katherine. *Systematic Theology*. Vol. 1, *The Doctrine of God*. Minneapolis: Fortress, 2015.

Sorabji, Richard. *The Philosophy of the Commentators, 200–600 AD: A Sourcebook*. Vol. 3, *Logic and Metaphysics*. London: Duckworth, 2004.

Soskice, Janet. "Why *Creatio Ex Nihilo* for Theology Today?" In *Creation Ex Nihilo: Origins, Development, Contemporary Challenges*, edited by Gary A. Anderson and Markus Bockmuehl, 37–54. Notre Dame, IN: University of Notre Dame Press, 2017.

Soulen, R. Kendall. *The Divine Name(s) and the Holy Trinity*. Vol. 1, *Distinguishing the Voices*. Louisville: Westminster John Knox, 2011.

———. "*Generatio, Processio Verbi, Donum Nominis*: Mapping the Vocabulary of Eternal Generation." In *Retrieving Eternal Generation*, edited by Fred Sanders and Scott R. Swain, 132–46. Grand Rapids: Zondervan, 2017.

Spicq, Ceslas. "La vertu du simplicité dans l'ancien et le nouveau testament." *RSPT* 22, no. 1 (1933): 5–26.

Sproston, W. E. "'Is Not This Jesus, the Son of Joseph . . . ?' (John 6.42): Johannine Christology as a Challenge to Faith." *JSNT* 24 (1985): 77–97.

Sterling, Gregory. "Prepositional Metaphysics in Jewish Wisdom Speculation and Early Christianity." *SPhiloA* 9 (1997): 219–38.

Strzelczyk, Grzegorz. *Communicatio Idiomatum: Lo scambio delle proprietà; Storia, status quaestionis e prospettive*. Rome: Pontifica Università Gregoriana, 2004.

Sturdevant, Jason S. *The Adaptable Jesus of the Fourth Gospel: The Pedagogy of the Logos*. NovTSup 162. Leiden: Brill, 2015.

Swain, Scott R. "The Bible and the Trinity in Recent Thought: Review, Analysis, and Constructive Proposal." *JETS* 60 (2017): 35–48.

———. "Divine Trinity." In *Christian Dogmatics: Reformed Theology for the Church Catholic*, edited by Michael Allen and Scott R. Swain, 78–106. Grand Rapids: Baker Academic, 2016.

————. "'Heirs through God': Galatians 4:4–7 and the Doctrine of the Trinity." In *Galatians and Christian Theology*, edited by Mark W. Elliott, Scott J. Hafemann, N. T. Wright, and John Frederick, 258–67. Grand Rapids: Baker Academic, 2014.

————. "The Mystery of the Trinity." In *The Essential Trinity: New Testament Foundations and Practical Relevance*, edited by Brandon R. Crowe and Carl R. Trueman, 213–21. Phillipsburg, NJ: P&R, 2017.

————. "Ruled Reading Reformed: The Role of the Church's Confession in Biblical Interpretation." *IJST* 14, no. 2 (2012): 177–93.

————. *The Trinity: An Introduction*. Wheaton: Crossway, 2020.

————. *Trinity, Revelation, and Reading: A Theological Introduction to the Bible and Its Interpretation*. London: T&T Clark, 2011.

Swart, G. "Aristobulus' Interpretation of LXX Sabbath Texts as an Interpretative Key to John 5:1–18." *JSem* 18 (2009): 569–82.

Swete, Henry Barclay. *The Apocalypse of St. John*. New York: Macmillan, 1906.

*Synopsis Purioris Theologiae: Synopsis of a Purer Theology—Latin Text and English Translation*. Vol. 1. Edited by Dolf te Velde and Rein Ferwerda. Translated by Riemer A. Faber. Leiden: Brill, 2014.

Tanner, Kathryn. *God and Creation in Christian Theology: Tyranny or Empowerment?* New York: Blackwell, 1988.

Tanner, Norman P., ed. *Decrees of the Ecumenical Councils*. Vol. 1, *Nicaea I to Lateran V*. London: Sheed & Ward, 1990.

Thiselton, Anthony. *The First Epistle to the Corinthians: A Commentary on the Greek Text*. NIGTC. Grand Rapids: Eerdmans, 2000.

Thomas Aquinas. *Latin-English Opera Omnia*. The Aquinas Institute. Steubenville, OH: Emmaus Academic, 2018–.

————. *Summa Theologiae*. Edited and translated by Thomas Gilby, T. C. O'Brien, et al. New York: McGraw-Hill, 1964–81. Reprint, Cambridge: Cambridge University Press, 2008.

Thompson, Marianne Meye. "The Living Father." *Semeia* 85 (1999): 19–31.

Thompson, Robin. "Healing at the Pool of Bethesda: A Challenge to Asclepius?" *BBR* 27 (2017): 65–84.

Thrall, Margaret E. *A Critical and Exegetical Commentary on the Second Epistle of Paul to the Corinthians*. Vol. 2, *Commentary on II Corinthians VIII–XIII*. ICC. Edinburgh: T&T Clark, 2000.

Tilling, Chris. *Paul's Divine Christology*. WUNT 2/323. Tübingen: Mohr Siebeck, 2012.

Toom, Tarmo. "Early Christian Handbooks on Interpretation." In *The Oxford Handbook of Early Christian Biblical Interpretation*, edited by Paul M. Blowers and Peter W. Martens, 109–25. Oxford: Oxford University Press, 2019.

Torrance, Thomas F. *The Trinitarian Faith: The Evangelical Theology of the Ancient Catholic Church*. London: T&T Clark, 1995.

Turretin, Francis. *Institutes of Elenctic Theology*. Edited by James T. Dennison. Translated by George Musgrave Giger. 3 vols. Phillipsburg, NJ: P&R, 1994.

Ursinus, Zacharias. *Commentary on the Heidelberg Catechism*. Translated by G. W. Williard. Grand Rapids: Eerdmans, 1954.

Vanhoozer, Kevin J. *Remythologizing Theology: Divine Action, Passion, and Authorship*. Cambridge: Cambridge University Press, 2010.

Vermigli, Peter Martyr. *Loci Communes*. 11th ed. Geneva: Petrus Aubert, 1624.

Vidu, Adonis. *The Same God Who Works All Things: Inseparable Operations in Trinitarian Theology*. Grand Rapids: Eerdmans, 2021.

Vos, Geerhardus. "The Idea of Biblical Theology as a Science and as a Theological Discipline." In *Redemptive History and Biblical Interpretation: The Shorter Writings of Geerhardus Vos*, edited by Richard B. Gaffin, 3–24. Phillipsburg, NJ: Presbyterian and Reformed, 1980.

Waaler, Erik. *The* Shema *and the First Commandment in First Corinthians*. WUNT 2/253. Tübingen: Mohr Siebeck, 2008.

Ward, Timothy. *Words of Life: Scripture as the Living and Active Word of God*. Downers Grove, IL: IVP Academic, 2009.

Warfield, B. B. *The Inspiration and Authority of the Bible*. Phillipsburg, NJ: Presbyterian and Reformed, 1948.

———. "'It Says:' 'Scripture Says:' 'God Says.'" In *The Inspiration and Authority of the Bible*, 299–348. Phillipsburg, NJ: Presbyterian and Reformed, 1948.

Watson, Francis. "The Scope of Hermeneutics." In *The Cambridge Companion to Christian Doctrine*, edited by Colin E. Gunton, 65–80. Cambridge: Cambridge University Press, 1997.

———. *Text and Truth: Redefining Biblical Theology*. Grand Rapids: Eerdmans, 1997.

———. "Trinity and Community: A Reading of John 17." *IJST* 1 (1999): 168–84.

———. "The Triune Divine Identity: Reflections on Pauline God-Language, in Disagreement with J. D. G. Dunn." *JSNT* 80 (2000): 99–124.

Webster, John. "Biblical Reasoning." In *The Domain of the Word: Scripture and Theological Reason*, 115–32. London: Bloomsbury T&T Clark, 2012.

———. *The Culture of Theology*. Edited by Ivor J. Davidson and Alden C. McCray. Grand Rapids: Baker Academic, 2019.

———. "Eternal Generation." In *God without Measure: Working Papers in Christian Theology*. Vol. 1, *God and the Works of God*, 29–42. London: Bloomsbury T&T Clark, 2016.

———. "Hermeneutics in Modern Theology: Some Doctrinal Reflections." In *Word and Church: Essays in Christian Dogmatics*, 47–86. Edinburgh: T&T Clark, 2001.

———. *Holy Scripture: A Dogmatic Sketch*. CIT. Cambridge: Cambridge University Press, 2003.

———. "Life in and of Himself." In *God without Measure: Working Papers in Christian Theology*. Vol. 1, *God and the Works of God*, 13–28. London: Bloomsbury T&T Clark, 2016.

———. "One Who Is Son: Theological Reflections on the Exordium to the Epistle to the Hebrews." In *The Epistle to the Hebrews and Christian Theology*, edited by Richard Bauckham, Daniel R. Driver, Trevor A. Hart, and Nathan MacDonald, 69–94. Grand Rapids: Eerdmans, 2009.

———. "Principles of Systematic Theology." In *The Domain of the Word: Scripture and Theological Reason*, 133–49. London: Bloomsbury T&T Clark, 2012.

———. "Resurrection and Scripture." In *The Domain of the Word: Scripture and Theological Reason*, 32–49. London: Bloomsbury T&T Clark, 2012.

———. "ὑπὸ πνεύματος ἁγίου φερόμενοι ἐλάλησαν ἀπὸ θεοῦ ἄνθρωποι: On the Inspiration of Holy Scripture." In *Conception, Reception, and the Spirit: Essays in Honor of Andrew T. Lincoln*, edited by J. Gordon McConville and Lloyd K. Pieterson, 236–50. Eugene, OR: Cascade Books, 2015.

Weinandy, Thomas G. "Cyril and the Mystery of the Incarnation." In *The Theology of St Cyril of Alexandria*, edited by Thomas G. Weinandy and Daniel A. Keating, 23–54. London: T&T Clark, 2003.

———. *Does God Change? The Word's Becoming in the Incarnation*. SHT 4. Still River, MA: St. Bede's, 1985.

———. *Does God Suffer?* Edinburgh: T&T Clark, 2000.

———. *Jesus Becoming Jesus: A Theological Interpretation of the Synoptic Gospels*. Washington, DC: Catholic University of America Press, 2018.

White, Devin L. *Teacher of the Nations: Ancient Educational Traditions and Paul's Argument in 1 Corinthians 1–4*. BZNW 227. Berlin: de Gruyter, 2017.

White, Thomas Joseph. *The Incarnate Lord: A Thomistic Study in Christology*. Washington, DC: Catholic University of America Press, 2015.

Whitsett, Christopher G. "Son of God, Seed of David: Paul's Messianic Exegesis in Romans 1:3–4." *JBL* 119 (2000): 661–81.

Wiles, Maurice. *The Spiritual Gospel: The Interpretation of the Fourth Gospel in the Early Church*. Cambridge: Cambridge University Press, 1960.

Williams, A. N. *The Divine Sense: The Intellect in Patristic Theology*. Cambridge: Cambridge University Press, 2005.

Williams, Catrin H. *I Am He: The Interpretation of 'Anî Hû' in Jewish and Early Christian Literature*. WUNT 2/113. Tübingen: Mohr Siebeck, 2000.

———. "'I Am' Sayings." In *Dictionary of Jesus and the Gospels*, edited by Joel B. Green, Jeannine K. Brown, and Nicholas Perrin, 396–99. 2nd ed. Downers Grove, IL: InterVarsity, 2013.

————. "Johannine Christology and Prophetic Traditions: The Case of Isaiah." In *Reading the Gospel of John's Christology as Jewish Messianism: Royal, Prophetic, and Divine Messiahs*, edited by Benjamin E. Reynolds and Gabriele Boccaccini, 92–123. AJEC 106. Leiden: Brill, 2018.

Williams, Rowan. *Christ the Heart of Creation*. London: Bloomsbury Continuum, 2018.

————. "Trinity and Revelation." In *On Christian Theology*, 131–47. Oxford: Blackwell, 2000.

Witherington, Ben, and Laura Ice. *The Shadow of the Almighty: Father, Son, and Spirit in Biblical Perspective*. Grand Rapids: Eerdmans, 2002.

Witmer, Stephen E. *Divine Instruction in Early Christianity*. WUNT 2/246. Tübingen: Mohr Siebeck, 2008.

Wittman, Tyler R. "*Dominium Naturale et Oeconomicum*: Authority and the Trinity." In *Trinity without Hierarchy: Reclaiming Nicene Orthodoxy in Evangelical Theology*, edited by Michael F. Bird and Scott Harrower, 141–64. Grand Rapids: Kregel, 2019.

Wodehouse, P. G. "Leave It to Jeeves." https://www.classicreader.com/book/3452/1/.

Wolff, Christian. *Der erste Brief des Paulus an die Korinther*. 3rd ed. THKNT. Leipzig: Evangelische Verlagsanstalt, 2011.

Wollebius, Johannes. *Compendium theologiae Christianae*. London: T. Longman, 1709.

Wright, N. T. *The Climax of the Covenant: Christ and the Law in Pauline Theology*. Edinburgh: T&T Clark, 1991.

Yeago, David S. "The Bible: The Spirit, the Church, and the Scriptures; Biblical Inspiration and Interpretation Revisited." In *Knowing the Triune God: The Work of the Spirit in the Practices of the Church*, edited by James J. Buckley and David S. Yeago, 49–93. Grand Rapids: Eerdmans, 2001.

————. "Jesus of Nazareth and Cosmic Redemption: The Relevance of St. Maximus the Confessor." *Modern Theology* 12 (1996): 163–93.

————. "The New Testament and the Nicene Dogma: A Contribution to the Recovery of Theological Exegesis." *Pro Ecclesia* 3 (1994): 152–64.

Young, Frances, and David F. Ford. *Meaning and Truth in 2 Corinthians*. London: SPCK, 1987.

Zehnder, Markus. "Why the Danielic 'Son of Man' Is a Divine Being." *BBR* 24 (2014): 331–47.

Zeller, Dieter. *Der erste Brief an die Korinther*. KEK 5. Göttingen: Vandenhoeck & Ruprecht, 2010.

Ziesler, J. A. *Pauline Christianity*. Oxford: Oxford University Press, 1990.

Zumstein, Jean. *L'Évangile selon Saint Jean*. 2 vols. CNT IVb, 2nd series. Geneva: Labor et Fides, 2007.

# Subject Index

and doctrine, xix, xx n26, 40, 57
and economy, 155–56
exactness of, 51–52
and faith, 22
and God, xxiii, 233
and judgments, xxiii, 52–53
New Testament, 156–61
partitive, 154–61, 163–78, 192–93, 228–29,
    241. *See also* rules: rule 9
and pedagogy, 40
and pressure, scriptural, 55
and retrieval, xxii–xxiii
rules of, xxi–xxii, 213
and theology, xviii–xix, xxi–xxii, 21, 41–42,
    52–57, 233
exegetical reasoning, xvii–xviii, xix, xxv, 20

faith, 14–18, 20, 22, 235–36. *See also* rules: rule 1
fallenness, 33–37
Father. *See* God: as Father
finitude, 32–36

glory
    of Christ, 5–6, 8–12, 17–18, 21, 105, 120, 127,
        135, 236–38
    and the cross, 9, 135, 236–38
    of God, 8–11, 68, 79, 92–93, 120, 237–38
    in Scripture, 5–6, 21
    and sight/visibility, 8–11, 17–18
    and the Trinity, 105, 238
God
    adaptability of, 29–30, 33–34, 36, 38
    anthropomorphism, 81–82
    and biblical reasoning, xxi, 42
    and communication of idioms, 142, 144–45
    and creation, 66–76, 80, 87
    as creator, 63, 77, 216–17
    and the cross, 34–35, 37, 121
    economy, 24–26, 28, 30, 33–34, 57–58, 155–
        56, 191–97
    essence of, 100–101, 103, 113
    and eternity, 69–72
    as Father
        and giving judgment to Christ, 220–21, 226,
            229–31
        greater than Son, 92, 167–70
        and oneness of works with Son and Spirit,
            109–16, 116, 192–200, 219, 223, 225–29
        and origin of Son, 83, 184–88
        and relation to Son, 223–24, 231–32
        and sending of Son, 122–24, 201, 206–7
        and Spirit, 124, 189–91

freedom of, 86, 87, 89
from-ness of, 207–8
glory of, 8–11, 68, 79, 92–93, 120, 237–38
holiness of, 68–69, 73, 90
and humanity, 134, 138–41, 144–45, 161–63
immutability of, 69–72, 77, 87
impassibility of, 87–88
knowledge of, 6, 11, 35–36, 182–83
name(s) of, 69–70, 101, 103–4
as one, 92–102, 112–15, 119, 125, 209
and pedagogical economy, 26, 28, 30, 33
and pedagogy, 26–32, 40, 42, 45, 51, 83,
    104–5
perfection(s) of, 81, 84
power of, 37, 115, 119–21
regret/repentance of, 84–90
and Scripture, 42, 45, 51, 55, 64, 79–80, 87,
    102, 119, 144–45
simplicity of, 95, 101–2
and Spirit, 10–11, 189–91, 196, 198–200,
    211–12
as teacher, 24–40, 42, 51
transcendence of, 69, 74, 75, 77
will of, 89, 90, 231
wisdom of, 34–37, 39, 119–21
works of 109, 114–15, 204
*See also* Jesus Christ; Trinity, the
Gregory of Nazianzus, 125, 144, 165–67, 177,
    188–91

Holy Spirit
    and contemplation, 18–19
    and divine economy, 196–97
    and the Father, 112–13, 121, 189–91, 198–99,
        211–12
    and inseparable operations, 111–12, 124
    mission of, 211–12
    name of, 188–91
    and oneness of works with the Father, 112–14
    person of, 188–89
    procession of, 83, 190–91
    and the Son, 189–91, 195–96, 199–202
    and sonship, 211–12
    spiration of, 101, 121
    and spiritual gifts, 112–13, 121
    and the visibility of God, 10–11
*homoousios*, xxiii, 53, 101, 105, 161, 190, 236
hypostatic union, 57–58, 126, 134–43, 162–63,
    204

idolatry, 94, 97–98
Ignatius of Antioch, 143

# Author Index

# Scripture and Other Ancient Sources Index

## Acts of the Apostles